GITA AND GANDHIJI

GITA AND GANDHIJI

DR. RAMESH S. BETAI
M.A. (Hindi)
M.A. (Sansk.)
Ph.D. (Sansk.)

NATIONAL GANDHI MUSEUM
Rajghat, New Delhi – 110002
in association with
GYAN PUBLISHING HOUSE
5 Ansari Road, New Delhi – 110002

First edition published in 1970 by Gujarat Vidyapith
with financial assistance from the Ministry of Education,
Government of India

Second revised edition 2002

ISBN 81-212-0799-1

Price: Rs. 450/-

Published by
The Director
National Gandhi Museum
Rajghat, New Delhi – 110002
Phones: 3311793, 3310168, 3328310
Fax: 91-01-3311793
e-mail: gandhimk@nda.vsnl.net.in
website: www.gandhimuseum.org

in association with

Gyan Publishing House
5, Ansari Road, Daryaganj
New Delhi 110 002
Phones: 3261060, 3282060, Fax: 3285914
E-mail: gyanbook@vsnl.com
Website: http://www.gyanbooks.com

Composed by: Sai Graphic Design, New Delhi

Contents

My Submission

The present work "*Gita and Gandhiji*" was published for the first time in 1970. It was a Central Government Project offered to Gujarat Vidyapith as a part of the celebrations of the centenary of the Father of the Nation. It was *entrusted* to me as a Reader in Sanskrit. All joy was ours because the book went out of print soon. This speaks for the value and relevance of the book then. It is more relevant to-day in modern India after more than 30 years. If India is to survive and be free from its turmoils, Gandhian values must be implemented. The present work was an humble contribution towards alleviation of Mother India's sufferings then. We in modern India feel its necessity all the more.

Before I worked on the project for two years around 1968-1970, my plan was okayed by my Gurus and Scholars of great eminence and of all India fame—late Dr. P.M. Modi and Dr. G.K. Bhat.

I find no words to express my thankfulness to Dr. Y.P. Anand (Director) and the authorities of National Gandhi Museum for taking interest in publishing the second impression of the work.

Ahmedabad
10 January 2002

R.S. BETAI

Publisher's Note to the Second Edition

Mahatma Gandhi's extensive writings on the Bhagavad Gita, and his interpretation of the philosophy propounded by it, have not yet received adequate attention from scholars and students of Gandhian thought or of the Gita. That Gandhiji claimed to have lived his life according to the teachings of the Gita and that it was his closest guide, is well-known. But few realize that Gandhiji not only wrote a verse-by-verse translation of it (अनासक्तियोग), but also delivered 218 discourses on it (गीताशिक्षण) at Sabarmati Ashram, compiled a comprehensive glossary (giving meanings) of words and phrases in the Gita (गीतापदार्थकोष), wrote 18 letters from jail, one on each chapter of the Gita (गीताबोध), compiled a 42-verse selection (गीताप्रवेशिका) (from the 700 verses of the Gita) for the guidance of his son Ramdas when both were in Yeravda Jail in 1932, and, above and beyond all this referred to the study, teachings and relevance of the Gita (often citing specific verses) about 1200 times in his articles, letters, speeches and discussions as recorded in the 'Collected Works of Mahatma Gandhi'.

A comprehensive compilation of all that Gandhiji is known to have said about the Gita is yet to be published. Equally important is the need for study of the eminently original and consistent interpretation given by him of what the Gita says. His is a total view and not merely an interpretation of some conveniently selected verses or paths to salvation.

Gandhiji accepts that the Gita was not written to propagate non-violence (अहिंसा) but to propagate selfless adherence to one's duty (धर्म) under all circumstances. Yet he contends—correctly, in my opinion—that according to the Gita, violence and war will not be indulged in by anyone who is truly stable-minded (स्थितप्रज्ञ), righteous (दैव), a devotee (भक्त), beyond the three-categories (गुणातीत), accomplished in Yoga (योगारूढ), wise (ज्ञानी), or joined with God (ब्रह्मभूत), or in general, has attained the high levels of virtuous living as adumbrated in the Gita. Ahimsa is described in the Gita as one of the vital human qualities proceeding from God (Gita-X:5), a virtue denoting wisdom (XIII:7), a quality of the righteous (XVI:2), and an essential component of austerity (तपः, XVII:14).

This is why Gandhiji says that the fight depicted in the Gita between the Pandavas and the Kauravas in fact represents the constant conflict going on between the forces of good and those of evil within the battlefield of every human heart, and also that non-violence (अहिंसा), truth (सत्य), sacrifice (यज्ञ), faith (श्रद्धा), service of God through the service of His creation (लोकसंग्रह, सर्वभूतहित), pursuit of detached action as an enjoined duty (अनासक्ति or कर्म-योग), non-possession (अपरिग्रह) and other such concepts (which Gandhiji himself pursued throughout his public and personal life) are also key concepts of the *Gita*.

There are not many critical appreciations of Gandhiji's interpretation of the Gita, so the subject is still wide open for scholarly research. It was, therefore, with a pleasant surprise that I received a letter from Dr. Varsha Das, Chief Editor and Jt. Director, National Book Trust of India, New Delhi, recommending that Dr. Ramesh S. Betai's book, 'Gita and Gandhiji', which was published in 1970 by Gujarat Vidyapith, Ahmedabad, but has been out of print for many years, may be reissued by the National Gandhi Museum. The book is a scholarly and painstaking work and National Gandhi Museum, therefore, considers it a privilege to take up its re-publication.

Dr. Betai's book contains mainly: (a) a critical appreciation of the principal interpretations of the Gita in ancient time and in modern time before Gandhiji; (b) an analytical review of Gandhiji's interpretation of the Gita as the 'Gospel of Selfless Action' (अनासक्तियोग); (c) a commentary on Gandhiji's views on various aspects of individual, social, economic, and ethical life, and on certain Gandhian concepts such as non-violence (अहिंसा), non-possession (अपरिग्रह), and 'bread labour' (शरीर-श्रम) as proceeding from his interpretation of the Gita; and (d) the place of Gandhiji among the principal interpreters (भाष्यकार) of the Gita.

The book has been re-edited with the kind help of Dr. Betai, and efforts have been made, as far as possible, to remove minor errors and omissions and to add English equivalents of the Sanskrit terms, phrases and lines wherever these were not given in the first edition. Dr. Betai has also added 'Glossary Two' for assisting the non-Sanskrit knowing readers.

We are grateful to him and also to Gujarat Vidyapith, who hold the copyright, for their approval of this re-publication by the National Gandhi Museum. I also express my gratitude to the staff in the Museum, who have worked so sincerely for the publication of this book.

10.3.2002

DR. Y.P. ANAND
Director
National Gandhi Museum
Rajghat
New Delhi-110002

Publisher's Note to the First Edition

Mahatma Gandhi was essentially a man of *Dharma*. His entire life and thought have a spiritual basis. Inspite of his heavy pre-occupation in political life of the country, he never under-stressed *Dharma* as the basis of entire human life including political life. He even went to the extent of attempting spiritualisation of politics.

The word *Dharma* was used by him to denote essential unity of all religions of the world. He never thought of *Dharma* as sectarian creed. He was wedded to universal brotherhood based on love and non-violence.

The influence of *Bhagavad Gita* in moulding the life and thought of Gandhiji is well-known. He himself has acknowledged the influence of *Gita* on him. His famous introduction to 'Anasaktiyoga' is an enlightened exposition of the teachings of *Gita* which he accepted as universal truth not confined to any one religion or sect.

During the Gandhi Centenary Year, the Gujarat Vidyapith felt that it would be valuable to make an academic study of this aspect of Gandhiji's life and thought. Dr. Betai, M.A., Ph.D., Reader in Sanskrit in the Gujarat Vidyapith, undertook this research project and worked very hard on it for over a year. The project became possible because of the generous help extended to us by the Ministry of Education, Government of India. It is proposed to bring out the Gujarati and Hindi versions of this work also at a later stage and Dr. Betai himself proposes to do so. This type of academic investigation of this very important influence on Gandhiji's life may probably be the first of its kind and is bound to be of interest to all students of teachings of *Gita* and Gandhiji.

We are grateful to Dr. Modi for writing an illuminating foreword to this volume and to the Ministry of Education, Government of India for their generous financial support.

9-12-1970 **Ramlal Parikh**

Foreword to the First Edition

I have read with interest Dr. Betai's work on '*Gita* and Gandhiji'.

Generally, people read only the translation of the *Gita* by Gandhiji. Such a reading is alright in a way, viz., only to know how Gandhiji would interpret consistently all the 700 verses of the *Gita*. But to know how the *Gita* influenced Gandhiji's entire life including his social, political and economic dealings as also his teachings, there is as yet no book available. This need has now been fulfilled by the present work of Dr. Betai.

Dr. Betai has shown in chapter ten that Gandhiji is a *Bhashyakara* on the *Gita* and as such he should find a proper place among the *Bhashyakaras*. To interpret all the 700 verses without being inconsistent as regards the interpretation of each single verse with the rest of the *Gita* is not a small thing. Even in Shri Shankaracharya, we find inconsistencies. To illustrate, Shankara takes Shri Krishna as his *Saguna* or comparatively real Principle throughout his interpretation of the *Gita*, but the same Acharya, while interpreting *Gita* XIV: 26-27, gives an interpretation in which he takes Krishna as the *Nirguna* or absolute Reality. But Dr. Betai's interpretation of the *Gita* clarifies to show that though Gandhiji follows the method of a *Bhashyakara* in understanding and interpreting the *Gita*, he is thoroughly consistent in his stand.

Dr. Betai has also shown how Gandhiji remarkably differed from Tilak, Radhakrishnan and others on the *Gita*. In the opinion of Tilak, *Himsa* as also *Asatya* (Telling a lie) would be possible to be committed without any selfish purpose. But Gandhiji held that such actions as killing, telling a lie, deceiving somebody etc., are never possible if a man is totally unselfish, totally *Anasakta*, as the *Gita* would tell in his opinion. Gandhiji holds that even if a man commits an act of killing even while working for the good of others or for the benefit of a nation or humanity that he loves or adores, his act of killing is selfish or done with *asakti*. Looking to our modern times, Gandhiji seems to be undoubtedly right, because we should, in our behaviour, look upon the whole world (and not only India) as our (or 'my') world, otherwise, one nation guided by its one disinterested leader would deeply harm another nation and would say that he has no self-interest. This viewpoint of Gandhiji has been brought out by Dr. Betai in his Chapters on Gandhiji's Interpretation of the *Gita* (Chapters 4 and 5).

In Chapters 6 to 9 Dr. Betai has collected all material from Gandhiji's other works to show how Gandhiji understood the *bhavartha*, the spirit, of the *Gita*, as distinguished from the *shabdartha* or the word, the verbal sense of the *Gita*. Thus, Dr. Betai has found that Gandhiji traced his Spining Wheel doctrine from Gita (*Shreyan svadharmo vigunah paradharmat svanushthitat Svadharme nidhanam shreyah paradharmo bhayavahah*). Gandhiji stated that *dharma* in the *Gita* means that which would save the economic and spiritual life of a nation, and according to Gandhiji, the Spinning Wheel would save the economic and spiritual life not only of India but of the whole world. The Spinning Wheel is meant by the *Gita's dharma*, for the present world.

Dr. Betai gathers information from Gandhiji's works (other than his comments on the *Gita*) to show Gandhiji's fight against untouchability. Gandhiji depended upon *Gita* (*Mam hi Partha vyapashritya ye api syuh papayonayah Striyo vaisyas tatha shudras te'pi yanti param gatim*). The same is the *Gita's* authority for Gandhiji to fight against the Indian Caste-system. Who can say that Gandhiji is wrong here? The *Gita* presented its fresh *Bhakti* doctrine to fight against the Caste-system supported by the followers of the *Jnana* doctrine. In fact, the present day untouchable is not the one mentioned in the *Manusmriti*. The modern untouchable is the creation of the old society which was later than Manu.

Dr. Betai has shown that Gandhiji takes *Satya* to be God Himself. This would mean that *Satya* according to Gandhiji is a living principle, omniscient, omnipotent, omnipresent and also omnigood. In fact, Gandhiji has really said so. Here also Gandhiji is adopting a terminology (word for the idea God) which our modern people of the world would understand, appreciate and follow. So, instead of speaking of God as Krishna, Govinda, Rama, or as *Sat-chid-ananda*,Gandhiji calls Him by the name *Satya* and this *Satya* is for him a Principle Supreme and working in the way in which God works as per our Scriptures. So, is not Truth or Truthfulness an attribute of God, not only in Indian Philosophy but in all Philosophies of the world? Gandhiji deserves credit and our respect for finding out a name and an idea about God which would appeal not only to Hindus but to the followers of all isms, all religions of the world.

These are only a few of the doctrines and ideas derived by Gandhiji, as he himself says, from the *Gita* and the spirit of the words and verses of the *Gita* as understood by him.

Dr. Betai is the first man to collect all the above and much more other information from Gandhiji's works, directly dealing with the *Gita* as well as indirectly telling us about Gandhiji on the *Gita*.

It is also good that Dr. Betai has brought out this 'Gandhi Dharma Shastra' as I would call it, not independently of the *Gita*, but in relation with the *Gita*, since the *Gita* is already known and believed in by Indians as well as by so many leaders all over the world. In India, of course, every literate man would also appreciate Dr. Betai's Labour of Love.

Dr. Betai's present work '*Gita* and Gandhiji' is a great need of the whole world, which does believe in the teaching, moral and religious, of Gandhiji as the sole cure of the modern day diseased life, even though such persons may find it difficult to practise it, even after they come to know about it.

This 'Gandhi Dharma Shastra' by Dr. Betai is like Manu's *Dharma Shastra* by Bhrigu. Manu taught *Ahimsa, Satya, Asteya, Shaucha*, and *Indriyanigraha* for the whole world known to him. Gandhiji teaches *Ahimsa* and *Satya* which two, of course, include also *Asteya*, *Shaucha* and *Indriyanigraha* for the whole world known to him. Manu based his *Dharma* on the Scriptures; Gandhiji also follows the Scriptures, the *Gita*, the Bible and others.

I congratulate and bless Dr. Betai on bringing out this 'Gandhi Dharma Shastra' as I would like to call it.

P.M. Modi
Ex-Prin. and Prof. of Sanskrit,
Samaldas College, Bhavnagar.
Director, Indological Research Institute, Dwarka.
Ex-member, Central Sanskrit Board,
Rashtrapati Award Holder, etc., etc.

Preface to the First Edition

The following pages are a result of about two years' study and investigation. The work of studying the problem of the influence of the *Gita* in the interpretation of Gandhiji's teachings and studying his own interpretation of the *Gita*, was entrusted to me when it was offered by the Government of India to Gujarat Vidyapith, specially in view of the centenary of Mahatma Gandhi. I was not only happy but proud when the work was entrusted to me because this gave to me an opportunity to probe into the life and mind of a great man who shaped the destinies of modern India, and through his service and struggle for the uplift of India, became a torch-bearer lighting the path of progress of humanity towards eternal peace and happiness. I knew then, and I know all the more today, the great difficulty of the work undertaken and completed by me. It is associated with a religious scripture that is given to humanity by Yogeshvara Lord Krishna and has commanded utter devotion and following of Hindus for more than 2000 years and has consequently been subjected to so many varied interpretations. It is again associated with a great man, whose principal doctrines of life were Truth, non-violence and world peace. He was the most difficult to understand, even though his life has been, throughout, an open book. It is not necessary for me to refer at this stage to the great importance of the *Gita* in Gandhiji's life and work, the problem of how the *Gita* shaped his mind and personality, the problem of his peculiarly interesting interpretation and the resultant teachings of the Mahatma and so on. I have discussed the problems in detail in the pages that follow. Here, I would only state that I have undertaken the study with devotional zeal, being careful all the while that the great devotion in which I hold the *Gita* and Lord Krishna and the veneration in which I hold Mahatma Gandhi, should not cloud and overcome my reason and evaluation. I have never forgotten that this is a scientific study and as a scientific study, it is expected to be perfectly impartial, unbiased and objective. I leave it to the worthy reader to judge whether or not I have succeeded in my effort in this particular approach.

Before I undertook the study, I was wondering and asking myself as to how far, we in India, have understood the secret of and real greatness of Mahatma Gandhi. After this study I have realized that very few of us know the secret of and his real greatness; he is far greater a man than we know him to be; very few of us understand him. The following pages are my humble effort to understand and evaluate the Mahatma in the light of a basic, fixed problem. It is again for the worthy reader to judge how far I have succeeded in my effort.

During the course of my study, I prepared two questionnaires—one for the devotees of and scholars on Gandhism, another for scholars of Sanskrit and Vedanta. I am grateful to all those scholars who discussed with me or answered my questionnaires. Their views have been of immense help to me in the evaluation of my own conclusions. I should particularly refer to Shri Kakasaheb Kalelkar, Shri Dolarrai Mankad, Late Shri Maganbhai Desai, Shri Chhaganlal Joshi, Dr. T.N. Dave, Dr. G.K. Bhat, Dr. P.M. Modi, and Prof. J.J. Pandya.

Dr. P.M. Modi and Prof. J.J. Pandya—two prominent scholars on Vedanta in general and the *Gita* in particular—took keen interest in my work and gave valuable suggestions during the course of my study and preparation of the work. No words of thankfulness can reward their love and regard for me and for my work.

In the end, I may take an appreciating note of the work of the assistants who took extracts, prepared copies, prepared the Bibliography etc., as I instructed them.

With this, I submit my work to the judgment of the worthy reader and that too with the deep, genuine and humble feeling that:

आपरितोषाद्विदुषां न साधु मन्ये प्रयोगविज्ञानम् ।

2-10-1969 **R.S. Betai**

ONE

Introduction

"I am but a poor struggling soul yearning to be wholly good, wholly truthful and wholly non-violent in thought, word and deed; but ever failing to reach the ideal which I know to be true. It is a painful climb, but the pain of it is a positive pleasure to me. Each step upward makes me feel stronger and fit for the next."

GANDHIJI[1]

"God, if I worship Thee in fear of hell, burn me in hell. And if I worship Thee in hope of paradise, exclude me from paradise; but if I worship Thee for Thine own sake, withhold not Thine everlasting Beauty."

RABI'A

Introductory

"In the evolution of civilization, if it is to survive, all men cannot fail to adopt his belief, that the process of mass application of force to resolve contentious issues is fundamentally not only wrong, but contains within itself the germs of self-destruction. Gandhiji, however was one of those prophets who lived far ahead of the times."

GEN. MACARTHUR

This was the tribute paid to Mahatma Gandhi, whom we know as a great prophet of peace (through universal brotherhood, love and non-violence towards all living beings) and a constant seeker after Truth. It was paid by a man who was a military General almost all his life, and it was paid at a time when the heartless, cruel and dastardly attack on the Mahatma resulted in his death. This led Dr. Radhakrishnan to exclaim: "When will the world be safe for its saints?" and a writer of international renown painfully stated: "It shows how dangerous it is to be too good."[2] This attitude of being good, had its roots in the attitude of the greatest saints of the world: Buddha, Christ, Mahavira, Socrates, Tolstoy, etc. He rightly adopted this attitude as an unstinted inner urge, that he would always and invariably put into practice in life.

Mahatma Gandhi has been accepted by most people in the world as a saint, a prophet of peace. For a saint, A. Huxley states: "The saint is one who knows that every moment of our human life is a moment of crisis, for, at every moment we are called upon to make an all-important decision to choose between the way that leads to death and spiritual darkness and the way that leads towards light and life, between interest exclusively temporal and the eternal order; between our personal will, or the will of some projection of our personality, and the will of God."[3] This applies to Gandhiji and he was clear about his mission in life. This knowledge and the practice that followed, came from his unstinted faith in God the Supreme, whose work he took to be essentially good. That led him to a unique faith in the ultimate goodness of man, a faith in the great potentialities of humanity and a faith that, inspite of all his limitations, weaknesses, violence in nature and all that man is, man will someday rise to divine heights. It will be a day when the world will be heaven itself and man will be divine. This naturally and logically led him to the service of humanity and that too by the path of non-violence that is love and the path of change of heart. His *Satyagraha* was a weapon chiefly to serve humanity and the basic qualification of an ideal *satyagrahi* was a living faith in love that is non-violence and living faith in God. To put in Gandhiji's own words: "He or she must have a living faith in non-violence. This is impossible without a living faith in God. A non-violent man can do nothing save by the power and grace of God. Without it he won't have the courage to die without anger, without fear and without retaliation."[4] Being a man of God, he was totally fearless and it is natural that such a man had the undaunted courage to declare that "For many years I have accorded intellectual assent to the proposition that death is only a big change in life and nothing more, and should be welcome whenever it arrives."[5] He says: "I have deliberately made a supreme attempt to cast out from my heart all fear whatsoever including the fear of death."[6] Where did this unique fearlessness, indomitable courage, the ever-readiness to lay down his life for truth and just cause, the will to die rather than kill, come from? So fearless was he that when Lady Mountbatten came to congratulate him when he was saved from the bomb-explosion on 20-1-1948, he could reply in perfect equanimity of spirit and perfect fearlessness: "On this occasion, I have shown no bravery. If somebody fired at me point-blank and I faced his bullet with a smile, repeating the name of Rama in my heart, I should indeed be deserving of congratulations."[7] Where did this equanimity of spirit and fearlessness come from? All this came naturally from the eternal word of God the Supreme. Gandhiji had partly inherited this great treasure through his parents and the extremely religious atmosphere of his family and childhood, partly from his study of the scriptures of different religions of the world—Christianity, Islam and Jainism in particular. This was of course in addition to Hinduism that was the religion of his birth and inheritance, and partly from his constant experiments with Truth. We are told: "No two of them inherit the same temperament and physical constitution, and their lives are passed in material, moral and intellectual environments that are profoundly dissimilar. Nevertheless in so far as they are saints, in so far as they possess the intuitive knowledge that makes them 'perfect, as their Father which is in heaven is perfect,' they are all astonishingly alike," states Huxley.[8] Saint Gandhiji is similar to many others though his moral, intellectual and spiritual environment is principally Hindu.

It is necessary that we accept the view of some students of Gandhiji that inspite of the glaring influence of Christianity and Islam, as also the acknowledged influence of Ruskin, Thoreau, Tolstoy, etc., Gandhiji's primary source of experience of and attitude to religion and the saintly work for every movement of his life that it led to, rests in Hinduism to which he remained attached like a child to its mother. This was inspite of its glaring limitations of which he was thoroughly conscious and for the eradication of which he fought throughout his life. T.K. Mahadevan is right when he states that "... the Gandhian teaching belongs strictly within this mainstream (of ancient Indian tradition) and any superficial resemblance it may have to western Christian tradition can only be accidental."[9] And here again, his greatest admiration was for the *Upanishads*, the *Gita,* the *Mahabharata*, and the *Ramayana* of Tulsidas. Of all these again his greatest dependence was on the word of the *Bhagavad Gita*, for which he rightly stated that: "Hinduism, as I know it, entirely satisfies my whole being and I find a solace in the *Bhagavad Gita* that I miss even in the *Sermon on the Mount*." And, "... but I must confess that when doubts haunt me, when disappointments stare me in the face, and when I see not even one ray of light on the horizon, I turn to the *Bhagavad Gita* and find a verse to comfort me; and I immediately begin to smile in the midst of over-whelming sorrow. My life has been full of external tragedies and if they have not left any visible and indelible effect on me, I owe it to the teaching of the *Bhagavad Gita*."[10] "To-day, the *Gita*, is not only my Bible or my Quran; it is more than that—it is my mother. I lost my earthly mother who gave me birth long ago; but this Eternal mother has completely filled her place by my side ever since."[11]

Why Interpretations Differ

But it should not surprise us to note, actually we should take it as a natural fact that his interpretation of the *Gita* should be very much different from that of Shankara, Ramanuja, Madhusudana, Madhava, Vallabha, etc., the ancients, and Shri Aurobindo, Tilak, Belvalkar, Radhakrishnan, Vinoba, Ranade, Dasgupta, etc., the moderns. In India, any interpretation of a religious and philosophical text is bound to be exactly in accordance with the personality, beliefs and outlook on life of the interpreter concerned. Interpretation can also differ in accordance with the interpreter being a philosopher, a saint, or a man of action. Here again the nature of the doctrines of the *Gita* is so very peculiar and remarkably different from other religious and philosophical texts of its kind that even though as it is, it looks very simple and flowing and easy to grasp, it is subject not only to varied interpretations, the remarkable fact is that normally no two interpretations of the *Gita* are similar in all respects. If Shankara states that the *Gita* teaches of the path of realization of final dissolution in the Divine that is of the nature of *Nirguna Nirakara Brahma* by the path of knowledge only after renouncing all *Karmas*,[12] if Ramanuja reads his doctrine of Qualified Monism with prominence of *Bhakti*, if the followers of Vallabha school insist on reading and interpreting the *Gita* only from the viewpoint of *Bhakti*,[13] if Tilak reads his *Karmayoga* doctrine in it, if Shri Aurobindo reads his peculiarly original doctrine of *Karmayoga* of the *Muktatma* in it, and if Gandhiji insists that the doctrine of the *Gita* is that of *Anasakti*—the *Gita* approves of all these interpretations. That is the reason why the *Gita* which is an *Upanishad* on its own claims (as the colophon— पुष्पिका —at the end of each *Adhyaya* specifies),[14] it is also the *Dohana* (essence) of the principal doctrines of the *Upanishads*. A famous verse praising the *Gita* tells: "All *Upanishads* are cows, the milkman is Lord Krishna, Partha is the calf, the learned the enjoyer: really great is the *Gita* with its nectar-like milk."[15] The *Gita* has been accepted as the basic religious book by almost all the sects in the country, and scholars take it as a book of religious guidance for humanity at large also.[16]

Rightly is it stated "The truth of the fact is that all 'isms' so far known to humanity and those that may be discovered in the future, find an appropriate place in the *Gita*."[17] Yet it is desirable and fruitful to try to know exactly what *Yogeshvara* Krishna himself has to say in the *Gita*. Of course all scholars and sects claim to interpret the *Gita* correctly, and even while they give varied interpretations the fact stands true that वादे वादे जायते तत्वबोध: (with every new thought there dawns the understanding of reality). But Avinashananda is right in stating that, "One of the customers watched all this with amazement. The dyer asked him, 'Well, what colour do you want for your cloth?.' The customer said, 'Brother, dye my cloth in your own colour.' So let us try to read the *Gita* in its own right colour and spirit and not seek our own pet theories."[18]

Popularity of the Gita

This naturally leads us to the causes of the immense popularity and universal appeal of the doctrine of the *Gita*, that is known as "...the most beautiful, perhaps the only true philosophical song existing in any known language"[19] by Humboldt, and that about which Radhakrishnan rightly states, "... if the hold which a work has on the mind of man is any clue to its importance, then the *Gita* is the most influential work in Indian thought."[20] That is the reason why it is translated in the maximum number of world-languages—probably only after the Bible. The reasons why the *Gita* extends beyond all limitations of time, place, culture and language, the reasons why the doctrine of the *Gita* knows no barriers as both eastern and western scholars accept, are as follows:

(1) The *Bhagavad Gita* is probably the only single work in Hindu Dharma that brings religion, ethics and philosophy in perfect unity in

the way of life of man. The *Gita* is a great religious work far above our usual concept of 'Religion', that lays down a path of life for humanity—this is man's religion. The *Gita* also shows how to follow it—this is man's ethics. The *Gita* also lays down in specific terms the ultimate purpose aimed at in pursuing this way of life by the path recommended—this is *Gita*'s philosophy.

(2) This is probably the first work in Hindu Dharma that talks directly to man in his own easy, flowing and straight language—a language that penetrates into the heart itself. Here too it talks on his problems—this-worldly and other-worldly both—and carves out for humanity a way that even the meek and mild, the humble and ordinary, can follow considerably if they have a will, if they cultivate the will. In this sense, the *Gita* can be called a work that is सर्वजनहितपरं शास्त्रम्। (A Shastra that is bent upon doing good to all men) or सर्वजनानुकूलतत्वप्रतिपादकं शास्त्रम्। (A Shastra that propounds a doctrine that will be suitable of attainment by all men). Man may hold in very high esteem the *Upanishads*—'the noblest part of the Vedic literature'[21]—as Vaidya stated. It will yet be the good luck only of an intellectual and philosopher of first rank like Schopenhauer to state that the *Upanishads* were a solace of his life and would become a solace of his death. Man may admire the sagely writings and doctrines of the षड्दर्शन *Shad-Darshanas* but when, say the Vedanta wants to establish that

ब्रह्म सत्यं जगन्मिथ्या जीवो ब्रह्मैव नापरः ।

(*Brahman* is true and this world false; the *Jiva* is *Brahman* only and not something different from It,) only a few *Sannyasins* can possibly act according to it. It is only the *Gita* that can become a solace of life and death both, to most of us.

(3) The added uniqueness of the *Gita* here is that it is a work almost equally appealing, may be in a variety of ways, to almost all men, whatever their age, understanding, intellect and status in life. It is likely that an ordinary man of the world, who engrosses only in this-worldly life may win his solace by just a concentrated daily and regular recitation of some verses in the *Gita*, a man of action might act according to the way shown to a कर्मयोगी *Karmayogi*, a *Bhakta* might act according to the way of a भक्त *Bhakta* in the *Gita* and men of

renunciation and *Jnana* might get solution of their problems also. But one fact stands that it is an unfailing guide and sure solace for all.

(4) This need not surprise us due to the fact that the *Gita* is, with its subject-matter and method and aim of approach to life, far above sectarianism and it has quite naturally become a work of reverence and authority for so many sects in Hinduism, though it may happen and it has happened that each sect interprets the meaning of the *Gita* in its own way. This is natural and in the fitness of things. Lord Krishna states about himself in the *Gita*: ये यथा मां प्रपद्यन्ते तांस्तथैव भजाम्यहम। (4:11) (In whatever way men resort to Me, even so do I render to them.) It is clear that the *Gita* itself says the same thing to all men.

(5) The *Gita* naturally therefore embraces humanity at large and carves out a way of life, an ethics of life and the ultimate aim of life. It assures equal success to man in this life and also eternal bliss in the life hereafter. It solves so many riddles of life. It is therefore extremely catholic in outlook, sympathetic, loving and ever prepared to take man as he is.

(6) For this, naturally enough, its approach is that of समन्वय *Samanvaya* (harmony) and संवाद *Samvada* (dialogue). It therefore holds no specified or bigoted attachment to one or the other way of life, ethics and philosophy. To state in the words of the Upanishads, the *Gita* seems just to lay down that यादृशी भावना यस्य सिद्धिर्भवति तादृशी (A man's success will be in accordance with his sentiments). All men can drink of its nectar according to capacity. The *Gita* also shows the way to enhance, sublimate one's personality in such a way that man at every stage in his life can drink deeper and deeper of its nectar and get more and more enlivened.

(7) The *Gita* therefore permits a variety of ways of life and accepts varied approaches in perfect equanimity. "Interpret the meaning of my words as your conscience tells you, and act according to it, and you have interpreted the meaning of my words correctly." This is what the *Gita* seems to tell men. Countless varied interpretations of the *Gita* therefore that are given and that are likely to be given in future, are correct for the interpreters and if they follow the meaning that

they read in the *Gita*, the purpose of the composition of the *Gita* is served. This is inspite of the fact that scholars might come to the conclusion that most of the interpretations put on the *Gita* are different from what is in the mind of the poet-sage Vyasa or whoever he might be.

(8) As the *Gita* accepts a variety of ways in life, it also permits three main and many more paths of the realization of God. It also approves of varied philosophical doctrines in several options as also varied views on the nature of God the Supreme and His relation to man and the world and so on.

(9) However, its principal doctrine and way of life is that of detached *Karma* and so, its approach is easier and more appealing to man.

(10) From the highest happiness offered to man in this life and the highest bliss promised, it is clear that the tone of the *Gita* is that of extreme optimism. Its faith in man and his potentialities is unique and the *Gita* experiments just on these. And the *Gita* actually proclaims in the last verse that:

यत्र योगेश्वरः कृष्णो यत्र पार्थो धनुर्धरः ।
तत्र श्रीर्विजयो भूतिर्ध्रुवा नीतिर्मतिर्मम ।।
(18:78)

(Wheresoever Krishna, the Master of Yoga is, and wheresoever is Partha the Bowman, there, rest assured, are Fortune, Victory, Prosperity and Eternal Right.) The *Gita* is therefore quite rightly put in the mouth of Krishna—God the Supreme, who is योगेश्वर (Master of Yoga). It thus becomes a word of highest authority and sacredness because this creates faith and confidence in man's heart. To the *Gita* no man, no soul is hopeless or lost.

(11) Sublimation and higher rise are all that all men on earth seek. To tell in the words of बृहदारण्यकोपनिषत् *Brihadaranayaka-Upanishad*, all men on earth are आत्मकाम *Atmakama* conscious or unconsicous though they might be with regard to this.[22] And it is *Gita*'s supreme effort, first to solve man's problems of this life and the ethics thereof and then to sublimate man and lift him higher and higher till he hears divine music and ultimately wins self-realization as Gandhiji would

say and till he wins परं निःश्रेयसम्, i.e., oneness with *Brahman*, as Shankara would say. Thus it is that the *Gita* is admired by almost all who read it.

Some Important Views

All these and many other varied traits are difficult to be found in just one work that is religious, ethical and philosophical—all in one, and so this speaks for the immense popularity of the *Gita* and it is no surprise for us to read so many words of admiration, some of which may be noted by way of illustration:

> गीता सुगीता कर्तव्या किमन्यैः शास्त्रविस्तरैः।
> या स्वयं पद्मनाभस्य मुखपद्माद्विनिःसृताः।।
> यस्माद्धर्ममयी गीता सर्वज्ञानप्रयोजिका।
> सर्वशास्त्रमयी गीता तस्माद् गीता विशिष्यते।।
>
> (वाराहपुराणे)

("The *Gita* should always be sung well; what use is the detailed study of other *shastras* when the *Gita* has come out of the lotus-like mouth of Padmanabha himself? The *Gita* is peculiarly great because it is religious, inspirer of all knowledge, and consisting of (the essence of) all scriptures."—In *Varaha Purana*).

> सर्वोपनिषदो गावो दोग्धा गोपालनन्दनः।
> पार्थो वत्सः सुधीर्भोक्ता दुग्धं गीतामृतं महत्।।

(All *Upanishads* are cows, the son of Gopala, Krishna is the milker, Arjuna the calf, the wise learned the enjoyer; great and noble (indeed) is the milk of the nectar of the *Gita*).

"To anyone who has eyes to see, the *Gita* is based on direct knowledge of Reality, and of the path that leads to that Reality..."
(KRISHNA PREM)[23]

"The *Bhagvadgita* holds forth before mankind the highest and the loftiest ideal by attaining which the soul is liberated from all limitations and enjoys peace and bliss of his inherent state of immortality."
(SWAMI RAMDAS)[24]

"This great handbook of practical living marked a positive

revolution in Hinduism, and inaugurated a great Hindu Renaissance for the ages that followed the Puranic Era."

(SWAMI CHINMAYANAND)[25]

"It is a philosophical work, yet fresh and readable as poetry; a book of devotion, yet drawing its main inspiration from speculative systems...."

(FARQUHAR)[26]

"It is a true scripture of the Race, a life rather than a book. For each age it has a new message, for each civilization a new record."

(ANNIE BESANT)[27]

"It gives utterance to the aspirations of the pilgrims of all sects who seek to tread the inner way to the city of God."

(RADHAKRISHNAN)[28]

"....the most beautiful, perhaps the only true philosophical song existing in any known tongue."

(WILLIAM VON HUMBOLDT)

"The *Gita* is not an aphoristic work; it is a great religious poem. The deeper you dive into it, the richer the meaning you get. It being meant for the people at large, there is pleasing repetition. With every age, the important words will carry new and expanding meanings. But its central teaching will never vary."

(GANDHIJI)[29]

"The *Gita* is not a book of ethics but of spiritual life. It teaches not human but divine action; not the disinterested performance of duties but the following of the Divine will; not a performance of social duties but the abandonment of all standards of duty to take refuge in the supreme alone....etc."

(AUROBINDO)[30]

"God-realisation according to us is the supreme teaching of the *Gita*."

(R.D. RANADE)[31]

"The *Gita* is neither a practical guide-book of moral efforts nor a philosophical treatise discussing the origin of immoral tendencies and tracing them to certain metaphysical principles as their sources; but, starting from the ordinary frailties of attachment and desires, it tries to show how one can lead a normal life of duties and responsibilities and yet be in peace and contentment in a state of equanimity and in communion with God."

(DASGUPTA)[32]

Causes of Popularity—Gandhiji

A study of the causes of the immense popularity of the *Gita* as Gandhiji understands, should naturally follow this broad review before we proceed to the problem of the varied interpretations of the work and Gandhiji's interpretation. This will also take us nearer to the characteristic approach and outlook of Gandhiji in his own interpretation of the *Gita*, that is based on his *Achara* according to the word of the Gita for almost 40 years. To put in his own words: "At the back of my reading there is claim of an endeavour to enforce the meaning in my own conduct for an unbroken period of forty years."

(*Anasaktiyoga*)

(1) The *Gita* is a book of life, free from all sectarianism and dogma and its appeal is universal. It is thus applicable to and therefore a prized treasure for all humanity.
(2) It gives an original rule of conduct, and by giving new meaning to *Karma, Samnyasa, Yajna*, etc., it has breathed new life into Hinduism.
(3) The *Gita* guides man on the path of light when his vision is darkended and blinded, when man is at sea with regard to what he should do and when he is under extreme conflicts.
(4) It shows the way of peace at the price of life itself because the finest words of Hindu religion, ethics and philosophy are put in extremely simple, straight and effective language that all can grasp.
(5) The *Gita* records the highest aspiration of the human species, self-realization, in Gandhiji's opinion.
(6) The spirit of the *Gita* is love for all humanity and it yields life-

giving milk of hope and confidence to all men like a mother to her child. It will appeal to the most ordinary man of the world as also to the best of ascetics.

It is clear that with regard to the immense popularity of the *Gita*, Gandhiji accepts most of the views laid down above and he has thoroughly grasped the secret of the popularity and acknowledged greatness of the *Gita*. However, he seems to emphasise the following points with regard to the popularity and greatness of the *Gita* that is looked upon by him as a mother, as we have already seen above:-

(i) The *Gita* is an all-time work for humanity at large, it is universal. To the *Gita* no one is lowly and lost.
(ii) The *Gita* lays down an original rule of conduct.
(iii) The *Gita* records the highest aspirations of the human species.
(iv) The *Gita* is a book of life and it lays down a religion and ethics that light up man's path when he is deluded by darkness and has lost hope.
(v) Self-realization is the highest end in view in the *Gita*.

It is in this spirit and confidence that Gandhiji resorts to the *Gita* like a child to the bosom of the mother and is confident ever of getting sweet life-giving nectar-like milk that enlivens him under all conflicts, problems and delusions in life. It is a spirit first of faith and devotion and then of action and knowledge. It suggests his own approach and view-point in the interpretation of the *Gita*. But to that we come after we study the problem of the varied interpretations of the *Gita*.

Varied Interpretations

Rightly has Dasgupta shown to us the peculiar structure and nature of the contents of the *Gita* when he states that:

"Neither the *Yoga-Vasistha* nor the *Gita* are systematic works on philosophy, and yet no treatment of Indian philosophy can legitimately ignore their claims. For, in a country where philosophy and religion have been inseparably associated, the value of such writings as breathe the spirit of philosophy cannot be overestimated and no history of Indian philosophy worth the name can do without them."[33]

Actually no philosophical system of note or no important *Acharya* has ignored it or has done without the *Gita* and all who resort to the *Gita* have worried to read their own doctrine in it and that also explains the varied interpretations of the doctrine of the *Gita*.

As we read the varied interpretations of the *Gita* by the *Acharyas* and scholars both of east and west, we find that "So many and varied are the existing introductions to, interpretations of and discourses on the *Bhagavadgita*," (V. Rele)[34] it is interesting that the *Gita* actually permits of all these interpretations. This is because, "One of the great charms of the book . . . is that the more it is read, the greater appears the possible number of interpretations of its teachings. The mirror of the *Gita* is so clear and untarnished that it reflects ideas from every side." (Rele)[35] One more reason why the *Gita* is interpreted from various angles is that, "Every teacher who wished to claim Vedantic authority for his teachings was obliged to write a commentary on it showing that it supported his views." (Krishna Prem)[36] This would of course be in addition to the commentaries on the *Upanishads* and *Brahmasutras*—the other two, with which the *Gita* forms the triple base on which the Vedanta is founded—the प्रस्थानत्रय (*Prasthantreya*).[37] One question of course arises in our mind. "Had the author all these interpretations in mind when he composed its teachings or had he, perhaps, an interpretation of his own that included and transcended all?" (Rele)[38] And scholars rightly express their feelings when they say that, "Enthusiasts for action, for knowledge (*Jnana* or Gnosis), or for devotion to a personal God, all find their special tenets in the *Gita* and though this universal appeal is proof of its catholicity, its authoritative status has had the drawback that the various commentators[39] have often devoted more energy to special pleading and refutation of opponents than to straight-forward inquiry into the real meaning of the text" (Krishna Prem).[40] So much of variety is there in man's mind and outlook and the resulting conception of religion, morality and ethics, and so much is the charm of the *Gita* that inspite of all varied interpretations from particular angles of vision, a study of every new interpretation added becomes interesting and with that the attempt on part of some scholars to probe into the mind of the original author by probing into the real meaning of the text is also interesting. Every such interpretation and attempt is bound to bring us nearer to the secret of the charm of the *Gita*. It may here be added that while some commentaries like *Amritatarangini* specifically and honestly state that:

श्रीविट्ठलपदाम्भोजकृपामधुसुपूरितः ।
व्याख्यास्ये भगवद्गीतां भक्तिमार्गानुसारतः ।।

("I, who am filled to the brim by the honey in form of favour of the lotus-like feet of Shri Vitthala, shall analyse the *Bhagavadgita* in accordance with the path of devotion"),

most of the Acharyas had not the idea that they were reading their own views in the *Gita*, and they were sincere in their belief that they were interpreting the doctrine of the original writer of the *Gita* and not their own. They opine that the philosophy that they read in the *Gita* is that of the *Gitakara* only. Yet the fact remains that the *Gita* has been interpreted in various ways by the Acharyas. That shows that interpreting the *Gita* to bring out the meaning of the *Gitakara* is very very difficult indeed, if not impossible.

The study therefore of every new interpretation becomes interesting, more so because in that study we get a new approach to the beauty of the *Gita* and we also read and interpret the mind of the interpreter. And it is not necessary to insist on giving a final interpretation to the *Gita*. With all interpretations that are given to the *Gita*, more are still likely to be given in future and it is not unlikely that many of these will read new doctrines and secrets in the *Gita*, even though some of its doctrines are commonly accepted almost by all. This shows that,

(i) The words of the epic poet Magha क्षणे क्षणे यन्नवतामुपैति तदेव रूपं रमणीयतायाः ("That is the charm of beauty indeed that assumes novelty at every moment")[41], will aptly apply to the *Gita* with its unique poetic charm, simple language, effective expression and deep religious, ethical and philosophical doctrines.

(ii) The limits of time, place and culture and barriers of language do not bind the *Gita*.

(iii) Men of all times are likely to seek a solace and sure guidance from the *Gita*.

(iv) The spirit of the *Gita* is large and universal and it enfolds humanity at large in its loving embrace.

That is the reason why Dr. Radhakrishnan admires the *Gita* in these words: "It gives utterance to the aspirations of the pilgrims of all sects who seek to tread the inner way to the city of God. We touch reality most deeply, where men struggle, fail and triumph. Millions of Hindus, for centuries, have found comfort in this great book which sets forth in precise and penetrating words the essential principles of a spiritual religion which are not contingent on ill-founded facts, unscientific dogmas or arbitrary fancies."[42]

Naturally therefore the interpretation of Mahatma Gandhi is bound to be partly new and interesting in its own way. As we will study his *Anasaktiyoga* and the views expressed therein and his hundreds of other utterances on the *Gita*, we will study the great work from a new angle. That will also help us in understanding the personality of the man and also his teachings better. The greatness of the *Gita* will be known to us still further when we come to know that Gandhiji and *Anasaktiyoga* are inseparable. The *Gita*, on which he looked as his mother, was his sure and unfailing guide in the midst of all strifes, problems and conflicts. His interpretation of the *Gita* gave much to him; actually it shaped his personality a lot. Consequently it continued to remain his life-long companion, friend, philosopher and guide till he breathed his last. To note from his own statements, this is what the *Gita* meant to Gandhiji:

(i) It gives peace and equanimity to spirit. (13-1-1940).
(ii) It fulfills the need of a scripture to serve as an unfailing guide through the trials and temptations of life. (24-8-1934).
(iii) The conflict about the rightness or otherwise of un-touchability is solved by the *Gita*.(24-8-1934).
(iv) The *Gita* is a universal mother turning away nobody. (24-8-1934).
(v) The *Gita* taught duty of perseverance in the face of deeming failure. (24-8-1934).
(vi) The *Gita* gives the milk that we need for spiritual sustenance.
(vii) In Harijan work, in the midst of calumny, mis-representation and apparent disappointments, her lap comforts and saves one from failing in the slough of despondency. (*Bapu's Letters to Mira*—p. 249).
(viii) The *Gita* teaches that to a true *Bhakta*, all are equal and so, it leaves no scope for belief in high and low.
(ix) The *Gita* is to him a key to the scriptures of the world. (18-4-1936).

All this makes his interpretation very much interesting because probably no other student of the *Gita* has singly admired the *Gita* to this extent. As we study his interpretation of the *Gita* and examine its impact on his life and personality, his teachings and search after Truth, we will also see that his personality has influenced his interpretation as it should be and has deeply shaped and influenced his personality and action in life.

Naturally therefore his interpretation is new and original and it reveals some secrets of the scholars and *Acharyas*. Gandhiji claims that, "I exercise my judgement about every scripture, including the *Gita*. I cannot let a scriptural text supersede my reason;"[43] and also that, "I ascribe to the *Gita*, a totally new meaning from that ordinarily given."[44]

These claims are amply supported by his translation in which he has taken utmost and scrupulous care to be exact, though as he frankly admits, he interprets the *Gita* from his own point of view. His claim stands true also by the interesting problems raised in his *Anasaktiyoga* and the answers to these as he finds them in the *Gita*, and also from his method of interpretation as specified in clear terms—the method is scientific and logical in its own way. It is the method that is usually followed by the भाष्यकार[s] (*Bhashyakars*) like Shankara, Ramanuja, etc.

If we take Aurobindo, Tilak, Radhakrishnan and Gandhiji to be the foremost of the modern eastern interpreters of the *Gita*, we find that their interpretations differ from each other glaringly and considerably. We also find that the interpretations of the *Gita* given by prominent Gandhiaites—Mashruwala, Vinoba, Kalelkar and Maganbhai Desai—differ from each other as also from that of Gandhiji. But Gandhiji's interpretation is authentic in its own way because he had tried to put into practice the teaching of the *Gita* as he read it, for forty years, when he published it. He claims that, "I never cite scripture unless I have subjected it to the test of personal experience," and also concedes that, "that of others may be different from mine, and they too, may perhaps find a *Gita* verse in support of it ... I may not, therefore, insist upon my experience being acknowldged as valid by all."[45]

We therefore undertake this study from various angles of vision and partly pushing aside the conventional approach, study the problem of the *Gita* as under:

As a background of the study, we will, first of all, make a brief and broad survey of important interpretations of ancients and moderns—of Shankara, Ramanuja, Madhusudana and the Vallabha school among the ancients and Hill, Tilak, Radhakrishnan and Aurobindo among the moderns. This will be the background on which our study of Gandhiji's '*Anasaktiyoga*' will be based. The study will naturally be broad and detailed and will cover up all other important statements of Gandhiji on the *Gita* in particular and Hinduism in general. On the basis of this we will proceed to examine in a rather descriptive chapter how the *Gita* worked in the life of Gandhiji, when his personality progressed and scaled greater and greater heights and ultimately made Gandhiji, *Mahatma* from *Mohan*. The next chapter will discuss how and why the *Gita* continued to help Gandhiji even in the worst of conflicts in life and how it became a source of consolation, inspiration and strength to him and unfailingly answered all his questions. This will establish the inner strength of the *Gita* and the great value of Gandhiji's own interpretation of its meaning. Gandhiji has made a few very important claims in his interpretation of the *Gita* such as: (i) The *Mahabharata* and the *Gita* are allegorical; the war described in the work is also purely allegorical and in no way a historical fact; (ii) The *Gita* teaches *Ahimsa*; (iii) The attitude of *Anasakti* is the very basis of *karma* and so on.

These will be analysed in detail in the next chapter and with that we will have come to almost a complete and all-sided study of Gandhiji's *Gita* and how far his important teachings are based on the *Gita*. We will also understand how the *Gita* helps us in understanding Gandhiji's teachings and philosophy of life. This will be the concluding chapter after which we will fix Gandhiji's place in the realm of scholars and *Acharyas* of the *Gita* and get a clear idea of the originality of the interpretation and its uniqueness because of the basis of its actual practice in life.

The whole study is thus an original one and one that, it is hoped, will be an important one in understanding the *Gita* as also the religious, ethical and spiritual teachings of Gandhiji. No such detailed study has been undertaken so far. It also helps us in understanding the greatness of the Mahatma. I have, after all the study of the works of Mahatma Gandhi, felt that we in India hardly know how great he was. He is far greater than we know him to be. It is hoped that our present study will open the door to the understanding of his greatness, and his greatness now of course means the greatness of his teachings.

NOTES

1. 'All Men are Brothers', p. 59.
2. George Bernard Shaw
3. 'Perennial Philosophy', p.53.
4. 'Harijan', 18-6-1938.
5. 'Satyagraha in South Africa', p. 186.
6. 'Satyagraha in South Africa', p. 186.
7. 'Last Glimpses of Bapu', Manuben Gandhi, p.222.
8. 'Perennial Philosophy', p.55.
9. 'An Approach to the Study of Gandhi'—An Article.
10. 'Young India', 6-8-1925.
11. 'Harijan', 24-8-1934.
12. Vide Shankara in Intro. to *Gitabhashya*.
13. व्याख्यास्ये भगवद्गीतां भक्तिमार्गानुसारतः । *Amritatarangini Tika.*
14. इति श्रीमद् भगवद्गीतासूपनिषत्सु etc.
15. सर्वोपनिषदो गावो दोग्धा गोपालनन्दनः । पार्थो वत्सः सुधीर्भाक्ता दुग्धं गीतामृतं महत् ।।
16. This is the contention of many eastern and western scholars.
17. '*Gita* Letters', Swami Avinashananda, p. 34.
18. '*Gita* Letters', p. 35.
19. Quoted by S. Radhakrishnan in his 'Bhagavadgita'—Introduction p. 2.
20. Bhagavadgita—Introduction, p. 1.
21. 'History of Vedic Literature', C.V. Vaidya.
22. बृहदारण्यकोपनिषद् 2-3-5 -न वा अरे सर्वस्थ कामाय सर्वं प्रियं भवति, आत्मनस्तु कामाय सर्व प्रियं भवति।
23. 'The Yoga of Bhgavadgita', p. xiv
24. '*Gita* Sandesh', p. 1.
25. 'The Bhagavadgita', Vol. 1, p. 35.
26. '*Gita* and the Gospel'
27. Quoted in 'The Gospel of Life' by F.T. Brooks p.v.
28. 'Bhagavadgita', Intro. p.11
29. 'Young India', 6-8-1931.
30. 'Essays on the *Gita*', p. 43.
31. 'Bhagavad Gita—As a Philosophy of God-Realization', p. 3.
32. 'History of Indian Philosophy', Vol. II. p. 501.
33. 'History of Indian Philosophy', Vol. II, p. vii.
34. 'Bhagavadgita—An Exposition', p.1.
35. 'Bhagavadgita—An Exposition', p. 1.
36. 'The Yoga of the Bhagavadgita', p. viii.
37. Kaka Kalelkar in his preface to the 'Anasktiyoga' gives a similar view.

38. 'Bhagavadgita—An Exposition', p. 2.
39. And shall we add—and almost all modern scholars, eastern and western?
40. 'The Yoga of the Bhagavadgita', p. viii.
41. शिशुपालवधम् of Magha –4-17.
42. 'Bhagavadgita', Introduction p. 2.
43. 'Harijan', 5-12-1935.
44. 'Young India', 5-4-1925.
45. 'The Diary of Mahadev Desai', p. 306, on 24-3-1932.

TWO

Survey of Principal Interpretations —The Ancients

विद्वद्भिः सेवितः सद्भिः नित्यमद्वेषरागिभिः।
हृदयेनाभ्युज्ञातः यो धर्मस्तं निबोधतः।।

(मनुस्मृति-2-1)

(Learn that sacred law which is followed by men learned (in the Vedas) and assented to in their hearts by the virtuous, who are ever exempt from hatred and inordinate affection.)

(Manusmriti 2.1)

"The Gita is a pure religious discourse, given without any embellishment. It simply describes the progress of the pilgrim soul towards the supreme Goal."—GANDHIJI.[1]

"When is a man in mere understanding? I answer, 'When a man sees one thing separated from another.' And when is a man above mere understanding? That I can tell you: 'When a man sees all in all, then a man stands beyond mere understanding'."—ECKHART.[2]

Introduction

"Philosophy in action is Religion. From time to time an ancient philosophy needs an intelligent reinterpretation in the context of new times and men of wisdom, prophets and seers guide the common man on how to apply effectively the ancient laws in his present life," states Swami Chinmayananda[3] in his 'Gita'.

We have seen in the previous chapter that every new interpretation on the *Gita* brings us to a clearer understanding of its secrets and greatness[4] and also that time and again new interpretations to this great work with a large spirit are likely to be given. It is known to those who scale the mountain top that their paths and efforts are different, but the wide vision of nature at the top is the same for all. Almost similar is the position of the various interpretations of the *Gita*. The approaches to life and divinity, ethics and religion, differ in the interpretations, but the realization at the end is almost the same for all.

Each new effort at interpretation is interesting in its own way. As Dr. Radhakrishnan rightly points out: "These writers are able to find in the *Gita* their own systems of religious thought and metaphysics, since the author of the *Gita* suggests that the one eternal truth derived cannot be shut up in a single formula."[5] No doubt it is true that it might be possible to come to a conclusion about the religious, ethical and metaphysical doctrine of the author of the *Gita* on the basis of a pure and impartial study of the text, very difficult though it is. It is also true that an effort on these lines is very much interesting, scholarly and it helps us in understanding the work better. On the other side it is also true that: "The various commentaries on the *Gita* were written by the teachers in support of their own traditions (सम्प्रदाय) and in refutation of those of others." But with this, the attempt of the *Acharyas*, each of whom has given a new interpretation to the *Gita* is scholarly, interesting and it has left a very deep impression on the life of the *Sampradaya* that he led. Each interpretation leaves a deep mark and shapes the lives of the followers of each *Sampradaya* and all its members breathe new hope and confidence and gain religious, ethical and metaphysical light. The *Gita* is like a mother with many children, each with a varied taste, outlook, temperament and intellectual grasp and the mother answers to the love call of one and all with the same loving warmth. Gandhiji states: "Well, that Immortal Mother gives all the milk we need for spiritual sustenance, if we would but approach her as babes seeking and sucking it from her. She is capable of yielding milk to her millions of babes from her exhaustless udders."[6] When Gandhiji states in his *Anasaktiyoga* that the interpretation given to it by him shows the way of life of the inmates of the *Ashrama* and also claims that: "But I am not aware of the claim made by the translators of enforcing their meaning of the *Gita* in their own lives. At the back of my reading there is the claim of an endeavour to enforce the meaning in my conduct for an unbroken period of 40 years," he is no exception to this rule.

But Gandhiji differs from the other *Acharyas* and scholars in many respects, as we shall see later on. Both as an interpretation like those of others and as an interpretation coming from the pen of Gandhiji, it will be of very great interest. When we get a clear grasp as to its real value, we will also get a glimpse of its deep impression on his teachings.

The originality of Mahadev Desai is specially referred to by Prof. R.D. Ranade in these words: "On account of his sound knowledge of Sanskrit and philosophy, Mahadev Desai was well qualified to undertake this great work that reflects the freshness and originality of the writer."[7]

Similar are Kaksaheb Kalelkar's remarks in Gujarati when he states the desire of Gandhiji in these words: "For this reason I do indeed harbour the wish that Gujarati men or women, wishing to shape their conduct according to their faith, should digest and derive strength from the translation here presented."[8]

If we come to know the secret of this greatness of the *Gita* and also know how it has influenced Gandhiji and examine how he valued the *Gita* for himself, we will also be able to get a glimpse of that essence of *Gita*'s teaching. We too might then be able to win that inspiration, solace, guidance and strength that Gandhji expects us to have.

We therefore start our study of the problem with a broad survey of the interpretations of ancients and moderns in this and the next chapter. This will be the proper background to the study of Gandhiji's interpretation of the *Gita* that follows next. It would be quite natural on our part to start the study of the interpretations of the ancients with Shankaracharya, whose *Gitabhashya* is very popular.

Shankaracharya

Shankara is less of a sectarian than most others, he is greater *ADHYATMAVADIN* than all others. In the opinion of the westerners, if at all there is any pure philosopher amongst the *Acharyas*, it is Shankara. He is, as we well know, the propounder of absolute monism and stands firm on the famous Upanishadic doctrine:

ब्रह्म सत्यं जगन्मिथ्या जीवौ ब्रह्मैव नापरः।

(Only *Brahman* is truth, the universe is false; the *Jiva* is *Brahman* and that only and not anything different.)

His God is *Nirguna Nirakara* and the path to the realization of this God the Supreme, and only reality, is that of *Jnana* alone. The path is ultimately open only to a *Samnyasin*. In his famous works *Vivekacudamani* and *Atmabodha* he preaches the same doctrine that he reads in the *Brahmasutra* of Badarayana as interpreted in his *Sharirakabhashya* and in the *Bhagavadgita* as interpreted in his *Gitabhashya*. He thus reads the same metaphysical and spiritual doctrine in all these works. In his commentaries on the ten conventionally accepted authentic Upanishads also, he tries, with twists and distortions of meanings even, to derive the same philosophy. Thus, in the opinion of Shankara, (i) *Moksha* is the final and highest and the only aim worth attaining for all living beings; (ii) *Moksha* means experience of the reunion of the *Atma*, that seems separate only apparently, with *Brahman*; (iii) *Brahman* is the only reality, the ultimate Truth that is *Nirguna* and *Nirakara*; (iv) The path to this realization is that only of *Jnana*—knowledge; (v) This realization is open only to a *Samnyasin*, who has completely renounced the world and has got over its *Maya*. Besides this, Shankara's important contribution is his doctrine of *Maya* and *Avidya*.

This explains his interpretation of the *Sthitaprajna* as a *Samnyasin* whom he defines in his *Bhashya* on *Gita* 2:55:

त्यक्तेपुत्रलोकैषणः संन्यस्यात्माराम आत्मक्रीडः स्थितप्रज्ञः इत्यर्थः।

(A *Sthiaprajna* is one who has completely renounced the attachment to sons, (family) and the world, who has embraced *samnyasa* and is thereby one delighting in his own self and playing also with his self.) He also takes the same stand in his comments on 2:56, when he states:

स्थितधीः स्थितप्रज्ञो मुनिः संन्यासी तदोच्यते।

(The *Sthitaprajan* is known as a man of steadfast intellect who is a sage, a *samnyasi*.) He calls him a *Yati* in his comments on 2:61, when he states:

"Steadfast is the intellect of that man, a steady *Yati*, whose senses act under his control, thanks to the power of study." His refutation of the *Samkhya, Vaisheshika, Nyaya Darshanas*, his rejection of Buddhism and Jainism in the तर्कपाद (*Tarkapad*) of his *Shankarabhashya* etc., are based on this. His concept of *Maya* follows from this. Accordingly he interprets the Vedanta-sutras of Badarayana and the ten Upanishads, in all of which he comes to the same conclusion and so does he in his *Bhashya* on the *Gita*. Sankaracharya's reading of the *Gita* is mainly philosophical and his conclusions are also derived on this line. That partly explains why he gives no importance to the 1st *Adhyaya* and the 10 verses of the 2nd *Adhyaya* and starts his comments with the famous verse:

अशोच्यानन्वशोचस्त्वं प्रज्ञावादांश्च भाषसे।
गतासूनगतासूंश्च नानुशोचन्ति पण्डिता:।।

(2:11)

(Thou mournest for them whom thou shouldst not mourn, and utterest vain words of wisdom. The wise mourn neither for the living nor for the dead).

We might start with the study of the famous conclusion that he has drawn in his preliminary discussion:

तस्यास्य गीताशास्त्रस्य संक्षेपत: प्रयोजनं परं नि:श्रेयसं सहेतुकस्य संसारस्यात्यन्तोपरमलक्षणम्। तच्च सर्वकर्मसंन्यासपूर्वकादात्मज्ञाननिष्ठारूपाद्धर्माद् भवति।

(The ultimate aim of the *Gita* is, in a word, the attainment of the Highest Good, characterised by the complete cessation of relative existence and its cause. This is realized by means of that *Dharma* whose essence is devotion, self-knowledge attained through the renunciation of all action). According to this statement, the purpose of composition of the *Gita*, in brief, is to describe these:

(i) *Moksha* and its attainment.
(ii) This should lead to destruction of (attachment to) the *samsara*.
(iii) This is possible only through *Atmajnana* preceded by renunciation of all actions.
(iv) This is the निवृत्तिमार्ग (*Nivrittimarg*) or निवृत्तिधर्म (*Nivrittidharma*) laid down by the Gita.
(v) As for the प्रवृत्तिमार्ग (*Pravrittimarg*) or प्रवृत्तिलक्षणो धर्म (*Pravrittilakshan dharma*) shown by the *Gita* with reference to the followers of *Varna* and *Ashrama*, it causes man's rise to the attainment of higher worlds like *svarga*, and if followed with a sense of submission to God, it leads to purity of *sattva* when attachment to the fruits of actions is lost.

(vi) When an individual has become शुद्धसत्त्व (*Shuddhasattva*), he deserves to attain to ज्ञाननिष्ठा (*Jnana-Nishtha*) and that leads to *moksha*.

According to Shankara, it is said that: "God created this universe and for its existence and destruction gave the two famous धर्मs (*Dharmas*) of प्रवृत्ति (*Pravritti*) and निवृत्ति (*Nivrtti*). Then when the धर्म (*Dharma*) in the universe was overcome by अधर्म (*Adharma*), Lord Vishnu named Narayana took birth in the womb of Devaki through Vasudeva. This God Krishna was ever endowed with knowledge, divine power, strength, heroism and lustre. He brought under control *Prakriti* that was *Maya* with the three constituent virtues. Since he was in reality God the Supreme that is unborn, indestructible, the Lord of all beings, and ever of the nature of purity, knowledge and freedom, he has as if, through his *Maya*, become one endowed with a human body; he is seen always engrossed in the good of the world. He instructed Arjuna, who indulged in the great ocean of sorrow and delusion, in the twofold *vaidikadharma*, even though therein he had no purpose of his own to serve and he was inspired only by the desire to protect the beings from sorrow. *Moksha* is the highest purpose of this philosophy of the *Gita*. It is of the nature of total annihilation of *samsara*. This annihilation is possible in due order only through following action constantly in a series of births. *Dharma* that is preceded by abandonment of all actions that are full of attachment and those that are prohibited, is to be followed by a sense of submission to God the Supreme. This is possible quickly to be attained to by *Dharma* of the nature of *Atmajnana* that is preceded by renunciation of all actions. This twofold means has *Moksha* for its purpose. The *Gita Shastra* shows that ultimately the परमार्थतत्व (*Parmarthatatva*) of the nature of Krishna is to be the final aim named परब्रह्म (*Parabrahma*)."[9]

The view is further supported and clarified when, in his comments on *Bhagavadgita* 2:11, he states that,

तस्माद्गीतासु केवलादेव तत्त्वज्ञानान्मोक्षप्राप्तिः।

(Therefore the *Gita* lays down the attainment of *Moksha* only through pure knowledge of Reality.)

He here rejects the theory of highest realization being possible by

ज्ञानकर्मसमुच्चय (*Jnanakarma Samuchchaya*) and thus strengthens his view that केवलाद्वैतरूप ब्रह्म (*Kevaladvaitrupa Brahma*) is to be realised by केवलज्ञान (*Kevaljnana*).[10] A question naturally arises here. If in 5:1 we were to accept this, how does Shankara reconcile himself to the constant talk of निष्काम कर्माचरण (following the path of desireless actions), in statements such as:

नियतं कुरु कर्म त्वं कर्म ज्यायो ह्याकर्मण:। (3 :8)

(Perform thou thy allotted task because action is superior to non-action);[11] and,

संन्यासस्तु महाबाहो दु:खमाप्तुमयोगत:। (5 :6)

(But *Samnyasa*, O Arjuna, is difficult to attain without resorting to *Karmayoga*);[12] and,

मयैवैते निहता: पूर्वमेव निमित्तमात्रं भव सव्यसाचिन्। (11 :33)

(I have already killed these warriors, O Arjuna, become just an instrument),[13] and so on? The reply is already given by Shankara in his introductory summary. It is that *Karma, Niskama-karma, Karma* in the name of God, etc., are necessary only upto a certain stage for the development of the personality of man and ultimately he comes to deserve the final bliss of *Moksha* by resorting to the path of ज्ञान (*Jnana*) and संन्यास (*Samnyasa*). This will be in addition to the rewards such as attainment of *svarga* and so on. To put in the words of Radhakrishnan, according to Shankara "even if *Karma* may not be the immediate cause of liberation, still it is a necessary means for acquiring saving wisdom."[14] (कर्मनिष्ठाया: ज्ञाननिष्ठाप्राप्तिहेतुत्वे पुरुषार्थहेतुत्वं न स्वातन्त्र्येण।) So, according to Shankara, by desireless action that is again submitted to God and performed in the name of God, and that too with full devotion, man raises his personality high and comes to that stage of mental quietude and preparedness for renunciation when the world by gradual steps, ceases to exist for him. His *Atman* comes to the realization of Itself and this आत्मज्ञान (*Atmajnana*) leads to ब्रह्मसाक्षात्कार (*Brahmasakshatkara*) that is मोक्ष (*Moksha*). He thus tries to assert even his सिद्धान्त (*Siddhanta*) of माया (*Maya*) in so far as for a संन्यासी (*Samnyasi* who has resorted to ज्ञानमार्ग (*Jnanamarga*), the external world does not exist as a reality and to him the only truth, one without a second, is ब्रह्म (*Brahma*).

It is known that according to Shankara, Krishna is, at the most *Sakara* and *Saguna*, i.e., lower *Brahman* and not *Parabrahma* that is *Nirakara* and *Nirguna* in his opinion. Madhusudana however believes tht Krishna is one with *Nirakara Brahman* that is *Parabrahman* in his opinion and he further stresses that *Nirguna –Nirakra Brahman* somehow appears in the form of Krishna or like Krishna. As a result of this, Krishna becomes God the Supreme. Similar is his attitude towards *Bhakti*. While Shankara gives to *Bhakti* a lower status than *Jnana*, as a path toward the highest realization, Madhusudana gives an equal status to *Bhakti* with *Jnana*. To him, *Bhakti* is in no way lower than *Jnana*. He naturally emphasises the verses referring to *Bhakti* such as,

चतुर्विधा भजन्ते मां नराः सुकृतिनोऽर्जुन।
आर्तो जिज्ञासुरर्थार्थी ज्ञानी च भरतर्षभ।। (7:16)

(Four types of well-doers are devoted to Me, O Arjuna; they are, O Bharatarshabha, the afflicted, the spiritual seeker, the material seeker and the enlightened,)

and,

तेषां ज्ञानी नित्ययुक्त एकभक्तिर्विशिष्यते। (7:17)

(Of these the enlightened, ever attached to Me in single-minded devotion, is the best.)

It is here clear that *Karma* is necessary upto a certain stage, a stage to which the sublimation of man's full personality is a necessity. He therefore interprets the word योगे in 2:39 as योगे तु श्रृणु (now hear my preaching from the point of view of *Karma-Yoga*). Once that limit, when he comes to deserve the highest knowledge, is reached, gradually all *Karmas* cease to exist for him. *Karmas* therefore are not a means to the end in the form of the attainment of *Brahman*, known in his introduction as परं निःश्रेयसम् (*Param Nishreysam*) by Shankara when the संसार (*Sansara*) ceases to exist for man. *Karma-Yoga* therefore is necessary only upto a certain stage. Shankara *literally* wants a stage of नैष्कर्म्यं (*Naishkarmyam*) for the मुमुक्षु (*Mumukshu*) and he reads just the same view in the *Gita*. Shankara propounded the theory that for a मुक्तात्मा (*Muktatma*), nay, even for a मुमुक्षु (*Mumukshu*) who has actually resorted to *samnyasa*, no actions are necessary. It is yet too well-known that for his whole life, for every minute of his life, Shankara had been a great *Karmayogin*. Rightly does Ranade state that "Shankaracharya, who fought for the uniqueness of *Jnana*, uncontaminated by *karma*, was himself one of the greatest intellectual activists the world has ever seen...one has only to remember that it becomes the mission of such a realiser to spread the gospel of God whenever and wherever it becomes possible for him to do so!"[15] So many verses in the *Gita* help him, he gives very long interpretations and explanations of verses 2:69, 3:1, 3:4, etc. where the letter of the *Gita* goes against his views, and gives distorted interpretations in verses 2:47, 4:4, 3:8, 5:5 to suit his own views. But he is consistent in his contention here. Shankara again fails to convince us when he interprets the important verses referring to *Bhakti* as the means to final realization (12:1, 12:2, 12:6, 12:14, 12:16, etc.). He even distorts the very clear words करिष्ये वचनं तव (18:73) in his interpretation when he comments thus, गतसंदेहो मुक्तसंशयः करिष्ये वचनं तवाहं त्वत्प्रसादात् कृतार्थो न मम् कर्तव्यमस्तीत्यभिप्रायः। (With all my doubts dispelled, I being devoid of all doubts, shall act according to your words, that is, my mission is fruitful through your favour (and) I have nothing to do, this is the opinion.) Ramanuja is very clear in his interpretation here when he says:

यथोक्तं युद्धादिकं करिष्ये इत्यर्थः।

(I shall resort to war, etc., as narrated by you. This is the meaning.) The interpretation of *Amritatarangini* is the same almost though under the deep stamp of the *Bhakti* cult:इदानीं तव वचनं पूर्वोक्तं युद्धादिरूपं सर्वधर्मत्यागरूपं त्वद्भक्तेष्वेतदुपदेशरूपं च करिष्ये। (Now I shall abide by your preaching to your devotees, given earlier, in the nature of war etc., that is also of the nature of renunciation of all *dharmas*,) and also the नीलकण्ठी टीका-करिष्ये वचनं तवेत्यनेन स्वधर्मे युद्धे चाधर्मधीरूपोऽपि मोहो नष्ट इति दर्शितम्। ("I shall abide by your word"- by these words it is shown that Arjuna's delusion of the nature of *Adharma* with reference both to *Svadharma* and war is destroyed.) Shankara has of course not been able to give convincing interpretation of तस्माद्युध्यस्व (2:38); तस्मादुत्तिष्ठ कौन्तेय युद्धाय कृतनिश्चयः। (2:37); युध्यस्व जेतासि रणे सपत्नान्। (2:34); युध्यस्व विगतज्वरः। (2:30), etc. because he takes for granted that all this *Karma* is simply to take Arjuna to a higher stage after which he will not fight or resort to any action.

This Vedantic and purely philosophical view has evoked admiration and criticism both and immediately after him, *Acharyas* started realizing and giving expression to the view that the *Gita* is not only or even predominantly a work on Advaita philosophy and that it is not a work that shows the path of the highest realization for a *samnyasin*, while the man of the world is to tread a long long path of *Karma-yoga* and *Bhakti-yoga* to raise his personality and mental stature high enough for *Jnana-yoga*. The first prominent *Acharya* to look upon the Gita as much more than a work on Advaita philosophy is Ramanuja. In Ramanuja we meet "...an Indian *guru* who explains a reverenced text to his disciples in the ancient and traditional manner, elucidating stanza after stanza passing at every word, enlarging upon every vital point and clarifying every difficulty."[16]

Interpretation of Ramanuja

God the Supreme is *Purushottama Narayana* whose basic trait is extreme and endless *kalyana*. He is the one abode of boundless *Ananda*, the one in whom rest the birth, maintenance and end of the world that is his *lila* and so on. He first created this whole universe and then took birth in it by His own form. His birth as an *Avatara* was for the ending of all sorrow of the world as also the living beings in it. For bringing an end to the sorrows of the world, he gave rise to his *Bhakti-yoga* that follow *Jnana* and *Karma*. When he interprets in this way, exactly in accordance with his doctrine of विशिष्टाद्वैत (*Vishishtadvaita*) in his श्रीभाष्य (*Shribhashya*), he clearly reads in the *Gita* these views:

(1) The *Gita* lays down the path of *Bhakti-yoga* that is particularised by *Jnana* and *Karma* that are subservient to it.
(2) The Gita teaches of God the Supreme as पुरुषोत्तम नारायण (Purushottama Narayana) i.e., Krishna who is पुरुषोत्तम (Purushottama) the Supreme Being, as the *Bhaktas* should realize.
(3) This पुरुषोत्तम नारायण (Purushottama Narayana) is born on earth with extraordinary divine traits to alleviate the sorrows that abound in the world.
(4) He is to be approached with utter devotion.
(5) Man should realize that this world is his play, his *Leela* and, He is the root cause of the universe.

(6) Man's life should be such that the truth of this God the Eternal, the highest reality is experienced and life is shaped in such a way that man approaches this divine more and more.
(7) Realizing that this *Narayana* is *Moksha*, the highest aim of life, Lord Krishna has taken birth for मोक्ष (*Moksha*) of all.
(8) This परब्रह्मभूत पुरुषोत्तमो नारायण: (*Parbrahmabhuta Purushottamo Narayanah*): is सगुण ब्रह्म (*Sagun Brahma*). He has clarified his position in his *Vedarthasamgraha* thus:
"True knowledge of the *Jivatma* and the supreme *atman*, applied to the performance of the obligations imposed by the *dharma* of the various stations and stages of life, accompanying humble and pious acts of reverence for and meditation on the Supreme Person—these and similar acts being held most dear by the devotee will result in the attainment of God." This has been the main thought of his philosophy in all his works including the गीताभाष्य (*Gitabhashya*).

When Ramanuja reads his own philosophy of God being *Saguna Brahman*, the path of Bhakti and मोक्ष (*Moksha*) in the form of realizing His greatness through life, his approach to the *Gita* is no better. He too reads his own typical doctrine in the *Gita*, and cares not much to read from the *Gita* the doctrines of the writer, whoever he is. But, as far as the nature, doctrine and philosophy of the *Gita* are concerned, he seems to be nearer to the truth of the writer than Shankara.[17]

It is now realized that,

(1) The *Gita* is not only a work on Advaita philosophy, it is much more than that.
(2) It is more a work on *Bhakti*, on theism, and philosophy of God is only in the background. *Bhakti* is the dominating doctrine.
(3) It teaches of attaining the divine heights through life, and so, even men of the world, *Samsarins* (अस्मदादीनाम् like us) can realize Him through *Bhakti*, and for that realization, resorting to *samnyasa* is not absolutely necessary.
(4) God as an *Avatara* is the subject of vision or all on earth, i.e., *Moksha*.
(5) This highest state, i.e., *Moksha* is not absolute identity of the soul with the Supreme. It is not of the nature of ब्रह्मविद् ब्रह्मैव भवति—the knower of Brahman becomes Brahman and that only.

In the Gita, the commentator does not read the Vedantic philosophy such as:

पूर्णमदः पूर्णमिदं पूर्णात्पूर्णमुदच्यते।
पूर्णस्य पूर्णमादाय पूर्णमेवावशिष्यते।।

(That is perfect, This is perfect. From the perfect the perfect arises. Taking out the perfect from the perfect, the perfect is the residue.)

Ramanuja has stressed that "liberation or *Moksha* is Service of and fellowship with God in *Vaikuntha* or heaven."[18]

(6) For everything, including the election for service to God, the soul is dependent upon God and it is only through His grace and favour that what Ramanuja understands as *Moksha* in the *Gita*, as in his own philosophy of विशिष्टाद्वैत (*Vishishtadvaita*), is realized. To Ramanuja "*Brahman*, the highest reality, is spirit, but not without attributes. He has self-consciousness with knowledge of Himself and a conscious will to create the world and bestow salvation on His creatures. He is the sum of all ideal predicates, infinite and eternal, before and above all world, without any second."[19]

This same God is the ultimate reality or the highest form of Krishna that Ramanuja visions in the *Gita*. There is an indirect admission that the *Gita* is not only a *Dohana* of the Upanishads, i.e., it is also influenced and perhaps more so by the *Bhagavad-dharma*. This becomes clear when in his own words God the Supreme (परं-ब्रह्म) is पुरुषोत्तमो नारायणः (*Purushottamo Narayanah*) who has created the world after Himself (अखिलं जगत् सृष्ट्वा स्वेन रूपेणावस्थितः), who is not visible by *Dhyana* and *Aradhana* (ध्यानाराधनाद्यगोचरः) and is yet, अपारकारुण्य सौशील्यवात्सल्यौदार्यमहोदधिः (*A great ocean of infinite compassion, extremely good nature, deep love and liberality*) and so on. As for the path of realisation, Ramanuja states: परमपुरुषार्थलक्षणमोक्षसाधनतया वेदान्तोदितं स्वविषयं ज्ञानकर्मानुगृहीतभक्तियोगमवतारयामास।

(Shri Krishna brought down on this earth *Bhakti-yoga* supported by *Karma* and *Jnana* about Himself, that is proclaimed in Vedanta because it is the means to *Moksha* that is of the nature of a great *Purushartha*.) Naturally therefore, Ramanuja is at an advantage when he comes to the *Bhakti-yoga* in the 12th *Adhyaya*. He is able to state that this *Bhakti* is said to be clearly the means of salvation for those who worship Lord Krishna, and "The highest *Bhakti* towards Me arises as a matter of course when the Soul that is the one form that is my residue is realized, after *Avidya* and the rest has all disappeared by *Adhyatma-jnana* when once *Karma*, that is of the nature of my worship and that is devoid of the desire for the fruits thereof, is resorted to" (12:11). This shows that in a man's rise there are three stages: (i) *Karma* that is devoid of desire for fruits and of the nature only of worship to God, (ii) *Jnana* that results from this, and (iii) *Bhakti* leading to *Moksha* that is its highest reward. But when it comes to interpreting the verses pertaining to सांख्य (*Sankhya*) as in 2:39, 3:3, 5:4, 5:5, and कर्मयोग (*Karamayoga*) as in 5:7, etc., he explains them in such a way that he will be able to emphasise that neither सांख्य (*Sankhaya*) nor योग (*Yoga*) is the final योग (*Yoga*) and that both are a means to the final and highest योग (*Yoga*), i.e., भक्ति (*Bhakti*). His comments on 4:3 न हि ज्ञानेन सदृशं पवित्रमिह विद्यते etc. यस्मादात्मज्ञानेन सदृशं पवित्रं शुद्धिकरमिह जगति वस्त्वन्तरं न विद्यते । (This is because in this world, there is nothing that is as purificatory as the knowledge of the Self,) confirm this view.

We have next to come to the problem of कर्मयोग (*Karmayoga*) or योग (*Yoga*) as it occurs in the work and to see how Ramanuja interprets it. While Shankara takes *yoga* normally in the spirit of योगः चित्तवृत्तिनिरोधः (*Yoga means control over the tendencies of the mind*) as in 5:7 योगयुक्तो विशुद्धात्मा विजितात्मा जितेन्द्रियः (One who is engrossed in *Yoga* is pure in Self, controlled in *Atman* and one who has conquered his senses), in 2:39 he takes योग (*Yoga*) as कर्मयोग (*Karmayoga*) in the normal course. By योग (*Yoga*) Ramanuja has understood only कर्मयोग (*Karmayoga*) that is to be adhered to in a spirit of detachment.[20]

In his comments on 2:39, he states: एवमात्मयाथात्म्यज्ञानमुपदिश्य तत्पूर्वकं मोक्षसाधनीभूतं कर्मयोगं वक्तुमारभते where he clarifies that *Karmayoga* precedes *Jnana-Yoga* and is of the nature of means to the attainment of *Moksha* (Salvation). This is because to him, the order of the three paths is *Karma-yoga*, *Jnana-yoga* and then *Bhakti-yoga*. But, Ramanuja in his comments on 2:48 understands योग (*Yoga*) as सिद्ध्यसिद्ध्योः समत्वरूपं चित्तसमाधानम् and on 2:50 he takes the word as बुद्धियोग (*Buddhi Yoga)* when he states: योगः कर्मसु कौशलं क्रियाक्रियमाणेष्वयं बुद्धियोगः कौशलमतिसामर्थ्यं अतिसामर्थ्यसाध्यमित्यर्थः *Karma-Yoga* is thus subsidiary to both *Jnana-Yoga* and *Bhakti-Yoga* in the opinion of Ramanuja.[21]

He just follows his principle that कर्मयोग (*Karma Yoga*) is a means to ज्ञानयोग (Jnana Yoga) and the fact still remains that भक्तियोग (*Bhakti Yoga*) is superior to both, or कर्मयोग (*Karma Yoga*), associated with ज्ञानयोग (*Jnana Yoga*) become a means to भक्तियोग (*Bhakti Yoga*). The three are taken in this sense by Ramanuja.

It is too well known and Ramanuja has acknowledged in different ways that his sole guide and fountain-head of inspiration was the famous scholar Yamuna, the author of the famous work गीतार्थसंग्रह (*Gita-arth Samgraha*). Ramanuja thus follows Yamuna and, to lay down his meaning of the *Gita* contends, that "In the first twelve lectures, then, the fundamental teaching of the *Gita* is laid down, culminating in the essential doctrine of *Bhakti*. The whole teaching of the *Gita* is declared to be the exposition of the *Mumukshu's* (one aspiring after salvation) progress to *Bhakti* and attainment of God. That progress is divided into two stages, the first of which, preparatory and ancilliary to *Bhakti*, is the subject-matter of the lectures 1:16."[22]

Much though we would like to go into details, this much of discussion of the view of Ramanuja would be sufficient for our purpose so as to come to the conclusion that, to Ramanuja,

(a) The *Gita* is not a mere work on Advaita Vedanta, it is not merely metaphysical or spiritiual.

(b) The *Gita* is a work of life and it shows the way that man should resort to in life in action, knowledge and devotion by which he gets over worldly pangs and sorrows, he conquers his Self and concentrates on God and ultimately attains *Moksha*. It is a book of religion, ethics and spiritualism in one.

(c) All this invariably requires favour of God, his *Krupa* and this is possible only by constant and unstinted *Bhakti* that has its basis in utter devotion and submission to the divine will. In this, ज्ञान *(Jnana)* supported by कर्म (*Karma*) as *yoga* is helpful. Ramanuja expects even a संन्यासी (*Samnyasi*) to become a भक्त (*Bhakta*). The *Gita* is a book of guidance not only for the attainment of *Moksha* by a *Samnyasin*, it is a work for all *Samsarins*. By regular and constant *Karma* followed by *Jnana*, *Samsarins* will rise to *Bhakti* that will lead to *Moksha*.

(d) The *Gita* will thus encompass in its fold humanity at large and will solve the problems of life not only of *Samnyasins* but also of *Samsarins*.

(e) When the philosophy of the *Gita* is interpreted as Ramanuja read it, the *Gita* became a work primarily on theism with him and it was a work for the alleviation of man's sorrows and his gradual rise to the divine. Getting over worldly sorrow and full engrossment in भगवद्भक्ति (*Bhagavad-Bhakti*) after *Jnana*, is an essential step in the rise of man to come to a stage when he will become an ideal *Bhakta* and thus deserve *Krupa* of God.

(f) Ramanuja thus emphasises that the *Gita* teaches man his *Dharma* in the Hindu sense of the term, and this religion is for life in the Hindu sense of the term i.e., "this plus that life is life."[23]

With this interpretation, it is noticed that the truth of the *Gita's* teaching is better realized and it is also understood that the *Gita* shows a specific leaning towards *Sakara* and *Saguna Brahma*. To Shankara, Krishna is *Ishwara* but not *Para Brahman*, but to Ramanuja, He is all in all. He is God the Supreme. He is to be realized by constant worship.

It should however, be conceded that while Ramanuja praised and brought to the forefront the doctrine of *Bhakti*, he has not given its due importance to *Karma-yoga*. The tendency to narrow down the doctrine of the *Bhagavadgita* to *Bhakti* still further continues in Vallabha and his followers.

Madhusudana Saraswati

Before we come to *Vallabha Sampradaya*, it is desirable that we refer in brief to the गूढार्थदीपिका (*Gudharthadeepika*) of the famous Acarya Madhusudana Saraswati. It is interesting to note that at the commencement of his *Bhasya*, Madhusudana Saraswati gives in 46 verses, more or less a clear cut summary of his own doctrine of the *Gita*. As the verses lay down, the *Gita* has propounded the following teachings:

(1) The purpose of this *Gita Shastra* is the highest bliss, परं निःश्रेयसम् (*Param Nishreyasam*) or मोक्ष (*Moksha*) that is of the nature of utter extinction of this *Samsara* that has a purpose of its own.

(2) This परं निःश्रेयसम् (*Param Nishreyasam*) is attainment to the feet of Lord Vishnu, it is the highest and perfect stage of the nature of *Sat*, *Cit* and *Ananda*.

(3) He is of opinion that the *Gita* is to be divided into three *Kandas*

(Parts) of six *Adhyayas* each and they are to be known as *Karmakanda*, *Upasanakanda* and *Jnanakanda*. There is a wide gap (अतिविरोध) between *Karma* and *Jnana* and therefore *upasana*, i.e., Bhakti is in the middle. भगवद्-भक्तिनिष्ठा (steadfastness in worship of God) is therefore in the middle. *Bhakti* is associated with both *Karma* and *Jnana*, it is threefold—कर्ममिश्रा (jointly with *Karma*), शुद्धा (pure) and ज्ञानमिश्रा (jointly with *Jnana*), it is the dispeller of all calamities (सर्वविघ्नोपपायिनी).

(4) The first six Chapters, (the first *Kanda*) describe *Atman* of the nature of '*Tvam*' (Thou) by *Karma* and *Karma-Samnyasa*. In the next six *Adhyayas* is described the meaning of the word 'तत्' (Tat) as '*Bhagawan*' who is परमानन्द स्वरूप (Supreme Bliss) and in the third *Kanda* is described the oneness of these two. This is the great Upanishadic sentence तत् त्वं असि ("Thou Art That"). This is the inter-relation of the three *Kandas* in the *Gita* that, in the opinion of Madhusudana, does the work of bringing together the two extremes of *Jnana* and *Karma* in *Bhakti*. According to Madhusudana this is the great achievement of the *Bhagvadgita*. Actually when Madhusudana opines that the *Gita* brings together the two extremes of *Karma* and *Jnana*, when both get fused in *Bhakti*, Madhusudana is stressing the great importance of *Bhakti* though, as we can well see, the concepts of *Bhakti* in Ramanuja and Madhusudana are glaringly different. It may, however, be stressed that the importance of *Bhakti* in Madhusudana's view is in no way less than in Ramanuja, even though the approach and concept differ.

(5) The author next takes up the stages of the development of the personality of the *sadhaka* in his progress towards the divine. The stages, as Madhusudana sees in the *Gita* are as follows:

   (a) Following the path of निष्कामकर्म (Nishkama karma) by the abandonment of काम्य (Kamya) (object of desire) and निमित्तकर्म (Nimitta Karma) (action with purpose), a stage in which the principal duty of the *sadhaka* is the muttering of God's names and singing of his glory. (12)

   (b) When, in this, all sins are annihilated, there arises in the mind the sense of distinction (*viveka*) by which man comes easily to realise the distinction between *Nitya* (lasting) and *Anitya* (Transient) objects. (13)

(c) With this, man comes to control his Self and there arises in him a sense of detachment with regard both to *Laukika* (worldly) and *Alaukika* (unworldy) objects. (14)

(d) This gives rise to *Samnayasa* because now he will be endowed with power in the form of शम (Shama), दम (Dama), श्रद्धा (Shraddha), समाधान (Samadhan), उपरति (Uprati) and तितिक्षा (Titiksha). (14)

(e) He then renounces every thing and experiences intense मुमुक्षुत्व (desire for salvation). He therefore retires to the feet of a teacher and gets instructed by him. (15)

(f) He next studies the Vedanta for dispelling all his doubts. (16)

(g) Then he engrosses himself in निदिध्यासन (constant contemplation) and with this end in view, the whole of *Yogashastra* is studied and practised.(17)

(h) It is then that he comes to experience the truth of the sentences such as अहं ब्रह्मास्मि ('I am Brahma') and by words comes to realize *Brahma-tattva.* This dispels all *Avidya.* All आवरण (Aavarna) and illusions are thus completely lost.

The development of man towards the divine is evidently described from the viewpoint of the *Bhakti* doctrine of Madhusudana. In his opinion, it reconciles the two extremes of *Jnana* and *Karma.*

Here again, there is greater emphasis on *Karma* and detachment but only as essential initial steps in man's rise to the Divine. The *Karmas* and even detachment become unimportant and a matter of course after a certain stage. The doctrine thus propounded will naturally apply to and give hope of rise to a larger mass of people no doubt. There is still no specific statement about the religion, ethics and philosophy of the *Gita.* Where Shankara has emphasised the cult of *Jnana*, the doctrine of Madhusudana has emphasised *Bhakti*, though of course in more clear light than Ramanuja in that he has reconciled *Bhakti* with *Jnana* and *Karma* both. He does not glorify *Bhakti* as does Ramanuja or later Vallabha, though his bias towards it is quite specific. But interesting is his very good reconciliation of the three paths with *Bhakti* in the middle, and, as we shall see at a later stage, this mutual relation and oneness of the three paths has been accepted as an important trait of the *Gita* by almost all moderns including Tilak, Belvalkar, Radhakrishnan, Ranade, Aurobindo, and Gandhiji as also Shri Vinoba. It is to be noted that while Shankara's contribution in the understanding of the *Gita* is his emphasis on *Jnana* and the realization of *Brahman*, while Ramanuja emphasises *Bhakti* and theism of the *Gita* with *saguna upasana*, Madhusudana lays great stress on the mutual relation of the three paths and develops a fine and systematic idea about the stages to the development of the *sadhaka*.

It is also notable that none of the three commentators takes any very serious notice of the *Vishada* by which Arjuna is overcome and even when the latter two comment on the first *Adhyaya* and the ten verses of the second one, in which the deep dejection of Arjuna is described, they do not study it philosophically. Shankara has no comments at all on these verses.

They therefore fail to stress the व्यामोह (Vyamoha) (delusion) that Arjuna has fallen in and the natural result is that when Arjuna is told कर्मण्येवाधिकारस्ते (Action alone is thy right), etc., Shankara interprets it as "You have a right only to action and not to knowledge", evidently implying thereby that Arjuna, though a fortunate soul, is not as yet a *sadhaka*, and, even when in 18:73 Arjuna states:

> नष्टो मोहः स्मृतिर्लब्धा त्वत्प्रसादान्मयाच्युत ।
> स्थितोऽस्मि गतसंदेहः करिष्ये वचनं तव ।। (18:73)

(My deusion is gone, I have regained the memory (of my duty) through your favour. O Krishna! I stand here (before you) with all my doubts dispelled (and) I shall act up to your words). Shankara adds that the fruit of study and knowledge of all the *shastras* goes only upto this limit as the reply to the question in 18:72 inquiring about the dispelling of delusion would show. This would mean that in the opinion of Shankara, Arjuna abides by the words of Lord Krishna and indulges in *Karma-yoga* only to raise his Self high.

The other two also interpret Arjuna's *Karma* and his *Yuddha* literally as physical warfare and do not take a serious note of the repeated appeal to action without attachment coming again and again and that too in asociation with all types of *sadhakas*. Naturally it has happened that the problems that have appealed to the modern writers have not appealed to them, in fact such an outlook was not conceivable for them. To all of them the *Bhagavadgita* is a work of *Sadhana* and philosophy; whatever their views about the doctrines.

Some are prone to omit the basic fact of the setting of the *Gita*. Arjuna is in *Vishada* and in utter dejection, he loses all power to fight, he refuses to fight. The second stage is that Krishna appeals to his conscience and awakens the real philosopher and hero in him, his doubts are dispelled and he decides to fight, to abide by the words of Lord Krishna. What is the significance of this? Is it to be taken in a metaphorical sense? Are we simply to forget the historical setting and *Gita's* place in the *Mahabharata*? Are we to neglect the fact that Arjuna is again and again asked to fight as a *Kshatriya*, in the spirit that it is his *Dharma*? Are we to forget that this teaching ultimately led Arjuna to fight in the spirit of a *yogi*? Shankara is silent over these questions and when he comes across तस्माद्युध्यस्व भारत etc., he takes it as 'Fight therefore Arjuna' taking all the while for granted that Arjuna is to fight only till he scales the higher heights of *Sadhana* and becomes a *Muktatma*. Ramanuja and Madhusudana take the words at their face value but do not go into the questions that we have raised. It goes only to the credit of moderns to tackle these and similar other questions. It may, in the end of this survey of the interpretation of Madhusudana, be noted that according to him, Krishna is the God of Gods and He is *Saguna* and *Sakara*. But it should be stressed that Krishna is *Saguna* and *Sakara*, not exactly in the sense in which Shankara takes Him to be. In Shankara's opinion, Krishna being *Saguna Sakara*, will be lower *Brahman*. But in the opinion of Madhusudana, Krishna is God of Gods in the sense that He is one with *Nirakara* and he stresses that *Nirguna-Nirakara*, somehow appears like Krishna. As a result it is clear that His *Bhakti* is in no way lower than *Jnana* as his comments on *Gita* 7:16 and 7:17 would show.

The followers of the Vallabha school do not fare better, even though it must be conceded that the supreme importance given by them to *Bhakti* does exist in the *Gita*, even when we insist on reading the *Gita* in this spirit: "So let us try to read the *Gita* in its own right colour and spirit and not seek for our pet theories" (Krishna Prem), as all ancients have done.

The Vallabha School

It was quite natural and in the fitness of things that the *Gita* should become the very basic religious and ethical scripture of this sect which has *Bhakti* as the be-all and end-all of its doctrine, so much so that the followers of this sect go to the length of stating that Lord Krishna teaches the पुष्टिमर्यादाभक्ति (*Pushti Maryada Bhakti*) to the Pandavas through Arjuna, meaning thereby that they read only their पुष्टिमर्यादाभक्ति (*Pushti Maryada Bhakti*) in the *Gita*.

Besides गीतातात्पर्यग्रंथ, the *Amritatarangini Tika* is an important contribution towards the understanding of the interpretation of the *Gita* by this school of Vallabha. The famous *Tika* at its commencement clarifies the central doctrine of the *Gita* in these words:

भक्तिमर्यादायाः लोकवेदातीतज्ञापनस्यैव प्रयोजनत्वादित्यत एव समाप्तौ फाल्गुनेन "नष्टो मोहःस्मृतिर्लब्धा त्वत्प्रसादान्मयाऽच्युत। स्थितोऽस्मि गतसंदेहः करिष्ये वचनं तव।।" इत्युक्तम्। अतोऽत्र मुख्यतया भक्तेरेवोपदेशः यत्पुनन्यत्तत्सर्वं तस्यैव शेषभूतमिति दिक्।

(Just like the knowledge of that which supercedes the world and the Vedas, it is (also) the purpose of the *Gitakara* to instruct Arjuna in the भक्तिमार्गमर्यादा (discipline for the path of devotion) and that is the reason why at the end Arjuna says: "My delusion is gone, and O Krishna! through your favour, I have regained memory (of my duty). Here I stand with all my doubts dispelled (and) I shall act up to your words." Here, therefore, the principal teaching is that of *Bhakti* only, and again, whatever else is narrated is only subsidiary.) Besides the firm resolve to read only the *Bhakti*-doctrine in the *Gita*, the writer of the *Tika* starts with this resolve:

श्रीविट्ठलपदाम्भोजकृपामधुसुपूरितः ।
व्याख्यास्ये भगवद्गीतां भक्तिमार्गानुसारतः ।।

(I, who am filled to the brim by nectar in form of the favour of the lotus-like feet of Shri Vitthala, shall comment on the *Bhagavad-gita*, following the *Bhakti-marga*). The principal tenets of the *Bhagavadgita*, as they read, are as follows:

(1) Everything including the great war of *Mahabharata* was dependent on the divine will (भगवदिच्छाविषयत्वं) and it is God who inspired the *Rajasuya* sacrifice and everything that follows in the minds of Yudhishthira and others,who are thus merely actors of the divine will.
(2) This is because God willed that the demons shall be killed and

Dharma shall be reinstated through Yudhishthira, etc. Thus, everything that happens on earth happens according to the divine will that wants to establish *Dharma* and uproot evil.

(3) It is precisely due to this that God Himself created dejection in the heart of Arjuna because He wanted him to uproot evil and also that he should become His devotee. Thus, all that happens on earth is due to divine will and resorting to the noble path of *Bhakti* is also through His favour. *Bhakti* will rise and raise man high when *Bhagavan* inspires and infuses it in his heart.

(4) Thus, the *Gita* teaches the great and noble doctrine of *Bhakti* to which everything else is subordinate. Arjuna's *Vishada* is just the beginning and it is brought out from the depth of his heart by *Bhagavan*, only because he ordains that concentration on the Divine (भगवत्तत्वम्) and the path of *Bhakti* (भक्तिमार्गत्वम्) also are not recommended to be resorted to all of a sudden even in case of a man who has faith in the path of *Bhakti* (भक्तिमार्गीयस्यापि).

(5) The primary purpose of the *Gita* is to show that it expounds *Pushtimaryadabhakti* that arises only when there is His favour (अनुग्रहात्) and man resorts to the path of *Shreya* consequently (श्रेयोद्धारेणा).

(6) Everything else that the *Gita* expounds, i.e., *Jnana, Karma, Dhyana*, etc., is subsidiary to *Bhakti* that is the principal teaching here. The *Amritatarangini* states in its comments on the last verse of the *Gita*[24] that:

"Where Shri Krishna and Arjuna are on one side, there exist prosperity, etc. What more is to be said, since they are bodily present! The suggested sense therefore is that for you also, resorting to the feet of the Lord would conduce to success of all aims... etc."

As a result, the स्थितप्रज्ञ (*Sthitprajna*) is one whose mind is fixed in full faith and devotion on the Divine. He is the best of the devotees who discards all desires other than those raised by Divine will (2:35); he everywhere sees भगवन्मयत्व (immanence of God) in everything (2:57) and does all things not for their own sake but for God; his interests as his own in the world are dispelled when he experiences divine *Rasa* (2:59). For a man, क्रोध (anger), संमोह (delusion), स्मृतिभ्रंश (loss of memory), etc. are all due to forgetting भगवतस्मरण (remembrance of

God) (2:63) and so on. The स्थितप्रज्ञ (*Sthitprajna*) is निःस्पृह (detached) with reference to worldly desires and attachments and he attains this state when he is one in devotion with *Bhagavan* (2:71). The *Amritatarangini* here states:

"Rare is that man who deserves to be one in Divine love, and, abandoning all desires and becoming free from attachments, moves in unstinted devotion to *Bhagavan*." Again, in his comments on 12:2, the *tika* states:

ये भाग्यवन्तो नित्ययुक्तवाः मत्सेवैकतत्पराः परया प्रेमैकलक्षणया श्रद्धया उपेताः युक्तास्ततो मामुपासते सेवन्ते ते युक्ततमाः उत्तमाः मे मताः संमताः इत्यर्थः।

(The meaning is that those fortunate persons who are ever engrossed in, that is, ever anxious only for service to me and are endowed with unique faith indicative of pure love, serve and pray to me are, in my opinion, the best and adjudged as the best by me.) Again, when Krishna states: न हि ज्ञानेन सदृशं पवित्रमिह विद्यते (There is nothing so sacred as knowledge on this earth), this ज्ञान (*Jnana*) is the means to divine favour, it is मत्स्वरूपात्मकं ज्ञानं (knowledge constituted of my real nature) and is therefore sacred but subordinate to *Bhakti*. The परा शान्ति (ultimate peace) that a man attains to is मोक्ष (*Moksha*) according to Shankara (तस्यास्य गीताशास्त्रस्य संक्षेपतः प्रयोजनं परं निःश्रेयसं) (The brief purpose therefore of this scripture that is the *Gita* (is to lay down) highest salvation), but it is *Bhakti* of God,

> अतोऽत्र मुख्यतया भक्तेरेवोपदेशः यत्पुनरन्यत्तत्सर्वं तस्यैव शेषभूतम्।
> (Therefore here, there is laid down principally the teaching of *Bhakti* and therefore all else that is there is only its subsidiary).

according to the Vallabha school. Even the त्रिगुणातीत (*Trigunatita*), all whose actions are dependent upon and decided by divine will (14:22), is a *Bhakta* of first order as the *Amritatarangini* would state in its comments on *Gita*, 14:22, and he too is a *Bhakta*. The verse line कर्मण्येवाधिकारस्ते मा फलेषु कदाचन (Thy right is to work only, but never to the fruit–2:47) is also interpreted in a different way and it is stated that (i) यावत्पर्यन्तं स्वपरेति ज्ञानं तावन्न कर्मत्यागः। (For the time that the knowledge of 'mine' and 'elses' persists, *Karma* is not renounced) and (ii) this attitude of योग also results from divine favour (2:47) and in 2:48, योगस्थ (steadfast in Yoga) is naturally interpreted thus: योगस्थः भगवत्संयोगे स्थितःकर्माणि तत्रोपयुक्तानि कुरु संगंत्यक्त्वा सर्वत्यागं कृत्वेति भावः।

"The meaning is, being engrossed in *Yoga*, that is, being firm in भगवत्संयोग, perform, after due detachment of everything, proper actions."

The ideal man of the Vallabha sect therefore is not essentially a *Samnyasi*, he is a man of the world and continues to perform works in the world, practises *Dhyana*, is merged in *Jnana* and is just an instrument of *Bhagavan* because God constantly goes on destroying evil and upholding good through men in whom he inspires these plus *Bhakti*, and takes birth on earth for both these, not Himself but in His devotees.[25] It is thus clear that the physical war that Arjuna fights is fought by him in a spirit of acting according to the will and wish of *Bhagavan* as his *Dasa* (servant, devotee) and this is to stress that Gods care constantly to destory अधर्म (Adharma) which means lessening of *Bhakti*.[26] The *tika* on 4:7 states: यदा यदा हि धर्मस्य मद्भक्त्यादिरूपस्य ग्लानिः संकोचो भवति।

(Whenever there is the lessening of *Dharma* of the nature of devotion to me and so on, etc.) The highest state therefore to which Arjuna rises is that of *Bhakti* of God who is of the nature of *Saguna Brahman*.

Other problems raised by the *Gita* are also to be explained accordingly.

Thus, it is clear that Shankara and Vallabha are the two extremes with regard to the interpretation of the *Gita* and all other commentators are in the middle. To Shankara the *Gita* is a book of philosophy like all other Upanishads and that only and Arjuna's fighting reveals his lower nature from which he rises higher, to come to a stage when he will deserve to resort to the higher path; the highest purpose of the *Gita* is to teach मोक्षमार्ग (the path to salvation). Thus, to Shankara, the *Gita* is not just a book of religion and ethics but predominantly a book on *Vedanta*. To Vallabha, the *Gita* is a work of philosophy no doubt, but the philosophy of theism and it is also a work on religion and ethics. The most remarkable and clear achievement therefore of this school with reference to the *Gita* is to accept that it is a work on religion, ethics and philosophy all in one. Another fact to be noted is that the Vallabha school accepts the *Gita* as a work on life because acording to it the *Gita* teaches the whole worldly conduct in a certain way. The *Gita* becoming a work of life, becomes a gospel for all men at all stages of life and all intellectual achievement. Yet one more fact stressed by the *Gita* in the view of this school is that no good action in life is to be discarded and also that we men should always pray for divine favour and always ascertain whether or not our actions will be to the liking of *Shri Bhagavan*. Even the smallest effort to come nearer to God, to reality is praiseworthy and therefore no effort is lost and no soul is lost to God. One more thing to be noted is that this school took the help of the *Bhagavata Dharma* to interpret the doctrines of the *Gita*, and our modern critical and analytical method in studying the *Gita* shows that in it there is a positively growing tendency to lean towards *Bhagavata Dharma* and a positive tendency to accept *Saguna Brahman* as God the Supreme. It is yet, not our purpose to state that the *Bhagavata Purana* and the *Bhagavata Dharma* thereof are known to the *Gita*. The *Gita* is earlier. Yet a current of *Bhakti* to *Shri Bhagavan* was probably growing stronger day to day and probably this is the common source of the *Purana* and the *Gita*. Thus, just like the *Bhashya* of Shankara, the commentaries of this school are a positive contribution in our better understanding of the doctrine and nature of the *Gita*, even though its effort at reading the doctrine of *Bhakti* in one and all verses has led to so many twists and distortions and misinterpretations. Again, we find it very difficult to accept that *Bhakti* is the only doctrine taught by the *Gita*.

So many other commentators are there. The most remarkable are Yamunacharaya, the *Guru* of Ramanuja in his *Gitarthasamgraha,* Madhava with his *Anandatirthabhasya*, the *Anandagiritika* that carefully follows Shankara and explains him further, the *Prameyadipikatika* and *Bharatabhavadipa*, etc. Last, but not the least is the *Jnaneshwari* that is valuable and important in its own way. For our purpose, however, the above-mentioned surveys of four interpretations would be enough.

NOTES

1. 'Harijan', 5-12-1936.
2. Quoted by A. Huxley in 'Perennial Philosophy', p. 70.
3. 'The Bhagavadgita', Vol. 1., p. 35.
4. *Vide* वादे वादे जायते तत्त्वबोध: "With every new thought, there dawns the understanding of reality."
5. 'Bhagavadgita', p. 16.
6. 'Bapu's Letters to Mira', p. 249.

7. 'Bhagavadgita—As a Philosophy of God-realization', p. 124.
8. *Vide* Kaka Kalelkar's Preface in Gujarati to Gandhiji's 'Anasaktiyoga'. Translation of quotation is mine.
9. As expounded in brief by the famous Sanskrit commentary on the Gita—*Amritatarangini.*
10. *Vide* also Shankara's comments on 4:18.
11. Gita, 3:8.
12. Gita, 5:6.
13. Gita, 11:33.
14. *Vide* also in Introductory remarks.
15. 'Bhagavadgita—As a Philosophy of God-realisation', p.121.
16. 'Ramanuja on the Bhagavadgita', J.A.B. Van Buitenan p.1.
17. Based on introduction to the *Amritatarangini.*
18. S. Radhakrishnan is his 'Bhagavadgita' Introduction, p. 19.
19. As above, p. 17-18.
20. Based on introduction to the *Amritatarangini.*
21. For this, *vide* 'Ramanuja on Bhagavad Gita', J.A.B. Van Buitenan, pp. 9 to 12.
22. *Vide* supra, p. 13.
23. I derive these on the basis of the *Amritatarangini tika.*
24. Gita, 18:78.
25. *Vide* comments of *Amritatarangini* on 4:7.
26. *Vide* comments of *Amritatrangini* on 18:73.

THREE

Survey of Principal Interpretations—The Moderns

"The *Gita* is strikingly original in teaching that the lasting foundations of a social order are to be built on the correct understanding with which the individual should do his work and the satisfaction that this will bring him."

J.C. Wadiyar.[1]

"Non-attachment to self and to what are called 'the things of this world' has always been associated in the teachings of the philosophers and the founders of religions with attachment to an ultimate reality greater and more significant than the self."

A.Huxley.[2]

"The revolutions of the years
Wherein we come and shall be gone,
No known beginning rests upon
Nor any end thereof appears."

Omar Khayyam.

Introduction

With the moderns, we come to quite a different approach. As the modern critical method and research methods are applied to the *Gita*, so many problems in which the ancients had no interest or which they could not conceive of as problems altogether, are discussed to-day by the moderns. Modern interpretation of the *Gita* has the added advantage of comparative study and analysis and application of the methods and approach of western philosophy. The results are,

(1) Problems pertaining to the text, its writer, its place in the Mahabharata, its place in Indian philosophy, its value as a religious scripture, its date, etc., are discussed.

(2) Problems of the nature and structure of the *Gita* and its comparison with other philosophical and religious works in India, are discussed.

(3) Several scholars have attempted a critical analysis of the *Gita* and we have countless translations of the work in all languages in India and so many languages of the world.

(4) Problems of the doctrines of the *Gita*, its place in life and Indian life, its status in all the sects of the country, etc., are discussed.

Vinoba Bhave states: "But from the *Gita* also several scholars have brought out varied isms. If we fall a prey to this, the *Gita* can also become a very much scholarly work and hence useless for life. I therefore always prefer to keep the *Bhashyas* apart from my outlook and also prefer directly to resort to *Gitamata*. I recommend the same approach for all."[3] While it is clear that by these remarks Vinoba intended to refer to the problems such as in (1), (2) and probably (3) also above, we must concede that the *Bhashyas* of the ancients and works of the moderns are not useless for life. As the learned *Acharya* opines, the works include those of Gandhiji and Vinoba himself. Actually, even Vinoba's famous work स्थितप्रज्ञदर्शन (Sthitpragyadarshan) is a highly technical and scholarly work, and judged by his own statement, we will have to say that his work is also useless for life! It would be too much and dangerous too, to state that scholarly things are useless for life, merely because they are scholarly. In all the cases, the *Bhashyas* and the works of important scholars result from their own approach and experiment in life and so, they are useful in their own way and they are learned no doubt. Even the problems in (1) and (2) cannot be considered to be quite useless and their study is no waste of energy or learning even after we accept that the *Gita* is a gospel of life and therefore it is to be practised in life. Moderns beginning with Dalhmann, Garbe, Hopkins, Hill, Edgerton and others have dealt with the problems. But we will not refer to these in so far as we are surveying the various interpretations of the *Gita* from the viewpoint of its doctrine, strictly as a background to the approach and understanding and interpretaticn of Gandhiji's views regarding the *Gita* and his main teaching. The contribution of the moderns towards a better understanding of the *Gita* is great and important in its own way. It can again not be denied that the moderns have given to us a new vision and approach towards the interpretation of the *Gita* and we have definitely come to a better understanding of the secret of the doctrine of the *Gita*. A study therefore of some prominent interpretations from among those of many will be a useful background to what Gandhiji reads in the *Gita* and under what circumstances and outlook. We will, as we have already stated above, discuss only the doctrinal interpretations and controversies and leave untouched the textual and historical and similar problems discussed by the scholars even though they are important in their own way. Garbe, Hopkins, Edgerton, Farquhar, etc., are known for their discussion of the latter type of problems, pertaining to the *Gita*. And even when we study the interpretation of the *Gita* as we have it in Hill, our interest lies only in his doctrinal interpretation.

Hill

With Hill there is more or less a continuation of the approach of Vallabha in this that he accepts the *Gita* to be almost a *Bhagavata* type of work and accepts that the *Bhagavata* religion has left a deep impression on the *Gita*. He starts his Introduction with the clear-cut argument that: "The *Bhagavadgita* presents the doctrine that Krishna Vasudeva, who helped the Pandava princes at the battle of Kurukshetra as Arjuna's charioteer, was supreme God, --- the Absolute into the world of men. Krishna is called *Bhagavat* and the poem is a product of the *Bhagavata* or *Vasudeva* sect, which at the time of its composition was beginning to identify Krishna with Vishnu."[4] This statement proves that according to Hill, in the *Gita*,

(1) The foremost of influences is that of the *Bhagavata Dharma*.
(2) Krishna, who is identified with Vishnu, is God the Supreme.
(3) Attaining to this God the Supreme is the highest aim of the path of life shown by the *Gita*.

Hill next takes up the various forms of Krishna as he finds them in the various *Adhyayas* and verses of the *Gita*. They are,

(1) Krishna is *Brahman*:
7:19; 10:12; 14:27; 12:1.

(2) Krishna is *Atman*:
7:4; 15:7; 15:17-18; 10:20; 6:29; 15:35; 13:2.
(3) Krishna is *Purusha*:
7:30; 8:4; 8:8-10; 9:23; 15:15-16; 13:22.
(4) Krishna is *Ishvara,*
(5) Krishna is not-self:
15:16.
(6) Krishna is *Avatara*:
10:21; 10:23; 9:24; 11:9; 18:77; 3:15; 5:29; 9:24.
(7) Krishna is Universe:
8:16-19; 7:6, 12; 9:5-10; 10:8; 15:4; 13:19.
(8) Krishna is Arjuna's charioteer,
(9) Krishna is Arjuna's comrade,
(10) Krishna is Arjuna's teacher, and so on.

Thus, Krishna of the *Gita* would be everything beginning from Arjuna's charioteer to God the Supreme, i.e., *Brahman*, according to Hill.

Hill has next stressed that even though the final attainment or aim of the teaching is knowing Krishna as all in all, "the author of the *Gita* is interested in man and his destiny; for man is the centre of creation . . .but to man is given a right denied even to the Lords of Heaven . . . man alone in all creation's scale can win release."[5] The *Gita* therefore is meant for the average, ordinary good man like Arjuna and it seeks to solve the problems and resolve conflicts of his life. He says: "The message of the *Gita* is a message to the ordinary man."[6] And the *Gita* takes man as he is, with all his weaknesses and strength and attachment to the world and takes him as essentially good. The message of the *Gita* is therefore for man's life, it is a message of resolution and it seeks to solve the varied riddles of man's life. For this, man is expected by Krishna to get over the evil in him, to control his Self, to rise higher though gradually and slowly; he is to be virtuous and is to resort to the path of righteousness so that he will act as a hero in the strife of life. Such a virtuous man will naturally perform his duties in life, and that too by a slow process of detachment.

Work is done ultimately for its own sake, for common good, in a spirit of social good, in a spirit of submission to God.

Once man comes to this state, he enters the higher plane and realizes that "when we turn our thoughts to absolute reality, and remember that 'Vasudeva is all', good and evil, virtue and vice lose their distinction and are seen for what they are—no more than elements of that great drama, which is the universe."

The next important thing stressed by Hill in his reading of the *Gita* is that the *Gita* accepts the conventional Hindu doctrine of transmigration and he adds that ". . . the purpose of its message is to teach Arjuna type of the ordinary man, that knowledge and devotion and performance of duty without desire form the threefold path of release."[7] In addition to the triple path round which interpretations of all moderns have moved, it is stressed that release from this transmigration is the ultimate aim of the *Gita*, and if we read this with the previous doctrine, release also leads man to extreme vicinity of Krishna, who is ultimately God the Supreme. Hill has also dealt with the exact meaning of the controversial word *Yoga*. In his opinion, it is used in the sense of "Control, or some particular method of control."[8] When used in contrast to *Samkhya-Yoga*, it means *Karma-Yoga* and at one place each, it is used in the sense of contemplation (5:21) and an ascetic of *Yoga* school. Actually the *Gita* teaches of three *Yoga*s that are mutually complementary and aids to each other and they are paid almost equal respect by Krishna. But the predominance of the one or the other depends upon the grade and intellectual status of man. Hill states: "Yet, while from first to last, work must be done, and knowledge sought, and devotion practised, the proportion of each will vary acording to the grade attained."[9] Thus, in the opinion of Hill, the *Gita* is not biased towards one or the other path and three paths are accepted by it as the principal ones. This also establishes the acceptance that a man's spiritual rise through life is only a gradual one and at each stage of man's sublimation, his *Yoga* may differ. This indirectly establishes Hill's acceptance that the *Gita* is a book of religion, a guide in ethics and a spiritual or philosophic discipline—all the three in one.

Hill has partly emphasised the doctrine of *Karma-Yoga* but, principally as a reply to the *Vedanta* in its dislike towards action in life. Hill states that *Karma-Yoga* in all its stages is taught by the *Gita* as a necessary step to man's rise and it is to be with man for all his life. Total inaction is not possible. Here, Hill is nearer to the secret of the *Gita* than Shankara and contributes towards establishing this *Yoga* to its proper place in the life of man. Hill adds: "Yet, nonetheless he combats the widespread fallacy that the man of knowledge should aim at complete inaction; inaction is neither right nor possible; theory and practice, knowledge and work, are not opposed but as the learned realize, two sides of one well-balanced mode of life. Knowledge must find its complement in work; its function is to bring all work to true fulfilment."[10]

Similarly does he analyse the *Bhakti-Yoga* from which we might note just one fine idea given by him. "One of *Gita*'s strongest claims to fame, one of the chief causes of its age-long popularity, is the fact that after centuries of pent up emotion it presented the worshipper with a visible object of devotion and taught the value of pure disinterested love in the religious life."[11] This happily establishes that the *Gita*'s approach to life and to man is positive, constructive and fully optimistic. When Hill sings the glory of *Bhakti* in the *Gita* in the fullest details and expounds how it helps man in his "personal relationship with Krishna Vasudeva,"[12] it shows that he is still nearer to the Vallabha doctrine and wants to stress the great influence of *Bhagavata Dharma* on the *Gita*. Scholars like Dr. Modi are of the opinion that even if we were to concede that some kind of *Bhagavata Dharma* is present as an important influence on the *Gita* as Hill contends, actually Krishna in the *Gita* can possibly be known to be Vishnu only if the idea of त्रिमूर्ति (Trimurti) is present in the *Gita*. But that is not so. Actually Krishna is one with पुरुष (Purusha), i.e., it is His personal conception of the final reality as we have it in the पुरुषसूक्त (Purushsukta) or *Chhandogya Upanishad*, or *Brihadaranyaka Upanishad* or *Katha Upanishad*, (1.3.9), etc. It should be noted as an illustration from the *Katha Upanishad* that the verse 1.3.9 states

विज्ञानसारथिर्यस्तु मनः प्रग्रहवान्नरः।
सोऽध्वनः पारमाप्नोति तद्विष्णोः परमं पदम्।।

(That man who acts with knowledge as his charioteer and is endowed with the reins of the mind, attains to the end of the path of life, that is the supreme state of attaining to Vishnu.)

On this even Shankara has to state:

तद्विष्णोः व्यापनशीलस्य ब्रह्मणः परमात्मनो वासुदेवाख्यस्य परमं प्रकृष्टं पदं स्थानम् . . . आप्नोति स विद्वान्।

(That is the highest or most glorious place or status of Vishnu that is

Brahman or *Paramatman* whose nature it is to encompass all and who is known as Vasudeva.) It might thus be seen that even this is an ancient Upanishadic influence.

A word might be added about the problem of free-will that Hill discusses. In his opinion, on one side the *Gita* asks man to make his choice, to do what he thinks fit and in the same tone warns about the grave consequences of choosing the wrong path. If a man does not desire fruit of his action and yet act he must, where is free will? How will man's पुरुषार्थ (Purushartha) work? What will be his impetus? These are the questions at the back of Hill's mind. And he states: "In actual fact, where man is God and personal being a delusion, the question of real freedom, and responsibility cannot arise. It is this double view of truth—the higher and the lower—that explains the apparent weakness of Hindu doctrine in general and the much blamed 'inconsistency of the *Gita*' on this subject of free will."[13] Western philosophy has given long discussions on free-will and in these remarks Hill is under the influence of the west. The reply is to be derived from the *Gita* itself in this that Krishna unfolds reality of man's life as it is, before Arjuna. He also shows what the ultimate aim of *Karma* is, as it is in accordance with human nature at all stages of life. He shows the path of action, devotion, sublimation and ultimate release. Now it is for Arjuna to decide whether or not he wants to rise, to sublimate himself. It is left to him, to his inner inclination. He is to choose only if he is fully convinced. And Krishna has specifically inquired in 18:72 whether he is convinced and is going to act up to the words of Lord Krishna. Performing all works of life without the slightest expectation of reward in the first stage and working in a spirit of renunciation to the divine in the last stage is a test no doubt. But the manner in which Vyasa, Valmiki, Janaka, Sḥankara, Ramakrishna, Aurobindo and Gandhi, etc., have worked has shown that this is possible. They have always worked with full enthusiasm and without the slightest attachment to work itself. To them work was worship and it was of their own free-will that they chose the path. What was the impetus? By gradual steps they took their personalities to a stage at which their expectation of reward was release, 'the supreme bliss', identity with God. When the *Kathopanishad* lays down two paths of श्रेय (Shreya) and प्रेय (Preya) and shows the results of both, choice is ultimately left to the person concerned. The Upanishadic mantra only lays down the results of following the one or the other path of श्रेय (Shreya) and प्रेय (Preya). The final choice is left only to the reader concerned when it states that:

श्रेयश्च प्रेयश्च मनुष्यमेतस्तौ सम्परीत्य विविनक्ति धीरः।
श्रेयो हि धीरोऽभि प्रेयसो वृणीते प्रेयो मंदो योगक्षेतमात् वृणीते।। (Valli 2.2)

A reply from another angle could be this. The reality of life has ever been against absolute free-will and there is a strong controversy even in western philosophers with regard to free-will, some accepting that such a thing as free-will does not exist at all. 'Man is born free but always finds himself in chains', states one proverb. Man is born with a heritage, a culture of centuries, a certain nature that normally he cannot give up, even the circumstances round him and his own nature under the influence of which he acts. This should not and cannot of course mean fatalism. Hinduism has never accepted what we call fatalism, it is a *Dharma* of पुरुषार्थ (Purushartha), of asking man to become a hero in the strife of life. That is the reason why "There is no such thing as a uniform, stationary, unalterable Hinduism whether in point of belief, or practice. Hinduism is a movement, not a position: a process, not a result, a growing tradition, not a fixed revelation." It should be accepted that when man is enabled to act according to his nature, his inherent ambition and latent capacities, he is acting under free-will. The most natural life of man will be to get a due opportunity, proper atmosphere and circumstances to act in accordance with his heritage, nature and inclination and win his happiness. When man gets such an opportunity, man is acting under free-will. Free-will is thus acting upto one's heritage, nature and inclination and the path shown by the *Gita* bases itself just on this. When Krishna on one side shows the path of life and reality of life and warns Arjuna that he will act only in a certain way inspite of himself and then asks Arjuna to act as he likes, this acting as he likes is going to be in the case of Arjuna, as in the case of any man on earth, acting not on the path of suicide or against social order and morality, but acting in accordance with his real inherent nature. In life therefore, free-will exists but within limits. To quote again from *Kathopanishad*, श्रेय (Shreya) and प्रेय (Preya) approach man as they are. A wise man prefers *Shreya* to *Preya* while a foolish man through ignorance chooses प्रेय (Preya). Both act according to their respective natures and this is their freedom. The scriptures show the path and leave man to act. They also show a path by which man will develop his personality on the right line according to his nature. We will therefore finally answer Hill here in the words of Radhakrishnan: "The *Bhagavadgita* asks us to raise the self by the Self. We can use the material with which we are endowed to promote our ideals. The cards in the game of life are given to us. We don't select them. They are traced to our past *Karma*, but we can call as we please, lead what suit we will, and as we play, we gain or lose. And there is freedom. . . But choice is not caprice. Free-will in the sense of an undetermined, unrelated, uncaused factor in human action is not admitted, but such a will defies all analysis. It has nothing to do with the general stream of cause and effect. It operates in an irregular and chaotic way. If human actions are determined by such a will, there is no meaning in punishment or training of character. The theory of *Karma* allows man the freedom to use the material in the light of his knowledge. Man controls the uniformities in nature, his own mind and society. There is thus scope for genuine rational freedom while indeterminism and chance lead to a false fatalism."[14] The truth of the last remark is proved by the explosive and extremely painful situation that prevails in the west even in the richest countries.

This rather long clarification was necessary to understand better, Gandhiji, who, when he interpreted the teaching of the *Gita* and wanted man to act according to it, wanted man to come in a situation in which he can act the best as man. He showed this natural way of life and applied brake whenever he had fear that man was likely to go astray.

I have given a rather detailed survey of Hill's reading of the *Gita* because he is the first important modern scholar to try to read the *Gita* with a thoroughly dispassionate mind and without the motives of the ancients. As clarified by Krishna Prem, "Every teacher who wished to claim Vedantic authority for his teaching was obliged to write a commentary on it showing that it supported his views,"[15] and "…its authoritative status has had the drawback that the various commentators have often devoted more energy to special pleading and refutation of opponents than to straightforward inquiry into the real meaning of the text."[16] It is clear that Hill has kept the slate of his mind clean and has asked the author of the *Gita* to paint the real picture. This is his very important contribution and difficult though it is, he has carved the real path for further interpretation.

It would be possible to criticise Hill from various points of view, but I do not refer to criticism of Hill by scholars or criticise him myself because that would be beyond the scope of my present Thesis.

Tilak

Shri Aurobindo has these words of admiration about Tilak: "He is a great Sanskrit scholar, a powerful writer and a strong, subtle and lucid thinker."

We will next refer to his view. He has given his epoch-making work, '*Gita Rahasya*' first in Marathi and then in other languages. Rightly does Ranade in a spirit of admiration state: "It is to-day, after the lapse of forty years, that I have been able to speak a few words about the great *Gita-Rahasya*."[17] Rightly does Gandhiji state: "The *Gita* enabled the Late Lokamanya Tilak out of his encyclopedic learning and study to produce a monumental commentary. . . I believe his commentary on the *Gita* will be a more lasting monument to his memory . . . His master work commentary on the *Gita* is unsurpassed and will remain so for a long time to come." Equally remarkable is the tribute paid by Shri Aurobindo: "His work on the *Gita*, no mere commentary but an original criticism and presentation of ethical truths, is a monumental work . . . and likely to become a classic."

These words of admiration lead us to the question as to what is great in the interpretation of Tilak and what his original contribution towards the interpretation of the *Gita* is. Tilak is specific when he states that: ". . . it follows clearly that the various interpretations, which have been put on the *Gita* by doctrine-supporting commentators, who have looked upon the *Karma-yoga* as inferior, are not correct."[18] He is again clear when he states that: "*Karma-yoga* fused with spiritual knowledge and Devotion, is the true purpose of the *Gita*."[19] He prefers to call the doctrine of the *Gita*, science of *Karma-yoga, Karmayoga-Shastra* and not mere *Karma-yoga* or even mere *Yoga-shastra*, the name given by Vyasa. As we try to understand Tilak's distinction between the two words, we find that to him, life-long action without attachment, is the central doctrine of the *Gita* and *Bhakti-yoga*—as also *Dhyana-yoga*, etc., are its means. *Karma-yoga* is the life-long companion of man at all times in his life. It is man's nature that,

न हि कश्चित्क्षणमपि जातु तिष्ठत्यकर्मकृत्।
कार्यते ह्यवशः कर्म सर्वः प्रकृतिजैर्गुणैः॥

(For none ever remains inactive even for a moment; for all are compelled to action by the *gunas* inherent in *Prakriti*.) (3:5)

If *Karma* is there at each movement of life, if forcibly man is to act, why not then act in a spirit of enthusiasm, in a spirit of detachment and lead a natural life while at the same time bringing one's Self higher in life? This means acting in accordance with the science of *Karma-yoga* and acting in accordance with science shows that Tilak reads applied philosophy in it. But it is not merely applied philosophy , it is theory also. Science is to be known, understood, grasped and also applied. Tilak therefore reads both applied and theoretical philosophy in the *Gita*.

He states, "Therefore the Blessed Lord has preached in the *Gita* the philosophy of life-long desireless action based on spiritual knowledge and in which the highest importance is given to Devotion, so as to effect a fusion between Intelligence (*Jnana*), Love (Devotion) and physical capacity (*Kartrutva*) . . ."[20] Work is worship and work as also concept of work must progress in such a way that man does his work and yet is free from the bondage of work. This is possible only by desireless action as also a growing non-attachment towards the work itself. That is the reason why he takes the verse

कर्मण्येवाधिकारस्ते मा फलेषु कदाचन।

(Action alone is thy province, never the fruits thereof) (2:47) as the most important and feels that, ". . .One may even safely say that these four parts of the stanza are the *Chatuh-sutri* (four axioms) of the *Karma-yoga*."[21] Again, when the *Gita* states

नियतं कुरु कर्म त्वं कर्म ज्यायो ह्यकर्मणः।

(Do thou thy allotted task; for action is superior to inaction.) (3:8)

the attitude of the *Gita* is not fatalistic. Action is to be performed in full enthusiasm in a spirit of service, in a spirit of contributing to universal welfare (लोकसंग्रह). To Tilak, the verse

न मे पार्थास्ति कर्तव्यं त्रिषु लोकेषु किञ्चन।
नानवाप्तमवाप्तव्यं वर्त एव च कर्मणि॥ (3:22)

(For Me O Partha, there is naught to do in the three worlds, nothing worth gaining that I have not gained; yet I am ever in action), is very important in stressing this doctrine of *Karma-yoga*. For a *Jnani*, for Lord Himself, *Karma* might not be necessary, yet even God the Supreme as Krishna should engross Himself in *Karma*. How much more is it necessary for others including Arjuna? And then Arjuna states with all his doubts dispelled that "Thanks to Thy grace, C *Achyuta*, my delusion is destroyed, my understanding has returned. I stand secure, my doubts all dispelled. I will do Thy bidding) (18:73)." He has been reminded of his duties as *Kshatriya*, just to abide by the words of Krishna. But with what difference! The difference that we see between Arjuna in the first *Adhyaya* and in the 18th is that now, he fights but he is a far higher personality, he is under the influence of a new attitude to life. This has dawned upon his mind through the instruction of Krishna, that he has understood and grasped clearly and thoroughly.

Tilak has called this Science of *Karma-yoga*. J. Bronowski states: "I define science as the organization of our knowledge in such a way that it commands more of the hidden potential in nature."[22] Taking this 'nature' also as human nature, we might state that this science of *Karma-yoga* has brought about for Arjuna a natural identity of *Jnana, Dhyana* and *Bhakti* in *Karma*. The *Gita* suggests that all men on earth can raise their personality high just as Arjuna did. The *Gita* is a work for all humanity. Yet one more aspect of this *Karma-yoga* is that unlike the western concept of *Karma* meant to lead "everybody to obtain happiness of worldly life,"[23] the *Gita* gives, to express in words of Tilak himself, ". . . greater importance to the happiness from self-identification, than to mere material happiness, and which preaches that all world affairs should be carried on."[24] This does not mean that the *Gita* is in any way indifferent towards the happiness in this life and in this world. The world is not *maya* to the *Gita* in the sense that Shankara puts on the word. But it can be stated that the *Gita* wishes with the famous Upanishadic *mantra* that सर्वेऽत्र सुखिनः सन्तु (May all attain happiness) with emphasis on सर्वे (all). The *Gita* does not and cannot end here. Self-identification with God is the higher way, the final goal of all activity as preached in the *Gita* as Tilak accepts. Ranade has rightly pointed out that Tilak regards "Realisation as being higher than service. It could hardly be expected from a great activist like Lokamanya Tilak that he would recognise this value of self-realisation, but that he has done it is beyond doubt."[25] This is inspite of the value of social service, maintenance of society, and universal welfare, etc., that he has accepted, as the cardinal facts of the doctrine of the *Gita*. It is thus clear that he accepts almost the metaphysics of Shankara as the basis of this ethics and religion of the *Gita*.

He has discussed this matter in his learned chapter IX 'The Philosophy of the Absolute Self' in which he particularly takes into consideration verses: 8:20, 15:18, 7:4, 7:5, 7:24, 13:12, 11:27, 13:15, etc. Here, three important views come up in this long discussion in about 90 pages:

(1) "But the fundamental proposition that all perceptible objects have come into existence in a gradual order out of the imperceptible matter as result of the development of the constituents, cannot possibly be altered."[26] "The second imperceptible substance which is higher than the *Samkhya* imperceptible substance, which is eternal and which is not destroyed even when all other living things are destroyed (8:20), is the ultimate goal."[27]

(2) "As in the *Bhagavad Gita*, so also in the Upanishads is the form of the imperceptible *Parameshvara* found described in three ways, that is sometimes as being *Saguna*, sometimes as *Saguna-Nirguna* and sometimes as *Nirguna*. . . .It is possible to worship a form which is indefinite (*Nirakara*), that is which is imperceptible to the eyes and the other organs of perception."[28]

(3) "Not only in the *Bhagavad Gita* but also in the *Bhagavata* or *Narayaniya* religion described in the *Mahabharata*, and even in the Upanishads, the imperceptible form of *Parameshvara* is considered superior to this perceptible form,. . . ."[29] and ". . .though the *parabrahman* is imperceptible to the organs and unrealisable by the mind, yet it is '*Svanubhavagamya*', that is , it can be realized by every man by his self-experience."[30]

Tilak thus accepts the supremacy of *Vedanta* and shows, in a scholarly manner, how all the important doctrines of *Vedanta* find a place in the *Gita* and how it is possible to reconcile these doctrines and establish the supremacy of *Vedanta* doctrine as accepted by the *Gita*. He in this context quotes the famous words: "Just like jackals in a forest, *Shastras* roar, till the lion of Vedanta with its great prowess does not roar."

He criticises the sectarian doctrines of old interpreters. As an illustration we may quote his attack on *Bhakti* doctrine: "But one cannot, on that account look upon as correct the opinion of some followers of the path of Devotion or of some commentators, that perceptible *Parameshvara* is considered to be the ultimate object of attainment in the *Gita*, because side by side with the descriptions referred to above of His perceptible form, the Blessed Lord has Himself stated that it is illusory, and that it is imperceptible by the organs, is His principal form."[31] He has stressed, in his comparison of the *Gita* and the *Upanishads* that the metaphysical knowledge in the *Gita* is taken from the *Upanishads*. He has, at the same time, stressed that the most important subject in the *Gita* is the exposition of the path of *Karma-yoga*. Ranade explaining this states: "All these criteria, according to Lokamanya Tilak, point to the real meaning of the *Bhagavadgita* as consisting in spreading the gospel of *Karma-yoga*, *Karma-yoga* being the be-all and end-all of its teaching. With *Karma-yoga* the *Bhagavadgita* begins, with *Karma-yoga* the *Bhagavadgita* ends and it is *Karma-yoga*, which pervades the *Bhagavadgita*."[32] Ranade is again right when he states that the doctrine is carried to the extreme and then adds that "in our opinion, as the title of the present work may show, God-realization constitutes the *Apurvata*, the novelty or the supreme contribution of the greatest works on mysticism that the world has ever seen and when God-realisation has been stressed, everything else will follow in its wake."[33]

Tilak's originality lies in the great stress that he has placed on the *Karma-yoga*, everything else including the ethics and philosophy of the *Gita* and all other path being subsidiary to, or shall we say, supporter of the *Karma-yoga*. Here it is that Tilak has read the *Gita* as per his own view of life based on the social, political, religious and ethical needs of contemporary India. He therefore could find justification for his doctrine of शठं प्रति शाठ्यं कुर्यात् (One should practice cunning towards the cunning.) or, to tell in his own words in the original—

शक्या तो शांतिनें, नहीं तो बलानें।

(The foreigner shall be thrown out if possible, peacefully, but otherwise, by force.)

To put in brief his claim in his own words: "I differ from almost all commentators when I say that the *Gita* enjoins action even after the perfection in *Jnana* and *Bhakti* is attained and the deity is reached through these mediums."[34] Tilak thus accepts the necessity of perfection in *Jnana* and *Bhakti* as Shankara and Vallabha insist, but to him this is subservient to *Karma*. He thus adds that, "I have thus solved the question for myself and I hold that serving the world and thus serving his will is the surest way to Salvation; and this can be followed by remaining in the world and not going away from it."[35] This is because "God does not help the indolent. You must be doing all that you can to lift your self up and then only may you rely on the Almighty to help you."[36]

This view of Tilak finds support of so many scholars. Thus, Nagarjana Rao taking *Yoga* to mean *Karma-yoga* when Arjuna is told तस्माद्योगी भवार्जुन (Therefore, Arjun, be a *Yogi*), says: "The superiority of *Karmayoga* is asserted in comparison to all the other ways of God-realisation. The *yogin* of the *Gita* is greater than the ascetic. He is considered to be greater than the man of rituals; then, therefore, become a *yogin*, is the instruction."[37] Dasgupta states that ". . . .the ideal of the *Gita* was decidedly an ideal of work,"[38] and ". . .the goodness or badness of an action does not depend upon the external effects of action, but upon the inner motive of action."[39] Krishna Prem, Modi, Munshi and many others agree.

Radhakrishnan

This brings us next to the view of Dr. Radhakrishnan, another great name in the expositon of Indian philosophy. His two famous writings on the *Gita* are in his 'Indian Philosophy (Vol. I)'[40] and another as an Introduction to his own *Bhagavadgita*, the latter being more useful in understanding his view.

We have seen that Hill and other contemporary western scholars—Hopkins, Edgerton, etc., tried to understand the *Gita* in its own ancient atmosphere, culture and setting and they tried to derive from the *Gita* the doctrine of the author himself. Howsoever we might appreciate the results that they arrived at and the most modern historical cum cultural, critical and analytical method that they applied to the work, the fact still stands that most of these western scholars were partly prejudiced and partly suffering from superiority complex. Their minds were not as open as they should have been. Another fact is that they did not have as intimate an acquaintance with Indian culture as they should have. Again, Christian missionary scholars have spread greater prejudices, Faruqhar being a prominent illustration in the matter. With all this, Beatrice Lamb is right when she states: "Probably no religion can be understood except by one of its believers –Hinduism perhaps least of all." Sanskrit scholarship therefore was in need of a scholar who is Indian by culture and inheritance and who, in addition to a very deep and scholarly study of our scriptures, is a good student of western philosophy and thoroughly acquainted with the western methods of interpretation. The world of Sanskrit learning, philosophy in particular, got this scholar in Dr. S. Radhakrishnan. Even though modern India has enriched the understanding of the greatness of the *Gita* by highly scholarly interpretations of *Karma*yogi Tilak, *Anasakta* Mahatma Gandhi and the great *Rishi* Aurobindo, when it comes to understanding the meaning of the *Gita* from the viewpoint of the original author, Radhakrishnan stands the best perhaps to lay down that meaning. His analysis of the doctrine and character of the *Gita* runs on these lines.

(1) Purpose of Composition

We may start our study of the interpretation of Radhakrishnan with purpose of composition of the *Gita*. It was too well known a fact in the ancient days that every activity must have a purpose and we are told that

> सर्वस्यैव हि शास्त्रस्य कर्मणो वाऽपि कस्यचित्।
> यावत्प्रयोजनं नोक्तं तावत्तत्केन गुह्यते।। (Author unknown)

(Who will accept any of the *shastras* or any action of anybody, unless and until its purpose is not mentioned?)

What then is the purpose of the *Gita*? As Radhakrishnan states: "The context in which the *Gita* is said to be delivered points out how its central purpose is to solve the problem of life and stimulate right conduct."[41] The *Gita*'s were the days in which diverse philosophical, ethical and religious points of view of life and conduct prevailed, and, in the interest of the unity of the country and society, a synthesis was necessary. To give only one illustration from Radhakrishnan, at least four views about ultimate reality were prominent then: The Upanishadic that was traditional, the *Samkhya*, the *Karma-mimamsa* and the *Bhagavata* views. What the *Gita* does is to attempt "to synthesise the heterogeneous elements and fuse them all into a single whole."[42] That is the reason why Dasgupta, another great exponent of Indian philosophy states: "The *Gita* is neither a practical guide-book of moral efforts nor a philosophical treatise discussing the origin of immoral tendencies and tracing them to certain metaphysical principles as their sources; but, starting from the ordinary frailties of attachment and desires, it tries to show how one can lead a normal life of duties, and responsibilities, and yet be in peace and contentment, in a state of equanimity and in communion with God."[43] In fact, with the rise of Buddhism and Jainism and their vast spread in the country, of the former in particular, a revaluation of almost all doctrines of Hinduism became necessary and so, in the fields of religion, ethics and philosophy all combined, the *Gita* revalued and synthesised Hinduism. The result was that, "It gives utterance to the aspirations of the pilgrims of all sects who seek to tread the inner way to the city of God," and, "It sets forth in precise and penetrating words the essential principles of a spiritual religion."[44] It is due to this that the structure of the *Gita* "is an ethico-religious treatise and not a system or philosophy,"[45] as Dasgupta contends.

(2) Not Primarily a Work on Philosophy

The *Gita* is not primarily a work on philosophy, of course in the Indian sense of the term. It means, that which deals primarily with the life of the embodied soul hereafter, the life in the world being either only a means to the higher end or *Maya*. Life from the viewpoint of the Hindus consists of three primary values—religion, ethics and spiritualism. The *Gita* is an authentic work on all the three; it is as much a work on ethics and religion as on spiritualism, and so, it meets the threefold need or thirst of man. That is the reason why Radhakrishnan states: "It crystalizes and concentrates the thoughts and feelings which were developing among the thinking people of its time,"[46] and, "It is set forth as a tradition which has emerged from the religious life of man-kind. . . . It represents not any sect of Hinduism, but Hinduism as a whole, not merely Hinduism but religion as such in its universality without limit of time or space, embracing within its synthesis the whole gamut of the Human spirit."[47] Thus, due to its typical structure and insistence on dealing with all the three yearnings of man at a time, the *Gita* has become a work of all Hindu sects and next a work for all mankind at all times. The *Gita* has therefore, with its typically catholic and wide outlook, accepted traditional values and views but not blindly. It is notable that the author ". . . draws all these living elements of Hindu life and thought into an organic unity. He adopts the method not of denial but of penetration and shows how these different lines of thought converge towards the same end."[48]

For this the *Gita* has adopted the method of refining and reconciling.

(3) Ultimate Reality

Radhakrishnan has rightly shown that the *Gita* does not take an absolute or extreme view of the ultimate Reality, because its problem is synthesis of the varied views on ultimate Reality, some of which—of *Samkhya, Bhagavata, Purva-mimansa* and of course the Upanishadic tradition—were prominent. The *Gita* has to find out a way and at the same time to take all these views into its fold. The *Gita* has supported of course the Upanishadic view of ultimate Reality as Supreme *Brahman*, one without a second, one without attributes, one that is identical with the deepest self of man, which creates a unity that overcomes all duality. This *Brahman* is described in negative and even contradictory terms in 2:25, 13:12, 13:15, 17, etc. After the acceptance of this ultimate Reality, the *Gita* has shown positive tendencies to emphasise the Supreme as the personal God who creates the perceptible world by this nature. Then follow His attributes in 18:61, 9:24, 7:22, and 7:4-5. When in the 15th *Adhyaya* the *Gita* says:

> द्वाविमौ पुरुषौ लोके क्षरश्चाक्षर एव च।
> क्षर: सर्वाणि भूतानि कूटस्थोऽक्षर उच्यते।। (15:16)

(There are two persons in this world, the perishable and the imperishable; the perishable is all these existences and the unchanging is the imperishable), it is trying to synthesise the views of the *Upanishads*, *Bhagavata* and the *Samkhya* in one. If there is emphasis on personal *Ishvara*, it is due to the *Bhagavata* influence and also due to the fact that the *Gita* embraces in its fold the common man at large who needs personal worship. Thus, after accepting *Nirguna Brahman* as the Ultimate Reality, the *Gita* shows two tendencies, (i) of worshipping the Supreme as the personal god and, (ii) a positive leaning towards *Saguna* worship as we go further and further in the *Adhyayas*. This explains also the status of Krishna and his varied personalities in the *Gita* as Hill has described and this reveals the *Gita*'s attitude to accept the prevalent views. It also brings them into a unity and gives its own personal view wherever necessary. That also explains the *Avatara* of Krishna who is identified with Vishnu and also *Narayana* and is also known as universal spirit—*Purushottama* and so on. Radhakrishnan states therefore that: "The God of the *Gita* cannot be identified with the cosmic process for, He extends beyond it. Even in it He is manifested more in some aspects than in others. The charge of pantheism in the lower sense of the term cannot be urged against the *Gita* view. While there is one reality that is ultimately perfect, everything that is concrete and actual is not equally perfect,"[49] and "The God of the *Gita* is personal as well as supra personal."[50]

(4) Individual Soul

Here also the *Gita*, being a *dohana* of the *Upanishads* and an *Upanishad* by its own right, accepts the position of the Soul in relation to *Brahman* on one side and the body on the other. The Lord Shri Krishna in the *Gita* states that the process in which the souls part from the Supreme and take these bodies, rebirth and so on, cannot be easily explained. It is His work. The individual soul that is embodied "is a portion of the Lord, a real, not imaginary form of the Supreme, a limited manifestation of God."[51] The meaning is that the soul in the body is supreme but in a limited sense and the soul, through all its activity in the world strives after liberation. Krishna knows that "Man is a complex multi-dimensional being including within him different elements of matter, life, consciousness, intelligence and the divine spark. He is free when he acts from the highest level and uses the other elements for the realization of his puprose."[52] The problem of man is, identification of the soul with the ultimate spirit at the root of the universe, God the Supreme, and that too in the opinion of the *Gita* without hating or disliking the body because "the life of the soul permeates the life of the body."[53] There is a vital unity of soul and body in man, the soul constantly struggles to expand and that explains the constant effort to get over the ego. The soul is tied to the body so long as the ego rules and the soul is liberated even while it is in the body and is active, once the ego is eliminated. Radhakrishnan therefore states that this is the opinion of the *Gita*. "Liberation is a return to inward being; bondage is enslavement to the objective world, to necessity, to dependenc."[54] It is known that the *Acharyas* and scholars are not unanimous with regard to what this liberation is; there are so many varied views and the *Gita* approves of all.

(5) The Status of the World

"Religion is the vision of something which stands beyond, behind and within; the passing flux of immediate things; something which is real and yet waiting to be realized; something which is a remote possibility, and yet the greatest of present facts; something which gives meaning to all that passes, and yet eludes apprehension. . ." and Christ has said: "Man does not live by bread alone but by every word that proceedeth from the mouth of God."[55] All these make the status of the world, its relation to the individual soul and its relation to God the Supreme, interesting questions. The *Gita* is remarkable with its optimistic outlook and its unique faith in the ultimate goodness of man. In one reference it is said by Krishna that मम माया दुरत्यया (7:14) (My divine mystery is hard to pierce), but the world with all its mortality and its limitations, is a creation of God and it is enveloped by Him. The world is supported and nourished by Him. It is not false or one from which one has to run away. The soul has no doubt to seek detachment and freedom from bondage due to this mortality but all that is to be sought in the world. The world is the place where the soul of man struggles and acts for its rise to the highest. The *Gita* therefore does not uphold a metaphysical dualism; the world is God's manifested aspect. In the opinion of the *Gita* therefore *Maya* is not the world itself; it is "God's power; which enables Him to produce the mutable world."[56]

(6) *Gita* A *Yoga-Shastra*

The word *Yoga* has been interpreted in different ways by different *Acharyas*. When the two prominent definitions of योग (*Yoga*) in the *Gita* state: समत्वं योग उच्यते (2:48) (Even-mindedness is *Yoga*), and योग:

कर्मसु कौशलम् (2:50) (*Yoga* is skill in action), actually these are in line with the definition of योग (*Yoga*) in योगशास्त्र *(Yogashastra)* as योग: चित्तवृत्तिनिरोध: (*Yoga* is control of the inclinations of the mind). Yet the basic meaning of योग (*Yoga*) in the *Gita* has been कर्मयोग (*Karmayoga*). Many have agreed that the *Gita* is a *Yoga-shastra* and the ending in each *Adhyaya* calls गीता (*Gita*) an Upanishad that is (ब्रह्मविद्यायां योगशास्त्रे) 'the science of the Eternal, the scripture of *Yoga*'. It is thus a *Yoga-Shastra*. But what is this *Yoga*? *Acharyas* and scholars are baffled and they give conflicting opinions. Shankara, Ramanuja and many others interpret it in the sense of कर्मयोग (*Karmayoga*) with their own reservations and modifications. Tilak takes this योगशास्त्र (*Yoga-shastra*) to mean कर्मयोग (*Karmayoga*) that is the highest path shown by the *Gita*. Aurobindo states that this *Yoga* is not *Yoga-shastra*.[57] He adds that it is कर्मयोग (*Karmayoga*) upto a certain stage but later on it means ". . . the selfless devotion of all the inner as well as the outer activities as a sacrifice to the Lord of all works, offered to the Eternal as master of all the souls, energies and austerities. *Yoga* is the practice of Truth of which knowledge gives the vision, and its practice has, for its motor-power a spirit of illumined devotion, of calm or fervent consecration to that of which knowledge seems to be the Highest."[58] Radhakrishnan following his own method of taking the *Gita* as a synthesis of divergent prevalent views, states: "The *Gita* gives a comprehensive *Yoga-shastra*, large, flexible and many-sided which includes various phases of the soul's development and ascent into the Divine. The different *Yoga*s are special applications of the inner discipline which leads to the liberation of the soul and new understanding of the unity and meaning of mankind."[59] Radhakrishnan therefore takes a very wide view of *Yoga*. It is the path of man's rise and progress towards God. Radhakrishnan acknowledges that according to the *Gita* there are more than three such paths; he accepts three as the principal ones. Remarkable is on this line the view of P.M. Modi that the *Gita* shows many *Yoga*s, at least one in each *Adhyaya*.[60] But Krishna Prem is exactly in line with Radhakrishnan when he states: "By *Yoga* is here meant not any special system called by that name, not *Jnana-yoga*, not *Karma-Yoga*, not *Bhakti-yoga*, nor the eightfold *yoga* of Patanjali, but just the path by which man unites his finite self with Infinite being."[61]

(7) The Three Paths

S.Radhakrishnan deals with the three principal paths shown in the *Gita* in some details. They are *Jnana*, *Bhakti* and *Karma*. He has specified that, "The *Gita* tries to harmonise the different ideals of life current at the time and correct their extravagancies. Intellectual inquiry, strenuous self-sacrifice, fervent devotion, ceremonial observance and Yogic exercises were looked upon as affording access to the Divine. The *Gita* synthesises them all and shows the exact place and value of each of them."[62] He also states that: "The *Gita* recognises that the one Infinite God can be approached and worshipped through any of his aspects."[63] While Radhakrishnan is not bigotted like Shankara in stating decisively that the only path to self-realization is that of *Jnana*, he has more or less accepted his doctrine that the order of the three paths is *Karma*, *Bhakti* and *Jnana*, even though he concedes that even after liberation is obtained, work is necessary. He says: "Work is inevitable till we attain freedom. We have to work for the sake of freedom and when we attain it, we have to work as instruments of the Divine."[64] The view without over-emphasising *Karma* or *Anasakti* comes very near that of Gandhiji when he further states: "The free souls have also the obligation to help others to discover the divine in themselves. Service of humanity is worship of God."[65] Thus, with due emphasis on the three paths forming a unity or identity in the personality of man, however he may start, Radhakrishnan states that: "It is a combination of *pravartti*, or work, and *nivartti*, or withdrawal, that the *Gita* upholds,"[66] and this is because "Action performed in the spirit indicated by the *Gita* finds its completion in wisdom. Egoism is eliminated and a sense of the divine is kindled."[67] And, "The *Gita*, however, recognises *Nirguna Bhakti* or devotion to the qualityless, as superior to all else . . . When devotion is perfected, the individual and his God become suffused into one spiritual ecstasy and reveal themselves as aspects of one life."[68] Thus, man can be principally a *Karmayogin* or *Jnanayogin* or *Bhaktiyogin* but in his life and in his onward march in the Divine oneness, ultimately all the three paths will be fused into one. Radhakrishnan suggests that *Karma-yoga*, *Jnana-yoga* and *Bhakti-yoga* at their highest have more or less the same definition and men who have raised their personalities to the highest by three paths are more or less the same person.

Shri Aurobindo

We now come to the next and the very important interpretation of the meaning of the *Gita* by Shri Aurobindo, the prophet and ascetic of Pondicherry. He has elaborated his views in his epoch-making work 'Essays on the *Gita*' and he comes to the level of a *Bhashyakara*. Very much remarkable is his perfectly logical argument that he bases on internal evidence of the verses in the *Gita*. His remarkable contribution in the assessment of the *Gita* doctrine is:

(i) His novel conception of *Karma-yoga* and his theory of three *Purushas*:

(ii) His stress on spiritiualism and explanation of the concept of *Ahimsa* in the *Gita* on the background of this.

For a clear understanding of the doctrine of the *Gita*, Aurobindo divides its eighteen chapters into three parts:

(i) *Adhyayas* 1 to 6 lay down the metaphysical doctrine of the *Gita* without elaboration and stress the great importance of *Jnana*, partciularly in the second *Adhyaya* and then associate it and bring it in unity with the doctrine of *Karma* in the third and the fourth *Adhyayas*. It is remarkable that most of the metaphysical doctrines are hinted at here.

(ii) In the chapters 7th to 12th, these doctrines are elaborated and properly explained. Again, the doctrine of *Bhakti* is introduced and brought into prominence. This is done with a view to lay down that *Anasakta Karma* is not possible without *Bhakti*. Thus, the doctrine of *Bhakti* is brought into unity with the doctrine of *Karma* and *Jnana*. On the basis of this Aurobindo wants to establish that *Karma* illumined by knowledge and inspired by *Bhakti* is *Karma-yoga*.

(iii) In the *Adhyayas* 13th to the 18th, further details of the three गुण (Gunas), दैवी and आसुरी संपत् (Divine and Demonical traits), etc., are given. In the 15th *Adhyaya* that is the most important from the viewpoint of Aurobindo, the spiritual doctrine finds the finest expression in the theory of the three *Purushas*. The *Gita* rightly calls this the subtlest of doctrines in the verse,

इति गुह्यतमं शास्त्रमिदमुक्तं मयानघ।
एतद्‌बुद्‌ध्वा बुद्धिमान् स्यात् कृतकृत्यश्च भारत।। (15:20)

(Thus, I have revealed to thee sinless one, this most mysterious *Shastra*;

he who understands this, O Bharata, is a man of understanding, he has fulfilled his life's mission.)

The eighteenth *Adhyaya* introduces the doctrine of *Samnyasa* and *Tyaga* in a unique manner and lays down that *Tyaga* is superior to *Samnyasa*. It is known that Madhusudana also divides the eighteen *Adhyayas* into three parts in this manner, but the approach is different, the details are different.

Shri Aurobindo bases his doctrine of the *Gita* on these grounds:

(i) Though, as we shall see at a later stage, Krishna teaches *Karma-yoga* to Arjuna, he specifically states that it is not the highest thing that the *Gita* intends to teach. To put in his own words: ". . .it is a mistake to interpret the *Gita* from the standpoint of the mentality of to-day and force it to teach us the disinterested performance of duty as the highest and all-sufficient law."[69]

(ii) Elaborating this point Aurobindo lays down the next ground further when he says: "The *Gita* does not teach the disinterested performance of duties but the following of the divine life. The abandonment of all Dharmas, *Sarvadharman*, to take refuge in the supreme alone, and the divine activity of a Buddha, a Ramakrishna, a Vivekananda is perfectly in consonance with this teaching."[70]

(iii) The *Gita* accepts the renunciation of works only as one way to the Divine. Other ways are there and the *Gita* accepts all these. The *Gita* refuses to be bigotted and sticky about just one way.

(iv) The cardinal doctrine, the very basis of the entire *Gita* is,

सर्वधर्मान्परित्यज्य मामेकं शरणं व्रज।
अहं त्वा सर्वपापेभ्यो मोक्षयिष्यामि मा शुचः।। (18:66)

(Abandon all duties and come to Me, the only refuge. I will release thee from all sins; grieve not!) and

मन्मना भव मद्भक्तः मद्याजीर्मां नमस्कुरु।
मामेवैष्यसि युक्त्वैवमात्मानं मत्परायणः।। (9:34)

(On Me fix Thy mind, to Me bring Thy devotion, to Me make thy obeisance; thus having attached thyself to Me and made Me thy end and aim, to me indeed shalt thou come, etc.)

(v) The *Gita* shows the way be which man rises from the human to the divine plane and ultimately comes to the state of super-mind and attains to the realization of पुरुषोत्तम (Supreme Spirit). This is what is known as तद्विष्णोः परमं पदम् (the highest state) in the Upanishads (*Kathopanishad*).

With this background based entirely on the internal evidence in form of the verses of the *Gita*, we now come to study Aurobindo's views on the *Gita*. His view is based on the three doctrines that we have referred to. This will help us in evolving a few more details.

Novel Conception of *Karma-yoga*

Aurobindo's conception of *Karma-yoga* is original and a very important contribution to the understanding of the *Gita*. He accepts the presence of all the three—*Karma*, *Jnana* and *Bhakti*—in man's life when he states that: "The first step is *Karma-yoga*, the selfless sacrifice of works, and here the *Gita*'s insistence is on action. The second is *Jnana-yoga*, the self-realisation and knowledge of the true nature of the self and the world. . . The last step is *Bhakti-yoga*, adoration and seeking of the supreme self as the Divine Being. . ."[71] But the *Gita*, in the opinion of Aurobindo does not preach merely mundane or worldly or physical action in a spirit of detachment as Gandhi and Tilak would state. If this were just what the *Gita* was to teach, the Lord of the universe, Shri Krishna, should not have taken the trouble. The *Gita*'s spirit is so large that it includes the whole universe in it and what it teaches is something far higher than this. Shankara states that for a *Samnyasin*, *Karma* is not necessary. *Karma*, even if it be detached, indicates only a lower stage of the development of man's personality. Shankara therefore lays stress on *Jnana-yoga* and believes that the path of *Jnana* is adjudged by the *Gita* as the highest and ultimately therefore the only path leading to spiritual rise and *mukti*. Aurobindo rejects Shankara's *Jnana-yoga* on the ground of *Gita*'s words:

सर्वधर्मान्परित्यज्य मामेकं शरणं व्रज।
अहं त्वा सर्वपापेभ्यो मोक्षयिश्यामि मा शुच:।। (18:66)

(Abandon all duties and come to Me, the only refuge. I will release thee from all sins; grieve not!)

To this may be added so many verses in which Arjuna is asked to fight. He is again asked to become an instrument in the hands of God and to act—

मयैवैते निहताः पूर्वमेव निमित्तमात्रं भव सव्यसाचिन्। (11:33)

(By Me have these already been destroyed; be thou no more than an instrument, O Savyasachin!)

Karma-yoga cannot thus be evaded by any argument whatsoever. Again, even *Samnyasa* is defined by the *Gita* as—

काम्यानां कर्मणां न्यासं संन्यासं कवयो विदुः।
सर्वकर्मफलत्यागं प्राहुस्त्यागं विचक्षणाः।। (18:2)

(Renunciation of actions springing from selfish desires is known as *Samnyasa* by the seers; abandonment of the fruit of all actions is called *Tyaga* by the wise).

Aurobindo does not say that the *Gita* does not teach *Jnana-yoga*, But he stresses that the *Gita* does not teach merely *Jnana-yoga*.

Aurobindo next rejects the view of *Bhakti-yoga*. If the *Gita* teaches *Bhakti* and that only, why is Arjuna again and again asked to fight? Why तस्माद्युध्यस्व भारत (Fight therefore, O Arjuna!) and तदर्थं कर्म कौन्तेय मुक्तसंगः समाचर। (For this purpose, O Kaunteya, resort to action in a spirit of detachment) and again

तेषां ज्ञानी नित्ययुक्तः एकभक्तिर्विशिष्यते। (7:17)

(Of these, the *Jnani* who is constantly indulging in sacrifice and is possessed of singular devotion exceeds all) and so on?

Aurobindo next rejects mere *Karma-yoga* on similar grounds. *Karma* can be possible only in union with something. If the union is with क्षर (the perishable), then *Karma* without attachment is not possible and it will not be *Yoga*. If it is union with अक्षर (*akshara*), then again *Karma* is not possible because once man attains to अक्षर (*akshara*), he is a *muktatma* and then for him no *Karma* remains (तस्य कार्यं न विद्यते), for him no action exists and (नैव तस्य कृतेनार्थो नाकृतेनेह कश्चन) he has no interest whatever in anything done, nor in anything not done.(3:18) Now, on one side the *Gita* again and again stresses the importance of *Karma* and *Bhakti* and on the other, Shankara stresses the need of man attaining to the निर्गुण निराकार (*Nirguna Nirakara*), the state that he takes to be the highest ever to be had. Here, the difficulty is that on one side the *Gita* preaches *Karma*, *Jnana* and *Bhakti* for all and in this state no *Karma* or *Jnana* or *Bhakti* will be possible, and on the other side the *Gita* states that *Muktatmas* Janaka and Krishna Himself have constantly resorted to *Karma* as we are told in the verses:

कर्मणैव हि संसिद्धिमास्थिता: जनकादय:। (3:20)

(For through action alone Janaka and others attained perfection;) and,

न मे पार्थास्ति कर्तव्यं त्रिषु लोकेषु किञ्चन।
नानवाप्तमवाप्तव्यं वर्त एव च कर्मणि।। (3:22)

(For Me, O Partha, there is naught to do in the three worlds, nothing worth gaining that I have not gained; yet I am ever in action.)

Aurobindo lays great stress on the fifteenth *Adhyaya* to get over all these difficulties. It refers to three *Purushas* in the following verses:

द्वाविभौ पुरुषौ लोके क्षरश्चाक्षर एव च।
क्षर: सर्वाणि भूतानि कूटस्थोऽक्षर उच्यते।। (15:16)

(There are two beings in the world: *Kshara* (perishable) and *Akshara* (imperishable); *Kshara* embraces all creatures and their permanent basis is in *Akshara*,)

and,

उत्तम: पुरुषस्त्वन्य: परमात्मेत्युदाहृत:।
यो लोकत्रयमाविश्य बिभर्त्यव्ययमीश्वर:।। (15:17)

(The Supreme Being is surely another called *Paramatman*, who, as the Imperishable *Ishvara*, pervades and supports the three worlds.) Aurobindo says: "The giving of the example of God himself to the liberated man is profoundly significant, for it reveals the whole basis of the *Gita's* philosophy of divine works. The liberated man is he who has exalted himself into the divine nature and accordingly to the divine nature must be his actions."[72]

The three *Purushas* referred to here are,

(1) The *Kshara*—mutable
(2) The *Akshara*—immutable
(3) The *Uttamapurusha* or *Purushottama*.

The stand of the *Gita* is that this *Purushottama* supports mutable and immutable both and at the same time it is greater and different from both. The अक्षर (*Akshara*) is अक्षरं ब्रह्म परमम् of Shankara and man's *advaita* with अक्षर (*Akshara*) as he says, makes him indifferent to and free from all actions. Aurobindo says that man's *advaita* with पुरुषोत्तम (*Purushottama*) is the highest ideal of the *Gita* and in this state the soul is प्रतिष्ठित (*pratishthita*) (established) in *Akshara* and yet *Kshara* is there! It cannot be avoided! *Karma* will therefore be there. To put in his own words: "To Him love and adoration and sacrifice of works have to be offered; the whole being has to be surrendered to Him and the whole consciousness so that the human soul may share in His divine transcendence of Nature and of His works and act in a perfect spiritual liberty."[73] At this highest stage also relation with क्षर (*kshara*) is there and so, *Karma* is also there. The *Gita* therefore brings in the second correction in the form of the two प्रकृति (*Prakritis*). They are, परा प्रकृति (*Para Prakriti*)—spiritual nature of पुरुषोत्तम (*Purushottama*) and अपरा प्रकृति (*Apara Prakriti*)—reflection of the प्रकृति (*Prakirti*) but not its truth or essence. It is distorted or limited due to ignorance.

In the opinion of Shri Aurobindo, these two—the concept of the three *Purushas* and the two *Prakritis*—are the greatest contribution of the *Gita* to Vedanta and without these the *Gita* would be meaningless, full of contradictions, and would not be God's word to man.

The matter may be clarified a little further even in this survey, in order to get a clear notion of कर्मयोग (*Karmayoga*) from the viewpoint of the *Gita*.

The first thing to be understood here is that the जीव (Jiva) that constantly struggles for divine illumination, is पुरुषोत्तम (Purushottama) but due to the influence of प्रकृति (Prakriti), due to the working of the three गुण (Gunas) and due to its ignorance he feels attached, feels dissatisfied. Here dissolution of the ego is the only solution. Not only are तमोगुण (*Tamo-guna*) and रजोगुण (*Rajo-guna*) indications of ignorance and are binding, even सत्व (*Sattva*) is in reality partial light and is binding, by the famous dictum सुखसंगेन बध्नाति (binds by attachment to happiness-4:6) These should be got over as Arjuna is told:

> त्रैगुण्यविषया वेदा निस्त्रैगुण्यो भवार्जुन।
> निर्द्वन्द्वो नित्यसत्त्वस्थो निर्योगक्षेम आत्मवान्।। (2:45)

(The Vedas are subject to the three *Gunas*, get yourself above the three *Gunas*, O Arjuna! Be thou without dualities, ever firm in reality, ever firm in *Atman* and above योगक्षेमः (Thought of acquisition and preservation.)

Arjuna is thus expected to try to transcend the effects of the three *Gunas*, to get over dualities, *yoga* and *Kshema*, (welfare) to be one in *Atman* and ultimately to be ever firmly established in सत्व (*Sattva*) that is *Purushottama* in the opinion of Shri Aurobindo. He states: "The real goal of the *yoga* is then a living and self completing union with the divine *Purushottam* and is not merely a self-extinguishing immergence in the Impersonal Being. To raise our whole existence to the Divine being, to dwell in him, to be at one with him, unify our consciousness with his, to make our fragmentary nature a reflection of his perfect nature, to be inspired in our thought and sense wholly by the divine knowledge, to be moved in will and action utterly and faultlessly by the divine will, to lose desire in his love and delight, is man's perfection, it is that which the *Gita* describes as the highest secret."[74]

He therefore states that so long as one is not united with the Divine *Purushottama*, so long as the ego is not completely dissolved, what the *Gita* calls निष्कामकर्म (*Nishkam-karma*) is not possible for man. He states: "In other words, man's way to liberation and perfection lies through an increasing impersonality. It is his ancient and constant experience that the more he opens himself to the impersonal and the infinite, to that which is pure and high and one and common in all things, the impersonal and infinite in Nature, the impersonal and infinite in life, the impersonal and infinite in his own subjectivity, the less he is bound by his ego and the circle of the finite, the more he feels a largeness, peace, pure happineess."[75] Aurobindo would thus insist that the कर्मयोग (*Karmayoga*) of Tilak and the कर्मयोग (*Karmayoga*) of Gandhiji with unique stress on *Anasakti* are not of the highest type; in both there is सात्विक कर्म (*Sattvik-karma*) and not what the *Gita* calls *Karma-yoga*. On one's unity with पुरुषोत्तम (Purushottama) the supporting divine consciousness, *Karma* illumined by knowledge and inspired by *Bhakti* would become *Karma-Yoga*. This leads to the प्रकृतिपुरुषविवेक (discrimination between Nature and Self) in the second *Adhyaya* and stress on प्रकृति (Prakriti) inspiring all action and so, the necessity of performing one's actions in a spirit of *Yajna*, sacrifice to the Lord as the *Adhyayas* 3 and 4 explain. That is the sense in which the Lord states:

यज्ञार्थात्कर्मणोऽन्यत्र लोकोऽयं कर्मबन्धनः।
तदर्थं कर्म कौन्तेय मुक्तसङ्गः समाचर।। (3:9)

(This world of men suffers bondage from all action save that which is done for the sake of sacrifice; to this end, O Kaunteya, perform action without attachment).

The *Karma-yoga* of the *Gita* will therefore be possible only for a *muktatma* and Aurobindo will understand ब्रह्मनिर्वाणं (Brahma-nirvana) as extinction of the ego in *Brahma*, and not as mere extinction as Lord Buddha would state. He states: "Losing our lower personality in the Impersonal, we arrive finally at union with that supreme Personality, which is not separate and individual, but yet assumes all individualities,"[76] and, "Reaching the inner actionlessness of the silent Purusha, *naishkarmya*, and leaving *Prakriti* to do her works, we can attain supremacy beyond the status of the divine Mystery which is able to do all works and yet be bound by none."[77] In all क्षर (Kshara) the पुरुषोत्तम (Purushottama) resides as spiritual consciousness, but the spiritual nature evolves and gradually too (i) from तमोगुण (Tamo-guna) to plant life, (ii) from plant life to animal life, (iii) from animal to human life and (iv) from human to divine life.

The word विभूति (*Vibhuti*) in the विभूतियोग (*Vibhuti-yoga*) is thus understood by Aurobindo as that which manifests the spiritual nature at its height at which the *muktatma*, saint and satan are one. The *Gita* says:

विद्याविनयसंपन्ने ब्राह्मणे गवि हस्तिनि।
शुनि चैव श्वपाके च पण्डिताः समदर्शिनः।। (5:18)

(The wise view as the same a brahmin endowed with learning and humility, a cow, an elephant, a dog and a *chandala*), and we have also a famous Sanskrit verse that states:

आत्मवत्सर्वभूतेषु यः पश्यति स पश्यति।

(That is the realiser who sees all living beings as his self.) But the difference is due to difference in manifestation, and it is the credit only of the Hindu philosophy and the *Gita* to see God even in destruction. Shankara therefore, in the process of man's rise to the divine, stops at अधिमनस् (*Adhimanas*), the overmind. At this stage, in Aurobindo's opinion प्रकृति (Prakriti) still dominates and so, man's realization is hazy. He should actually come to the stage of अतिमनस् (Atimanas), the super mind and Aurobindo knows this as the highest state (तद्विष्णोः परमं पदम्।). This is a stage in which प्रकृति (Prakriti) and पुरुष (Purusha) both are fully evolved and still *Advaita* is there. According to Aurobindo, at this stage there is unity in mulitplicity, i.e., visioning *Advaita* in *dvaita* and *dvaita* in *Advaita*. पुरुष (Purusha) is *Jnana* and प्रकृति (Prakriti) is शक्ति (Shakti), they are one and undividable at this stage. At this stage ज्ञान (*Jnana*) is all energy and शक्ति (Shakti) is all-knowing. So, where Shankara's approach is that of नेति नेति, Aurobindo's is that of both नेति नेति (not this, not this) and स इति स इति (He is this, He is this). Actually at that stage God is transcendent and immanent both because even after the निषेध (denial) of the whole Universe by the approach of नेति नेति (not this, not this) पुरुषोत्तम (Purushottama) is still there. Gandhiji and Shankara have emphasised the सत् (sat) aspect of God from सत् (sat), चित् (chit), and आनन्द (anand); but Shri Aurobindo emphasises all the three that are ultimately one. Acceptance of all the three and proceeding on the path of spiritual illumination is philosophy.

In brief, the *Karma-yoga* of the *Gita* is the performance of actions that are illuminated by *Jnana* and inspired by *Karma* and performed in spiritual nature. This sort of *Karma-yoga* is possible only for a *muktatma*. To put in his word: "All truth of work must depend upon the truth of being. All active existence must be in its inmost reality a Sacrifice of works offered by *Prakriti* to *Purusha*, nature offering to the supreme and infinite soul, the desire of the multiple finite soul within her."[78] It is a sacrifice to the Divine, that goes on even after man has attained *Brahmanirvana*. The performance of the mundane or physical *karma* in a spirit of detachment is not the highest doctrine of the *Gita*. It is at the lower level, it is *Karma* while man is a मुमुक्षु (*Mumukshu*) and it will become कर्मयोग (*Karmayoga*) when man is a मुक्तात्मा (*Muktatma*). He says: "All individual, all social action, all the works of the intellect, the heart and the body are still his, not any longer for his own separate sake, but for the sake of God in the world, of God in all beings and that all those beings may move forward, as he has moved, by the path of works towards the discovery of the Divine in themselves."[79]

Aurobindo thus goes far ahead of Shankara and of course reads his own philosophy in the *Gita*. His view can explain away most of the contradictions in the work. By putting the *Karma-yoga* of the *Gita* in new light with greatest emphasis on one becoming a *Trigunatita* and without rejecting outright the *Karma-yoga* of Tilak and Gandhi, he sets it on a new glorious height. It is an all-embracing view that gives new glory to the *Gita* and makes its claim of being the word of God the Supreme, full of meaning.

Other Scholars

Dasgupta, Ranade, etc., have also made a positive contribution towards the understanding of the *Gita*, but we take here only a note of this because our survey would otherwise be too long. Dr. Modi also interprets the *Gita* with an original view.

NOTES

1. 'The Gita and Indian Culture', p. 14.
2. 'Ends and Means', p. 4.
3. Vide his Hindi preface (*Amukha*) to the Gujarati translation by Gantbal entiled 'Jain Drshtie *Gita*.' Translation is mine.
4. 'The Bhagawadgita', W.D.H. Hill, p. 1.
5. Vide supra, p. 33.
6. Vide supra, p. 33.
7. Vide supra, p. 33.
8. Of course in a spirit of detachment.
9. 'The Bhagavadgita' Introduction.
10. Vide supra, p. 48.
11. 'The Bhagavadgita', p. 51.
12. Vide supra, p. 52.
13. Kathopanishad.
14. Radhakrishnan in 'Bhagavadgita' Introduction.
15. 'The *Yoga* of Bhagavadgita', p.3.
16. Vide supra.
17. "Bhagavadgita—as Philosophy of God-Realization".
18. '*Gita*-Rahasya', Introduction.
19. '*Gita*-Rahasya', Introduction.
20. Vide supra.
21. Vide supra
22. 'Science and Human Values'.
23. '*Gita*-Rahasya', p. 698.
24. Vide supra, p.699.

25. "Bhagavadgita—as Philosophy of God-Realization", p.122.
26. '*Gita*-Rahasya', p. 268.
27. Vide supra, p. 268, Foot note.
28. Vide supra, p. 282.
29. Vide supra, p. 286.
30. Vide supra, p. 318.
31. Vide supra, p. 279.
32. 'Bhagavadgita—as Philosophy of God-Realization', p. 123.
33. Vide supra, p. 123.
34. '*Gita* Rahasya', p. xxv-vi.
35. Vide supra, p. xxvi.
36. Vide supra, p. xxvii.
37. 'Introduction to Vedanta', p. 14.
38. 'History of Indian Philosophy' Vol. II, p. 504.
39. Vide supra, p. 507.
40. 'Indian Philosophy' Vol. I, p. 532.
41. Vide supra, p. 529.
42. 'History of Indian Philosophy' Vol. II, p. 501.
43. S. Radhakrishnan—'Bhagavad *Gita*' Introduction, p.111.
44. Vide supra p. 11.
45. 'History of Indian Philosophy' Vol. II, p. vii.
46. 'Bhagavadgita' Introduction, p. 13.
47. Vide supra, p. 12.
48. Vide supra, p. 13-14.
49. Vide supra, p.28.
50. Vide supra, p. 28.
51. Vide supra, p. 45.
52. Vide supra, p. 46
53. Vide supra, p.46.
54. Vide supra, p. 47.
55. Holy Bible.
56. 'Bhagavadgita' Introduction, p. 40.
57. 'Essays on the *Gita*', p. 91.
58. 'Essays on the *Gita*', p. 93.
59. 'Bhagavadgita', p. 51.
60. Vide 'Bhagavadgita—A Fresh Approach' Introduction.
61. 'The Yoga of Bhagavadgita', xiii.
62. 'Indian Philosophy' Vol. I, p. 554.
63. Vide supra, p. 563.
64. Vide supra, p. 567.
65. Vide supra, p. 568.
66. Vide supra, p. 569.
67. Vide supra, p. 572.

68. Vide supra, p. 565.
69. 'Essays on the *Gita*' p. 42. This is probably hinting at Gandhiji and his followers, may be even Tilak.
70. 'Essays on the *Gita*', p. 43.
71. Vide supra, p. 50.
72. Vide supra, p. 188.
73. Vide supra, p. 50.
74. Vide supra, p. 179.
75. Vide supra, p. 173.
76. Vide supra, p. 170.
77. Vide supra, p. 181.
78. Vide supra, p. 169.
79. Vide supra, p. 187.

FOUR

Anasaktiyoga—An Analysis

गीतागंगोदकं पीत्वा पुनर्जन्म न विद्यते।

(There is no rebirth after taking the water of river Ganges in form of the *Gita*).

"It is only later, when we come to the days of the *Bhagawadgita*, that we see how even in the midst of the life of action, actionlessness may be secured only if attachment to action is annihilated once for all and no calculating desire is entertained for the fruit of action."

R.D. Ranade[1]

"As ever he eludes us, though outwardly none can be more obvious than he is."

R.J. Walsh[2]

Introductory

With this background of the survey of interpretations by prominent ancients and moderns, we now take up Gandhiji's interpretation of the *Gita*. To put in his own words: "The *Gita* is the universal mother. She turns away nobody. Her door is wide open to anyone who knocks. A true votary of the *Gita* does not know what disappointment is. He ever dwells in perennial joy and peace that passeth understanding,"[3] and that is the reason why he added: "Today the *Gita* is not only my Bible or my Koran; it is more than that, it is my mother. I lost my earthly mother who gave me birth long ago; but this eternal mother has completely filled her place by my side ever since. She has never changed, she has never failed me. When I am in difficulty or distress I seek refuge in her bosom."[4] This was the feeling of Gandhiji and he became firmer in his faith and conviction with the passing of years when he passed through the worst of conflicts, trials and tribulations.

Gandhiji had realized in the later years that the *Gita* stood by him and guided him as no other work did. On his first reading of the *Gita* when in England, in the translation "Song Celestial" by Edwin Arnold, he derived immense joy and then he studied more and more of it. About this he writes: "I have read almost all the English translations of it, and regard Sir Edwin Arnold's as the best. He has been faithful to the text and yet it does not read like a translation."[5] Once more later he said: "I have read many English translations but there is nothing to equal Edwin Arnold's metrical translation which he has beautifully and aptly called, 'The Song Celestial.'"[6] Even as early as in 1925, he had claimed: "I ascribe to the *Gita* a totally different meaning from that ordinarily given."[7] His *Anasakatiyoga* was published on 12-3-1930 just as he was proceeding on his long march of humanitarian service to awaken the children of mother India; this happened some 40 years after his first reading of the *Gita*. During these years, his admiration had gone deeper and deeper with his constant practice of the teaching of the *Gita* that commanded as much of his attention as no other religious work did. Gandhiji took scrupulous care and great pains after the study of the *Gita* and the result of it all is his '*Anasaktiyoga*', the Gujarati translation, the index of technical words known as गीतापदार्थकोश (Gitapadarthakosha) and this is in addition to so many other things that he said and wrote on the *Gita* before and after 1930. We therefore have ample material; he has even explained with great care his method of interpretation of the work in 'Young India' issue of 12-11-1925. We will start our study with a clear view of his ideas about the correct method of interpretation.

Method of Interpretation

He first of all wants to stress that any and every man cannot understand and interpret the *Shastras*. One should be qualified, competent to interpret the word of the *Shastras*. What are the qualifications of a man to interpret the *Shastras*? What should be his approach to the work? Gandhiji has laid down the following canons of correct interpretation of the *Shastras*:

(1) A prayerful study and experience.
(2) For interpretation of the scriptures, man should have spiritual experience.

(3) Added to this is study at the feet of a Guru, or, in his absence, *Bhakti* to cultivate faith in the work.
(4) Only that of the experienced will be the true interpretation, not of the learned.
(5) For the inexperienced also there are certain canons, which if followed, can lead him to correct interpretation.
(6) One should always scan the spirit and not the letter.
(7) Anything that is vicious and goes against the spirit should be rejected.

We may now analyse these details from Gandhiji's point of view and thus get a correct perspective of his method of interpretation of the *Gita*, that he has acknowledged as "the book par excellence for the knowledge of Truth;" the book that afforded him invaluable help in moments of gloom; the scripture that was ever to him "an infallible guide of conduct;" the book that worked as the "dictionary of daily reference for the solution of all troubles and trials" and so on.

(i) A Prayerful Study and Experience

Gandhiji would not agree with the view that "philosophy is an adventure of the mind. It is an intellectual interpretation of Reality."[8] He would not agree to take philosophy only as "...the thinking consideration of things" as Hegel opines. To him no philosophy that is not useful in life is acceptable and he courageously states that he would not accept anything that conflicts with reason and his conscience. Here his view is similar to the view of Manu, about Dharma:

> विद्वद्भि: सेवित: सद्भि: नित्यमद्वेषरागिभि:।
> हृदयेनाभ्यनुज्ञात: यो धर्मस्तं निबोधत।। (2.1)

(That is to be known as Dharma which is ever practised by the learned gentlemen without attachment or hatred and which is approved by man's conscience).[9] Gandhiji had very great respect for *Shastras*, scriptures of all religions and so much the more for Hindu scriptures. He therefore insists particularly on the qualification of the man who interprets the scriptures. The first principle and qualification is "Prayerful study and experience." To put in his own words: "A prayerful study and experience are essential for a correct interpretation of the scriptures."[10] And then, inspite of his very great regard for the untouchables and extreme love for humanity he adds: "The injunction that a *Shudra* may not study the scriptures is not entirely without meaning. A *Shudra* means a spiritually uncultured, ignorant man. He is more likely than not to misinterpret the Vedas and other scriptures."[11] So, supreme faith in the scriptures and a consequent devoted study is the first qualification. If I have no faith in the word of the scriptures, if I do not take the scriptures as divinely inspired and I proceed to interperet the *Shastras*, Gandhiji is right to say that I would not be the right person to interpret them. But mere faith as faith does not and cannot exist unless and until it is supported by experience. This means acting in one's life according to the word of the *Shastras*. Rao rightly states: "The Vedantic sages affirm what they accept as a working hypothesis the authority of Scriptures by their own spiritual experience. Experience is the ultimate test for the existence of the spirit. Such an attitude can hardly be called dogmatic or unscientific."[12] In fact Gandhiji seems to accept the view of Eckhart that, "we must think like men of action and act like men of thought."[13] Study will guide the understanding and the consequent experience will then strengthen our conviction and understanding of and faith in the *Shastras*. That is the reason why Gandhiji states that, "Man therefore, who would interpret the scriptures must have the spiritual understanding."[14] The great Indian Sociologist Manu, while stressing the glory of Vidya states:

> विद्या ब्राह्मणमेत्याह शेवधिष्ठेऽस्मि रक्ष माम्।
> असूयकाय मां मादाः यथा स्यां वीर्यवत्तमा।। (2-114)

(Learning approached a Brahmana and said: 'I am the best of treasures, protect me. Hand me over not to any selfish person, so that (in your or deserving minds) I (grow to) yield the best power.) The idea is that only the deserving can have right to grasp and interpret, protect and make fruitful, one's study. It is very near the view stressed by Gandhiji. The meaning of the word *Acharya* also goes to establish this first and basic qualification that Gandhiji lays down. It is more than clear that one would not be able to do justice to the *Shastras* if he does not hold this first qualification. If man has no faith in the *Shastras* that he interprets, if he is not rightly devoted to his work, he would in all probability misinterpret the holy scriptures. A. Huxley gives the same idea when he states: "Faith is a pre-condition of all systematic knowing, and purposive doing and all decent living."[15] This will be strengthened by man's spiritual experience and here Gandhiji suggests the practice of the various *Yamas* and *Niyamas*. To quote him, "A man, therefore, who would interpret the scriptures must have the spiritual discipline. He must practise the *Yamas* and *Niyamas*, the eternal guides of conduct."[16] This is because, as Radhakrishnan puts it: "Men on a lower level of feeling and thought cannot all of a sudden be lifted up into a higher state. The humanising process takes a long time, sometimes several generations."[17] This view is no surprise to India in which most of the *Acharyas* of old who have interpreted the scriptures have been learned holy men who always tried to practise what they preached. They were adept in spiritual practice and learning.

(ii) Study at the Feet of a Guru or *Bhakti*

This is laid down as the next qualification of a man who wants to come to a stage when he will desrve to interpret the *Shastras*. Man must study with a prayerful attitude and spiritual discipline and experience. Here the Hindu ideal of learning at the feet of a *Guru* is laid down and this is accepted by Gandhiji. In the old days when Vedic study was deemed to be higher learning, the best teacher was said to be the "*Acharya*" and he is defined by Manu in these words:

> उपनीय तु यः शिष्यं वेदमध्यापयेद् द्विजः।
> सकल्पं सरहस्यं च तमाचार्यं प्रचक्षते।। (2-140)

(He is an *Acharya* who ceremoniously initiates a pupil and teaches him the Veda together with the *Kalpa* and the *Rahasyas* (secrets, mysteries). This is a great qualification for Sanskrit learning and Gandhiji accepts the necessity of study at the feet of a Guru. He here follows the Hindu tradition. But for studying the scriptures, no ordinary Guru will be useful. Guru must be worth the word. He must be one who stands the test of the sentiment:

> गुरुर्ब्रह्मा गुरुर्विष्णुः गुरुर्देवो महेश्वरः।
> गुरुः साक्षात्परब्रह्म तस्मै श्री गुरवे नमः।।

(A Guru is Brahma, Vishnu, the God Maheshwara; He is *Parabrahma* incarnate. My salutation to such a respectable Guru) If however one fails to find such a Guru as it has happened with many, the next thing is *Bhakti* for the work undertaken, for the *Shastra* to be interpreted. In other words, this means accepting the work itself as Guru and getting proper guidance therefrom. Gandhiji puts it this way: "The *Shastras* have enjoined the necessity of a Guru. But a Guru being rare in these days, a study of modern books inculcating *Bhakti* has been suggested by the sages. Those who are lacking in *Bhakti*, lacking in faith, are ill-qualified to interpret the scriptures."[18] A man might be highly learned and he might interpret the *Shastras*, but the interpretation will not be acceptable to Gandhiji. He is clear and firm in his conviction that: "The learned may draw an elaborately learned interpretation out of them, but that will not be the true interpretaion. Only the experienced will arrive at the true interpretaion of the scriptures."[19] Similarly Vinoba, following Gandhiji writes in his introduction to the Hindi book '*Jain Drshtie Gita*' by Muni Santbal: "But those intent upon it have deduced several isms from the *Gita*. If we fall a prey to this, even the *Gita* can become a book of high learning and thus, can become useless for life."[20] Let not Gandhiji be misunderstood here. He has always respected learning and scholars, he always approaches them with veneration. But to him learning and practice of the same combined, was the best combination, the best qualification, to interpret the *Shastras*.

(iii) How to Become Experienced

Naturally Gandhiji discusses this problem of how a man can become experienced. Natural it is that following in the foot-steps of the great ancient seers and saints, Gandhiji gives three canons to a man who is inexperienced and who wants to become experienced so that he can become duly qualified to interpret the *Shastras*. These are:

(a) In any scripture worth the name, truth is the first and last problem. Man will therefore always try to strike at truth.
(b) That which conflicts with truth is not and cannot be correct.
(c) Non-violence is the mature fruit of truth and therefore acceptance of truth leads to acceptance of non-violence.

To put in the words of Gandhiji: "That interpretation is not true which conflicts with truth. To one who doubts even truth, the Scriptures have no meaning. No one can contend with him. There is danger for the man who has failed to find *Ahimsa* in the Scripture, but he is not doomed. Truth—*Sat* is positive. Non-violence is negative. Truth stands for the fact. And yet, non-violence is the highest religion. Truth is self-evident, non-violence is its maturest fruit. It is contained in truth, but as it is self-evident, a man may seek to interpret the *Shastra* without accepting it. But the acceptance of truth is sure to lead him to the aceptance of non-violence."[21] It is natural that Gandhiji takes truth and non-violence as the basis for a correct interpretation of the *Shastras*—these two are the most important principles of his approach to life. To him, they are a must for a man who wants to become experienced and enlightened so that he possesses the key to correct interpretation of the *Shastras*. The approach of our ancient *Shastrakaras* has been more or less on the same lines. Thus Gandhiji, who seeks truth from the *Shastras*, stresses the need for love of truth in a man who wants to raise his personality high enough to become as learned and experienced as to be able to interpret the *Shastras*. Here, the principal cannons accepted by Gandhiji are:

सत्यान्नास्ति परो धर्मः।

(There is no Dharma higher than *Satya*) and,

सत्येन सत्यं ज्ञातव्यं सत्यात्सत्यं प्रवर्तते।

(By *Satya* should *Satya* be known, for, *Satya*, springs from *Satya*.)

(iv) Examine the Spirit and not the Letter

This is a very important recommendation from Gandhiji. He expects the interpreters not to go by the letter of the Scriptures but by their spirit that should be accepted as the central theme of the work. There might be a few things in the work that go against the spirit of the Scripture. In that case, these things should be rejected as interpolations or suprefluities. Gandhiji would thus believe that the authority of the *Shastras* lies in their spirit and not in their letter and surely one who goes by the letter is likely to make mistakes, to misinterpret and commit blunders. Gandhiji states: "Another cannon of interpretation is to scan not the letter but to examine the spirit."[22] He has clarified this point by an illustraton from the *Ramayana* of Tulsidas, which consists of the famous words: "Animals, fools, Shudra and woman, all these deserve to be beaten."[23] He adds: "A man who cites that verse to beat his wife is doomed to perdition. Rama did not only not beat his wife, but never even sought to displease her. . . But the *Ramayana* was not written to justify beating of their wives by their husbands. It was written to depict Rama, the perfect man, and Sita the ideal wife, and Bharata the ideal of devoted brother. Any justification incidentally met with therein of vicious customs should, therefore by rejected."[24]

(v) A Scientific Approach

After this long discussion of the method of interpretation adopted by Gandhiji, it needs hardly to be stated that the approach is very much scientific and in accordance with the nature, outlook and personality of the man that he is. We would also be inclined to accept the view of Vincent Sheean that "...but the receptivity of his nature, its instinctive and immediate response, indicates that the teaching of the *Gita* was in him already in some unformed, some latent state."[25] The approach is positive, constructive and helpful in knowing the eternal truths of the Scriptures. We see that with all due respect for and faith in the Scriptures, Gandhiji retains his freedom to reject a few things from the *Shastras*, if they revolt against truth as we conceive of it and against the spirit of the work. He, in another context admitted that: "The written word undobtedly helps" but hastened to insist that: "But even that has to be interpreted and, when there are conflicting interpretations, the seeker is the final arbiter."[26]

And everyone knows that along with the lasting truth for the welfare of humanity, Scriptures refer to so many timely truths and old customs that sound to us strange to-day and even revolt against our common-sense and sense of justice, our sense of truth. We seek only the eternal or lasting truths from the Scriptures and reject the rest or remain silent over the rest. He has of course acknowledged that all cannot know the truth and know it easily. The path of truth is very hard indeed to tread The test of a man's competence to know truth is bound to be very high. Thus, indirectly Gandhiji would accept that the best course for others would be to follow those who are competent. If after this test, it happens that two equally competent persons derive different truths from the same *Shastra*, Gandhiji would not mind it. He would expect that man follows the truth and spirit that he has grasped from the *Shastras*; but he knows the secret of the mantra एकं सद्विप्राः बहुधा वदन्ति। (Truth is one but the learned interpret it variously) and is confident that ultimately all would be led to the same God, and also that the knowledge and interpretation of the *Shastras* is not for its own sake, but to know truth and follow it. It is exactly in this spirit that he says: "I know that ultimately one is guided not by the intellect, but by the heart. The heart accepts a conclusion for which the intellect subsequently finds the reasoning. Argument follows conviction. . . I shall therefore appreciate the position of those who are unable to accept my interpretation of the *Gita*. All I need do is to indicate how I reached my meaning, and what canons of interpretation I have followed in arriving at it. Mine is but a fight for my meaning, no matter whether I win or lose."[27] He therefore is able to state with confidence and in a firm and challenging tone that, "Only they have no answer to my interpretation of the *Gita*, except to say that mine is wrong and theirs is right. The *Gita* is not a theoretical treatise. It is a living but silent guide whose directions one has to understand by patient striving."[28]

The Analysis

With this, now it would be proper to take up an analysis of Gandhiji's famous small Introduction to his Gujarati translation, his *Anasaktiyoga* that clearly and pointedly lays down his own reading of the *Gita*. He is clear in his approach and adds that, "The *Gita* has sung the praises of knowledge, but it is beyond the mere intellect, it is essentially addressed to the heart and capable of being understood by the heart. Therefore, the *Gita* is not for those who have no faith."[29] His analysis runs thus as the development of the argument in the *Gita*.

(i) Mahabharata—An Allegory

His very first contention is that the *Gita* is the crown in the great work, known as the *Mahabharata*. The great work is like a mine of diamonds in which the more and deeper you dig, more lustrous diamonds you get. Gandhiji states specifically and again and again that to him great *Mahabharata* is not a historical work in the accepted sense. To him, "It is the spiritual history of man considered as an immortal being, and as used with a magnifying lens a historical episode considered in his times of moments for the tiny world around him, but in terms of present day values of no significance."[30] He further specifically calls the *Mahabharata* an allegory. He writes: "The *Mahabharata* and the *Ramayana*, the two books that millions of Hindus know and regard as their guides, are undoubtedly allegories as the internal evidence shows. . .Each epic describes the eternal duel that goes on between the forces of Darkness and of Light."[31] He takes his stand on this and believes that the *Gita* is also an allegory and further states on *Gita* (1:1) that: "The human body is the battle-field where the eternal duel between right and wrong goes on,"[32] and also that, "All the names given in the First Chapter of the *Gita* are, in my opinion, not so much proper nouns as names of qualities. In describing the eternal warfare between the heavenly and the devilish natures, the poet has personified them as the characters in the *Mahabharata*."[33] He also adds: "I regard Duryodhna and his party as the baser impulses in man, and Arjuna and his party as the higher impulses. The field of battle is our body."[34] Again, "The *Mahabharata* depicts for all time the eternal struggle that goes on daily between the forces of good and evil in the human breast and in which, though good is ever victorious, evil does put up a brave show and baffles even the keenest conscience."[35]

(ii) *Gita* Describes Futility of Physical Warfare

Once that he accepts the *Mahabharata* as an allegory, he next tries to establish the central doctrine of its philosophy, the doctrine that is the be all and end all of its philosophy, that of *Ahimsa*. He therefore first of all establishes that once the *Mahabharata* is taken as an allegory, it proves the futility of physical warfare. The *Gita* is remarkable with its fine definition of the स्थितप्रज्ञ (Sthitprajna) in the second *Adhyaya*, it teaches the doctrine of निष्काम कर्मयोग (*Nishkama Karmayoga*) and once a man is a स्थितप्रज्ञ (Stithprajna) that is, a निष्काम कर्मयोगी (Nishkama Karmayogi), war ceases for him. He will not even think of entering into physical warfare. In fact he feels that in the *Gita* there is nothing that corresponds to physical warfare. Gandhiji says: "The author of the *Mahabharata* has not established the necessity of physical warfare; on the contrary he has proved its futility. He has made the victors shed tears of sorrow and repentance, and has left them nothing but a legacy of miseries."[36] Again, "In the characteristics of the perfected man of the *Gita* I do not see any to correspond to physical warfare. Its whole design is inconsistent with the rules of conduct governing the relations between warring parties."[37] At a later stage in the *Anasktiyoga* he agrees that: ". . . it may be freely admitted that the *Gita* was not written to establish *Ahimsa*." Actually it is an earlier doctrine taken for granted by the *Gita*. The *Gita* believed in *Ahimsa*. He has, in so many later references taken pains to prove that the *Gita* accepts *Ahimsa* as a doctrine. To quote just one such reference. ". . .but as a commentator draws innumerable interpretations from a poetic text, even so I interpret the *Gita* to mean that, if its central theme is *Anasakti*, it also teaches *Ahimsa*."[38] In the face of the facts (i) that this is a teaching in the midst of the cries of battle, (ii) that during his teaching Krishna specifically states again and again तस्माद्युध्यस्व भारत (therefore fight O Bharat, etc.), (iii) that in the chapter विश्वरूपदर्शन (Vision of the cosmic form) Krishna states in so many words:

तस्मात्वमुत्तिष्ठ यशो लभस्व
जित्वा शत्रून् भुंक्ष्व राज्यं समृद्धम्।
मयैवैते निहता: पूर्वमेव
निमित्तमात्रं भव सव्यसाचिन्।। (11:33)

(Therefore, do thou arise and win renown! Defeat thy foes and enjoy a thriving kingdom. By Me have these already been destroyed; be thou no more than an instrument, O Savyasachin!), (iv) that when he appeals to Arjuna's sense of *svadharma*, he clearly states धर्म्याद्धि युद्धात् श्रेयोऽन्यत्क्षत्रियस्य न विद्यते। (2:31) (For there is no higher good for a Kshatriya than a righteous war.), and in the end (v) that Arjuna says करिष्ये वचनं तव (I will act according to thy word–18:73), it is rather bold to try to prove that the central doctrine of the *Gita* is *Ahimsa*, but we will analyse the problem in a later chapter.

(iii) Krishna The Perfect is the Teacher

To Gandhiji this is a very important fact of the *Gita*. Krishna might be historical, but he is not interested in that Krishna, because, as he says: "I believe in Krishna. But my Krishna is the Lord of the Universe, the creator, preserver and destroyer of us all. He may destroy because He creates."[39] But about the place of Krishna in the *Gita* he clearly and firmly holds that Krishna the perfect is imagined, Krishna as the perfect incarnation पूर्णावतार (Purnavtaar) is an aftergrowth.

(iv) Belief in Incarnation

But to Gandhiji, this belief in incarnaton, this faith that God takes a human birth when the world is overcome by sin and evil, is a very important matter. He further analyses the matter to stress that belief in incarnation is a testimony of man's lofty spiritual ambition to become like unto god. Gandhiji states: "This belief in incarnation is a testimony of man's lofty spiritual ambition. Man is not at peace with himself till he has become like unto God." Hill has stated that the *Gita* is the first to talk on incarnation theory and Gandhiji interprets it in this manner. Other scholars there are who follow the same lines. But he is original in his contention when he states that: "In Hinduism, incarnation is ascribed to one who performed some extraordinary service of mankind. All embodied life is in reality incarnation of God, but it is not usual to consider every living being an incarnation. Future generations, pay this homage to one who, in his own generation, has been extraordinarily religious in his conduct . . . It is in accordance with this train of thought that Krishna enjoys in Hinduism, the status of the most perfect incarnation."[40] This is to show that man by his own deeds and moral, religious and spiritual uprise can become God; Gandhiji thus accepts the theory of Incarnation but not in the conventional sense. He gives a new colour and glory to it. This is worth comparison with the view of Radhakrishnan: "The theory of *Avatara* is an eloquent expression of the law of spiritual world. An *Avatara* is a descent of God into man and not an ascent of man into God,"[41] and "Though the *Gita* accepts the belief in *Avatara* as the Divine limiting Himself for some purpose on earth, it also lays stress on the eternal *Avatara* of God in man, the Divine consciousness always present in the human being."[42] It is clear that Gandhiji emphasises in his interpretation of the theory of *Avatara* the latter part in the statement of Dr. Radhakrishnan and this is just in consonance with his peculiar view of humanity and God. That is the reason why Ranade takes the meaning of Incarnation as one of the five chief points in his discussion of Gandhiji's view.[43] He has rightly shown that Gandhiji's view, in line with the view of Garbe, Hopkins and Edgerton, finds its support in its great emphasis on verse

यद्यद्विभूतिमत्सत्त्वं श्रीमदूर्जितमेव च।
तत्तदेवावगच्छ त्वं मम तेजोंऽशसंभवम्।। (10:41)

(Whatever being there is that is glorious, prosperous or powerful, that know thou to be a part of thy splendour.)

The view is in line with the thinking of Hegel and rightly does Ranade add: "This raises the conception of the essence or incarnation to a philosophic level."[44]

(v) Self-realization

And Ranade is quite right in so far as immediately in continuation with his view of incarnation, Gandhiji hastens to add: "And this is self-realization. This self-realization ('*Atmadarsan*' as he has written in original Gujarati) is the subject of the *Gita*, as it is of all scriptures." Self-realization is the aim, the end of the whole vast teaching of the *Gita*. Gandhiji sepcifically told, more than once that his only aim in life was attainment of *Moksha*, the same as self-realization for him and he did not seek rebirth. In the introduction to his Autobiography that he rightly and significantly calls "My Experiments with Truth", he states: "What I want to achieve, and what I have been striving and pining to achieve these thirty years, is self-realization, to see God face to face, to attain *Moksha*. I live and move and have my being in pursuit of this Goal." Again, to put in his own words: "I have not yet found Him, but I am seeking after Him. I am prepared to sacrifice the things dearest to me in pursuit of this quest."[45] And, "Life is an aspiration, its mission is to strive after perfection, which is self-realization. The ideal must not be lowered because of our weaknesses or imperfections."[46] And, "I count no sacrifice too great for the sake of seeing God face to face. The whole of my activity whether it may be called social, political, humanitarian or ethical is directed to that end."[47] He has not gone into the details of the controversies regarding the nature of this God, either in his Introduction to this translation, or anywhere else. To him, it is enough to say that God exists. Whatever the nature and attributes and form of God, to him it is enough that He is God the Supreme, the all-pervading ultimate Reality, the be-all and end-all of the Universe. About His existence he is supremely confident. He states: "I am surer of His existence more than that of the fact that you and I are sitting in this room. Then I can also testify that I may live without air and water but not without Him."[48] And with this unstinted faith that has resulted in this conviction, he gives some remarks about God who is to him Truth, and his main dictum is 'Truth is God'. He says: "God is not a person . . . God is the force. He is the essence of life. He is pure and undefiled consciousness. He is eternal,"[49] and, "To me God is ethics and morality; God is fearlessness. God is the source of Light and Life and yet He is above and beyond all these. He is conscience. He is even the atheism of the atheist." He does not therefore enter into any controversy with regard to the nature of God as our *Shastrakaras* do, as the great *Acharyas* of old have done. He is not interested in these controversies. To him it is sufficient that God is and He appears in the form in which His devotee conceives of Him. If therefore, we were to press Gandhiji into the controversy with regard to the nature of this Supreme Reality in the *Gita*, he will at the most state that any form of God that we adore is acceptable to the *Gita*. And this will be in line with the general metaphysical ideology of the *Gita* plus the words of Krishna that ये यथा मां प्रपद्यन्ते तांस्तथैव भजाम्यहम् (4:11) (I adore my devotees just as they approach me.) This is inspite of the metaphysics of the *Gita* with its growing leaning towards *Saguna Sakara Brahman.*

But Gandhiji is clear in his conviction that the *Gita* is not sung by *Shri Bhagawan* simply to establish that doctrine of self-realization. In his opinion the *Gita* is an ancient Hindu scripture and like all other ancient scriptures its subject is self-realization. But actually it is not written only for this. To put in his own words: "But its author surely did not write it to establish that doctrine. The object of the *Gita* appears to me to be that of showing the most excellent way to attain self-realization." Thus, the *Gita* as Gandhiji opines, accepts or takes for granted the end that is self-realization. Its real contribution, value, originality and glory lies in the means, the way shown to attain the end in form of self-realization. This sort of approach and reading is in consonance with Gandhiji's conviction that 'means' is more important than the 'end.' Many other saints like him have cultivated this attitude. In a way, this also explains one of the reasons why he calls his reading *Anasaktiyoga* and not *Karma-yoga.*

(vi) Renunciation of the Fruits of Action

Gandhiji is firm in his conviction that means justify the ends and not vice-versa. He very clearly states that: "Means and ends are convertible terms in my philosophy of life." And, "They say 'means are after all means.' I would say means are after all everything. As the means so the end..." Realization of the goal is in exact proportion to that of the means. This is a proposition that admits of no exception. The *Gita* is great and important, original and revered due to its peculiar approach to the means while the end is found to be the same in all the Hindu scriptures. It is too well known that the major controversy of the *Gita* in the world of scholars is with regard to the path of this highest realization, known as supreme bliss, *Moksha*, self-realization and so on. Gandhiji values the *Gita* for the means that it lays down, and according to him the means is 'renunciation of the fruits of action'. It is on the basis of this that Gandhiji calls the *Yoga* of the *Gita* *Anasaktiyoga*. As we will see at a later stage, it is *Karma-yoga* and the views of Tilak and Gandhiji have glaring similarities. But when he calls it *Anasaktiyoga*, he is again emphasising the means.

Gandhiji bases his view on Krishna's words such as these:

> अनाश्रित: कर्मफलं कार्यं कर्म करोति य:।
> स संन्यासी च योगी च न निरग्निर्न चाक्रिय:।। (6:1)

(One who performs his duty without resorting to the fruits of his actions, is a *Samnyasi*, a *Yogi* and not one who does not propitiate the sacred fire or who is actionless,)

and,

> कर्मण्येवाधिकारस्ते मा फलेषु कदाचन। (2:47)

(Your right is only of *Karma* (and so) you should never (desire) the fruits thereof), and,

> यं संन्यासमिति प्राहुर्योगं तं विद्धि पाण्डव। (6:2)

(What is called *Samnyasa* (by the seers), know that to be *Yoga* O Pandava!)

In life, how can *Samnyasa* become *Yoga*? Gandhiji seems to ask himself and he gets this reply.

Let us now go into a few details, and understand what Gandhiji means by this 'renunciation of the fruits of action', that is to him the central, the basic theme of the *Gita*. He states: "This is the centre round which the *Gita* is woven. This renunciation is the central sun, round which devotion, knowledge and the rest resolve like planets." He does not very clearly and in details elaborate what he means by renunciation. But his theory goes some how on these lines. It is very clear that wherever the soul is embodied, that is, wherever there is a body with life, action is unavoidable. The *Gita* specifically states that:

न हि कश्चित्क्षणमपि जातु तिष्ठत्यकर्मकृत्। (3:5)

(Really, even for a moment, no one can stand without performing any action). The result of this is that even if man becomes intent on non-action, his nature will force him to act—

प्रकृतिस्त्वां नियोक्ष्यति। (18:59)

(Your nature will force you to action).

The next fact is that wherever there is action, there is taint or sin. If we were to put it a little differently, all action good or bad, binds man to worldly attachment and keeps him tied to the world while self-realization is the highest goal to be attained and it can be attained only if man's soul is free and light enough to rise to the highest. That is the reason why Arjuna is told.

त्रैगुण्यविषया वेदा निःस्त्रैगुण्यो भवार्जुन। (2:45)

(O Arjuna, the Vedas are subject to the three *Gunas*, while you should attain to a state above the *Gunas*). A problem arises for man. Action is unavoidable, and all action binds. What is a man to do then? To put in the words of Gandhiji: "There must be action where there is body. Not one embodied being is exempt from labour. . . Every action is tainted, be it so trivial." So, what is the way out? The way out is renouncing the fruits of action, i.e., performing all acts with a consciousness first that our right is only to action and not to the fruit thereof:

कर्मण्येवाधिकारस्ते मा फलेषु कदाचन। (2:47)

and next, performing all actions in a spirit of dedication to the Lord and yet a stage higher, man performing all acts just in a spirit of becoming an instrument in the hands of God. To put again in the words of Gandhiji: "And yet all religions proclaim that it is possible for man, by treating the body as the temple of God, to attain freedom. . ." How can the body be made the temple of God? In other words, how can one be free from action i.e., from the taint of sin? The *Gita* has answered the question in decisive language: "By desireless action; by renouncing fruits of action; by dedicating all activities to

God, i.e., by surrendering oneself to Him body and soul." Thus, unlike Vallabha who stresses that *Bhakti-marga* is the supreme path for the final realization, Gandhiji like Tilak accepts that the path of *Karma-yoga*, known by him as the path of renunciation of the fruits of action, is the final and unavoidable path that leads to self-realization. No doubt there is some glaring and interesting difference of opinion between Tilak and Gandhiji, but we shall take up that problem later. If we were to study the view of Gandhiji a little further, it is clear to him that this state of renunciation of fruits of actions is a state in which man rises by slow but sure steps in such a way that ultimately he comes to a stage when he does not renounce action. He still practises the highest possible renunciation in that even when he acts, he is as good as not acting because his actions are such that they do not bind him. They cease to bind him because he has got over his personal interest, his attachment to the fruit by a spirit of dedication not only of fruits, but also of all activities to God. This is possible only by complete self-surrender. When a man like Arjuna, advised by Krishna in the words:

मय्येव मन आधत्स्व मयि बुद्धिं निवेशय। (12:8)

(Keep your mind attentive only on Me and engross your *Buddhi* also in Me,) acts accordingly, he will consciously work only for God and in the name of God. To Gandhiji, only such a man is a *Yogi* and his attitude is as it is explained in *Gita* 4:18 thus:

कर्मण्यकर्म यः पश्येदकर्मणि च कर्म यः।
स बुद्धिमान्मनुष्येषु स एव कृत्स्नकर्मकृत्॥

(He who sees inaction in action and action in inaction, is enlightened among men, he is a *Yogi*, he has done all he need to do.) On this Gandhiji notes: "The action of him who, though ever active, does not claim to be the doer, is inaction, and the 'inaction' of him, who, though outwardly avoiding action, is always building castles in his own mind, is action. The enlightened man who has grasped the secret of action knows that no action proceeds from him, all proceeds from God and hence he selflessly remains absorbed in action. He is the true *Yogi* . . . The soul's natural progress is towards selflessness and purity and one might therefore, say that the man who strays from the path of purity strays from selflessness."[50] Gandhiji's view about renunciation would be very nicely explained in the words of Nagaraja Rao: "It is not world-negation, but is self-negation. It is not freedom from action but freedom in action."[51] Thus the final goal of a man who cultivates this spirit is to come to a stage when his experience is:

ब्रह्मार्पणं ब्रह्महविर्ब्रह्माग्नौ ब्रह्मणा हुतम्।
ब्रह्मैव तेन गन्तव्यं ब्रह्मकर्मसमाधिना।। (4:24)

(The offering of sacrifice is *Brahman*; the oblation is *Brahman*; it is offered by *Brahman* in the fire that is *Brahman*; thus he whose mind is fixed on acts dedicated to *Brahman* must needs pass on to *Brahman*)—The highest stage of self-rise is that of स्थितप्रज्ञ (Sthitprajna) or त्रिगुणातीत (Trigunatit), also known as भक्त (Bhakta) and ज्ञानी (Jnani). The attitude of such a man who has got over all desires and all attachment, is to remain unruffled, firm like a stone under all odds, all joys and sorrows in life. Gandhiji in his notes on 14:23 to 25 states: "The difference between a stone and a *gunatita* is that the latter has full consciousness and with full knowledge he shakes himself free from the bonds that bind an ordinary mortal. He has, as a result of his knowledge, achieved the repose of a stone. Like the stone, he is witness, but not the doer of the activities of the *gunas* or *prakriti*."[52]

It is natural that when one starts on this path that is hard to tread, he starts with his *svadharma* that he has to resort to in a spirit of absolute *Anasakti. Svadharma* is what man gets by birth, by heritage and inherent culture and that is the best course of action to start with. So has Gandhiji explained in his notes on 2:37 with reference to 2:31—

स्वधर्ममपि चावेक्ष्य न विकम्पितुमर्हसि।
धर्म्याद्धि युद्धाच्छ्रेयोऽन्यत्क्षत्रियस्य न विद्यते।। (2:31)

(Again seeing thine own duty, thou shouldst not shrink from it; for there is no higher good for a *Kshatriya* than a righteous war.) "Krishna reminds Arjuna that a *Kshatriya* may not flinch from a fight which comes unsought,"[53] and on the same lines, commenting on 18:47, Gandhiji states: "The central teaching of the *Gita* is detachment, abandonment of the fruits of action." Ultimately and in its highest state, this leads one to total surrender of one's full personality to divine will, to God. The next step to this is what Gandhiji calls self-realization. And there would be room for this abandonment of the fruits of action if one were to prefer one's own duty to another's. Therefore one's own duty is said to be better than another's. "It is the spirit in which duty is performed that matters, and its unattached performance is its own reward." Similarly he writes: "We see others as we are. Hence the central teaching of the *Gita* is, acquisition of the capacity to see things with detachment as perfect as it is humanly possible."[54] Following his own ideology, he emphasises service to humanity, social welfare, etc., as unattached *Karma*. He even traces the great importance of physical labour or bread labour in the *Gita* and so on. But we shall refer to these in a later chapter when we discuss the implications of *Anasaktiyoga* as Gandhiji understood them.

(vii) *Jnana* and *Bhakti* necessary stages in *Anasakti.*

After stressing this *Anasakti* as 'matchless remedy' Gandhiji accepts in his *Anasaktiyoga*: "But desirelessness or renunciation does not come for the mere talking about it. It is not attained by intellectual feat. It is attainable only by a constant heart-churn. Right knowledge is necessary for attaining renunciation ...In order that knowledge may not run riot, the author of the *Gita* has insisted on devotion accompanying it, and has given it the first place. Knowledge without devotion will be like a misfire." Thus, it is clear that to Gandhiji the order of the three paths comes to (i) Action in a spirit of renunciation, (ii) *Bhakti* and (iii) *Jnana*. He states: "The *Gita* contains the gospel of work, the gospel of *Bhakti* or devotion, the gospel of *Jnana* or knowledge. Life should be harmonious whole of these three. But gospel of service is the basis of all . . ."[55] Here Gandhiji follows his own theory and interprets *Karma* as service. And Gandhiji is of firm opinion on this and states in clear cut terms that "but such knowledge and devotion, to be true, have to stand the test of renunciation of fruits of action." Gandhiji emphasises this on the strength of the verse:

कर्मणैव हि संसिद्धिमास्थिताः जनकादयः।
लोकसंग्रहमेवापि संपश्यन् कर्तुमर्हसि।। (3:20)

(For through action alone Janaka and others attained perfection; even with a view to the guidance of mankind thou must act). King Janaka was a liberated soul and he was at that mental stage when he could say:

मिथिलायां दह्यमानायां न मे दहति किञ्चन।

(When Mithila is burning, nothing belonging to Me, burns.) He yet went on with his work. Gandhiji therefore says: "But the *Gita* says: No one has attained his goal without action. Even men like Janaka attained salvation through action. If even I were lazily to cease, the world would perish. How much more necessary then for the people at large to engage in action?"[56] It is true that Gandhiji's view finds full support in the verses:

कर्मणैव हि संसिद्धिमास्थिताः जनकादयः। (3:20)

(For through action alone Janaka and others attained perfection).

and

न मे पार्थास्ति कर्तव्यं त्रिषु लोकेषु किञ्चन।
नानवाप्तमवाप्तव्यं वर्त एव च कर्मणि।। (2:22)

(For me O Partha, there is naught to do in the three worlds, nothing worth gaining that I have not gained; yet I am ever in action) and even though Gandhiji does not refer to the other verses, he will also get ample support in

न मां कर्माणि लिम्पन्ति न मे कर्मफले स्पृहा।
इति मां योऽभिजानाति कर्मभिर्न स बद्धयते।। (4:14)

(Actions do not affect Me, nor am I concerned with the fruits thereof. He who recognizes Me as such is not bound by actions),
and

एवं ज्ञात्वा कृतं कर्म पूर्वैरपि मुमुक्षुभिः।
कुरु कर्मैव तस्मात्त्वं पूर्वैः पूर्वतरं कृतम्।। (4:15)

(Knowing this did men of old, desirous of Freedom perform action; do thou then, just as they did—the men of old in days gone by) and,

काम्यानां कर्मणां न्यासं संन्यासं कवयो विदुः। (18:2)

(Renunciation of actions springing from selfish desire is known as *Samnyasa* by the seers) and,

नियतस्य तु संन्यासः कर्मणो नोपपद्यते। (18:7)

(It is not right to renounce one's allotted task.)

It does not become necessary for Gandhiji to distort the meaning of these verses as Shankara has done by stressing that here the importance of *Karma* is stressed only for आत्मशुद्धि (Purity of self) (4:15) because it is only a means to सत्त्वशुद्धि (Purity of being) (3:20), and Janaka resorted to कर्म (*Karma*) only till he had not attained *siddhi* (3:20) and so on. Here we may note the clarification given by Shri Aurobindo: "All works in their totality find their culmination and completeness in the knowledge of the Divine. (सर्वं कर्माखिलं पार्थ ज्ञाने परिसमाप्यते।) They are not an absolute, but the way to supreme knowledge."[57] The view of Gandhiji can be explained on these lines.

(viii) Salvation of *Gita*

Gandhiji does not fight for or about words. He does not mind calling self-realization आत्मदर्शन (Atmadarshan) what others know as salvation (मोक्ष). He sticks to his view that just as for कर्मयोगिन् (*Karma-yogin*), for ज्ञानयोगिन् (*Jnana-yogin*) and भक्तियोगिन् (*Bhakti-yogin*)also, renunciation of action in the spirit of renunciation of the fruit of action is unavoidably necessary. In other words, all men in this world must necessarily become अनासक्त (*Anasakta*) while they constantly resort to their *Svadharma* in a spirit of renunciation. This is to establish that no one can give up action, while one has to cultivate the spirit of action. Gandhiji makes use of the facts of human life, unavoidable stark realities of life with regard to *Karma* and creates his citadel of *Anasakti* and *Karma* on it. Only this path elevates and ultimately sublimates man's personality, his Self. He does not say in so many words but accepts the basic tenet of the *Upanishads* that all men on earth struggle for liberation, all are therefore *Atma-Kama* as *Brihadaranyaka Upanishad* will state. He states: "I do believe that it is possible for every human being to become perfect. It is necessary for all to aspire after perfection, even as God is perfect."[58] The *Gita* shows the best and in the opinion of Gandhiji the only right path to man in his progress towards the Divine.

(ix) Religion of Man in the *Gita*

All this discussion brings us to the conclusion that religion, ethics and philosophy are one and indivisible in the opinion of the scriptures of Hindu life and culture. Gandhiji also tends to accept the same view. To him the *Gita* is primarily a work of religion and ethics. In this connection, quite interesting is the view of [Kakasaheb] Kalelkar, a staunch follower of Gandhiji and a prominent Gandhiaite: "Actually, the *Gita* is not a book of religion but much more than that. I have always felt that the day the *Gita* has to act as a work on religion, it has lost its natural, living atmosphere."[59] Then only is it a work on philosophy—philosophy of course from the point of view of the Hindus. According to Gandhiji the religion of the *Gita* is *Karma-yoga* of life and its ethics is that of cultivation of a spirit of renunciation by renouncing the fruit of action performed. In this religion man starts with *Svadharma* and gradually with the spirit to be cultivated, goes on sublimating his notion of *Karma*, and ulitmately comes to a stage of complete surrender of all actions to God, a total disappearance of the ego and strict adherence to the spirit of renunciation. Ethics thus combined with religion leads to philosophy in form of visioning of God or self-realization. Thus, the order of the importance of the three in Gandhiji is ethics followed by religion, followed by philosophy, and of course ulimately they form a unity, an identity. To put in his own words: "In my opinion the author of the *Gita* has dispelled this delusion. He has drawn no line of demaraction between salvation and worldly pursuits. On the contrary he has shown that religion must rule even our worldly pursuits. I have felt that the *Gita* teaches that what cannot be followed in our day-to-day practice cannot be called religion. Thus, according to the *Gita*, all acts that are incapable of being performed without attachment are taboo. This golden rule saves mankind from many a pitfalls. According to this interpretation murder, lying, dissoluteness and the like must be regarded as sinful and therefore taboo. Man's life then becomes simple, and from that simpleness springs peace." Peace is the ultimate goal and it means self-realization. This peace is to be attained by the sublimation of man's personality, his *Atman* into Divinity, and this is possible by *Anasaktiyoga* or *Karma-yoga* that is supported by and therefore ultimately identified with *Bhakti* and *Jnana*. Here it is that ethics, religion and philosophy form an identity. He has further elaborated the same point when he says that: "The *Gita* is not a theoretical treatise. It is a living but silent guide whose directions one has to understand by patient striving,"[60] and "The *Gita* is a pure religious discourse given without any embellishment. It simply describes the progress of the pilgrim soul towards the supreme goal. Therefore, there is no question of selection,"[61] and, "If Hindu students may not read the *Gita*, they may not read any religious work at all."[62] To Gandhiji, who sought comfort, guidance and solace from the *Gita* in everyday life as also in the midst of all conflicts and sorrows, the *Gita* was the work that enhanced man's joy of life, his enthusiasm, his sense of living in a certain peculiar way. The *Gita* taught man to become a pilgrim of progress by following its religion and ethics and the consequent refusal to treat the world just as an illusion. The *Gita* taught man to lead to better, higher, progressive life, it taught him how to live as a human being. The *Gita* is a work for all humanity, for all time with its unique religion of life. Gandhiji has described this religion in this manner: "The *Gita* inculcates upon them the duty of perseverence in the face of seeming failure. It teaches us that we have a right to actions only but not to the fruits thereof and that success and failure are one and the same thing at bottom. It calls upon us to dedicate ourselves body, mind and soul, to pure duty, and not become mental voluptuaries at the mercy of chance desires and undisciplined impulses."[63]

Beatrice Lamb asks: "What then is Hinduism?" And she answers the question thus: "The only possible answer is that it is a wide variety of beliefs held together by an attitude of mutual tolerance and by the characteristically Hindu conviction that all approaches to God are equally valid."[64] When we in the words of the old sages say, एकं सद्विप्रा बहुधा वदन्ति (Truth or God is one and the learned describe it in a variety of ways) and सर्वदेवनमस्कार: केशवं प्रति गच्छति (Salutation to all the Gods goes to Keshava (the Supreme)) and when the *Gita* states

ये यथा मां प्रपद्यन्ते तांस्तथैव भजाम्यहम्। (4:11)

(In whatever way men resort to Me, even so do I render to them), the typical Hindu approach finds expression. Gandhiji could read the same catholic attitude in the *Gita* and therefore accepted the *Gita* as the basic religious scripture of the Hindus. He could find that the *Gita* combined the problems of this life with the life hereafter. In fact, according to the *Gita*, this life plus that life is life. That explains the Hindu attitude to religion in these words: "The great purpose in life should be to enhance spiritual values, to free the spirit from the drag of matter, to realise the spirit within one's self." Emile Durkheim defines religion in these words: "A religion is a unified system of beliefs and practices relative to sacred things, that is to say, things set apart and for hidden beliefs and practices which united into one single moral community called a church, all those who adhere to them."[65] But the concept of religion is far wider than this in Hinduism in general and in the *Gita* in particular. That is the reason why Gandhiji felt that the *Gita* is a religious work of daily reference and it shows that religion is associated with all its sacred practices and its lofty ethics, with all acts in life. Hinduism has taken for granted through its experience of men, culture and inheritance what some westerners come to generalise on the basis of their study thus: ". . .religion is and seems likely to remain an inevitable part of human life." Gandhiji has rightly stressed the point that the religion of the *Gita* makes man a real hero in life, a real *Yogi*, an ideal *Satyagrahi*, though submitting his entire self in all humbleness before God the Supreme. This is in line with what Yinger says about religion: "Religion then can be defined as a system of beliefs and practices by means of which groups of people struggle with these ulimate problems of human life. It is the refusal to capitulate to death, to give in the face of frustration, to allow hostility to tear apart one's human association."[66] Gandhiji's religion as derived from the *Gita* will be ready to accept this in essence.

(x) Stress on Renunciation

Remarkable in this context is Gandhiji's stress on renunciation. He wants men, as devotees of the *Gita*, to cultivate a spirit of constant activity together with mental renunciation. This is a state of अकर्म (Ak*arma)* in कर्म (*Karma*) and it is here that he is diametrically opposed to Shankara. Shankara's reading of the *Gita* shows that *Karma*s, even *Karma-yoga* in a spirit of detachment is necessary only upto a certain stage, upto a certain limit beyond which once the soul rises, it indulges in *Jnana*. Gandhiji is emphatic and clear in his conviction that in the *Gita Karma* without any attachment to fruit is the basic need for all men, whether *Bhaktas* or *Jnanins*. Gandhiji clarifies in *Anasaktiyoga*: "The *Samnyasa* of the *Gita* will not tolerate complete cessation of all activity. The *samnyasa* of the *Gita* is all work and yet no work." *Karma* is not to be renounced but attachment to fruit and so, while Shankara's is renunciation from life, Gandhiji's is renunciation in life. The advantage is that the attitude embraces this as also the other life, the life of the society as also the ultimate rise of man's soul. Gandhiji further clarifies the point when he states that: "But renunciation of fruit in no way means indifference to the result. In regard to every action one must know the result that is expected to follow, the means there to, and the capacity for it. He, who, being equipped, is without desire for the result, and is yet wholly engrossed in the due fulfilment of the task before him, is said to have renounced the fruits of his actions." He believes that this is the real *purushartha* of man in life. Let every man worry the least for himself and worry more for others, for the society, for the world. Let man's ego gradually widen itself and ultimately become as wide as the universe. Once egoism is lost, man is in the greatest happiness, in greatest freedom.

But this is the reality of human life. While Manu states that man should behave decently, normally, justly and morally in the midst of desires (काम), and become immortal, the approach of Gandhiji differs in this that the desires of man should be gradually sublimated so that he gradually ceases to be selfish and personal and develops desire for doing good to others, to humanity at large. The ideal of Gandhiji's life was:

न त्वहं कामये राज्यं न स्वर्गं नापुनर्भवम्।
कामये दु:खतप्तानां प्राणिनामार्तिनाशनम्।।

(I desire no kingdom, not *Svarga*, not *Moksha*. I desire the destruction of the suffering of beings that are afflicted with sorrow). This was possible only through this spirit of renunciation. But to make this spirit firm, Gandhiji says in *Anasakatiyoga*: "Again let none consider renunciation to mean want of fruit for the renouncer. The *Gita* reading does not warrant such a meaning. Renunciation means absence of hankering after fruit. As a matter of fact, he who renounces reaps a thousandfold." The emphasis is on renunciation becoming a mental attitude. Gandhiji has not explained how he gets a thousandfold, but from the context it is clear that the renouncer reaps in two ways: (i) The impersonal satisfaction that he derives from the service to society and service to humanity at large, and (ii) The elimination of his ego by slow but sure steps and his going nearer and nearer to self-realization, to come to a stage when his only consciousness, to tell in the words of the *Gita*, would be,

ब्रह्मार्पणं ब्रह्महविर्ब्रह्माग्नौ ब्रह्मणा हुतम्।
ब्रह्मैव तेन गन्तव्यं ब्रह्मकर्मसमाधिना।। (4:24)

(The offering of sacrifice is *Brahman*; the oblation is *Brahman*; it is offered by *Brahman* in the fire that is *Brahman*; thus he whose mind is fixed on acts dedicated to *Brahman* must needs pass on to *Brahman*.) This attitude develops as a result of following the instruction given to Arjuna by Krishna.

> मय्यैव मन आधत्स्य मयि बुद्धिं निवेशय।
> निवसिष्यसि मय्येव अत ऊर्ध्वं न संशयः॥ (12:8)

(On Me set thy mind, on Me rest thy conviction; thus without doubt shalt thou remain only in Me hereafter). We know that Buddha, Janaka, Shankara, Vallabha, Gandhiji and Aurobindo, etc., were such great *Karma-yogins* who acted in life in the most impersonal manner, with full detachment and with their lofty and noble mental renunciation, performed their actions in greatest of enthusiasm. Their lives were a unique saga of constant activity. This is the great good of Gandhiji's ideas of renunciation as he reads in the *Gita*. This is his orginality of interpretation.

(xi) Truth and *Ahimsa*

Naturally and in a logical sequence Gandhiji comes to the view that for a man who constantly practises this sort of renunciation and who constantly rises in renunciation, the basic facts of life should be Truth and *Ahimsa*. He agrees that the *Gita* is not written to preach *Ahimsa*; "the *Gita* had to deliver the message of renunciation of fruit of one's actions." But Gandhiji takes for granted that as "it was an accepted and primary duty even in the *Gita* age," the *Gita* accepts *Ahimsa* as the basic fact and teaching of life. He has given so many different statements at different times to express this view. He is fully conscious that in the work as it is, Arjuna through attachment and working of the ego was forgetting his duty as a *Kshatriya* (Warrior Class) to fight the battle, that it is the intention of Krishna to inspire him to fight the battle, that Krishna reveals his *Viratarupa* (Cosmic form) to Arjuna and orders him to kill his enemies, that in the end, when Arjuna says करिष्ये वचनं तव (I shall act up to your words), it means that he is going to fight this battle and so on. It is clear therefore that when Gandhiji says that the *Gita* accepts the basic principle of *Ahimsa*, he is making a rather bold statement. We will analyse the problem in a later chapter.

Here we would just state that Gandhiji comes to this view exactly in continuation of his line of thinking and analysis. He says in *Anasakatiyoga*: "Thinking along these lines, I have felt that in trying to enforce in one's life the central teaching of the *Gita*, one is bound to follow Truth and *Ahimsa*. When there is no desire for fruit, there is no temptation for untruth or *Himsa*. Take any instance of untruth or violence, and it will be found that at its back was the desire to attain to cherished end." He also contends and rightly too, in accordance with his theory that experience and action are the proper way of knowing reality and secret of the doctrine of Scriptures. It is said that आचार: प्रथमो धर्म: (The first duty is good action) and this आचार (*Achara*) will lead to a better understanding and appreciation of the scriptural doctrines. When Gandhiji differs from the interpretations given by others, he boldly and honestly gives his views. The views are shaped by his understanding plus experience. He has the support of the famous definition of *Dharma* in the *Manusmriti* (2-1) that we have referred to earlier in this chapter. Similar is the view of Aristotle: "He is best who acts on his own convictions, while he is second best who acts in obedience to the counsel of others."[67] Gandhiji therefore rightly contends that "But after 40 years of unremitting endeavour fully to enforce the teaching of the *Gita* in my own life, I have, in all humility, felt that perfect renunciation is impossible without perfect observance of *Ahimsa* in every shape and form." And if he gives a view entirely different from that of others, it is mainly due to the peculiar style of the *Gita* in addition to the approaches of the different *Shastrakaras* (Those well-versed in Scriptures). Gandhiji has known through his reading that various scholars have derived varied meanings from this 'great religious poem', He seeks the reason therefore and comes to the conclusion that: "The deeper you dive into it, the richer the meaning you get. It being meant for the people at large, there is pleasing repetition. With every age the important words will carry new and expanding meanings. But its central teaching will never vary. The seeker is at liberty to extract from this treasure any meaning he likes so as to enable him to enforce in his life the central teaching."[68] How nicely this goes with the definition of *Vidya* as we get it in the *Manusmriti*,

विद्या ब्राह्मणमेत्याह शेवधिष्ठेऽस्मि रक्ष माम्।
असूयकाय मां मादा: यथा स्यां वीर्यवत्तमा।। (2-114)

to which we have referred earlier. We will of course have to analyse the problem and examine how far this view of Gandhiji is in line with the view of the *Gita*. But that will be done in a later chapter. Here for our purpose of analysis, it will be sufficient to note that Gandhiji, through his own reading and experience in following the teaching of the *Gita* in life, comes to the conclusions that:

(i) The main purpose of the *Gita* is to lay down the path of self-realization, and not to preach the doctrine of *Ahimsa*.
(ii) Still *Ahimsa* that was an earlier doctrine is taken for granted as the basic doctrine of life following this central teaching of the *Gita*.
(iii) Experience and observance have convinced him that perfect renunciation is impossible without perfect *Ahimsa*.
(iv) This would be in line with the stand of Gandhiji that the Mahabharata is an allegorical poem and the characters in the *Gita* as also the battle are only symbolical and in reality they indicate that "The human body is the battle-field where the eternal duel between Right and Wrong goes on."[69]
(v) As we will see at a later stage, the स्थितप्रज्ञ (Sthitprajna), कर्मयोगी, (Karmayogi), भक्त (Bhakta), गुणातीत (Gunatita), etc., described and defined in the *Gita* are more or less similar and for all, the final approach will be that of absolute *Ahimsa*.

(xii) An Ideal Devotee

Gandhiji establishes in his peculiar doctrine of *Anasakti* and renunciation that *Jnana*, *Bhakti* and *Karma* are "entirely dependent on and governed by the doctrine of *Anasakti*." Faith and devotion were the very basis of Gandhiji's life, and it was natural of him to be enamoured of the *Adhyayas* that deal with *Bhakti* in the *Gita*. He specifically stated that: "Then, as you are aware, I have, for years past, been swearing by the *Bhagavad Gita*, and have said that it answers all my difficulties and has been my *Kamadhenu*, my guide, my open sesame, on hundreds of moments of doubt and difficulty. I cannot recall a single occasion when it has failed me."[70] This happened because of his perfect devotion and absolute faith in the greatness of the teaching of the *Gita*. Even though he read his life's favourite doctrine of *Anasakti* in the *Gita* and took *Karma* to be the very basis of life, he contended that *Bhakti* was the foundation on which the gradual cultivation of *Anasakti* and the elevation of *Atma* to the higher heights rested. *Anasakti* was ultimately for self-realization and this was to be attained on the path of *Bhakti* and "it requires a prayerful study before the *Kamadhenu* yields the rich milk she holds in her udders."[71] It is due to this exactly that scholars are enamoured of Gandhiji's definition of *Bhakti*, doctrine number two according to him in the *Gita*, and Ranade therefore calls Gandhiji's description of a devotee 'sublime' and adds that: "Neither in his work on the *Bhagavad Gita* nor probably anywhere else has Mahatma Gandhi described the qualification of a devotee in the manner in which he has done here. It is a superb illustration of what a devotee ought to be. Not merely does he gather together utterances from the *Bhagavad Gita* but inserts some of his own reflections in order to present a full picture of a devotee."[72]

The first and the most remarkable thing that Gandhiji wants to lay down is that *Bhakti* is not external, it has nothing to do with externals. It is an inner experience of a devotee of unstinted faith in God and it guides his unconscious and conscious attempt to strengthen his faith and act according to the divine will, to keep God ever in the heart and to act with Him as the witness. Gandhiji is not opposed to the use of the externals as he is not opposed to idol-worship, even though he states that idols creat no sense of respect in his heart. He states in the present context that: "A devotee may use, if he likes, rosaries, forehead marks, make offerings, but these are not test of his devotion." Gandhiji would permit these as necessary only as means to enhance inner faith, concentration and experience. If these help the devotee to deepen his experience of *Bhakti*, to concentrate on the divine and thus to take him nearer to God, he has no objection against their use. But Gandhiji would insist that these are not for show, not superfluities, not ends in themselves. They should not reveal the popular notion of *Bhakti* as "soft-heartedness, telling beads and the like" and lead one to disdain "to do even a loving service lest the telling of beads etc., might be interrupted." *Bhakti* is an inner experience to keep man firm in his action and gradually to raise high his concept of *Anasakti* so that ultimately he comes to a stage, the final blessed stage, when he continues to act in a spirit of absolute surrender by body, mind and heart to God. *Anasakti* cannot develop if it has not this impetus as the basis. *Bhakti* thus gives an impetus to *Anasakti* and keeps man constantly on the right path, the path of God. Gandhiji cannot conceive of *Bhakti* that is devoid of *Anasakti*, or, as we would like to put it, that is not subsidiary to *Anasakti*, and ever helpful in it. He specifically states and in very clear terms that: "But such knowledge and devotion to be true, have to stand the test of renunciation of fruits of action." In actual fact, *Bhakti* is constant activity in a spirit of extreme goodness. Man on one side constantly goes on practising activity in a spirit of detachment and on the other side, goes on with the development of his personality, his soul. A stage comes when man has cultivated that spirit of activity by which he submits at the feet of God, not only fruits of activity, not only activities themselves, but his entire self. He then comes to a stage of total elimination of the ego, when his experience is that his activities, their fruits and his entire self, everything, is for God and only for God. This will happen to be also the highest stage of *Bhakti*. It is the stage about which Krishna says:

> मय्यावेश्य मनो ये मां नित्ययुक्ता उपासते।
> श्रद्धया परयोपेतास्ते मे युक्ततमा: मता:।। (12:2)

(Those I regard as the best *yogins* who, riveting their minds on Me, ever attached, worship me, with the highest faith.) and,

> ये तु सर्वाणि कर्माणि मयि संन्यस्य मत्परा:।
> अनन्येनैव योगेन मां ध्यायन्त उपासते।। (12:6)

(But those who, casting all their actions on Me, making Me their all in all, worship Me with the meditation of undivided devotion) and,

> तेषामहं समुद्धर्ता मृत्युसंसारसागरात्।
> भवामि न चिरात्पार्थ मय्यावेशितचेतसाम्।। (12:7)

(Of such, whose thoughts are centered on Me, O Partha, I become ere long the Deliverer from the ocean of this world of death.)

And that is why Arjuna is instructed:

> मय्येव मन आधत्स्व मयि बुद्धिं निवेशय।
> निवसिष्यसि मय्येव अत ऊर्ध्वं न संशय:।। (9:26)

(On Me set thy mind, on Me rest thy conviction; thus without doubt shalt thou remain only in Me hereafter.) It can therefore be clearly seen, that accroding to Gandhiji the highest stage of *Bhakti* and the highest stage of *Anasakti* are one and the same. The two are mutually dependent and mutually complementary. A man who practises *Anasakti* is essentially a *Bhakta* of the ideal of Gandhiji. Of Gandhiji it is said by Vincent Sheean: "He wanted to be good, to live the good life, and goodness was for him very much associated and almost identical with innocence" (Mahatma Gandhi-15). It was natural that such a man should be a great devotee of God the incarnate that he worshipped as Truth; it is too well-known that the cardinal doctrine of Gandhiji was "Truth is God". He therefore gives a unique definition of *Bhakta* thus: "He is the devotee . . . who has a disciplined reason."[73] It is natural of him to state: "Such devotion is inconsistent with the existence at the same time of strong attachments." In a way *Anasakta* is essentially a *Bhakta* and a *Bhakta* is essentially an *Anasakta*. We can see how original Gandhiji is here in his emphasis. His greatest contribution towards the interpretation of the *Gita* is his doctrine of *Bhakti*. It finds ample support in the *Gita* even though some element of reading personal views in the *Gita* does exist, as we will examine at a later stage.

Conclusion

We have taken this rather detailed view of Gandhiji's small introduction "*Anasaktiyoga*" because in this simple article, Gandhiji has been a man of few words, he writes almost in an aphoristic style. As we go deep and think, we find that the article is only apparently simple. We have analysed his views on the *Gita* with the help also of so many other statements and writings on the *Gita*.

Acharya Kripalani is right when he states that Gandhiji is not a systematic thinker and on any subject, he has not given a fully systematic and consistent philosophy. He explains clearly to state that: "He is pre-eminently a man of action and is rightly called a *Karmayogin*. It may not therefore be possible to find in his speeches, writings and action any logical or philosophical system. In this he is like the prophets and reformers of old."[74] We may not call him a philosopher in this sense, and surely he did not claim to be one. There are repetitions and even contradictions in his views. But, it is clear that with every word that he uttered, scholars the world over thought and analysed and wondered, even his opponents admired him, and of course the common masses followed him in utter devotion and accepted as word of God, every little sentence that he uttered. We have been able to see that unlike the other topics, here, in the interpretation of the *Gita*, he has adopted a certain approach and has done so in consistency. Even those who do not agree with him concede that he has adopted a system and his interpretation of the doctrine of the *Gita* evolves as a system. This is unlike anything else that he has written. He of course claims, that "What I have done is perfectly historical. I have followed in the footsteps of our forefathers," and his finding is this: "I hold that the logical outcome of the teaching of the *Gita* is decidedly for peace at the price of life itself. It is the highest apiration of the human species."[75] He thus claims to be logical and historical. He had also clarified his point when he stated that: "I have endeavoured in the light of a prayerful study of the other faiths of the world and, what is more, in the light of experience in trying to live according to the teaching of Hinduism as interpreted in the *Gita*, to give an extended but in no way strained meaning to Hinduism, not as buried in its ample scriptures, but as a living faith speaking like a mother to its aching child." Here he further claims that his approach is comparative and experimental and no doubt faith and devotion are the very basis of his approach. The analysis of the various important issues raised by Gandhiji in his *Anasaktiyoga* and in his other writings on the *Gita* will prove how far his claim stands in the interpretation. Here we draw a few very important conclusions on his interpretation. As we draw the conclusions, we will be in a position to state that while Gandhiji in his various fields of activity and writing is not a systematic philosopher, the personality of Gandhiji in all activity, thinking and writing is guided by a definite system of philosophy of life. This philosophy is derived from the *Gita*.

(i) The first important and a basic factor is that Gandhiji has treated *Gita* as a work on religion, ethics and philosophy all combined into one. Here, religion is *Karma-yoga*, ethics is *Anasakti* and *Bhakti* and philosophy is *Jnana* as also self-realization after absolute submission of the Self to God.

(ii) Religion, ethics and philosophy form an integral whole or an identity in the *Gita* for strictly following the law of *Karma* or *Karma-yoga*. Gandhiji lays greater stress on *Anasakti*, so much so that if we were not to say that the means has exactly become the end, it is almost the end. All this is for the constant uplift of the soul, the gradual elimination of the ego and with full and firm state of renunciation in action, coming to the stage of self-realization. This is eternal peace or *Mukti*.

(iii) *Jnana* and *Bhakti* are both subsidiary to *Karma* and all the three are subsidiary to *Anasakti*, which means cultivation of the spirit of non-activity or renunciation in the midst of constant activity that is accompanied by detachment.

(iv) Gandhiji has laid great stress on renunciation that gradually enhances man's personality, ennobles and sublimates him even while he is in life. He wants man to become *Anasakta* even while he is in the midst of life and its activity.

(v) The order of the three important paths is *Karma*, *Bhakti* and *Jnana*. Gandhiji has stressed that just like a man following the path of *Karma*, the *Bhakta* and *Jnanin* should also practise detachment or renunciation of the fruits of action so that they loose nothing and gain hundredfold.

(vi) To Gandhiji, *Bhakta, Jnani, Karma-yogi, Sthitprajna, Trigunatita* all are more or less one, almost identical and all perform actions constantly in a spirit of detachment.

(vii) Once a man cultivates this spirit of detachment, Truth and *Ahimsa* lead him to self-realization.

(viii) Gandhiji agrees that the *Gita* is written to preach detachment and not to spread the doctrine of *Ahimsa*. But *Ahimsa* is an earlier doctrine that the *Gita* takes for granted and accepts as the basic doctrine.

(ix) This view rests on Gandhiji's firm belief that the *Mahabharata*, the war in the *Gita*, etc., are to be taken as allegorical and that the forces of Pandavas and Kauravas symbolise the good and evil in human nature. The human heart is the battle-field in which a constant war is going on between these good and evil forces. Lord Krishna preaches the *Gita* to Arjuna not to justify physical warfare, but to teach *Anasakti*.

(x) Gandhiji has a peculiar view about *Avatara*. He is of the opinion that an *Avatara* or an incarnation of God is one who has performed extraordinary service to mankind, The theory of *Avatara* symbolises man's constant effort and struggle to become like unto God. In brief, it is a rise from down upwards and not vice-versa. His faith in Krishna is unstinted, but the

Krishna of his heart is not the lover of the *Gopis*, the diplomat, the killer of the demons and so on. He is Lord of the universe, the Creator, Preserver and Destroyer of all, the inspirer of the *Gita*, the inspirer of millions of human beings; he is *Yogeshvara*.

(xi) The *Gita* is a scripture not only for the Hindus but for humanity at large. Its spirit is large and eternal. It is Gandhiji's spiritual guide, an unfailing mother, the work that helps him through all thick and thin of life, through all strifes, calamities and conflicts. It answers all his questions and never fails him.

It might be possible to criticise Gandhiji here or there in one or the other aspect, in one or the other stand that he takes. We are to examine this criticism in a later chapter. But the fact remains that Gandhiji has derived immense strength and inspiration from the *Gita* and the greatness that he finds in the *Gita* has made him the great saint and prophet of peace that he is, through his constant effort to put into practice in life, the doctrine that he reads in the *Gita*. This is his own reading of the doctrine of the *Gita*. Gandhiji is what he is because of what he read in the *Gita*. The result is that his own reading has its unique value because it reveals that inner strength of the *Gita* that can make a man that Gandhiji became. Shankara, Ramanuja and many ancients as also Tilak and Aurobindo the moderns read their views in the *Gita* and derived immense satisfaction, the unique *achara*, supreme bliss from it. That is the value of this bold interpretation that is original in its own way.

NOTES

1. 'Constructive Survey of Upanishadic Philosophy', p. 218
2. 'Nehru on Gandhi,' p. x.
3. 'Harijan', 24-8-1934.
4. 'Harijan', 24-8-1934.
5. 'Autobiography', pt. 1. Ch. xx.
6. 'Harijan', 16-12-1938.
7. 'Young India', 25-8-1925.
8. P. Nagaraja Rao in 'Introduction to Vedanta,' p. 17.
9. Manusmriti, 2-1.
10. 'Young India', 12-11-1925.
11. 'Young India', 12-11-1925.

12. 'Introduction to Vedanta' P. Nagaraja Rao, p. 50.
13. Quoted in 'Perennial Philosophy', A. Huxley, p. 72.
14. 'Young India', 25-11-1925.
15. Quoted in 'Introduction to Vedanta', P. Nagaraja Rao, p. 59.
16. 'Young India', 12-11-1925.
17. 'Indian Philosophy', Vol. 1, p. 570.
18. 'Young India', 12-11-1925.
19. 'Young India', 12-11-1925.
20. Translation is mine.
21. 'Young India', 12-11-1925.
22. 'Young India', 12-11-1925.
23. Translation is mine.
24. 'Young India', 12-11-1925.
25. 'Mahatma Gandhi', p. 15.
26. 'Harijan', 22-12-1933.
27. 'Young India', 12-11-1925.
28. 'Harijan', 26-9-1936.
29. 'Young India', 6-3-1931.
30. 'Harijan', 5-2-1936.
31. 'Harijan', 3-10-1936.
32. '*Gita* According to Gandhi', p. 132.
33. 'Diary of Mahadev Desai', p. 172.
34. 'Young India', 12-11-1925.
35. 'Harijan', 5-9-1936.
36. 'Young India', 6-8-1931.
37. 'Young India', 6-8-1931.
38. 'Young India', 6-8-1931.
39. 'Young India', 9-4-1925.
40. 'Young India', 6-8-1931.
41. 'Bhagavadgita', Introduction, p. 28.
42. 'Bhagavadgita', Introduction, p.35.
43. Vide 'Bhagavadgita –as Philosophy of God-Realization', pp. 124-125.
44. Vide Supra, p. 129.
45. 'All Men are Brothers', p. 66.
46. 'All Men are Brothers', p. 71.
47. 'All Men are Brothers', p.75.
48. 'All Men are Brothers', p.68.
49. 'All Men are Brothers', p. 65.
50. '*Gita* According to Gandhi', pp. 198-199.
51. 'Introduction to Vedanta', p. 95.
52. '*Gita* According to Gandhi', p. 332.
53. '*Gita* According to Gandhi', p. 154.
54. Letter on S. Ghosh on 14-11-1945. Quoted in his 'Gandhiji's Emissary' p. 190.

55. 'Young India', 3-11-1927.
56. '*Gita* According to Gandhi', p. 127.
57. 'Essays on the *Gita*', p. 153.
58. 'Young India', 22-9-1927.
59. 'Jeevan Pradeepa', p. 35.
60. 'Harijan', 3-9-1931.
61. 'Harijan', 5-12-1936.
62. 'Young India', 8-12-1927.
63. 'Harijan', 24-8-1934.
64. 'India—A World in Transition', p. 98.
65. Durkheim in 'Religion, Culture and Society', Ed. L. Schneider, p. 35.
66. 'Philosophy of Religion', Ed. Aberenethy and Longford, p. 77.
67. 'Ethics', 1-4-7.
68. 'Young India', 7-8-1931.
69. Gandhiji on *Gita* 1-1, '*Gita* According to Gandhi', p. 132.
70. 'Harijan', 30-1-1937.
71. 'Harijan', 30-1-1937.
72. 'Bhagavadgita—As a Philosophy of God-Realization', p. 129.
73. '*Gita* According to Gandhi', p. 126.
74. 'The Gandhian way', p. 158.
75. 'Harijan', 3-10-1936.

FIVE

Anasaktiyoga—An Analysis (Continued)

It would now be proper to discuss further four important aspects of Gandhiji's interpretation of the *Gita*. These are:

(1) Gandhiji's conception of an ideal *Bhakta*;
(2) Gandhiji's conception of *Samnyasa*.
(3) His conception of God in the *Gita*.
(4) Gandhiji's concept of Krishna and *Avatara*; *Samnyasi*, *Bhakta*, *Yogi, Trigunatita* and so on.

A clear idea about these can give to us a perfect understanding of Gandhiji's conception of the doctrine of the *Gita*.

(1) An Ideal *Bhakta*

When Gandhiji says: "The *Gita* contains the gospel of work, the gospel of *Bhakti* or Devotion, and the gospel of *Jnana* or knowledge. Life should be a harmonious whole of these three,"[1] he is not saying anything new. This is stated by other *Acharyas* and scholars. But, Gandhiji's originality lies in the great stress that he places on *Karma-yoga*, that he knows as 'Gospel of Service.' It was the guiding principle of his life and he found it to be the basis in the *Gita*. He says: "The human body is meant for service, never for indulgence. Renunciation is life. Indulgence spells death."[2] Service to humanity has been the ideal of all saints and prophets of peace and so it is with Gandhiji. He therefore specifically states: "But the gospel of service is the basis of all, and what can be more necessary for those who want to serve the country than that they begin with the chapter enunciating the Gospel of work?"[3] His argument will find support in so many verses in the *Gita* that is *Karma-yoga shastra*.

Gandhiji conceives of *Karma-yoga* as *Anasaktiyoga*. This is due to greater stress on the spirit at the back of the action rather than on the action itself. It applies to all men in all stages of life. One such man is the *Bhakta*, described in the 12th *Adhyaya* and also at some other places. Being a *Vaishnava* by birth and inheritance and being a typical *Vaishnava* all through his life, naturally greater is the stamp of *Bhakti* than of *Jnana* on Gandhiji's personality. It is therefore rightly stated that: "The *Vaishnava* mode of thinking made a permanent impression on Gandhiji's mind in his early childhood. And his philosophy is more or less the *Vaishnava* philosophy. Though he is a Hindu, he is more a *Vaishnava* Hindu than a *Shakta* Hindu."[4] This can be particularly evidenced in the last three or four years of his life when he experienced a spirit to the full of complete dedication to the will of God and a spirit of absolute submission of all his activities to His will, with the keenest desire to act only as an instrument in His hands. This *Bhakti* of Gandhiji's experience was mainly the outcome of his love for the *Gita* and the concept of *Bhakti* and *Bhakta* that he read in it. The concept comes more or less to this.

(i) Gandhiji states that renunciation of the fruits of one's actions is the basic teaching of the *Gita*. Action is not to be avoided and cannot be avoided. For a man who follows the teaching of the *Gita*, *Samnyasa* is not actual renunciation of all action, it is renunciation of the fruits of action as Gandhiji states, and it is also renunciation of the mental attachment to fruit as we would add. So, becoming free from attachment to the fruit, which is freedom from all bondage and all sin, is the state of *Akarma* (non-action) in the *Gita*. This is, becoming free from action, before one becomes fit to receive divine insight and spiritual knowledge. A question naturally arises as to how this state can be attained because, as Gandhiji says: "The detachment prescribed by the *Gita* is the hardest thing to achieve, and yet it is absolutely necessary for perfect peace and for the vision of both the little self and the greatest self."[5] For this also, Gandhiji's ideas are crystal clear. He says: "In other words, how can one be free from action, i.e., from the taint of sin? The *Gita* has answered the question in decisive language: 'By desirelss action; by renouncing fruits of action; by dedicating all activities to God, i.e. by surrendering oneself to Him body and soul.' But desirelessness or renunciation does not come for the mere talking about it. It is not attained by an intellectual feat... Right knowledge is necessary for attaining renunciation. . . . In order that knowledge may not run riot, the author of the *Gita* has insisted on devotion accompanying it, and has given it the first place."[6] So, *Bhakti*, in the opinion of Gandhiji finds the first place in the *Gita* and this is of course after accepting the fact that *Anasakta Karma* is an unavoidable necessity applicable to all. Gandhiji therefore believes that all who are followers of God must necessarily cultivate a spirit of devotion, actually Gandhiji states almost that after *Karma*, *Bhakti* is necessary for all for success in their effort at the cultivation of the spirit of *Samnyasa*.

(ii) The next important thing about this active *Bhakti* of Gandhiji's concept is that it is essentially an inner urge and trait and man may or may not use external modes. Gandhiji is clear in saying that "The devotion of the *Gita* has the least to do with externals."[7] Gandhiji does not protest against the use of externals as he has not protested against idol-worship, even though he personally does not need either and has therefore no regard for both. The common man may require these external modes for cultivation of concentration and so on.

(iii) Yet the next thing to be noted about this *Bhakti* is that a real *Bhakta* is perfectly non-attached and cultivating a spirit of समत्व *(samatva)*, looks on all as alike. With his Self above even *Sattva Guna*, he acts with his Self perfectly above dualities. He is thus a *Sthitaprajna* we might say. It is here that for Gandhiji *Bhakta* and *Sthitaprajna* are more or less one and the same. He thus possesses all the fine qualities as they are described in the verses 12:13 to 19. Arjuna is again in the 18th *Adhyaya* asked to become such a *Bhakta* –

> मन्मना भव मद्भक्तो मद्याजीमां नमस्कुरु।
> मामेवैष्यसि सत्यं ते प्रतिजाने प्रियोऽसि मे।। (18:65)

and,

> सर्वधर्मान् परित्यज्य मामेकं शरणं व्रज।
> अहं त्वा सर्वपापेभ्यो मोक्षयिष्यामि मा शुचः।। (18:66)

("On Me fix thy mind, to Me bring thy devotion, to Me offer thy sacrifice, to Me make thy obeisance; to Me indeed shalt thou come; solemn is my promise to thee, thou art dear Me."

"Abandon all duties and come to me, the only refuge. I will release thee from all sins; grieve not!")

(iv) It is again important that such a real devotee indulges in a constant striving to attain to self–realisation. Self-realisatioin is the ultimate goal for all men, conscious or unconscious though they might be. For the fine way in which a devotee acts and behaves, the ultimate ideal is sublimation of his self to the highest goal of life, self-realization. This is the goal of the *Gita*, it is also that of an ideal *Bhakta*. Such *Bhakta*s constantly act in life with a spirit of detachment and in a spirit of total submission of the self and actions to God. For such *Bhakta*s the highest reward is promised in *Adhyaya* 12, when we are told:

ये तु सर्वाणि कर्माणि मयि संन्यस्य मत्पराः।
अनन्येनैव योगेन मां ध्यायन्त उपासते।।

तेषामहं समुद्धर्ता मृत्युसंसारसागरात्।
भवामि न चिरात् पार्थ मय्यावेशितचेतसाम्।।

मय्येव मन आधत्स्व मयि बुद्धिं निवेशय।
निवसिष्यसि मय्येव अत ऊर्ध्वं न संशयः।। (12:6 to 8)

("But those who, casting all their actions on Me, making Me their all in all, worship Me with the meditation of undivided devotion, of such, whose thoughts are centred on Me, O Partha, I become ere long the deliverer from the ocean of this world of death."

"On Me set thy mind, on Me rest thy conviction; thus without doubt shalt thou remain only in Me hereafter.")

Similar is the assurance given in 16:68-69. To put in Gandhiji's words: "We must see that to be a real devotee is to realize oneself. Sef-realization is not something apart . . . The extreme of means is salvation—salvation of the *Gita* is perfect peace."[8]

(v) Gandhiji would go a step further and say that such a *Bhakta* will quite naturally be endowed with the knowledge of the Divine, though he might not make a show of it. But to such a *Bhakta*, even knowledge is a means and not the end. The dominant factor in his life is devotion and that only. King Janaka was a *muktatma* and Gandhiji knows him as a *Jnanin* as also a *Bhakta* and of course he is a great *Karma*-yogi. The *Gita* has stated:

कर्मणैव हि संसिद्धिमास्थिताः जनकादयः। (3:20)

(For through action alone Janaka and others achieved perfection.) Actually the whole leaning of Gandhiji is to identify even *Jnani* with *Bhakta* and *Bhakta* with *Sthitaprajna*, though ultimately his own admiration is for *Bhakti*. After *Anasakti-yoga*, he reads the doctrine of *Bhakti* as the most dominant one in the *Gita*.

(vi) A question might arise in our mind as to how best a *Bhakta* will remain engrossed in self-less service. What is the best detached service for a *Bhakta*? He recommends the Religion of Service for such a man, and wants that even this service should be towards the lowly and the lost, the suppressed and the poverty-stricken. A famous verse tells us:

अयं निजः परो वेति गणना लघुचेतसाम्।
उदारचरितानां तु वसुधैव कुटुंबकम्।।

(Only persons with a small mind have these considerations—He is mine, he is an enemy, etc.; but for large-hearted souls, the whole earth is a family). And so, when a *Bhakta* looks upon the world as his family, naturally his ideal as expressed in this famous verse will be:

न त्वहं कामये राज्यं न स्वर्गं नापुनर्भवम्।
कामये दुःखतप्तानां प्राणिनामार्तिनाशनम्।।

(I do not hanker after a kingdom or *svarga* or *moksha*; I desire the removal of the sufferings of the beings afflicted with sorrow). The idea is based on this and similar verses of the *Gita*:

पत्रं पुष्पं फलं तोयं यो मे भक्त्या प्रयच्छति।
तदहं भक्त्युपहृतमश्नामि प्रयतात्मनः।। (9:26)

(Any offering of leaf, flower, fruit or water, made to Me in devotion, by an earnest soul, I lovingly accept.)

Gandhiji states: "He who would be a *Bhakta*, therefore, must serve these by body, soul and mind. How can he who regards the 'suppresed' classes as untouchables serve them by the body?"Actually Gandhiji states that the *Gita* knows no untouchability because its attitude can be thus stated:

आत्मवत्सर्वभूतेषु यः पश्यति स पश्यति।

(He is a real seer who visions all living beings as his own self.)

And the *Gita* states:

> मां हि पार्थ व्यपाश्रित्य येऽपि स्युः पापयोनयः।
> स्त्रियो वैश्यास्तथा शूद्रास्तेऽपि यान्ति परां गतिम्।। (9:32)

(For finding refuge in Me, even those who, though born of the womb of sin, women, *vaishyas* and *shudras* too, reach the supreme goal.)

(vii) The next step is to prove that the path of *Bhakti* is actually the path of *Karma*. This is because active service and that too with perfect detachment, first in a spirit of service to others and then, in the end, in a spirit of devotion and total submission to the Divine will, are the basis of successful ideal *Bhakti*. All the best of men served the people and lived for the good of mankind, all the *Avatara*s fought evil for protecting and upholding the good, not of their own selves, but of humanity at large. Krishna the *Purna Avatara*, who is God the Supreme for his devotees, *Divya Akara* higher than *Nirakara* as Dasgupta suggests, constantly remains active. Krishna says:

> न मे पार्थास्ति कर्तव्यं त्रिषु लोकेषु किंचन।
> नानवाप्तमवाप्तव्यं वर्त एव च कर्मणि।। (3:22)

(For Me O Partha, there is naught to do in the three worlds, nothing worth gaining that I have not gained; yet I am ever in action) and, as a result, he constantly worries about the welfare of the world, for uplift of *Dharma*, for the good of humanity and so on. He therefore says:

> यदा यदा हि धर्मस्य ग्लानिर्भवति भारत।
> अभ्युत्थानमधर्मस्य तदात्मानं सृजाम्यहम्।।
>
> परित्राणाय साधूनां विनाशाय च दुष्कृताम्।
> धर्मसंस्थापनार्थाय संभवामि युगे युगे।। (4:7-8)

(For whenever Right declines and Wrong prevails, then O Bharata, I come to birth.

To save the righteous, to destroy the wicked, and to re-establish Right I am born from age to age.)

How much more of *Karma* is necessary in the same spirit for a *Bhakta*! Gandhiji therefore finds *Karma-yoga* and *Bhakti-yoga* to be almost identical.

He therefore states: "The difference, between one who is a devotee of God and another who is not, is that the former is active in service of others, never gives up Truth in the midst of activity and gradually overcomes his likes and dislikes . . ." and "Shri Krishna served the people all his life, he was a real servant of the people . . . His whole life was an unbroken *Gita* of *Karma*", and so, "In *Bhagavadgita*, Lord Krishna has shown the path of *Bhakti* which means the path of *Karma*."[9] This speaks for the very great importance that Gandhiji gives to *Karma* and the internal unity that he conceives of among the paths of *Karma*, *Jnana* and *Bhakti*. His clear contention is that the basis of the whole life and therefore of all men in all stages and stations of life is in *Karma* and further that a real *Karma-yogi* should be both a *Bhakta* and a *Jnani*; a real *Bhakta* should be both a *Karma-yogi* and a *Jnani* and so on.

This whole approach is again in line with the *Bhakti* doctrine. As Survira Jaiswal rightly states: "Nonetheless, in the *Bhagavadgita* the doctine of *Bhakti*, in its wider sense, becomes a religious principle and a way of life. In practical application, this doctrine does not mean mere enjoyment of escstatic trances fancying the nearness of the deity; it means carrying out of one's duties and other social actions in a spirit of renunciation."[10]

(viii) Yet one more thing stressed by Gandhiji in this concept of *Bhakti* is that spiritually, a *Bhakta* cultivates a sense of oneness of all life (आत्मवत् सर्वभूतेषु) and with all the qualities of an ideal *Bhakta* laid down in the 12th *Adhyaya*, Gandhiji extendes his ideal to state that the *Gita* makes no distinction of caste and creed, higher and lower. To the *Bhakta*, all are God's creation and so all are good. Krishna has stated:

> सर्वस्य चाहं हृदि संनिविष्टो मत्तः स्मृतिर्ज्ञानमपोहनं च।
> वेदैश्च सर्वैरहमेव वेद्यो वेदान्तकृत् वेदविदेव चाऽहम्।। (15:15)

and,

> यद्यद्विभूतिमत्सत्त्वं श्रीमदूर्जितमेव च।
> तत्तदेवावगच्छ त्वं मम तेजोंऽशसंभवम्।। (10:81)

(And I am seated in the heart of all, from Me proceed memory, knowledge and the dispelling of doubt; it is I who am to be known in all the Vedas; I, the author of Vedanta and the knower of the Vedas.

Whatever is glorious, beautiful and mighty, know thou that all such has issued from a fragment of My splendour.)

These and similar verses can bring about Gandhiji's concept of unity of all life and lack of distinction between one and the other living being. To put in his words: "Lord Krishna has also taught that to be a true *Bhakta* we should make no difference between a *Brahman* and a scavenger. If that is true, there can be no place for untouchability in Hinduism,"[11] and, "The great message of the *Bhagavadgita* is: "Treat the *Brahman* and *Bhangi* alike, if you would but know God. But how are they alike? A *Brahmin* is any day superior to the *Bhangi* in learning and how am I to treat both alike? The *Bhagavad Gita* says that you should treat them even as you would wish to be treated by them, or even as you would treat yourself." (Young India, 13-1-1927)

This will be in line with the *Gita* verse:

शुनि चैव श्वपाके च पण्डिताः समदर्शिनः। (5:18)

(The men of self-realization look with an equal eye on a dog and even a dog-eater,)

and,

ब्रह्मभूतः प्रसन्नात्मा न शोचाति न कांक्षति।
समः सर्वेषु भूतेषु मद्भक्तिं लभते पराम्।। (18:65)

(One with *Brahman* and at peace with himself, he grieves not, nor desires; holding all beings alike, he achieves supreme devotion to Me.)

स्त्रियो वैश्यास्तथा शूद्रास्तेऽपि यान्ति परां गतिम्। (9:32)

(Women, *Vaishyas* and *Shudras* too, reach the supreme goal), and also verses 13:27-28, etc.

Gandhiji has thus given an original interpretation to the meaning of the word '*Bhakti*' in the *Gita*, and, whether the ancient social conventions justify this interpretation or not, Gandhiji is thoroughly consistent and logical in deriving the interpretation that differs from all others in certain matters. And the fact remains that throughout his life and particularly during the last days when he faced the worst of mental conflicts and ordeals, the *Bhakti* gave him unique strength to withstand the worst of calamities. He did not lose his equanimity of mind and spirit only because of this unstinted devotion to God. He says: "God binds me for a while, and then He flashes the truth across my mind like lightning. Therefore, I feel no remorse,"[12] and, "God has made me as I am. He will do what he wills. He can put an end to my life if it pleases Him. I think I obey the word of God,"[13] and so on.

This interpretation seems to give new life and meaning to *Bhakti* and *Vaishnavism* and Ranade rightly states that it is an original interpretation that should rightly be acknowledged as a very important and positive contribution to knowledge and also interpretation of the meaning of the *Gita*. To put in Ranade's words: "We shall now deal with Mahatma Gandhiji's sublime description of a devotee. Neither in his work on the *Bhagavadgita* nor probably anywhere else has Mahatma Gandhi described the qualifications of a devotee in a manner in which he has done here. It is a superb illustration of what a devotee ought to be. Not merely does he gather together utterances from the *Bhagavadgita*, but inserts some of his own reflections in order to present a full picture of a devotee."[14]

(2) Gandhiji's Conception of *Samnyasa*

As Gandhiji is a man of action and desires for himself and others spiritual uplift through action and that only, he has conceived of action in such a way that its concept goes on from refinement to refinement. Surendranath Dasgupta rightly states that: "The *Gita* is neither a practical guide-book of moral efforts nor a philosophical treatise discussing the origin of immoral tendencies and tracing them to certain metaphysical principles as their source; but, starting from the ordinary frailties of attachment and desires, it tries to show how one can lead a normal life of duties and responsibilities and yet be in peace and contentment, in a state of equanimity and in communion with God."[15] In the *Gita* that is rightly adjudged as a scripture giving expression to the best and noblest that is in Hinduism in the spheres of religion, ethics and spiritualism, a very important word is '*Samnyasa*' and scholars have taken great interest and pain in defining *Samnyasa* from the view point of the *Gita*. To Shankara, a *Samnyasi* is one who has actually renounced the world, has put on bark garments and taking to the vow of complete *Brahmacharya*, he is completely absorbed in the realization of *God*. The same view is not acceptable to other *Acharyas*, the *Acharyas* of the *Bhakti* cult in particular, because they expect the highest spiritual uplift *through* life. Gandhiji is a *Vaishnava* and a *Bhakta* first and last and so, his conception of *Samnyasa* will not agree with that of *Samnyasa* in Shankara and he will not agree with an attitude of inaction or an attitude only of self-rise. He has no word of sympathy for the man who actually renounces the world. Even in the last years of his life, he was consistent with his interpretation and was clear about his ideas and said that: 'The lesson of the *Bhagavadgita* is meant not for those who have forsaken the world, but for every house-holder inrrespective of his birth and state,"[16] and, "I know that there is a school of philosophy which teaches complete inaction and futility of all effort. I have not been able to appreciate that teaching. In my humble opinion, effort is necessary for one's own growth. It has to be irrespective of results."[17] The problem before Gandhiji is to reconcile action with life of renunciation or *Samnyasa*. He therefore naturally takes recourse to *Gita*'s word:

काम्यानां कर्मणां न्यासं संन्यासं कवयो विदुः। (18:2)

(*Samnyasa* is so known by the learned due to its being the renunciation of actions resorted to with a desire for personal gain.) Gandhiji extends the meaning of this to say that the *Gita* does not preach *Samnyasa* in the sense of actual renunciation of the world. It has shown the attitude of *Samnyasa* or mental detachment or renunciation while actions constantly go on and get gradually sublimated as we have seen earlier. Dasgupta is right in stating that: "The *Gita* wants us to control our senses and mind and to approach sense-objects with such a controlled mind and senses, because it is by this means alone that we can perform our duties with a peaceful and contented mind and turn to God with a clean and unruffled heart."[18] Gandhiji in his very simple and clear language states: "I believe in the doctrine of renunciation, but I hold that renunciation should be sought for in and through action. That action is the *sine qua non* of life in the body; that the wheel of life cannot go on even for a second without involving some sort of action, goes without saying. Renunciation can, therefore, in these circumstances, only mean detachment or freedom of the spirit from action, even while the body is engaged in action."[19] To Gandhiji, law of *Karma* is the law of life and instead of taking *Karma*, *Jnana* and *Bhakti*—all three as simultaneously preached by the *Gitakara*, he takes *Karma* as the basis and applies it to all. *Samnyasa* therefore cannot in any way mean a state of total incaction as Shankara might take it. Actually Gandhiji expects the *Samnyasi* to be more vigilant with regard to his *Karma*; he wants that he should be constantly engrossed in

Karma, that is performed in a spirit of detachment. What Gandhiji expects is that a *Samnyasi* becomes a man of action and yet in such a manner that the actions do not bind him in any way. Following the famous dictum laid down above (18:2), Gandhiji states that: "*Samnyasa* in the *Gita* is renunciation of actions inspired by desire (*Kama*),"[20] and in his '*Anasktiyoga*' he is very clear in stating that: "The *Samnyasa* of the *Gita* will not tolerate complete cessation of all activity. The *Samnyasa* of the *Gita* is all work and yet no work." Gandhiji thus accepts that for complete freedom from the bondage of life, a state of inaction is necessarily to be attained to. It is only in such a state that man will scale real spiritual heights. The *Gita* has described that highest state in this way:

नैव तस्य कृतेनार्थो नाकृतेनेह कश्चन।
न चास्य सर्वभूतेषु कश्चिदर्थव्यपाश्रयः।। (3:18)

(He has no interest whatever in anything done, in anything not done, nor has he need to rely on anything for personal ends,)

and,

सर्वकर्माणि मनसा संन्यस्यास्ते सुखं वशी।
नवद्वारे पुरे देही नैव कुर्वन् न कारयन्।। (5:23)

(Renouncing with the mind all actions, the dweller in the body, who is master of himself, rests happily in his city of nine gates, neither doing nor getting anything done,)

and,

न कर्तृत्वं न कर्माणि लोकस्य सृजति प्रभुः।
न कर्मफलसंयोगं स्वभावस्तु प्रवर्तते।। (5:14)

(The Lord creates neither agency nor action for the world; neither does he connect action with its fruit. It is nature that is at work.) But along with this it is added,

तस्मादसक्तः सततं कार्यं कर्म समाचर।
असक्तो ह्याचरन् कर्म परमाप्नोति पुरुषः।। (3:19)

(Therefore, do thou ever perform without attachment the work that thou must do; for performing action without attachment man attains the Supreme,)

and,

कर्मणैव हि संसिद्धिमास्थिता: जनकादय:।
लोकसंग्रहमेवापि संपश्यन्कर्तुमर्हसि।। (3:20)

(For, through action alone Janaka and others attained perfection; even with a view to the guidance of mankind thou must act,) (3:20)
and,

न मे पार्थास्ति कर्तव्यं त्रिषु लोकेषु किञ्चन।
नानवाप्तमवाप्तव्यं वर्त एव च कर्मणि।। (3:22)

(For me Partha, there is naught to do in the three worlds, nothing worth gaining that I have not gained; yet I am ever in action.) (3:22)

Gandhiji is therefore very clear and firm in his conviction when he states that: "Renunciation can, therefore, in these circumstances, only mean detachment or freedom of the spirit from action, even while the body is engaged in action."[21] *Samnyasa* is therefore more of a mental state and not physical. When Shankara states that for a *Samnyasin* who is a *muktatma*, no action is necessary, he is opposed in his views to Gandhiji's and his view is against the very basic spirit of the *Gita*. Shri Aurobindo evidently tries to reconcile these apparent contradictions in Shankara's views and those of the *Gita* when he takes the *Karma* taught by the *Gita* as divine action. He is specific in his statement when he says: "The *Gita* does not teach the disinterested performance of duties but the following of divine life, the abandonment of all *Dharmas* to take refuge in the Supreme alone, and the divine activity of a Buddha, a Ramakrishna, a Vivekananda is perfectly in consonance with this teaching."[22] He explains the divine works thus: "Transcending the lower nature of the three *gunas* and seeing the soul in the immobile *Purusha* beyond the three *gunas*, we can ascend finally into the higher nature of the infinite Godhead which is not bound by the three *gunas* even when it acts through nature. Reaching the inner actionlessness of the silent *Purusha, naishkarmya*, and leaving *Prakriti* to do her works, we can attain supremely beyond to the status of the divine Mastery which is able to do all works and yet be bound by none."[23] Shri Aurobindo thus seems to emphasise that highest state of activity is when man's body acts only as an instrument in the hands of God, when, as the *Vaishnava*s tell us, man has surrendered his entire self and all his actions to the divine will in perfect devotion. Gandhiji modifies even the *Vaishnava* view of action in *Bhakti* when he states that even for a *Samnyasi* all physical actions, bread-labour, action in a spirit of devotion and detachment are absolutely necessary. Shri Aurobindo insists on divine work for divine nature, Gandhiji stresses all works with detachment so that man's personality rises higher to attain to divine nature. Aurobindo adds again: "To attain to the divine birth, divinising new birth of the soul into a higher consciousness, and to do divine works both as a means towards that before it is attained and as an expression of it after it is attained, is then all the *Karmayoga* of the *Gita*."[24] Gandhiji on the other hand says: "The object of the *Gita* appears to me to be that of showing the most excellent way to attain self-realization. That which is to be found, more or less clearly, spread here and there in Hindu religious books, has been brought out in the clearest possible language in the *Gita* even at the risk of repetition. That matchless remedy is renunciation of fruits of action." Actually the *Gita* will approve of both the views on the basis of the emphasis placed on different verses. Gandhiji, from his own angle of vision, and consistently with his own outlook, states that: "This renunciation is the central sun, round which devotion, knowledge and the rest revolve like planets. . . There must be action where there is body. Not one embodied being is exempted from labour. And yet all religions proclaim that it is possible for man, by treating the body as the temple of God, to attain freedom." This conception of *Samnyasa* with a very hard life, very severe *Vratas*, with constant activity and no desire for reward of any kind is a challenge that few can face. And these few will be towering personalities far above the striving common man; they will be leaders of the people and they will incidentally work for the welfare and happiness of the common masses of humanity at large. This is *lokasamgraha* (लोकसंग्रह) in the opinion of Gandhiji. The *Samnyasi* of Gandhiji's ideal as he found in the *Gita*, leads a life in which these things are attained all at a time:

(1) His own self-realization for which he constantly strives in his life.
(2) The rise of the common masses before whom he sets himself as an example.
(3) A mental state of inaction in the midst of constant activity.
(4) The good of the people, the unity of worldly life.
(5) He thus keeps the world-order going, he contributes to its movement, though mentally he is unconcerned about these.

(6) He is thus doing God's work with his *Samnyasa* that ultimately comes to his complete dedication to God the Supreme.

This emphasis is the originality and greatness of Gandhiji's conception of *Samnyasa* and it finds full support in the *Gita*.

Vinoba rightly follows this conception of Gandhiji in *Samnyasa* when he states: "But there is a way of renouncing action, and that is to devise a method by which, though we do all actions in the world, they melt and flow away from us. It is only when this becomes possible that we can say that *Samnyasa* has been reached." And for this, the attitude required is:

कर्मण्यकर्म यः पश्येदकर्मणि च कर्म यः।
स बुद्धिमान्मनुष्येषु स युक्तः कृत्स्नकर्मकृत्।। (4:19)

(Who sees inaction in action and action in inaction, he is enlightened among men, he is a *yogi*, he has done all he need do,) and,

त्यक्त्वा कर्मफलासंगं नित्यतृप्तो निराश्रयः।
कर्मण्यभिप्रवृत्तोऽपि नैव किंचित्करोति सः।। (4:20)

(He who has renounced attachment to the fruit of action, who is ever content and free from all dependence, he though immersed in action, yet acts not.)

This is thus, a very important contribution of Gandhiji towards the understanding of the great value and message of the Gita.

(3) Gandhiji's Conception of God in *Gita*

We should, first of all fix up, or try to fix up *Gita*'s conception of God, very difficult though it is. The *Bhashyakaras*, who wanted to justify and uphold their peculiar teachings by reading these in the *Gita*, have made our work more difficult because they derive their own peculiar conceptions of God from the *Gita*. Again, the *Gita* is a scripture for all men, and man's mind and notions of God are so much varied that the *Gita* has encompassed all these. Naturally therefore,

(i) When Shankara and Tilak take *Nirguna-nirakara Brahman* as the highest Reality in the *Gita*;
(ii) When to Ramanuja, *Brahman* of the *Gita* is *Saguna*;
(iii) When to the Vallabhites He is Krishna *Purushottama*;

(iv) When to Shri Aurobindo, He is *Purushottama*, higher than even *Akshara Brahma*;

(v) When Dasgupta opines that Krishna as *Divyapurusha* is higher than *Nirguna Brahman* even, and lastly when;

(vi) Many others agree that the *Gita* finds worship of Krishna the personal God as the best and thus accepts Krishna as the highest Reality and says that: कृष्णात्परं किमपि तत्त्वमहं न जाने। (I know of no Reality higher than Krishna),

all will find verses here and there to justify their views with regard to God in the *Gita*. The *Gita* will accept any and every conception of God, and it is very much likely that many more and varied conceptions of God might be found in the *Gita* in future; the *Gita* will justify these also. It will therefore by very difficult to state in clear and concise terms as to which of these conceptions is justified by the *Gita* as the final secret of God in its opinion. Two prominent influences have worked on the *Gita*, the *Upanishads* or *Vedanta* and the *Bhagavatadharma*, whatever it probably was in the days of the *Gita*. When the conception of God is to be studied from the point of view of the *Gita* from amongst these varied views, we find the working of three very important facts:

(i) There is a gradual evolution in the conception of God from the *Vedanta* concept of *Nirguna Brahma* to the *Bhagavata* concept of *Saguna Brahma*. This will be found as we proceed from *Adhyaya* to *Adhyaya*.

(ii) There is a slow but sure leaning towards *Sagnuna* worship and even the worship of a personal God.

(iii) Attempt is also made by the author of the *Gita* to synthesise the two.

We will trace the truth of these three facts as we proceed from *Adhyaya* to *Adhyaya* and even at the end in the 18th *Adhyaya*.

Before we try to synthesise (if at all synthesis is possible) the varied views on the conception of God in the *Gita* and trace how these find justification on the basis of a few verses here and there, it would be desirable actually to note the verses that justify the varied views on God as scholars and *Acharyas* find in the *Gita*. We may take even these as different forms of Krishna, because almost everywhere he has talked in the first person. To illustrate,

विष्टभ्याहं जगत्सर्वमेकांशेन स्थितो जगत्। (10:42)

(With but a part of Myself I stand, upholding this Universe,) and,

यद्यद्विभूतिमत्सत्त्वं श्रीमदूर्जितमेव च।
तत्तदेवावगच्छ त्वं मम तेजोंऽशसंभवम्। (10:41)

(Whatever is glorious, beautiful and mighty, know thou that all such has issued from a fragment of My splendour) and,

अहमात्मा गुडाकेश सर्वभूताशयस्थितः।
अहमादिश्च मध्यं च भूतानामन्त एव च।। (10:20)

(I am the *Atman*, O Gudakesha, seated in the heart of every being; I am the beginning, the middle and the end of all beings)

There are a few verses that refer to Krishna as *Brahman*. These verses make a specific reference to *Brahman* of the *Upanishads*. There are other verses, particularly in the second *Adhyaya* that refer to this God the Supreme as *Atman* in the human body. The verses referring to Krishna as *Brahman* are—7:19; 10:12; 14:27; 12:1, etc., and the verses referring to *Brahman* and *Brahman* as *Atman* are 2:17; 2:18; 2:19; 2:20; 2:22; 2:23; 2:24; 2:25; 2:29; 6:29; 8:3; 15:17; 15:18 and so on.

In these verses the following traits are notable:—

(i) *Brahman* is referred to as अक्षर (Akshara) (8:3) and in negative traits (2:17; 2:24; 2:25). Thus *Brahman* in negative aspect, realised by the नेति नेति (not this, not this) approach is described. Here, *Brahman* is निर्गुण (Nirguna). In the 15th *Adhyaya*, He is said to be above both क्षर (Kshara) and अक्षर (Akshara) and He is known as पुरुषोत्तम् (Purushottama). The interpretation normally given is that He is above प्रकृति (Prakarti) and पुरुष (Purusha) and He stands far above all (अत्यत्तिष्ठद्दशांगुलम्).

(ii) He is known as *Saguna* in the other verses, and, as *Saguna Brahman* He supports, the Universe and He is the creator, destroyer etc., of the whole universe. He is thus both निर्गुण (Nirguna) and सगुण (Saguna) and if we were to read the verses together, our impression will be that *Brahman* is *Saguna* and *Nirguna* both, or *Sakara* and *Nirakara* both. To the *Gita* it seems, both the aspects are necessary for a clear understanding of the real nature of *Brahman*. The two aspects belong to *Brahman* like the two sides of a rupee coin we might say.

(iii) The third important trait here is that *Saguna Brahman* and *Nirguna Brahman* both are conceived of as Krishna. Krishna is thus in a way God the Supreme, even though this is not acceptable to Shankara and Tilak who accept more or less the same concept of *Brahman* in the *Gita*. But we can see a positive attitude, a leaning to vision this unique form of *Brahman* with His two aspects in Krishna, who is constantly before the eyes of the worshipper and the *Jnani*. This sows the seeds of worship of a personal God in the *Gita*. As Krishna states:

> मन्मना भव मद्भक्तः मद्याजीमां नमस्कुरु।
> मामेवैष्यसि सत्यं ते प्रतिजाने प्रियोऽसि मे।। (18:65)

(On Me fix thy mind, to Me bring thy devotion, to Me offer thy sacrifice, to Me make thy obeisance, to Me indeed shalt thou come – solemn is My promise to thee, thou art dear to me)

and,

> अव्यक्तं व्यक्तिमापन्नं मन्यन्ते मामबुद्धयः।
> परं भावमजानन्तो ममाव्ययमनुत्तमम्।। (7:24)

(Not knowing My transcendent, imperishable, supreme character, the undiscerning think Me who am unmanifest, to have become manifest,) and,

> बहूनां जन्मनामन्ते ज्ञानवान्मां प्रपद्यते।
> वासुदेवः सर्वमिति स महात्मा सुदुर्लभः।। (7:19)

(At the end of many births the enlightened man finds refuge in Me; rare indeed is this great soul to whom *Vasudeva* is all.)

It is clear that Krishna is being identified by the *Gitakara* with *Brahman*, God the Supreme. The climax comes in the fifteenth *Adhyaya* when Arjuna is told by Krishna that there are three *Purushas*, अक्षर (Akshara), क्षर (Kshara) and पुरुषोत्तम (Purushottama) and then Krishna adds:

> यो मामेवमसंमूढो जानाति पुरुषोत्तमम्।
> स सर्वविद् भजति मां सर्वभावेन भारत।। (15:19)

(He who, undeluded, knows Me as *Purushottama*, knows all; he worships Me with all his heart, O Bharata.)

This is again known as गुह्यतमं शास्त्रं "the subtlest of all secrets" in the next verse. The references naturally have inspired scholars like Shri Aurobindo and Dasgupta to opine that according to the *Gita*, Krishna as *Purushottama* is superior even to *Akshara* that is known as *Para Brahma* by the *Gita* (अक्षरं ब्रह्म परमम्) and that Krishna as दिव्यपुरुष (Divine Being) has दिव्याकार (Divine Form) and He is superior even to *Para Brahma*.

There are some verses that refer to Krishna as *Atma* (7:4; 6:29; 10:20; 15:17-18; 13:2, etc.) These verses show that *Brahman* and *Atman* are one and also that the realization of *Atman* is realization of *Brahman*. This is again a Vedantic concept that is accepted. But the author, as in the previous case, does not stop here. He asks his devotee to conceive of *Atman* in Krishna. Krishna is *Atman*, He is all, and therefore, worship of Krishna is the worship of *Atman* and through it *Brahman*. The author thus tries to unify the two influences, the *Vedantic* and the *Bhagavata* and he finds this necessary in the interest of the rise of the common man. The *Gita* wants to give the hope of the highest rise (परमगति)even to lowly and the lost in the society.

Then there is a positive leaning of the author towards the *Bhagavata* cult and therefore, towards devotion to a personal God. This brings us across the conceptions of (i) Krishna as *Purusha* (7:30; 8:4; 8:8-10; 9:19; 13:22, etc.); and (ii) as *Ishvara* (भूतानामीश्वरोऽपि सन् 4:6, in 16:14, 18:61, etc.); as *Purna Avatara* to which the *Gita* is the first work to refer (4:6; 4:7; 4:8; 4:9 also 10th *Adhyaya* etc.), because of which Krishna's birth and work, personality and everything is divine and through this worship to the personal God Krishna, the devotee gradually comes to the stage when he feels that

कृष्णात्परं किमपि तत्त्वमहं न जाने।

(I know of no reality higher than Krishna.) There is thus actually an evolution in the sense that in this worship of a personal God in form of Krishna, we find the following aspects that are worshipped by different men of different strata and with the gradual uprise in personality, man will worship each following aspect as the higher one.

(i) Krishna is Divine
(ii) Krishna is *Purna Avatara.*
(iii) Krishna is *Ishvara.*

(iv) Krishna is *Purusha*.
(v) Krishna is *Paramatma-tattva*

With these stages, man's mind will enter the realms of the Upanishadic doctrine and he will experience gradually that,

(vi) Krishna is *Atman*.
(vii) Krishna is *Saguna Brahman*.
(viii) Krishna is *Nirguna Brahman*.
(ix) Krishna is *Divya Purusha* or *Purushottama*.

Thus, with the conception of God in the *Gita* is associated the fact that the author has made a supreme effort at synthesising the *Vedanta* and the *Bhagavata* conceptions of God and so, wherever there is *Brahman*, *Atman*, *Purusha*, *Ishvara*, etc., there is Krishna.

Scholars have also been of opinion that the *Gita* prominently preaches *Bhakti* and worship to a personal God and this personal God is Krishna who rises to be superior even to the *Akshara* of the *Upanishads*. The *Gitakara* does not openly show his greater regard towards Krishna the personal God and his worship, but still that greater liking is there, and there is preference over the *Vedanta* concept but without any criticism whatsoever of *Vedanta*. Here, the effort at synthesis is complete. And this is the reason why the *Gita* succeeds in giving a God and mode of worship to any and every man at all stages of life and all stages of *Sadhana*, even though it is a fact that even amongst the *Bhakta*s there are four or even more types:

चतुर्विधा भजन्ते मां नराः सुकृतिनोऽर्जुन।
आर्तो जिज्ञासुरर्थार्थी ज्ञानी च भरतर्षभ।। (7:16)

(Four types of well-doers are devoted to me. O Arjuna, O Bharatarshabha; they are, the afflicted, the spiritual seeker, the material seeker, and the enlightened.)

The question is this. Who are dear to His heart? Krishna says ते मे युक्ततमाः मताः (Those devotees are exceedingly dear to Me.) Who are they? The reply is this. The *Bhakta* to the best liking of Krishna is a *Jnani Bhakta*.
Krishna says:

तेषां ज्ञानी नित्ययुक्तः एकभक्तिर्विशिष्यते।
प्रियो हि ज्ञानिनोऽत्यर्थमहं स च मम प्रियः।। (7:17)

(Of these the enlightened, ever attached to me in single-minded devotion is the best; for to the enlightened I am exceedingly dear and he is dear to Me.)

This leads us to the conclusion that real renunciation lies not in the renunciation of the fruits of action only, but actually in a mental state that renounces the desire also for the fruits of action. Actually even becoming pleased when others win the fruits of one's action is not freedom from the fruits of action. Even if a man constantly serves others and is happy when others enjoy the fruits of his actions, this *Karma* is binding.To Shri Aurobindo this is *Karma* and not *Karma-yoga*. We may put it better this way. When a man's renunciation of the fruits of action will be free from all bondage, he will attain to a state of अकर्म (*Akarma*) in कर्म (*Karma*).

But this will happen only when he attains to a state when even the desire for the fruit ceases to exist. This state of mind will be possible only by attaining to a state of ज्ञान (*Jnana*). Thus, the love of Krishna for a ज्ञानी (*Jnani*) type of भक्त (*Bhakta*) is associated with the central doctrine of the *Gita*. It is attaining to a state not only of renunciation of the fruit of action, but renunciation even of the desire for the fruit. Arjuna is told,

यज्ञार्थात्कर्मणोऽन्यत्र लोकोऽयं कर्मबन्धनः।
तदर्थं कर्म कौन्तेय मुक्तसंगः समाचर।। (3:9)

(This world of men suffers bondage from all action save that which is done for the sake of sacrifice; to this end, O Kaunteya, perform action without attachment.)

Here the word 'मुक्तसंगः' 'free from attachment' should mean freedom even from the desire for the fruit. It is thus freedom of the mind. And only this will make man's mind rise higher to God.

(4) Gandhiji's Conception of Krishna and *Avatara*

With this background, if we were to come to Gandhiji's conception of God as he found it in the *Gita*, we find that first of all, he has made a few clear remarks about Krishna. These remarks show that to him the historical Krishna with all his deeds is surely not the highest God, he does not come in any way near to his own conception of Krishna. In the life of Krishna there are a few things like his so-called relations with the *Gopis*, and his killing of the demons and his wars, that revolt against Gandhiji's sense of morality and *Ahimsa*. He says; "I have no knowledge that the Krishna of *Mahabharata* ever lived. My Krishna has nothing to do with any historical person. I would refuse to bow my head to the Krishna who would kill because his pride is hurt, or the Krishna whom non-Hindus portray as a dissolute youth,"[25] and, "But if it was proved to me that the *Mahabharata* is history in the same sense that modern historical books are, that every word of the *Mahabharata* is authentic and that the Krishna of the *Mahabharata* actually did some of the acts attributed to him, even at the risk of being banished from the Hindu fold, I should not hesitate to reject that Krishna as God-Incarnate."[26] Here, *Vaishnavas* with their unstinted devotion to Krishna might see *Leela* in these so-called acts, not to the liking of Gandhiji and even we might not reject these acts just at their face value and even add that: लोकोत्तराणां चेतांसि को हि विज्ञातुमर्हति? ("Who could possibly deserve to probe into the minds of extraordinary persons?")[27] But being so clear, Gandhiji states: "I believe in Krishna of my imagination as a perfect incarnation, spotless in every sense of the word, the inspirer of the *Gita* and the inspirer of the lives of millions of human beings." Millions of human beings have taken Krishna known by tradition with all his acts a God the Supreme and inspirer of their lives. They believe in and are devoted to that Krishna and feel purified even by uttering his name. But Gandhiji would insist that: "I believe in Krishna. But my Krishna is the Lord of the Universe, the Creator, Preserver and Destroyer of us all. He may destroy because He creates."[28] Gandhiji of course does not enter here in the controversy of the nature of God he believes in. But it is clear here that he takes it as *Trimurti* and Lord of the Universe and so, it is worship of *Saguna Brahma*. It is also notable that to him, He is above the concept of *Himsa* and *Ahimsa* both. But this is Krishna of his imagination, Krishna after his heart, and probably not Krishna even of the *Gita*. In his '*Anasaktiyoga*' he says this about Krishna: "Krishna of the *Gita* is perfection and right knowledge personified; but the picture is imaginary. That does not mean that Krishna, the adored of his people, never lived. But perfection is imagined. The idea of a perfect incarnation is an aftergrowth." Gandhiji does not clarify here or elsewhere why he takes the idea of a perfect incarnation as an after-growth. But to him Krishna of the *Gita* is perfection and right knowledge and that only. With reference to the idea of incarnation he further clarifies his position when he says that: "In Hinduism, incarnation is ascribed to one who has performed some extraordinary service of mankind. All embodied life is, in reality, an incarnation of God, but it is not usual to consider every living being an incarnation. Future generations pay this homage to one who, in his own generation, has been extraodinarily religious in his conduct...And therefore, he who is the most religiously behaved has most of the divine spark in him. It is in accordance with this train of thought, that Krishna enjoys, in Hinduism, the status of the most perfect incarnation." (Young India, 6-8-1931). The important notions in the paragraph are two with regard to the incarnation:

(i) Extraordinary service to mankind, and (ii) Extraordinary religious conduct. Verses such as these:

> यदा यदा हि धर्मस्य ग्लानिर्भवति भारत।
> अभ्युत्थानमधर्मस्य तदात्मानं सृजाम्यहम्।
> परित्राणाय साधूनां विनाशाय च दुष्कृताम्।
> धर्मसंस्थापनार्थाय संभवामि युगे युगे।। (4:7-8)

(For whenever Right declines and Wrong prevails, then O Bharata, I come to birth. To save the righteous, to destroy the wicked and to re-establish Right, I am born from age to age,)

and,

> तेषामहं समुद्धर्ता मृत्युसंसारसागरात्।
> भवामि न चिरात्पार्थ मय्यावेशितचेतसाम्।। (12:7)

(Of such, whose thoughts are centred on Me, O Partha, I become ere long the deliverer from the ocean of this world of death), might be interpreted on these lines. But the fact is clear that Gandhiji's conception of God is peculiar to his own religious ideas and his notion of the needs of the present age. It is hardly philosophical and probably not according to the spirit of the *Gita*, great and original though it is. In contrast may be placed the views about *Avatara* from Radhakrishnan, Aurobindo and Tilak as follows:

(a) Radhakrishnan

In his book 'The Bhagavadgita', he writes about Lord Krishna: "Krishna the teacher of *Gita*, becomes identified with Vishnu, the ancient Lord of the sun, and Narayana-an ancient God of cosmic character and the goal or resting place of Gods and men."[29] Even here he differs from Gandhiji's view of Krishna of the *Gita*. He next adds: "So far as the teaching of the *Bhagavad Gita* is concerned, it is immaterial whether Krishna the teacher, is the eternal incarnation of the Divine, the everlasting bringing forth of the perfect and divine life in the universe and the soul of man,"[30] and adds further that: "The theory of *Avatara* is an eloquent expression of the law of spiritual world. An *Avatara* is a descent of God into man and not an ascent of man into God."[31] Here, the author hits right at the conventional views of *Avatara*, the view that most of the Hindus accept even today. Krishna's greatness and the great veneration and admiration of Him with all deep *Bhakti* is due to this faith that man is safe in the hands of God, that God the Supreme always looks to man's safety and welfare, and that He will assume human form and come down on earth and set right things in man's life. This gives new hope, new enthusiasm, new life to the man of the world. He is totally dependent on his faith in the Divine. It might then happen that when some towering personality, some extrarodinarily great man does so much of good to mankind, mankind in later years might adjudge him to be an *Avatara* of God. This is possible though rare. And this will be indicative of man's faith in the presence of the divine in him. This is its philosophical side.

Radhakrishnan therefore adds: "Though the *Gita* accepts the belief in *Avatara* as the Divine limiting Himself for some purpose on earth, possessing in His limited form the fullness of knowledge, it also lays stress on the *eternal avatara, the God in man*, the Divine consciousness always present in the human being. Krishna's *avatara*, is an illustration of the revelation of the spirit in us, the Divine hidden in gloom."[32]

(b) Shri Aurobindo

Shri Aurobindo bases his view of the *Avatara* on the following verses in addition, of course, to the verses 4:7-8.

जन्म कर्म च मे दिव्यमेवं यो वेत्ति तत्त्वतः।
त्यक्त्वा देहं पुनर्जन्म नैति मामेति सोऽर्जुन।।
वीतरागभयक्रोधा मन्मया मामुपाश्रिताः।
बहवो ज्ञानतपसा पूता मद्भावमागताः।। (4:9-10)

(He who knows the secret of this My divine birth and action is not born again after leaving the body: He comes to Me, O Arjuna. (4:9)

(Free from passion, fear and wrath, filled full with Me, relying on Me, and refined by the fiery ordeal of knowledge, many have become one with Me.) (4:10)

Sri Aurobindo accepts the conventional view in 4:7-8, but laying greater stress on the verses that follow he says: "But we have to remark carefully that the upholding of *Dharma* in the world is not the only object of the descent of the *Avatara*, that great mystery of the Divine manifest in humanity; for the upholding of the *Dharma* is not an all-sufficient object in itself, not the supreme possible aim for the manifestation of a Christ, a Krishna, a Buddha, but is only the general condition of a higher and a more supreme and divine utility. For there are two aspects of the divine birth; one is a descent, the birth of God in humanity, the God head manifesting itself in the human form and nature, the eternnal *Avatar*; the other is an ascent, the birth of man into the Godhead, man rising into the divine nature and consciousness, *Madbhavam agatah*; it is the being born anew in a second birth of the soul."[33] He states that while the upholding of *Dharma* etc., may be accepted as a general purpose, this other purpose which is ever likely to be missed, should be emphasised because "otherwise the *Avatara* idea would be only a dogma, a popular superstition or an imaginative or mystic deification of historical or legendary super-men, not what the *Gita* makes all its teaching, a deep philosophical and religious truth and an essential part or step to the Supreme mystery of all, *rahasyam uttamam*."[34] The second purpose, though less popularly known, is more important from the viewpoint of Sri Aurobindo and it is the descent of God to help the rise of man to Divinity. Avatarahood thus guides man to the higher paths, to the real aim of man's life, and that is just to strive constantly and persistently, to rise higher and higher from humanity to divinity. Aurobindo again bases his interpretation of *Avatara* on the relation between Arjuna and Krishna, specially as we see it in the *Vibhuti-yoga* and philosophically comes more or less to the same conclusion, i.e., the greater emphasis on the second aspect of Avatarhood. To put in his own words: "The *Avatara* therefore is a direct manifestation in humanity by Krishna the divine soul of the divine condition of being to which Arjuna, the human soul, the type to arise, by climbing out of ignorance and limitation of his ordinary humanity. It is the manifestation from above of that which we have to develop from below; it is the descent of God into the divine birth of the human being into which we mortal creatures must climb; it is the attracting divine example given by God to man in the very type and form and perfected model of our human existence."[35] The theory is consistent with the spiritual doctrine and the peculiarly original meaning of *Karma-yoga* derived by Sri Aurobindo from the *Gita* and it creates a better understanding of *Avatara* for us.

(c) Tilak

Against the background of these two views of Radhakrishnan and Aurobindo, we may take the view of Tilak from his comments on verses 4:7-8 to which he gives greater importance for understanding the concept of *Avatara*, while he takes verses 4:9-10 to refer to quite something else. The view runs as follows:

> In both these stanzas, the word '*Dharma*' does not mean 'the vedic religion relating to life in the other world.' The word principally means and includes the duties of the four castes, justice, morality and other similar things. The import of these stanzas is in the statement that when injustice, immorality, cruelty and tyranny begin to rule in the world, the righteous are harassed and the unrighteous dominate, the blessed Lord becomes incarnated in the shape of a brilliant and powerful human being, in order that proper order should rule in the world which He created, and that the world should derive happiness. He thus re-establishes the order of the world. It has been stated in the previous chapter that *lokasamgraha* (universal welfare) is only another name for the work which, the Blessed Lord does by becoming incarnated in this manner; and that the self-realised (*Atma-Jnanin*) must do the same work as far as his power or authority extends.

Comparing these views with the view of Gandhiji, it must be conceded that he is consistent with his own doctrine of the *Gita*. But we also feel that he does not enter into the detailed controversy of the conception of God and the theory of *Avatara*, probably because he is afraid that the common man for whom he has interpreted the *Gita* might get confused. We know that he writes and interprets exclusively for the common man. His idea is that for man only one feeling and experience is sufficient that God is God and that God is Supreme. But it is our feeling that his conception of God and *Avatara* in the *Gita* could have been better explained, it could have been far higher than what it is and that too without any offence to his own doctrine of the *Gita*.

The truth of this will be found as we give a few further details of his remarks about the nature of God in the *Gita* on the basis of his varied general views of God. We find that without entering into any controversy or any logical argument or systematic development of his theory, he has given so many statements that prove that he worships God as Truth and his famous views also refer to whether God the Supreme or God the Almighty is *Saguna* or *Nirguna*, *Sakara* or *Nirakara* and so on. He makes several statements to clarify his position in the matter. Some of these may be noted as under:

(1) "My uniform experience has convinced me that there in no other God than Truth. . . The little fleeting glimpses that I have been able to have of Truth can hardly convey an idea of the indescribable lustre of Truth, a million times more intense than that of the sun we daily see with our eyes."[36]

(2) "But search for Truth is search for God. Truth is God. God is because Truth is and that can be found by diligent search and meticulous observance of the well-tried rule of the search."[37]

(3) "He sees without eyes, and hears without ears. He is formless and indivisible. He is uncreated, has no father, mother, wife or child, and yet he allows himself to be worshipped as father, mother, wife and child. He allows himself even to be worshipped as stock and store, although He is none of these things—He is the most elusive. He is the nearest to us, if we would know the fact. But he is farthest from us when we do not want to realize His omnipresence."[38]

(4) "I am an Advaitist and yet I can support Dvaitism. The world is changing every moment and is unreal; it has no permanent existence. But, though it is constantly changing, it has something about it which persists and it is, therefore, to that extent real."[39]

(5) "God may be called by many other names so long as it connotes the living Law of Life—in other words, the Law and the Law giver rolled into one."[40]

(6) "Everyone has faith in God though everyone does not know it. For everyone has faith in himself and that multiplied to the nth degree is God. The sum total of all that lives is God. We may not be God, but we are of God, even as a little drop of water is of the ocean."[41]

We have already referred to Gandhiji's unstinted faith in God the Supreme and how he is conscious of His presence and how that faith inspires him to live and work. Commenting on the *Gita* one scholar says: "Humanity and complete submission arise when it is realised that there is one supreme source of all strength and all joy and there is none other. The power behind all power and the light behind all light, is the supreme self and it is better for a man to submerge his individual consciousness of petty importance in that submission, realisation and identification."[42] This will apply fully to Gandhiji and when he approaches God through Truth, it is just to find for God a word that will be acceptable to all, even the atheists. As a saint and prophet again, it is natural that his approach to God should be through Truth, सत् (Sat), even though his appeal for सत् (Sat) does not reject the possibility of realising God through and as चित् (Cit) and आनन्द (Ananda). If we conceive of God as सत्यं शिवं सुन्दरम् (Truth, Goodness, Beauty), he will desire to realise God through सत्य (Truth) but will not reject the possibility of realising God through and as शिव (Goodness) and सुन्दर (Beauty). In a later chapter, when we study how Gandhiji derived greater and greater strength from his unstinted faith in God and could withstand the worst of the calamities and continue to work in his own way, we will get a glimpse of what strength this faith in God gives to man. God was the greatest strength, the greatest wealth of the Mahatma.

But it is a matter of great surprise to us that even though Gandhiji concedes that the ultimate aim of all detached action in life, all action undertaken with renunciation of the fruit and even the desire of it, all action undertaken in a spirit of sacrifice, is self-realization, that is *Moksha*, he does not go into the details of his conception of God in the *Gita*. He actually refused to enter into the controversies of the philosophical problem. To him as a man of action, faith in God of the *Gita* and a total submission of his entire Self to Divine will was all. After refusing to bow his head to the historical Krishna "who would kill because his pride is hurt" and "whom non-Hindus portray as a dissolute youth," he goes a step further and states that the concept of Krishna as *Purna Avatara* is a later growth. His Krishna, and Krishna that he feels is portrayed in the *Gita* is "the Lord of the Universe, the Creator, Preserver and Destroyer of us all. He may destroy because he creates."[43] He also states: "I believe in Krishna of my imagination as a perfect incarnation, spotless in every sense of the word, the inspirer of the *Gita* and the inspirer of the lives of millions of human beings."[44] These two views about Krishna will not prove that Krishna is to Gandhiji, God the Supreme because of the faith in whom his ego is completely dissovled and he consciously and constantly feels that every action of his is a sacrifice to God. It is also interesting to note that Gandhiji's sources of strength and inspiration in the last years of his extremely active life were the *Gita* and Rama. His conception of Rama is God the Supreme. Still, however Gandhiji's belief in Krishna and Rama has some vital and basic differences even though one might feel that in the ultimate sense, Rama and Krishna are only different names of the same God. But the fact remains that as far as the *Gita* is concerned, Gandhiji refuses to be drawn into the controversy of God's nature, the metaphysical aspects, whether He is *Saguna* or *Nirguna* and so on. And even though he is a *Vaishnava* of the highest order, he does not positively read *Saguna Upasana* in the *Gita* and being a great ascetic, he does not insist on finding *Nirguna Brahman* as God the Supreme. To him God is God as we saw and that is sufficient for his purpose as also for the purpose of an ideal devotee and follower of the *Gita*. He would have no objection even if different persons derive different concepts of God from the *Gita* because all such concepts will be true to the spirit of the *Gita*. The *Gita* specifically states that,

ये यथा मां प्रपद्यन्ते तांस्तथैव भजाम्यहम्। (4:11)

(In whatever way men resort to Me, even so do I render to them). And actually his own conception of God outside the *Gita*, be it Truth or anything else, is yet subtle and not very clear. He accepts God as the highest reality, the only reality. God will be creator, preserver and destroyer of the Universe and yet far above the whole Universe. He will be present in everything and yet above all. It is known that after his love for the *Gita*, came his love for the *Ishopanishad* and the conception of God as it is found in this *Upanishad* with all its subtlety will be acceptable to Gandhiji. It will not be too much to state that to Gandhiji the concept of God in the *Ishopanishad* is more or less the same as that in the *Gita*. Being enamoured of the first verse of the *Ishopanishad* Gandhiji stated: "The *Gita* is a commentary on the first verse of the *Ishopanishad*...The verse, therefore, seems to me to mean only one thing: Recognize that everything you fancy you have is God's and from God, and take only what you really need for life,"[45] etc.

NOTES

1. 'Young India', 3-11-1937.
2. 'Harijan', 24-2-1946.
3. 'Young India', 3-1-1927.
4. B.G. Ray in 'Gandhian Ethics', p. 6.
5. 'Harijan', 6-2-1937.
6. 'Young India', 6-8-1931.
7. 'Young India', 6-8-1931.
8. 'Young India', 6-8-1931.
9. 'Young India', 1-9-1927.
10. 'Origin and Development of Vaishnavism', p. 114.
11. 'Young India', 1-9-1927.
12. 'Last Glimpses of Bapu', Manuben Gandhi, p. 115.
13. Vide supra, p. 291.
14. 'Bhagavadgita—As a Philosophy of God-realization', p. 129.
15. 'History of Indian Philosophy', Vol. 2. p. 501.
16. 'Harijan', 5-1-1947.
17. 'Young India', 21-10-1926.
18. 'History of Indian Philosophy', Vol. 2., p. 492.
19. 'Young India', 25-10-1928.
20. 'Diary of Mahadev Desai', p. 113.
21. 'Young India', 25-10-1928.
22. 'Essays on the *Gita*', pp. 42-43.
23. 'Essays on the *Gita*', p. 181.
24. 'Essays on the *Gita*', p. 238.
25. 'Young India', 1-10-1925.
26. 'Young India', 1-10-1925.
27. 'Uttararamacarita', 2.7.
28. 'Young India', 9-4-1925.
29. 'Bhagavadgita', Introduction, p. 27.
30. Vide supra, p. 28.
31. Vide supra, p. 35.
32. Vide supra, p. 35.
33. 'Essays on the *Gita*', p. 199.
34. 'Essays on the *Gita*', p. 199.
35. 'Essays on the *Gita*', p. 211.
36. 'My Experiments with Truth', Ed. Of 1945, p. 404.
37. 'Harijan', 21-9-1934.

38. 'Young India', 25-9-24.
39. 'Young India', 21-1-1926.
40. 'Harijan', 14-4-1924.
41. 'Harijan', 3-6-1939.
42. '*Gita* Explained', M. Subedar, p. 8.
43. 'Young India', 9-4-1925.
44. 'Harijan', 23-6-1947.
45. 'Harijan', 23-6-1947.

SIX

Impact on Gandhiji's Life

"You Gandhiji, you and your Jain ancestors, long ago, left their chanting and singing and telling of beads. He is there where the tiller tills the hard ground. He is with them in sun and shower, and His garments are dirty."

Rabindranath Tagore

न त्वहं कामये राज्यं न स्वर्गं नापुनर्भवम्।
कामये दुःखतप्तानां प्राणिनामार्तिनाशनम्।।[1]

(I desire not kingdom or *Svarga* or *Moksha*; I desire the removal of the sufferings of beings that are afflicted with sorrow.)

Introduction

"I knew that he was a man who had given all he had of his possession and mind and body, and was therefore the freest human I had ever known."[2] In these words Mrs. W.H. Fisher, the wife of an American bishop gives her impression of Mahatma Gandhi. How Gandhiji came to this state, how slowly and steadily he developed his prized inheritance and ultimately how he became the greatest man of the twentieth century as Holmes states, is a matter of deep and interesting study. Equally interesting is the study of how various authorities and scriptures of various religions influenced him and how the influence of the *Gita* that came to possess him when he was about twenty, became deeper and deeper with him and after becoming paramount, remained with him for life. How these influences have contributed towards shaping the evolution of the personality of Gandhiji in his scaling of heights higher and higher in greatness and how ultimately the influence of the *Gita* reigned supreme, are matters that have not been systematically studied so far. I here make an humble effort in this direction.

When we here confine ourselves to examining how the *Gita* influenced the man and his teachings, we start with two important facts:

(i) That Gandhiji's rise to greatness has been an uphill task, almost what we might call Everest –climb in which he has seen so many ups and downs, each ultimately taking this man of indomitable will-power and courage to higher and higher heights, and,

(ii) That the life of Gandhiji is the history of man who became a greater and nobler Hindu day be day, ultimately to become 'an ideal Hindu, why the only Hindu' as Smt. Sarojini Naidu said in her tribute to him when he died. Thus, the great son returned as if to his religion of birth and inheritance and environment, of course after placing his religion before the world in its proper perspective and in its proper glory. It is here that the *Gita* has worked in a unique manner. Gandhiji has clearly stated that it is the *Gita* that has been the greatest scripture for him, the scripture of his life and it continued to act as his best guide and consolation in his last years. What Schopenhauer said of the *Upanishads*—"*Upanishads* are solace of my life, they will be a solace of death",—can be said to have been accepted by Gandhiji with reference to the *Gita*.

Growing Influence of *Gita*—An analysis

In this chapter we will examine how Gandhiji adopted the *Gita* and how it came to have greater and deeper influence on his mind, life and action. This will form the background of our study of the impact of the *Gita* on his teachings and their interpretation and here, when we say the impact of the *Gita*, it of course means impact of his own interpretation of the doctrine of the *Gita* that he put into practice in life. Gandhiji, we concede, is the *Sthitaprajna* of the *Gita* in flesh and blood. His has been a constant and sincere attempt to rise higher and higher in life with the ideal of *Sthitaprajna* before him. Even in the last years, he has remained alert about examining whether or not he is a *Sthitaprajna* and the result is that his ideal of *Sthitaprajna* is higher even than the ideal in the *Gita*. His ideal combines *Jnani*, *Bhakta*, *Samnyasi* and *Trigunatita* all in one. Gandhiji wipes out all technical difference among these. It is in this sense that to Gandhiji, all these are one, though, on the basis of their definitions in the *Gita*, we will have to concede that the *Trigunatita* is the *Sthitaprajna* at his highest stage of development.

Gandhiji's Personality and Heritage

Two factors are noticeable right from the beginning, right from Gandhiji's childhood; (i) That he has inherited from the culture of the family what is popularly known as *Vaishnava dharma* and way of life, and (ii) That the whole atmosphere of the family when he was young and growing was strictly *Vaishnava* in everything. Credit for this should mainly go to Gandhiji's mother, to whom Gandhiji was deeply attached and towards whom therefore he had great devotion. His mother was a staunch *Vaishnava* in faith and practice both and so, both in inheritance and atmosphere Gandhiji acquired, though unconsciously, the *Vaishnava dharma* in childhood.

(a) The *Vaishnava* heritage

It is necessary that we do not underestimate this heredity and environment in so far as (i) this shaped Gandhiji's personality till the age of 18 when he went to England. (ii) It acted as his strength in the midst of a totally different atmosphere and inspite of his anxious and devoted reading of the Scriptures of several religions that raised conflicts in his mind and even some doubts with regard to the Hindu religion. Again, (iii) after a long life of *Vaishnava* religious practice and ideology, even when he died, he was a Hindu and a *Vaishnava* of first rank. It can be stated without hesitation that Gandhiji took birth, lived and died as a *Vaishnava* Hindu. It is conceded that for many years, Gandhiji was hardly conscious of the deep impression of Vaishnavism on his mind and personality and that he had hardly any conscious faith in this. But one thing is clear that Gandhiji remained firm in ideology and practice of Vaishnavism that he acquired both by heredity and environment. Gandhiji practised Vaishnavism in which he was born. In spite of so many western influences, inspite of varied conflicts, it is clear that at no stage in his life has Gandhiji's religious ideology and practice changed; it only took a more concrete shape and became more and more clear to him day by day, so that when he died after a life of constant work and constant thinking, he was not only an ideal Hindu but an ideal *Vaishnava*. To put in his own words the description of his mother: "The outstanding impression my mother has left on my memory is that of saintliness. She was deeply religious. She would not think of taking her meals without daily prayers. Going to Haveli—the *Vaishnava* temple—was one of her daily duties . . . To keep two or three consecutive fasts was nothing to her".[3] Again, "The Gandhis were *Vaishnavas*. My parents were particularly staunch *Vaishnavas*. They would regularly visit the Haveli. The family had even its own temples. Jainism was strong in Gujarat, and its influence was felt everywhere and on all occasions. The opposition to and abhorrance of meat-eating that existed in Gujarat among the Jains and *Vaishnavas* were to be seen nowhere else in India or outside in such strength. These were the traditions in which I was born and bred. And I was extremely devoted to my parents."[4] Again, "In Rajkot, however, I got an early grounding in toleration for all branches of Hinduism and sister religions. For my father also visited Shiva's and Rama's temples, and would take or send us youngsters there. Jain monks also would pay frequent visits to my father, and would even go out of their way to accept food from us—non-Jains."[5] All these words decisively prove that Gandhiji's schooling in religion and ethics is rooted in the traditional *Vaishnava* heritage of the family and the similar *Vaishnava* environment of the childhood days. He has thus acquired Vaishnavism as ideology from the inheritance and *Vaishnava* religious practice from his environment plus of course his very great devotion to his parents, his mother in particular. He has got his first lessons in truth, religion, morality, attachment to God, toleration of other faiths and religions, nay, the basis of everything religious, ethical and spiritual in him, from this *Vaishnava* heredity and environment plus his utter devotion to the parents. The whole ideology is in its infancy, in its initial stages only, but it was destined to develop into a unique ideology and practice that gave to us Gandhiji that he became in his life, the 'Mahatma', the great saint in line with Buddha and Christ, the great prophet of peace, the unique humanitarian. Pyarelal therefore rightly states: "The ancestral faith of the Gandhis was Vaishnavism, a school of *Bhakti* which teaches that, with intense love and complete self-surrender, God is accesible to all, irrespective of rank and even culture."[6] Unstinted faith in God the Supreme, as sense of total self-surrender to Him and His will, a unique sense of devotion that led him first unconsciously and then consciously to believe that he is doing God's work, is the basis of Gandhiji's philosophy of religion, ethics and spiritualism. And this has its basis in Vaishnavism. To put in his own words: "But one thing took deep root in me—the conviction that morality is the basis of things, and that truth is the substance of all morality. Truth became my sole objective. It began to grow in magnitude every day, my definition of it also has been ever widening."[7] And Gandhiji said: "I am surer of His existence than of the fact that you and I are sitting in this room. I may live without air and water, but not without Him."[8] This was precisely the reason why "No important decision of his was taken without consulting the 'inner voice'."[9]

(b) In Childhood

We know that all these religious, ethical and spiritual leanings were just in their infancy in Gandhiji's early life and other things were also ingrained in his mind. But the whole mental make up was in line with this inheritance and atmsophere.That explains the deep impression that the story of Shravan's devotion and the drama of 'Harishchandra' had on his mind; the grave conflict that he, as a boy underwent, when he ate meat and had to steal and that led to the consequent confession before his father; the confusion and dumbness that he felt when he paid a visit to a brothel. Gandhiji in this particular incident of course attributes his being saved, to God when he states: "But I have ever since given thanks to God for having saved me" and "I can recall four more similar incidents in my life, and in most of them my good fortune, rather than any effort on my part, saved me." Actually Gandhiji is saved only on account of the deep-rooted influence of this inheritance and environment that have become his invaluable treasure all his life, conscious or unconscious though he was about it.

(c) In England

We may now examine a little how the same *Vaishnava* culture accompanied him and saved him when he was in England, in a totally different atmosphere. He went there of course without much of a religious consciousness, without any marked reading of the Hindu scriptures, without much of a love for Hinduism. But he went there with his three vows, his extreme devotion to his mother and of course unconsciously with the *Vaishnava* religious culture that he inherited from her and the family. Shy as he was, these three things shielded him and made him uncompromising and adamant in so many respects. He was saved, in the very first year, twice, (i) from eating meat and drinking, inspite of the persistent efforts of a friend and well-wisher, and, (ii) from close companionship and marriage with an English girl as so many Indian boys used to do. To put in his own words: "My shyness has been in reality my shield and buckler. It has allowed me to grow. It has helped me in my discernment of truth."[10] And in the matter of persistent argument by a friend for meat-eating: "The more he argued the more uncompromising I became. Daily I would pray to God for protection and get it. Not that I had any idea of God. It was faith that was at work—faith of which the seed had been sown by the good nurse Rambha."[11] And of course the seed took to sprouting only on the strength of the culture based on faith, devotion and constant religious practice that he had unconsciously inherited. Again, after he clarified his position with regard to the young girl in question, he writes: "But who dare harm whom God protects?" And "But it lifted a burden that was weighing me down" and "I thus purged myself of the canker of untruth . . ."[12] It can easily be seen how inherited culture works, shields man and makes him adamant and asks him to indulge in constant experimentation. The inheritance shapes the personality of the young man in the direction of truth, faith, devotion, prayer, high morals and so on as these are the very basis of *Vaishnavism* and these became the basis of the personality of the Mahatma later on.

(c) First Reading of *Gita*

Then comes his first reading of the *Bhagavad Gita* in the translation of Edwin Arnold, 'Song Celestial' by name. This opens his eyes in a new direction. On one side, he becomes anxious to know more and more about his religion of birth—Hinduism—and on the other side he reads the scriptures of other religions. Remarkable is the very first impression of the *Gita*, of the second *Adhyaya* in particular and there also of the definition of the *Sthitaprajna* and there also the verses:

ध्यायतो विषयान्पुंसः संगस्तेषूपजायते।
संगात्संजायते कामः कामात्क्रोधोऽभिजायते।।

क्रोधाद्भवति संमोहः संमोहात्स्मृतिविभ्रमः।
स्मृतिभ्रंशाद् बुद्धिनाशो बुद्धिनाशात्प्रणश्यति।। (2:62-63)

(If a man is brooding on objects of the senses, attachment to them springs up; attachment begets craving and craving begets wrath. Wrath begets stupefaction, stupefaction leads to loss of memory, loss of memory leads to ruin of reason and the ruin of reason spells utter destruction.) He got this in the able translation of Arnold as,

If one
Ponders on subject of the sense, there springs
Attraction; from attraction grows desire,
Desire flames to fierce passion, passion breeds
Recklessness; then the memory—all betrayed—
Lets noble purpose go, and saps the mind,
Till purpose, mind, and man are all undone.

He writes: "The verses in the second chapter . . . made a deep impression on my mind and they still ring in my ears. The book struck me as one of priceless worth. The impression has ever since been growing on me with the result that I regard it to-day as the book *par excellence* for the knowledge of Truth. It has afforded me invaluable help in my moments of gloom"[13] Actually it has happened that even though he read lots on religion, even though the western influences now followed for many years to come took hold of his mind and activity, even though under these influences he made a supreme humanitarian effort to unite men of the world and raise down-trodden India high in self-respect and to bring about religious unity, (and due to these facts, the value of the western influences cannot be underestimated) actually in these matters and in many others the widening influence of the *Gita* and behind it Hinduism in general is at work. There is nothing in Gandhiji's ideology including his principle of *Satyagraha*, principle of bread-labour, principles of Truth and non-violence, attitude to fast, service to humanity and so on, which may not be found in one form or another in Hinduism, for which it is rightly stated by a westerner that: "What then is Hinduism? The only possible answer is that it is a wide variety of beliefs held together by an attitude of mutual tolerance and by the characteristically Hindu conviction that all approaches to God are equally valid."[14] Basham says: "To us the most striking feature of ancient Indian civilization is its humanity."[15] Nehru states correctly that: "Gandhiji was essentially a man of religion, a Hindu to the innermost depths of his being, and yet his concept of religion had nothing to do with dogma or custom or ritual. It was basically concerned with his belief in the moral law, which he calls the Law of Truth or Love,"[16] and, "Influenced by modern thought currents, he never let go of his roots and clung to them tenaciously."[17] As he has stated time and again, Gandhiji calls himself a Hindu and he is proud of belonging to Hinduism. But it is to be noted that he is not prepared to accept anything that goes against his conscience and reason.

He is never a blind follower of anything and actually he has *discovered* his religion by a study of the Hindu and other scriptures and by a constant practice of the same. And it can easily be seen that the religion that he discovered, followed, practised and preached is *Vaishnavism* minus of course its sectarianism and several other things, to which we shall refer later. Here, it is enough to state that when he read the *Gita*, his own views that were not clear to him though he followed many of them, took concrete shape and they dawned on his mind in growing clarity. He discovered much of *Vaishnavism* in the *Gita* even at the first reading, and, as years passed and he read more and more of and on the *Gita* and he practised what he read and understood, the practice led to further clarity and the process went on for years. He translated the *Gita* and wrote his famous '*Anasaktiyoga*' some 38 years after his first reading and he has specifically claimed, as we have already seen, that: "But after 40 years' unremitting endeavour fully to enforce the teaching of the *Gita* in my own life, I have, in all humility, felt that perfect renunciation is impossible without perfect observance of *Ahimsa* in every shape and form."[18] Looking to the years of study and practice of the teaching, it is clear that the interpretation of Gandhiji can, in no way, be underestimated. Before we proceed to study its importance, it would be desirable to see how Gandhiji's religious views developed while in South Africa and how the *Gita* played its own part in shaping them. The years that Gandhiji passed in South Africa are the most important as far as the all-sided development of the personality of the man is concerned, and his personality has developed through the religious views that he read and developed then.

(e) His Years in South Africa

Within a year of his reaching South Africa he underwent several experiences of humiliation that gave to Gandhiji a clear picture of the condition of the Indians in South Africa. He settled there and attributed his stay to God's will. Here, four things are notable in the mature man that Gandhiji has become: (i) He has now got a clearer notion of his 'inner voice'; (ii) He takes to service of Indians as service to humanity in South Africa, (iii) He gets himself absorbed in service to the community and "the reason behind it was my desire for self-realization";[19] (iv) He now consciously studies scriptures of various religions and becomes a conscious, firm and intelligent follower of Hinduism, his religion of birth, of course after consulting Raychandbhai and others on matters of conflict. Naturally this brings him nearer to Hinduism and consequently to the *Gita* and this faith in his religion of birth and in its scriptures that he discovered, becomes the be-all and end-all of his life till the last. Now, Gandhiji becomes an ideal Hindu in faith and thought and consequently in deed. He becomes the best illustration of what Hinduism can give a man (a) in whose life thought and deed are consistent, and (b) whose life itself becomes a symbol of the three famous Hindu dicta—

आचार: प्रथमो धर्म:।

(Conduct is the first *Dharma*.)

अयं तु परमो धर्म: यद्योगेनात्मदर्शनम्।

(The visioning of the soul through *Yoga* is the supreme *Dharma*.)

उदारचरितानां तु वसुधैव कुटुम्बकम्।

(For persons with a liberal attitude, the earth itself is a family).

It has now become clear to Gandhiji that his path is the path of self-realization, through life and through service to humanity, and at every moment of his life he makes efforts and experiments to come nearer to this realization. That enhanced the spirit of service in him, that led him to the resolution of complete *Brahmacharya* at a rather young age of 37 years.

Gandhiji does not specifically state so, but he is following the word of the *Gita*, he is trying and striving hard to become an ideal

Sthitaprajna and *Trigunatita*. He has quite realized that

न हि कल्याणकृत्कश्चिद्दुर्गतिं तात गच्छति। (6:40)

(O Arjuna, no one who does good to others meets a sad end.) To put in his words: "*Brahmacharya* means control of the senses in thought, word and deed. Every day I have been realizing more and more the necessity for restraints of the kind . . . There is no limit to the possibilities of renunciation even as there is none to those of *Brahmacharya*. . . . the existence of God within makes even control of the mind possible . . . It is the highest goal, and it is no wonder that the highest effort should be necessary to attain it." Now, the famous verse of the *Gita*.

विषया विनिवर्तन्ते निराहारस्य देहिनः।
रसवर्जं रसोऽप्यस्य परं दृष्ट्वा निवर्तते।। (2:59)

(When a man starves his senses, the objects of those senses disappear for him, but not the yearning for them; the yearning too departs when he beholds the Supreme,) becomes the very basis of his life, thought and activity. He is now on way to realize that ". . .His name and His grace are the last resource of the aspirant after *moksha*." And now Gandhiji consciously becomes an aspirant after *moksha* through the supreme influence of the *Gita*. He is now on way to become an ideal *Bhakta* and *Jnanin* in addition to *Sthitaprajna* and *Trigunatita*. A stage is set for all these four to become an identity in one personality that Gandhiji became. Unstinted devotion and complete submission to the Divine Will mark a clear development in him, he is now conscious of this plus the supreme bliss in the limitless compassion of God. Gandhiji cannot even conceive of finding fault with God as did Nietzsche, the famous western philosopher. If man suffers, it is due to his own faults,; if man is happy, it is due to the will and favour of God. This attitude of finding fault with man and his grave limitations and weaknesses when he is unhappy and miserable, and attributing to God's limitless compassion all happiness that a man derives in life is peculiarly Hindu and it gives a unique strength and confidence coupled with humility to man. Gandhiji had all the three virtues in him and these came mainly from the *Gita*. He sees the dirt and filth, unbearable noise and hypocrisy in Benares and remarks: "If anyone doubts the infinite mercy of God, let him have a look at these sacred places. How much hypocrisy and irreligion does the Prince of Yogis permit to be perpetrated in His holy name? He proclaimed long ago:

ये यथा मां प्रपद्यन्ते तांस्तथैव भजाम्यहम्। (4:11)

(Whatever a man sows, that shall he reap.) The law of *Karma* is inexorable and impossible of evasion. There is thus hardly any need for God to interfere. He laid down the law and, as it were, retired."[20] And God retired so that man may progress in life and to the divine through life by his own action, by the indomitable law of *Karma* that he can influence and shape if he so wills. God does not favour those "who stand and wait" as Milton tells us in his famous poem "On his Blindness." Hinduism expects man to act and to act rightly and shape his destiny. According to Hinduism, providence—नियति—is not cruel and ruthless and man is not its helpless play-toy. Man can even partly shape his नियति. This is based on the famous Law of *Karma* that Hinduism has given.

We can thus see that Gandhiji's life and activity in South Africa had considerable influence in shaping his personality and character, in brining him to maturity and calm and firm spirits together with humbleness. His religious, moral and spiritual outlook is shaped considerably and it evolves and develops in a certain direction. It is the direction of becoming a better and better Hindu, a real *Vaishnava*, a constant and firm devotee of God, who takes up all acts in the name of God. This has its climax when man acts only as an instrument in the hands of God.[21] He works in a spirit of total submission to the divine will, his eternal bliss is in complete *Bhagvatkrupa*, and his whole life is an opportunity to rise to those heights when he comes to deserve this. Here the *Gita* has worked and he now consciously tries to come to experience this Godliness.

To put in his own words: "But when my mode of life changed in South Africa, my outlook changed too. All the steps I took at this time of trial were taken in the name of God and for His service."[22] And the consciousness of taking up everything in the name of God, that is, of living constantly, not only in communion with God but with God, grows on him. He now turns with greater faith to the *Gita*, reads it in the original, commits verses of the *Gita* to memory, is simply fascinated by it and now consciousness grows on him that the *Gita* and only the *Gita* is his infallible guide henceforth. To put in his own words again: ". . .but to me the *Gita* became an infallible guide of conduct. It became my dictionary of daily reference. Just as I turned to the English dictionary for the meanings of English words that I did not understand, I turned to this dictionary of conduct for a ready solution of all my troubles and trials."[23] Words like अपरिग्रह *(Aparigraha)* (Non-possession) and समभाव *(Sambhava)* grip him. He understands the implication of the word 'trustee' from the *Gita*, he discovers religion in it, and naturally enough he acts upon these. The *Gita* grips his mind as his guide in matters of religion and conduct and the same is destined to become in later life his guide for all matters spiritual. Of course, the reading of the scriptural works of different religions continues. 'Unto this Last' of Ruskin leaves a permanent impression on his mind, but, as it becomes clear in the years that follow, the influence of Hinduism is enhanced and the influence of the *Gita* grows deeper and deeper. Gandhiji is now a man of his own natural heritage, environment, cultural background and religious as also spiritual leanings.[24] Here the *Gita* is his guide. Now and again, he takes recourse to the *Gita* to justify one or the other of his acts. He allowed his insurance policy to lapse and decided to put his wife and children to God's care as he did his own self. He found justification for fasting in the following verse of the *Gita*:

> विषया विनिवर्तन्ते निराहारस्य देहिनः।
> रसवर्जं रसोऽप्यस्य परं दृष्ट्वा निवर्तते।। (2:59)

and in the fine translation of Edwin Arnold:

"For a man who is fasting his senses outwardly, the sense-object disappears, leaving the yearning behind; but when he has seen the Highest, even the yearning disappears." Quite relevant and to the point is his remark in this connection: "Fasting and similar discipline is, therefore, one of the means to the end of self-restraint, but it is not all, and if physical fasting is not accompanied by mental fasting, it is bound to end in hypocrisy and disaster."[25] After this, even in the midst of extremely active political life, various *Satyagraha* movements, and all-sided work for the uplift of the ignorant Indian masses, Gandhiji's religious, ethical and particularly spiritual personality develops in a fixed direction, it is the direction first, of his sincere attempt to take the masses with him on the spiritual path of truth and non-violence. He is developing his ideology, when he preaches non-violence for the common man also. His is an attitude peculiar to his personality in the doctrine

शठं प्रति सत्यं कुर्यात्

(One shall resort to truth even towards the cunning)

Next comes, his gradual rise to the divine heights, when he gradually realises that it is not possible for the common masses to rise with him even if they willed and his acceptance more or less that man has to seek his spiritual uplift individually and singly and not collectively. This realization comes late in his life, in the midst of the severest trials and tribulation culminating in the worst of communal riots and the most humiliating rapes of women and the mass slaughter of brother by brother which blackened the horizon just when the sun of independence was dawning.

During the period between 1920 and 1930, Gandhiji took greater interest in the *Gita*, he wrote his famous '*Anasaktigoya*' in Gujarati and so much more on the *Gita*, not to speak of countless statements now and again on the *Gita*.

(f) Back in India

It is during this period that Gandhiji, in the midst of a heated public life when every second is allotted to the welfare of mankind, becomes a man of greater introspection. He consults his heart more and more and he is very clear in his conviction that faith dominates over intellect in life and to him as a saint, as a prophet of peace, this is the only desirable attitude. To put in his own words: "I know that ultimately one is guided not by the intellect but by the heart. The heart accepts a conclusion for which the intellect subsequently finds a reasoning. Argument follows conviction. Man often finds reason in support of whatever he does or wants to do."

A similarly applicable view is found in Kalidasa's '*Shakuntalam*' when we are told:

सतां हि संदेहपदेषु वस्तुषु प्रमाणमन्तःकरणप्रवृत्तयः।

(In matters of doubt the activity of the inner conscience is the proof for noble men.)

In the beginning he accepts that even a great work like the *Gita* is not a panacea for all modern ills. It would be too much in his opinion to expect answers to all our problems from the *Gita* in the modern days. To put in his words: "To look upon Krishna as a *Purna Avatara* should not mean that we can obtain from the *Gita* direct answers to all the questions that arise from day to day. . . . This would not be desirable even if it were possible; for, in that case, there would be nothing like progress or discovery for mankind. Human intelligence would then simply atrophy from disuse. . . . Real help can come only from our endeavours and struggles."[26] But it is interesting to note that all his endeavours and struggles follow the word now principally of the *Gita*, of course as he interpreted it, and with the passing of days and months and years, he resorts more and more to the *Gita*; in fact after 1935, he is positively in the direction of seeking answers to all his questions from the *Gita* adopting it as his religious, ethical and spiritual dictionary. It was as early as in 1918, i.e., the beginning almost of his career in India that Gilbert Murray said of Gandhiji: " Persons in power should be very careful how they deal with a man who cares nothing for sensual pleasure, but is simply determined to do what he believes to be right. He is a dangerous and uncomfortable enemy because his body, which you can always conquer, gives you so little purchase upon his soul."[27] Yes, Gandhiji was a seeker after soul, a man constantly practising in self-realisation, and the path of the man was the path of *Sthitprajna* and the *Trigunatita* as it is laid down in the *Gita*. The period after 1920 is a peculiar period in the life of Gandhiji. His spiritual path is fixed, his aim of life is clear, his concept of ends and means is clear, he is a man seeking his own self-realisation through life, through service to humanity and he even seeks men's rise to higher heights by the path of truth and non-violence as he visioned these. Holmes is right in his statement that: "It is not often in human history that men join at once the inner and the outer life, and thus make saint and statesmen one. But when they do, they shake the world, and turn the tides of destiny."[28] Yes, Gandhiji stood on the strength derived from Hinduism in general and the *Gita* in particular, and when he tried, through life and practice to become a स्थितप्रज्ञ (*Sthitprajna*) and त्रिगुणातीत (*Trigunatita*), he became this rare combination and turned the tides against the vast British Empire in which, it was said, 'the sun never sets!' When India had Gandhiji in the centre of all political, social, moral, religious, cultural and economic activity in the country, he was just the embodiment of the ideal of स्थितप्रज्ञ (*Sthitprajna*) and त्रिगुणातीत (*Trigunatita*) of the *Gita*. Dr. Holmes states: "Humanity, beset by encompassing ills, waits, with amazing patience, confident that sooner or later her redeemer will come."[29] Gandhiji was this redeemer for humanity through his becoming the redeemer of the millions in India. Gandhiji as India saw him is a rare embodiment of the best that Hinduism and the *Gita* could give. Sayud Hossain says of Gandhiji: "But no one who has really looked into Gandhiji's eyes can ever forget him. Those eyes are certainly the windows of his soul. This man, you would say, is carrying the sorrows and burdens of humanity. His is an anguished and consecrated life."[30] And now, inspite of all influences Eastern and Western, Gandhiji has returned to his natural surroundings, the religion and ethics and spiritualism of his birth, and he is now on the path of self-realisation as the *Gita* has laid down. With the passing of days and years he seeks greater and greater solace in Hinduism through the grand influence of the *Gita* of course. We therefore only partly, not fully agree with the statement of Sayud Hossain that: "His philosophy of life is not solely derived from Hinduism or from Buddhism, from Jainism or the *Vedanta*. Gandhiji represents a rare synthesis of the ancient and modern, of the East and the West."[31] If this were true, this should speak of the universal spirit and applicability of the teaching of the *Gita* for which it is rightly stated that: "it is catholic in its message, comprehensive in its outlook and concrete in its suggestions."[32] The *Gita* has laid down the ideal of *Karma-yoga* that Gandhiji has interpreted as *Anasaktiyoga* because of his peculiarly original views regarding means and ends and it is stated by the same author that: "The ideal of *Karma-yoga* is the best way to God–realisation. It included knowledge of God (*Jnana*), devotion to God (*Bhakti*), renunciation (*Samnyasa*), action and service (*Karma* and *Seva*). With all this, it does not renounce action."[33] And the *Gita* influenced Gandhiji the most just because of this unique sort of *Karma-yoga,* that suited his work and way of life the most. His enthusiasm about the path adopted by him became enhanced and he become firmer on it. The *Gita* gave consent to him about the path adopted by him, or, to put it otherwise, he discovered the path of life through the *Gita*. On the other side, it made him more clear and firm in his mission. The *Gita* thus clarified his mission to Gandhiji.

(g) 1920 to 1944

The period between 1920 and 1944 is the period of conflict and consequent introspection for Gandhiji with regard to the propriety of taking the masses with him. He felt that both truth and non-violence were on trial. He himself was on trial. In the beginning, say in the *Satyagraha* at Kheda, or the strike by labourers at Ahmedabad, people were not properly trained for it. Later on, his sympathies towards the masses were enhanced even though now and again he experienced failure in bringing the masses to adopt his path. Gandhiji's correspondence with the then Viceroy Lord Linlithgo is proof of this. The masses failed him and yet Gandhiji loved them, because he had realised how difficult his path was, and, it is interesting to note that Gandhiji became firmer personally in his attachment to his own principles. He blamed his own self, his own *tapas* for the failure of the masses and now and again he undertook penance in form of fasts to get over his own sins as he said. It is of interest to note that not once has he lost faith in the masses or has he blamed them. But his vow of self-realisation is day by day becoming more of a personal matter, and in this, he is firm as a rock. Gandhiji takes recourse to the *Gita* more and more. Time and again, references to the *Gita* are there, they are increasing day by day. Inspite of the worst of trials, inspite of the incidents that might shake any man's faith from its very roots, inspite of conflicts that would tend to make a man mad, in the worst of incidents when momentarily he starts doubting the rightness of his cause and path, Gandhiji remains firm and calm and for all this, credit goes to his adoption of the *Gita* doctrine in theory and practice. Rajagopalachari rightly states: "The other is that human being is basically good and reasonable, and if the approach is properly made, with disinterested love and self-sacrifice, he will be converted from evil and unreason to good and right conduct. Gandhiji swore by the latter philosophy."[34] Gandhiji very often had great doubts in the propriety of his faith and his philosophy, but ultimately he did not change his views, he resorted to his philosophy, stuck to it and consequently he continued to work for the welfare of humanity at large.

(h) The Last Three Years

The worst of trials and tribulations came in the last three years of his life, when he failed to bring about Hindu-Muslim unity. India was partitioned, terrible communal riots broke out, and even though the Congress went to power, tales of horror, insult, shame and woe were heard from all corners of the country. It created a feeling that his creed of non-violence had failed or it was thrown away. Surely he could not be a silent spectator to all this. Surely he would suffer. To put in his own words: "This is a unique experiment in self-sacrifice. I am undergoing austere self-immolation in order to create fraternal love by winning all hearts . . .Either I am, or I am not, a real Mahatma. If I am, the world can gain by learning from me whatever there is worth learning."[35] "I am at present heavily laden both with mental pressure and physical work."[36] "The city is quiet for fear of the police. But there is fire in the hearts of the people. I must either perish in that fire or put it out."[37] "There was a time when people immediately carried out whatever escaped from my lips. Truly, I was then the commander of a non-violent army. But to-day mine is a cry in the wilderness."[38] "Why don't I go mad when I see all this work?"[39] and so on. Again, "But the rulers of the country have no faith in non-violence . . . In this age perhaps I am the only believer in non-violence. I pray to God to give me enough strength so that at least I, if none else, may be able to practice non-violence."[40] In these days he invokes the help of the *Gita* again and again. It is rightly stated by Suvira Jaiswal that ". . . in the *Bhagavad Gita*, the doctrine of *Bhakti* in its wider sense, becomes a religious principle and a way of life. In practical application this doctrine does not mean mere enjoyment of ecstatic trances fancying the nearness of the deity; it means the carrying out of one's caste duties and other social actions in a spirit of renunciation."[41] Gandhiji, even till last, adopted this view. He agreed that he constantly tried to become an ideal *Sthitaprajna* of the *Gita*, even though, to put in his own words: "My dreams of an ideal India are being shattered, but I do not mind it much. My inner voice is, however, prompting me to do my duty."[42] It is thus clear that during this period the *Gita* in particular and Hinduism in general sustained him and made him firmer in his convictions though he has realized that he is doing everything now as a duty at the bidding of God and that he is constantly going nearer and nearer to his aim of life—self-realization. To put in his own words again: "I am not yet a Mahatma. If people call me a Mahatma, what is it to me? I am only an ordinary man. If I have truly kept vows of truth, non-violence, non-stealing, celibacy, etc., calling upon God as my witness, I shall die a death I have longed for."[43] "I am a servant of God. I shall carry out His work so long as it pleases Him."[44] "I am a prisoner of God."[45] "It is God who has always been my sole guide and physician. He never errs. He is almighty . . . I am in the hands of God."[46] "Therefore, I have to acquire that inner vision for which I have been striving for the last sixty years, I do not claim that I have been fully successful in it, but at the same time, it is true that I am drawing nearer to it and all my activities are being directed to that end."[47] It is remarkable that absolute devotion to God, total surrender to His will, directing all one's activities and one's very Self towards becoming an instrument in the hands of God etc., are the most remarkable features of Gandhiji's utterings in these last days. And he had read just this in the *Gita*. All this leads him to self-realisation, that is to him the basic end proclaimed by the *Gita* for man. Gandhiji is at the highest heights of his greatness just when he undergoes the worst of mental conflicts. Here it is that the *Gita* sustains him and nourishes him. Catlin, in his fine estimate of Gandhiji states: "And I was fairly certain that the Mahatma only remained a Hindoo precisely because he believed that he could reconcile faith with waging the very western fight against evil (but not by violence in resisting evil), while also affirming the Eastern mysticism by which all belonged to and was sustained by God. In brief, it is just here that the Mahatma was the evangelist of the West to the East as well as apostle of the East to the West."[48] Whether we accept this fully or not, one fact stands out glaringly clear that Gandhiji is a *Sthitaprajna* and *Trigunatita* of the *Gita* and he has remained a Hindu because of the *Gita*, he has constantly progressed in life and from greatness to greatness due to the *Gita*. In the last years of his life he has very often stated that he is a perfect Hindu. Even in the last days, he felt that: "I am, so to say, in a furnace. What will happen, it is difficult to say; possibly some result may come out soon."[49] He has yet stated and followed the view that: "How wonderful are His ways of helping me in this sacrifice! The more I find myself opposed in my mission, the more determined I get in my resolve to fulfill it. God is with me." Gandhiji has thus reached a stage very much similar to the one described by Sri Aurobindo in these words: "Losing our lower individual personality in the Impersonal, we arrive fully at union with that Supreme Personality which is not separate and individual, but yet assumes all individualities. . . . Reaching the inner actionlessness of the silent *Purusha*, *naishkarmaya*, and leaving *Prakriti* to do her works, we can attain supremely beyond to the status of the divine Mastery which is able to do all works and yet be bound by none."[50] This shows the greatness of the doctrine of the *Gita* and the inner strength of Hinduism as also the grand potentiality and power of the personality of Gandhiji, who adopted it as his own both in theory and practice for more than sixty years of his life. In the last years, he experienced frustrations of the worst kind with reference to the uplifting of Indian masses, the eradication of the evil of untouchability, the practice of truth and non-violence by the masses, the problem of Hindu-Muslim unity etc. He was so much overcome with sorrow that when Miss Margaret inquired of him whether he wanted to live upto 125 years, he replied: "I have lost that hope because of the terrible happenings in the world. I don't want to live in darkness."[51] Again he said: "I am fully conscious that my views are not shared by others and I am the only one who holds them, but those views cannot be changed now. The more I reflect upon them, the greater the conviction they carry with me."[52] It is remarkable that inspite of what he suffered, (i) his conviction about his Truth and non-violence and the life adopted by him has not only not changed, it has become firmer, and (ii) he now prefers to go nearer and nearer to God all alone to experience perfect happiness by complete submission of his full self at the feet of God. He has, after all his work in the world, become a *yogi* who seeks self-realization for himself, leaving the rest to the care and will of God, even though he is in the midst of the world and continues to act as an instrument in the hands of God. That is why he stated: "*Ahimsa* is a mightier weapon by far than the atom bomb. Even if the people of Hiroshima could have died in their thousands with prayer and good will in their hearts, the situation would have been transformed as if by a miracle."[53] Again "I am a servant of Rama, I shall continue to do my work so long as He commands me; and I shall depart when He orders me."[54] And again to blind men he said: "My Himalayas are here. To remove your sufferings and to die in your service is tantamount to going to the Himalayas for me."[55] Again, "If I am unworthy, God will not let me survive. Because I am a perfect Hindu, I am much distressed to see that Hindus do not perform their duty .. . . Therefore this fast is really for the purification of my own soul. It is an appeal to God to purify the souls of all and make them sane."[56] Gandhiji is satisfied in his last year that he is a perfect Hindu, he also feels satisfied that, "I am a true Mahatma."[57] This shows that he feels he is going nearer and nearer to the goal that he had conceived many years earlier in his life and set before himself as an ideal. It is the goal of self-realization.

Throughout all these years, at every moment of his life, Gandhiji tries to live up to the doctrine of the *Gita*, in fact his whole life has been a living activity of the *Gita* doctrine. When, in 1930, he claimed that he had tried to live and act up to the doctrine of the *Gita* for forty years, hardly had he realised that his living according to the *Gita* would be so severely tested in the last years, and he will have to state that: "I am, so to say, in a furnace."[58] "My ideas of truth and non-violence are at present being weighed in a delicate sensitive balance, like the one used for weighing pearls."[59] And firmly he states that: "And you know I am a student of the *Bhagavad Gita*. 'It is ours' says Mother *Gita* 'to do our part of work in all fervour and honestly and without any craving for results."[60] again, "So, it is the first and foremost duty of a man to satisfy the inner self, i.e., to follow its dictates with the utmost sincerity and honesty of feeling," and, "Why should we worry over the question of victory or defeat?"[61] "But God in His unbounded grace bears with me and sustains me."[62] "If I attain the state of a *Sthitaprajna*, whatever happens will leave me unaffected and calm."[63] Gandhiji's is thus a soul lifted high in the midst of trials and tribulations, mental tortures and the worst of sorrows.

Gandhi and Buddha

At this stage, it is worth comparing Gandhiji's mental state with that of Buddha. Buddha it is known, lived in the midst of luxury of the highest type and was not permitted even to imagine of the sorrows of the world. His father, fearing that Gautama would renounce the world and thus the royal family and the kindgom would be orphaned, saw to it with scrupulous care on his part that no sorrow of the world came to his eyes. Gautama was by nature and inheritance kind, affectionate, compassionate, simple, honest, heroic, fearless, in fact he possessed all the best qualities in abundance that would make a very good king or an ideal ascetic, and the father wanted to make a very good king of him. Then, he happened to see old age, sickness and death in their most pitiable and, shall we say, horrible form. He was, first of all shocked, though he withstood the shock. He thought, brooded and meditated over the problem. Several questions struck his mind. Why do old age, sickness and death overcome man? Why does man take birth if he is to suffer these things and ultimately be lost in oblivion? If these sorrows are unavoidable, how is it that man is able to enjoy worldly joys? With this state, is man learned or ignorant? Cannot old age, sickness and death, i.e., sorrows of this transitory life, be conquered? What is Gautama's duty in this? Since he is already awakened to sorrows, what should he do?

Evidently the questions that struck the mind of Gautama are philosophical questions. He came thus on the verge of his philosophical and spiritual uplift. The questions indicate the first entrance of man into the world of philosophical secrets about life and hereafter. The striking of these questions immediately on witnessing sorrows of the world should not surprise us. We are already told that Gautama possessed, right at birth, all the qualities and traits that would go to make an ideal king or an ideal ascetic. This possession, according to the Hindu faith comes (i) from parental heritage and (ii) from the influence of works and thought in the earlier births because psychic effects of this come with the soul. This led Gautama to renunciation of royalty and family and all personal love and tenderness of and towards his father, son, wife and so on. Gautama renounced the sorrowful world to seek an end to this grim sorrow. He sought *Gurus* but was not happy. He then entered into meditations and tortured the body till it was reduced to bones while all the time he was meditating on the secret and origin of this sorrow and was in search of the way by which this sorrow could be overcome. Even though he tortured the body, he failed to come to reality. The way of *Hathayoga* failed him. He ultimately took food and nourishment. Study and meditation awakened his 'inner voice' and he gained real knowledge and gave it to the world. We may state that this inner voice, be it in the case of Lord Buddha, Vardhaman Mahavira or Mahatma Gandhi, is actually the sum total of all the thinking process that is constantly going on in the minds. The reply to the problem seems to come like lightning but actually that is not so; it is actually the culmination into a striking reply of a whole process of thinking that goes on constantly. The *Jnana* therefore that strikes to the mind actually comes from it and Hindus are prone to attribute it to some higher powers and so they call it "inner voice". All doubts of Buddha are resolved and then it is that he starts his preaching.

The case is very much dissimilar as compared to that of Gandhiji, whose personality has developed by slow, gradual and sure steps from its meek and mild character to that of a man of steel, of indomitable will. What Bhavabhuti tells of Rama in his *Uttararamacharita*—

वज्रादपि कठोराणि मृदूनि कुसुमादपि।
लोकोत्तराणां चेतांसि को हि विज्ञातुमर्हति।। (2:7)

(Who can possibly probe into the depths of the hearts of persons extraordinary, who are harder than *Vajra* and milder than flowers), aptly applies to Gandhiji. Gandhiji inherited Vaishnavism and lived and died in Vaishnavism. His religious, ethical and philosophical views have developed, but they have never substantially changed; these have become more clear to him but they have never reversed. The philosophical and all other questions have come to him in their natural course, and these have been duly answered. Gandhiji never had questions that found no answer, questions that his heart could, in all possibility, not answer. It was again not a philosophical question, when Gautama put the sad reality of old age, sickness and death in one scale and life in the other. He no doubt failed to understand how, inspite of the constantly hanging sword of death on man's head, man could freely indulge in worldly joys and be constantly tied to worldly attachments. The sight of old age, death, etc., brought him to the threshold of philosophical knowledge and renunciation at the same time. He first wondered at the vast ignorance of men who could enjoy themselves inspite of fear of death.

विस्तीर्णमज्ञानमहो नराणां हसन्ति ये रोगभयैरमुक्ताः।
(*Buddhacharitam*, 33-46)

(Vast indeed is the ignorance of men of the world, who enjoy life inspite of the fear of death,) he felt. But here the other reading is,

विस्तीर्णविज्ञानमहो नराणां हसन्ति ये रोगभयैरमुक्ताः।

(Vast indeed is the knowledge of men of the world, who enjoy life inspite of the fear of death.) In this comes his realization that real knowledge of the secret of birth, life and death will answer the problems of joys of life and death.

So, three things strike his mind at a time:

(1) The Philosophical problems,
(2) Renunciation is the path,
(3) He should widen the bounds of his knowledge to get to the secret of reality.

And Buddha retires from the world. No such conflict arises in Gandhiji's mind at any time in life. It is only in due natural course of activity and work that (i) the spirit of service to humanity, to help it get over its sorrows, (ii) the necessity of renunciation in married life, and (iii) the necessity of knowing reality through service and finding his self-realization and that of humanity just in this, arise in his mind. He wants to wipe the tears of suffering humanity but *through life, through service, through activity, through selfless action*. He thus becomes an ascetic, a *Yogi* in life. His personality rises by a slow process from ordinary to extraordinary, from mundane to spiritual, and all this happens in a natural manner, and ultimately he becomes Mahatma from Mohan. His whole life is a proof of this, His detachment, *Yoga* and spiritual rise are similar to those of Buddha. But their approach is different, their process of uplift is different. To clarify the whole position, in the ultimate stage, the attainment of both is the same, but the path resorted to by Buddha is that of the Upanishadic *Samnyasin*, the path of Gandhiji is that of the *Samnyasin* of the *Gita*, about whom it is rightly stated:

ज्ञेयः स नित्यसंन्यासी यो न द्वेष्टि न कांक्षति।
निर्द्वन्द्वो हि महाबाहो सुखं बन्धात्प्रमुच्यते।। (5:3)

(Him one should know as ever renouncing who has no dislikes and likes; for he who is free from the pairs of opposites is easily released from bondage). And Gandhiji, on the basis of the definition of *Samnyasa*:

काम्यानां कर्मणां न्यासं संन्यासं कवयो विदुः। (18:2)

(Renunciation of actions springing from selfish desire is known as *Samnyasa* by the seers) and on the basis of the verse

आत्मवत्सर्वभूतेषु यः पश्यति स पश्यति।

(One who visions all living beings as his own self is the real seer), was very clear when he stated that the path of the *Gita* is not for a man of inaction, a man who has renounced the world. He says: "The lesson of the *Bhagavad Gita* is meant not for those who have forsaken the world, but for every householder, irrespective of his birth and state. Everybody's duty should be to attain the state described therein, and this can only be done if life is built on the rock of fearlessness,"[64] and "I know that there is a school of philosophy which teaches complete inaction and futility of all effort. I have not been able to appreciate that teaching. In my humble opinion, effort is necessary for one's own growth. It has to be irrespective of results."[65] This view is worth comparison with another view of his: "There is a stage in life when a man does not need even to proclaim his thoughts much less to show them by outward action. Mere thoughts act. They attain that power. Then it can be said of him that his seeming inaction constitutes his action."[66] It will be seen here that the principle of the *Gita* for a man at this stage of life constitutes almost a complete absence of difference of opinion between Shankara and Aurobindo on one side and Gandhiji on the other. When Shankara states that for a संन्यासी, no action is necessary, and Gandhiji refers to a stage in the rise of man when 'mere thoughts act', there is not much difference of opinion.

नैव तस्य कृतेनार्थो नाकृतेनेह कश्चन। (3:18)

(For him there is no interest whatsoever in what is done or what is not done.)

The difference between Budhha and Gandhiji therefore would come to this, even though both sought the eradication of the deep sorrows of suffering humanity through life:

(1) The conflicts of Buddha forced him to renounce the family and the world to find out in solitude a solution of the infinite and grave problems of the world; while in the case of Gandhiji no such conflicts arose, he was rising to higher heights gradually, and by stages his mission on life was becoming more and more clear to him.

(2) Both preferred to stay in the world and in the midst of suffering humanity to serve it by constant *Karmayoga*, while in their own person, both were attaining higher and higher heights day by day.

NOTES

1. In Mahabharata.
2. 'My Gandhi'. J.H. Holmes.
3. 'My Experiments with Truth', p. 2
4. 'My Experiments with Truth', p. 2
5. 'My Experiments with Truth', p.24.
6. 'Mahatma Gandhi—Early Phase', p. 178.
7. 'My Experiments with Truth', p. 25.
8. 'Mahatma Gandhi—Early Phase', p. 99.
9. Vide supra, p. 99.
10. 'My Experiments with Truth', p. 46.
11. 'My Experiments with Truth', p. 34.
12. 'My Experiments with Truth', 49.
13. 'My Experiments with Truth', p. 50.
14. Beatrice P. Lamb in "India—A World in Transition', p. 98.
15. Quoted by Beatrice P. Lamb in 'India—A World in Transition', p. 33
16. R.J. Walsh—'Nehru on Gandhiji' p. 22.
17. Vide Supra, p. 23.
18. '*Gita* According to Gandhi', p. 130.
19. 'My Experiments with Truth', p. 118.
20. 'My Experiments with Truth', p. 183.
21. निमित्तमात्रं भव सव्यसाचिन् (10:33) (Be thou no more than an instrument, O Savyasachin!) says Krishna to Arjuna.
22. 'My Experiments with Truth', p. 196.
23. 'My Experiments with Truth', p.198.
24. 'My Experiments with Truth', p. 198-99.
25. 'My Experiments with Truth', p. 250.
26. 'Diary of Mahadev Desai', p. 105.
27. Quoted by Dr. Holmes in his 'My Gandhi' p. 2.
28. 'My Gandhi', p. 160.
29. 'My Gandhi', p. 174.
30. 'Gandhi—As Saint and Statesman', p. 10.
31. 'Gandhi—As Saint and Statesman', p. 15.
32. P. Nagaraja Rao in his 'Introduction to Vedanta', p. 102.
33. 'Introduction to Vedanta', p. 95.
34. 'Gandhiji's Teachings and Philosophy', by Rajagopalachari, p. 25.
35. Manubehn Gandhi 'Lonely Pilgrim', p. 196—on 12-2-1947.
36. 'Lonely Pilgrim', p. 208 on 17-2-1947.
37. 'Last Glimpses of Bapu', p. 10 on 1-1-1948.
38. Vide supra, p. 67.
39. Vide supra, p. 70.
40. Vide supra, p. 225.

41. 'Origin and Development of Vaishnavism', p. 114.
42. 'Last Glimpses of Bapu', Manuben Gandhi p. 42.
43. Vide supra, p. 252.
44. Vide supra, p. 252.
45. Vide spra, p. 141.
46. Vide supra, p. 164.
47. Vide supra, p. 8.
48. 'In the Path of Mahatma Gandhi', George Catlin, p. 125.
49. 'Last Glimpses of Bapu',p. 19.
50. 'Essays on the *Gita*', Sri Aurobindo, p. 180-181.
51. 'Last Glimpses of Bapu', p. 284.
52. Vide supra, p. 254.
53. Vide supra, p. 285.
54. 'Last Glimpses of Bapu', Manuben Gandhi, p. 245.
55. Vide supra, p. 286.
56. Vide supra, p. 28.
57. Vide supra, p. 234 dt. 22-1-1948.
58. Vide supra, p. 19.
59. 'The Lonely Pilgrim', by Manuben Gandhi, p.24
60. Vide supra, p. 177.
61. Vide supra, p. 195-196.
62. Vide supra, p. 214.
63. Vide supra, p. 217.
64. 'Harijan', 5-1-1947.
65. 'Young India', 21-10-1926.
66. 'Harijan', 26-10-1947.

SEVEN

Gita and Gandhiji's Teachings

"Hinduism, as I know it, entirely satisfies my soul, fills my whole being and I find a solace in the *Bhagavad Gita* and *Upanishads* that I miss even in the *Sermon on the Mount*."

Gandhiji[1]

"To-day, the *Gita* is, not only my Bible or my Quran; it is more than that—it is my mother. I lost my earthly mother who gave me birth long ago; but this Eternal mother has completely filled her place by my side ever since."

Gandhiji[2]

"If I am unworthy, God will not let me survive. Because I am a perfect Hindu, I am much distressed to see that Hindus do not perform their duty . . ."

Gandhiji[3]

Introductory

Gandhiji, as we have seen earlier, stated: ". . .but I must confess that when doubts haunt me, when disappointments stare me in the face, and when I see not one ray of light on the horizon, I turn to the *Bhagawad Gita* and find a verse to comfort me; and I immediately begin to smile in the midst of overwhelming sorrow. My life has been full of external tragedies and if they have not left any visible and indelible effect on me, I owe it to the teaching of the *Bhagavad Gita*."[4] He has, at several places, uttered words of unique admiration for the *Gita*. Gandhiji acknowledges the invaluable and sure help of the *Gita* in his life and still it is interesting to note that he has not stated how and at what times, under which conflict, the *Gita* has helped him and how it has answered his questions.

Specific Reference on Untouchability

He has accepted just one fact that when he was haunted with the question whether the *Shastras* sanction untouchability, the *Gita* gave to him a positive 'No' in the famous verse:

> मा हि पार्थ व्यपाश्रित्य येऽपि स्यु: पापयोनय:।
> स्त्रियो वैश्यास्तथा शुद्रास्तेऽपि यान्ति परां गतिम्।। (9:32)

(O Partha, even those who are of low birth, as also women, Vaishyas and Shudras attain to the highest bliss by resorting to me.)

To put in his own words: "Often in the course of my struggle against untouchability, I am confronted with conflicting opinions delivered by doctors of learning. Some of them tell me that untouchability as it is practised today has no sanction in Hinduism and they bless my efforts to eradicate it; but there are some others who maintain that untouchability is an essential part of Hinduism from the very beginning. Which authority should I follow under the circumstances? I feel absolutely at sea. The Vedas and the *Shastras* are of no avail to me. I then approach the Mother and say, 'Mother, these learned Pandits have put me in a predicament. Help me out of my perplexity.' And the Mother, with a smile says in reply: 'The assurance held out by me in the ninth chapter is not meant for the *Brahman*as only, but for the sinner and the outcaste, the downtrodden and the disinherited, too.'"[5]

Except for this specific reference, we do not know of any other in which Gandhiji accepts that the *Gita* answered his questions in conflicts. He had his own peculiarly original interpretation of the *Gita* as we saw earlier and he lived up to it. But this great man who, at every moment of his life constantly breathed of the spirit of the *Gita* and lived in the *Gita*, has not clarified as to how the *Gita* helped him again and again. The question therefore assumes great interest and importance and we try to answer it. We thereby indirectly come closer to his teaching and examine how it is related to the *Gita*, even though the conclusions that we try to arrive at might not be very clear and fully systematic. It is rightly stated that: "Not having had the time or the training for the systematic development of his thought, Gandhiji's ideas are in the main, of an existential kind: they grew as he grew up."[6]

The Background

For this it is necessary that even at the risk of repetition, we note the first impressions of the *Gita* on his young mind when he read Sir Edwin Arnold's 'The Song Celestial.' Before that, probably he must have heard the *Gita* recitation either at his house or somewhere else. He must have heard of the greatness of the *Gita* from so many religious persons who came to see his father when Gandhiji was just a boy. He definitely knew that it was a great scripture. Then it was in England that two friends requested him to read the *Gita* with them. His immediate reaction was that of shame because he had not read it either in Sanskrit or in Gujarati. He agreed to read it with them, in Arnold's translation. To put in his own words: "Towards the end of my second year in England, I came across two Theosophist brothers, both unmarried. They talked to me about the *Gita*. They were reading Sir Edwin Arnold's translation—'The Song Celestial' and they invited me to read the original with them. I felt ashamed, as I had read the Divine Poem neither in Sanskrit nor in Gujarati; I was constrained to tell them that I had not read the *Gita*, but that I would gladly read it with them, and that though my knowledge of Sanskrit was meagre, still I hoped to be able to understand the original to the extent of telling where the translation failed to bring out the meaning." On reading it, we find that the very first verses that struck him to be unique are these:

ध्यायतो विषयान्पुंसः संगस्तेषूपजायते।
संगात्संजायते कामः कामात्क्रोधोऽभिजायते।।
क्रोधाद् भवति संमोहः संमोहात्स्मृतिविभ्रमः।
स्मृतिभ्रंशाद् बुद्धिनाशो बुद्धिनाशात्प्रणश्यति।। (2:62-63)

In Arnold's translation it is:

"If one
Ponders on objects of the sense, there springs
Attraction; from attraction grows desire,
Desire flames to fierce passion, passion breeds

Recklessness; then the memory—all betrayed—
Lets noble purpose go, and saps the mind,
Till purpose, mind, and man are all undone."[7]

To put in his own words: "The verses in the second chapter . . . made a deep impression on my mind, and they still ring in my ears." So, the verses that made the very first deep impression on Gandhiji's mind and remained ever his prized ideal are the verses that speak of the necessity of absolute self-control and keeping one's self away from attractions and in God and *Yoga*. This would next lead to rejection of *Preya* in favour of *Shreya* as that famous Upanishadic mantra lays down:

श्रेयश्च प्रेयश्च मनुष्यमेतस्तौ सम्परीत्य विविनक्ति धीरः।
श्रेयो हि धीरोऽभि प्रेयसो वृणीते प्रेयो मन्दो योगक्षेमाद् वृणीते।।
(*Kathopanishad*—1.2-2)

(*Shreya* and *Preya* approach man; a wise man ponders over both and properly distinguishes between the two. The wise man prefers *Shreya* to *Preya*, while through the desire for worldly prosperity the ignorant selects *Preya*.)

The immediate reaction after these verses made a deep impression on his mind was: "The book struck me as one of priceless worth." And as he read more and more of its translations and the original, he came nearer to the secret of its greatness. He says: "The impression has ever since been growing on me with the result that I regard it today as the book *par excellence* for the knowledge of Truth."[8]

So, even when he had at first reading not studied it in details, it took hold of his mind and created a deep impression on him, an impression that grew stronger day by day and that he nourished for his whole life-time. To put in brief, the immediate reactions are these:

(i) He was fascinated by it and took the book to be of priceless worth.
(ii) The impression grew deeper and deeper till he came to realize that it is the best book ever written for the knowledge of Truth.
(iii) The verses that immediately took hold of his mind are those that form a part of the definition of the *Sthitaprjana*. They stress the need of absolute self-control so that the mind is trained to form an identity with the self and the whole personality is

controlled, so that man becomes a real Yogi. While he does everything in life that he should, his self is on its way to sublimation and oneness with the Divine, his self is on its way to ब्रह्मनिर्वाण (Brahma-Nirvana) while it is steady in ब्राह्मी स्थिति (communion with *Brahman*). Gandhiji thus got exactly what he required for his mission of life. This was his first lesson we might say in *Yoga*; The definition that the verse gave to him was योग: चित्तवृत्तिनिरोध:।

(iv) He next stresses that from this very first reading: "To me the *Gita* became an infallible guide of conduct. It became my dictionary of daily reference." He also realized that the *Gita* shows the way of right conduct for a man and that in everyday life also the *Gita* would be the right guide-book.

Definition of *Sthitaprajna* and Gandhiji

The very first impression is thus very much significant in that it has shown to Gandhiji the way of conduct of life, the way of his *Yoga* and the way of self-realization –everything that a Hindu will be expected to do and follow in this worldly life and in the life hereafter, so that the purpose of the whole life is fulfilled. Thus, the *Gita* occupies the central position in his life right with its first reading and paves the way for Gandhiji constantly trying to become a *Sthitaprajna* and shaping his life and activities on this line. The first peculiar impression also fixed up the line of interpretation of the meaning of the *Gita* that was to follow later. Gandhiji's later claims also show that with the very first reading of the *Gita*, he had moulded his activities of life on the lines of the *Gita* as he had understood it. Influences of other religions—Christianity in particular—followed and Gandhiji was deeply influenced by the works of Thoreau, Ruskin and Tolstoy and their idealism. He then underwent a grave conflict and had his own doubts. He felt that Hinduism could not resolve these and he had a very much interesting correspondence with Shrimad Rajachandra, whom Gandhiji called Raichandbhai through affection and intimacy. But, all through this period, Gandhiji was under the impression of the *Gita*, that had already occupied the central position in his life and the impression was growing firmer day by day, both unconsciously and consciously. The place that the *Gita* occupied in his heart is thus a very important factor in the evolution of his personality and in the shaping of his ideas that resulted in his teachings. It is thus clear that the conviction about the teachings of the *Gita that was growing to greater and greater clarity day by day*, must have, both unconsciously and consciously weighed itself against the other religious and ethical and spritual influences that came to his mind, and even took hold of it for some time. That he has weighed these can be seen from one illustration in his own words thus: "Hinduism, as I know it, entirely satisfies my soul, fills my whole being and I find a solace in the *Bhagavad Gita* and *Upanishads* that I miss even in the 'Sermon on the Mount.' Not that I do not prize the ideal presented therein, not that some of the teachings in the 'Sermon on the Mount' have not left a deep impression upon me, but I must confess that when doubts haunt me, when disappointments stare me in the face, and when I see not one ray of light on the horizon, I turn to the *Bhagavad Gita* and find a verse to comfort me and I immediately begin to smile in the midst of overwhelming sorrow."[9] Also remarkable is another statement of his that: "I find the greatest consolation from the *Bhagavadgita* and Tulsidas's *Ramayana*. I frankly confess that the Quran, the Bible and the other scriptures of the world, inspite of my great regard for them do not move me as do the *Gita* of Krishna and the *Ramayana* of Tulsidas."[10] And even earlier his feeling was: "Nothing elates me so much as the music of the *Gita* or the *Ramayana* by Tulsidas, the only two books in Hinduism I may be said to know. When I fancied I was taking my last breath, the *Gita* was my solace."[11] Shri V.B. Kher therefore rightly states that: "*Bhagavadgita* was for Gandhiji a book of reference. He found it of great help and called it his *Kamadhenu*. It offers an excellent synthesis of the very best that is in Hindu spiritual thought and culture."[12]

Gita and Path of Life

Gandhiji has made several references to his mental comparison of the teaching of the *Gita* with the teaching of the other religions and to weigh what appeals to him more in the light of the path of life that he has carved for himself. It is by now clear that the *Gita* has its own vital contribution in Gandhiji carving out his path of life and in this comparison, ultimately it is the *Gita*, the *Upanishads* and the

Ramayana that continue to dominate. To put in his own words: "But the New Testament produced a different impression, especially the 'Sermon on the Mount' which went straight to my heart. I compared it with the *Gita* . . . My young mind tried to unify the teaching of the *Gita*, the 'Light of Asia' and the 'Sermon on the Mount'. That renunciation was the highest form of religion appealed to me greatly."[13] And again: "The spirit of 'Sermon on the Mount' compares almost on a par with the *Bhagavadgita* for the domination of my heart."[14] Now and then he even puts 'Sermon on the Mount' etc., on equal terms with the *Gita*. But, ultimately he agrees and specifies in very clear terms his strongest liking, admiration, love and devotion for the *Gita*. Rightly does he state: "The *Gita* is a pure religious discourse given without any embellishment. It simply describes the progress of the pilgrim soul towards the supreme Goal. Therefore, there is no question of selection."[15]

That spirit of renunciation found in the *Gita* appealed to him the most, and the spirit of absolute self-control overtook his mind at the very first reading. He therefore later on consciously took to becoming an ideal *Sthitaprajna*, a man of renunciation and *Yoga*. He understood this as self-less service on the basis of the two fine and highly significant definitions of *Yoga* in the *Gita*—

योगः कर्मसु कौशलम् (2:50) समत्वं योग उच्यते। (2:48)

(*Yoga* is skill in action, and even-mindedness is *Yoga*). His experiment of becoming an ideal *Sthitaprajna* continued right up to his last days when his spirit of equanimity was put to the worst of fire-ordeals we might say. From very early years of his activity in South Africa, a conscious effort at cultivation of equanimity of spirits started and for this he has given clear credit to the *Gita*. To put in his words: " I enjoy peace and equanimity of spirit which has excited the envy of many Christian friends. I have got it primarily through the *Gita*."[16] Here it is that the definition of the *Sthitaprajna* in the *Gita* (Verses 2:49 to 73) has come to his rescue and particularly the verses:

विषया विनिवर्तन्ते निराहारस्य देहिनः।
रसवर्जं रसोऽप्यस्य परं दृष्ट्वा निवर्तते।। (2:59)

(When a man starves his senses, the objects of those senses disappear for him but not the yearning for them; the yearning too departs when he beholds the Supreme,) and,

रागद्वेषवियुक्तैस्तु विषयानिन्द्रियैश्चरन्।
आत्मवश्यैर्विधेयात्मा प्रसादमधिगच्छति।।
प्रसादे सर्वदु:खानां हानिरस्योपजायते।
प्रसन्नचेतसो ह्याशु बुद्धि: पर्यवतिष्ठते।। (2:64-65)

(But the disciplined soul, who, moving among sense-objects with the senses weaned from likes and dislikes and brought under the control of *Atman*, attains peace of mind. Peace of mind means the end of all ills, for the understanding of him whose mind is at peace stands secure,) and

त्रैगुण्यविषया वेदा नि:स्त्रैगुण्यो भवार्जुन।
निर्द्वन्द्वो नित्यसत्त्वस्थो निर्योगक्षेम आत्मवान्।। (2:45)

(The Vedas have as their domain the three *gunas*; eschew them, O Arjuna. Free thyself from the pairs of opposites, abide in eternal truth, scorn to gain or guard anything, remain the master of thy soul.)

Gita Saves Him in Early Life

And Gandhiji takes this as a matter of natural course because very early the idea is developing in his mind that the most natural and realistic course of action for a man is to take shelter in his religion of birth and in the normal course, it is bound to answer his questions. When in England, attempts were made on him to convert him to Christianity, he was hardly conscious of this reality. He still humbly refused to be converted, on the ground that he must know his religion of birth thoroughly before he thinks of conversion to some other religion. And once Gandhiji read the *Gita*, the *Upanishads*, etc., he became conscious of the greatness and even uniqueness of Hinduism. This supported him again in Africa when conflicts and doubts did arise in his mind. While answering all his questions Shrimad Rajachandra advised him to dive deeper in his own religion. Gandhiji realized the necessity to adhere to one's religion acquired by birth and through heritage and that again brought him later to his opposition against conversions. That is the reason why, while he accepts the *Gita* in these terms: "The *Gita* is not a theoretical treatise. It is a living but silent guide whose directions one has to understand by patient striving."[17] He advises students in these words: "And so I say to a Hindu boy that he must not uproot the traditions in which he has been brought up, as I say to a Mussalman or a Christian boy that he must not uproot his traditions," and, "And so, whilst I would welcome your learning the Gospel and your learning the Quran, I insist on all of you Hindu boys, learning the *Gita*," and again, "And it is because I see the same God in the *Bhagavad Gita*, as I see in the *Bible* and the *Quran*, that I say to the Hindu boys that they will derive greater inspiration from the *Bhagavad Gita*, because they will be tuned to the *Gita* more than to any other book."[18] This realization that had far-reaching consequences, later even in saving Hindus from the onslaught-like process of conversions by Christian missionaries in India, came to him through the deep study of the *Gita* and he took the *Gita* as the most representative scripture of Hinduism. The *Gita* and *Upanishads* have, in fact, been the works through which he has rightly comprehended Hinduism and the best thing that he liked about Hinduism was renunciation that finds the finest expression in the *Gita*. He clearly states: "We will have to imbibe the virtue of control of our senses. This in my view, is the essence of the teaching of the *Gita*. I think that the chief merit of the *Gita* is that certain basic truths are explained in the attractive form of a dialogue. Human beings must restrain their senses if they do not want to go mad."[19]

We have seen already in an earlier chapter that at no stage in one's life, even at the stage of a man becoming a *Muktatma*, is this renunciation, renunciation of actions. It is renunciation, of one's personal desire and attachment, one's desire for regard of fruits of the actions that a man performs. Gandhiji gave a totally new and unique turn to this renunciation in that he, after stressing the uniqueness of *Karma-yoga*, interpreted the spirit of *Yajna*, or, shall we say, *Yoga*, as duty and service to mankind. Service to others was the be-all and end-all of his life and all his activity and he stresses: "*Yajna* is duty to be performed, or service to be rendered, all the twenty-four hours of the day. . .But renunciation here does not mean abandoning the world and retiring into the forest. The spirit of renunciation should rule all the activities of life. A householder does not cease to be one, if he regards life as a duty rather than as an indulgence."[20] And, "The human body is meant for service, never for indulgence. The secret of happy life lies in renunciation. Renunciation is life, indulgence spells death."[21] This is worth comparison with the ideal of service given to the householder—*Grihastha*—and the educated one—the *Snataka*, in particular in the *Manusmriti*. Manu describes mainly the duties of a householder and expects the educated one to follow a stricter code of duties, so that he can stress in the end that:

> सर्वेषामपि चैतेषां वेदस्मृतिविधानतः।
> गृहस्थ उच्यते श्रेष्ठः स त्रीनेतान्बिभर्ति हि।।
> यथा नदीनदाः सर्वे सागरे यान्ति संस्थितिम्।
> तथैवाश्रमिणः सर्वे गृहस्थे यान्ति संस्थितिम्।। (6-89, 90)

(Of all these four, through the words of the Vedas and Smritis, the householder is said to be the best because he maintains the other three. Just as all rivers—big and small—get ultimately merged in the ocean, so are the members of the other *Ashramas* merged in the *Ashrama* of the householder). Actually, the life of the ideal *Grihastha* is that of all duties and almost no rights and the spirit of renunciation persists in his life; it is more or less a life of service. Similar is the reference to the kings of the *Raghuvamsha* given by the great poet Kalidasa:

> त्यागाय संभृतार्थानां सत्याय मितभाषिणाम्।
> यशसे विजिगीषूणां प्रजायै गृहमेधिनाम्।।
> शैशवेऽभ्यस्तविद्यानां यौवने विषयैषिणाम्।
> वार्धक्ये मुनिवृत्तीनां योगेनान्ते तनुत्यजाम्।। (1-7, 8)

(I shall talk to you of the family of the Raghus, the kings in which were collecting wealth for donations, were speaking less for truth, were conquering countries for fame and were householders only for progeny. In young days they engrossed themselves in learning; in youth in enjoying various sense –objects; in old age in the life of a *muni* and in the end giving up the mortal frame through *Yoga*.)

Actually the *Gita* represents the ideal of renunciation found generally in Hinduism at its best and so, it is natural of Gandhiji to adopt it. He says: "The detachment prescribed by the *Gita* is the hardest thing to achieve, and yet it is so absolutely necessary for perfect peace and for the vision of both the little self and the greatest self."[22] And, "By detachment I mean that one must not worry whether the desired result follows from your action or not, so long as your motive is pure, your means correct. Really, it means that things will come right in the end if you take care of the means and leave the rest to Him."[23] This makes Gandhiji a sage in life and a prophet who seeks his highest uplift through life, through action and through constant service to humanity. Shankaracharya's *muktatma* has for his ideal, renunciation of action that is renunciation *from* life while the same ideal of renunciation of action with Gandhi is renunciation *into* or *through* life; Shankaracharya's ideal is that of *Samnyasa from* life, that of Gandhiji is *Samnyasa in* life. And even this two-fold way of *Samnyasa*, finds support in the *Smritis*. Manu talks of those who embrace *Samnyasa* directly from *Brahmacharyashrama* and those who renounce the world after passing through the first three stages of life; the others are those who stay with family and with the world and are yet *Samnyasins* in the best sense of the term. Gandhiji's concept of renunciation and *Samnyasa* is nearer to the latter. He read this ideal of *Samnyasa* in the *Gita* partly due to his *Vaishnava* heritage in which actual renunciation of the world has little place. The result was that even in the last years of his life, when he began to feel and feel deeply "Who hears me now?" and he was even advised to retire to the Himalayas by some, he, after proper thought on the matter, decided not to do so. We have the most touching incident of some blind-men coming to see him and pay their respects to him when he said: "My Himalayas are here. To remove your sufferings and to die in your service is tantamount to going to the Himalayas for me."[24] This great ideal of renunciation and *Samnyasa* that Gandhiji stresses, is read by him in the *Gita* and in the *Upanishads* and they have been a guide of Gandhiji through life and all its ordeals. If he could withstand the worst of trials and tribulations, if he could stand in equanimity in the most terrifying crisis, credit goes to this attitude.

Yet another fine feature of this ideal is that along with it, Gandhiji tried to lift high, not only himself but the masses at large. He constantly strived for his own sublimation and self-realization, but he also tried to take the masses with him. Gandhiji therefore had this clear conviction right upto the last years of his life when he stated that: "The lesson of the *Bhagavad Gita* is meant not for those who have forsaken the world, but for every householder, irrespective of his birth and state. Everybody's duty should be to attain the state described therein, and this can only be done if life is built on the rock of fearlessness."[25] His attempt to take the masses with him to those spiritual heights is rooted in his faith about their ability to rise high. It is the tendency of all saints of the world, never, under all odds, to lose their faith in the ultimate goodness of humanity and to believe that as man is essentially good, a day will come when he will be on the right path, there will be eternal peace and universal brotherhood in man's life and heaven will dawn on earth. This is what he says even as late as in 1946; "If we accept that ideal (of a *Sthitaprajna* i.e., 'The man of steady wisdom,' i.e., a *Satyagrahi*) we would not regard anybody as our enemy, we must shed all enmity and ill-will—that ideal is not meant for the select few—the saint or the seer only; it is meant for all . .. As an humble fellow toiler, then, let me bear witness that anyone, even a simple-minded villager who wants to and tries, can attain the state of mental equipoise decribed in the *Gita* verses."[26] The appeal of Krishna to Arjuna—"The Vedas have, as their domain the three *gunas*; eschew them, O Arjuna! Free thyself from the pairs of opposites, abide in eternal truth, scorn to gain or guard anything, remain the master of thy soul"(2:45), was also Gandhiji's appeal to the masses of India, and through them, to humanity at large. We must confess that he failed in this effort. Many years earlier, Tagore had forecast that he will fail. To put in his words: "Perhaps he will not succeed. Perhaps he will fail as the Buddha failed and as Christ failed to wean men from their iniquities; but he will always be remembered as one who made his life a lesson for all ages to come."[27] The effort is great and noble and unique in its own way, the effort needs repetition in human life and history again and again. It is therefore rightly stated that "Influenced by modern thought currents, he never let go off his roots and clung to them tenaciously."[28] If this happened, credit goes to the *Gita*, adopted by him in all activities of life on the basis of his *Vaishnava* heritage, by which he has interpreted the meaning of the *Gita* and followed it in life.

Unstinted Faith in God

The basis of this whole unique attitude lies in Gandhiji's unique faith in God. This faith has its roots in his heritage and his environment, and, as more and more time passed, his conviction grew stronger and stronger. He not only refused to lose his faith in God when the events in the country had shaken many from their very roots, when brother cut the throat of brother, and countless men were killed and thousands of women were raped and abducted; actually his faith in God grew stronger and stronger. As late as in 1946 he writes: "So long as we believe that all is from God, we should have no cause for perturbation. The only condition is that whatever we do, we should do with God as witness. It is He who makes the world go and we only reap the consequences of our actions. Therefore, ours is only to obey His law and then be indifferent as to the result."[29] During his mission of brotherhood, love and peace in Noakhali, Gandhiji says: "How wonderful are His ways of helping me in this sacrifice! My faith in His divine power goes from strength to strength. The more I find myself opposed in my mission, the more determined I get in my resolve to fulfil it. God is with me."[30] And at the time of the horrible slaughter, arson, rape and abduction in Delhi and Pakistan, he says: "All I say every day is a part of my prayer. Whatever I possess is dedicated to God,"[31] and, "My sole counsellor is God and I am taking this decision without consulting anybody."[32] This shows that Gandhiji's faith in God was constantly growing and it was at its highest in the last years. In fact, unique faith in God and an unquestioning acceptance of his working are the basis of Gandhiji's whole life, activity and his teachings as it is of the Hindu religion. All the views that Gandhiji has read in the *Gita* as we have seen so far in this chapter, are based on this faith in God. Gandhiji does not worry himself about the characteristics of this God whether He is *Saguna Sakara* or *Nirguna Nirakara*, etc., on which our old *Acharyas* have raised countless controversies. Actually he is not interested in this. If we were to ask a straight question to Gandhiji in the matter, he would say that he believes in both. Statements such as this are not wanting in him: "To me God is Truth and love; God is ethics and morality, God is fearlessness, God is the source of light and life, and yet He is above and beyond all these," and "God and God's law are not different things or facts, in the sense that an earthly king and his law are different. Because God is an idea, Law Himself; therefore, it is impossible to conceive God as breaking the Law."[33] As we saw earlier, to him God is God and that is sufficient. He is a matter of faith and conviction. Gandhiji as we know, would not accept anything that his conscience and conviction do not accept. He would never become a blind follower of the *shastras* or anything at that. To put in his own words: "I exercise my judgment about every scripture, including the *Gita*. I cannot let a scriptural text supersede my reason."[34] We may of course agree that even the reason that he used will be guided by his conviction that will be based on his heritage.

The commentators no doubt explain the origin of धर्म—(*Dharma*) as विद्वद्भिः सद्भिः अद्वेषरागिभिः सेवितः धर्मः (That is righteousness that is practised by the noble learned without prejudice or attachment). Here they understand the word विद्वद्भिः (The learned or enlightened or knowers of the Vedas) as वेदविद्भिः and stress that the learned and even their सम्यक्संकल्पजः कामः and आत्मनः तुष्टि will be guided by the Vedas. But this proves that reason will also be guided by man's heritage of beliefs. With this he boldly states that his Krishna is quite different from the historically-known Krishna. It is natural that only *Yogeshvara* Krishna appeals to him. His Krishna is God the Supreme. To put in his own words: "I would refuse to bow my head to Krishna who would kill because his pride is hurt, or the Krishna whom non-Hindus portray as s dissolute youth. I believe in Krishna of my imagination as a perfect incarnation, spotless in every sense of the word, the inspirer of the *Gita* and the inspirer of the lives of millions of human beings,"[35] and "I believe in Krishna. But my Krishna is the Lord of the Universe, the Creator, Preserver and Destroyer of us all. He may destroy because he creates,"[36] and "Krishna failed to do nothing He wished to do, so says the author of the *Mahabharata*. He was omnipotent. It is futile to drag Krishna from his heights. If he has to be judged as a mere mortal, I fear He will fare badly and will have to take a back seat."[37] We can here see the peculiar *Vaishnava* philosophical attitude reflecting itself in the conception of Krishna. For the average *Bhakta* who is on his way to rise, Krishna is गोपीजनवल्लभ (Gopijan Vallabha), पूर्णावतार (Purnavatara), पुरुषोत्तम (Purushottama) and so on. But to the *Bhakta* who has raised his personality fairly high in pursuit of *Moksha* that is experience of absolute bliss in total submission at the feet of the Lord, Krishna besides being पूर्णावतार (Purnavatara), is God the Supreme. It is therefore natural that Gandhiji should speak in the most adorable terms of Him. It is naturally accepted that "कृष्णात्परं किमपि तमहं न जाने।" (I know no other object higher than Krishna.) But Gandhiji, even though a staunch *Vaishnava* in practice and so in his philosophy, would naturally go a step futher and stress that Krishna and Rama are one and the same. He has time and again referred to the glory of *Ramanama* and as he grew in age, he referred to Rama as his God the Supreme. It was his ambition to face the bullet of the murderer, with the name of 'Rama' in his heart and we are told that the last words in his mouth, when he faced the bullets, were हे राम (Hey Rama). He again and again referred to God in his hours of trial and he stated: "I am a servant of Rama. I shall continue to do my work as long as He commands me; and I shall depart when He orders me to do so."[38] That shows that in Gandhiji's worship of Krishna or Rama, there is not an iota of worship of personal God or sectarianism. Not only Krishna and Rama are the same to him because he worships God the Supreme by these names, to him Krishna, Rama, God, and Truth are synonymous words. He goes a step further and finds oneness in all the names of God found in all religions. That was the reason why when, due to his worship of Rama, he was charged with worship of a human as a God, he clarified that his Rama is God the Supreme. That is the reason why when he worships Krishna of the *Gita*, this Krishna is God the Supreme, i.e., more than even the *Purna Avatara* that he is. As we have seen, Gandhiji has never liked to indulge into questions such as whether the God of the *Gita* is *Saguna* or *Nirguna* and so on. He is God the Supreme that commands all his devotion, adoration, activities, his whole self and the supreme bliss of Gandhiji is in total surrender of his entire self at His feet and at His bidding. Self-realization to him is bathing in His eternal blessing. His view of self-realization comes very near the view that यमेवैष वृणुते तेन लभ्य: (The one who is chosen by the Divine, attains to Him) and he seeks ब्रह्म कृपा हि केवलम् (only through His grace can one attain to Him). Actually he agrees and contends that human being is too frail and weak to know Him and sing of His praises. Man is too small to know Him. This is very near the view that:

श्रवणायाभिर्बहुभिर्यो न लभ्य:
श्रृण्वन्तोऽपि बहवो यं न विद्यु:।
आश्चर्यो वक्ता कुशलोऽस्य लब्धा-
श्चर्यो ज्ञाता कुशलानुशिष्ट:।।

(*Kathopanishad* 1.2-7)

(God is He who is not attainable by many by hearing his descriptions and even those few who hear about him, do not know him. A man who can describe God the Supreme is a surprise and clever is he who can attain to Him; one who can know Him is a surprise and clever is he who can grasp the teaching about Him,) and so, it is rightly stated in another *Upanishad* that:

अन्धं तम: प्रविशन्ति ये अविद्यामुपासते।
ततो भूय इव ते तम: य उ विद्यायां रता:।।

(*Ishopanishad*—9)

(In binding darkness enter they who worship *Avidya*; deeper darkness than this is the lot of those who are engrossed only in *Vidya*.) The attitude to God necessary is,

अविज्ञातं विजानतां विज्ञातमविजानताम्।

(*Kenopanishad*)

(Grasp thoroughly the unknown and forget totally the known.)

This is precisely Gandhiji's view and the *Gita* has done a lot in the evolution of this concept. His devotion to the *Gita* has shaped his conception of God as it has shaped all his activities and his whole life. It is again because of this that for his whole life he has gone on experimenting with Truth.

'Truth is God' and Gandhiji

A word may be added here about Gandhiji's conception "Truth is God" and its bearing in his interpretation of the meaning of the *Gita* and how far the *Gita* accepts this. As we have already stressed earlier, right from the beginning, his deep reverence towards the *Gita* made him feel: "The book struck me as one of priceless worth. The impression has ever since been growing on me with the result that I regard it to-day as the book par excellence for the knowledge of Truth." Gandhiji's whole life has been a constant experiment with Truth, that is, with God, and his constant effort has been at self-realization, and in this, he says: "It became my dictionary of daily reference. Just as I turned to the English dictionary for the meanings of English words that I did not understand, I turned to this dictionary of conduct for a ready solution of all my troubles and trials." This shows that the *Gita* has an important bearing on his experiments with Truth, by which he expected ultimately to be led to self-realisation or *Moksha*. As for the reasons why Gandhiji began to say 'Truth is God' rather than 'God is Truth', he mainly contends that he wants for God the Supreme a term that will be acceptable to all religions and even to the atheists because he seeks unity of mankind. There can be varied views in different religions about God, his relation with man and his characteristics. But there can be no differing views on Truth, even the atheists and all will accept Truth. Christianity conceives of God as "Truth, Goodness and Beauty," Hinduism knows *Brahman* as सत्यं शिवं सुन्दरम् (Satyam

Shivam Sundaram) or सच्चिदानंद (Sat-chit-ananda). Gandhiji, in the manner of a prophet and a practical philosopher, actually accepts the dominance of सत्य (*Satya*), (Truth), in his pursuit of God, and he wants his views to be acceptable to all. To him God conceived of as सत्य (*Satya*) has greater appeal and so of the three सत्यं (Satyam), शिवं (Shivam), सुन्दरम् (Sundaram), and सत्, चित्त, आनन्द (Sat, Chit, Ananda), he knows God as सत्य (*Satya*) or सत् (Sat) and would naturally accept that other traits are included in it. Thus: "Reality is truth and where truth is, knowledge exists. That is why the word *chit* or pure knowledge is associated with God. Again, true knowledge is accompanied with bliss or *Anandam*. Gandhiji views reality as *sat-chit-ananda* or Truth-Knowledge-Bliss. God is the conserver of all values—Truth, Beauty and Goodness. To Gandhiji, the truth-value is the most important and he thinks that the others are only its corollaries."[39] The idea is worth comparison with a statement in the *Mundakopanishad*. Shaunka approaches Angirasa and asks

कस्मिन्नु भगवो विज्ञाते सर्वमिदं विज्ञातं भवति। (1.1.2)

(What is it, O Bhagavan, by the knowledge of which all this will be known?)

The Guru answers him in these words:

द्वे विद्ये वेदितव्ये परा अपरा च।
परा ययैतदक्षरमधिगम्यते। (1.1.3)

(Two *Vidyas* should be known, the *Para* and *Apara*. *Para* is that by which this *Akshara* is known.)

There are again several other *mantras* that guide Gandhiji. His concept 'Truth is God' is very much near these from the *Upanishads*:

(1) सत्यान्नास्ति परो धर्मः।

(There is no *dharma* higher than truth).

(2) सत्येन सत्यं ज्ञातव्यम्। सत्यात्सत्यं प्रवर्तते।

(Truth should be known from truth, Truth arises from Truth.)

(3) सत्यानृते विनिश्चित्य ततो भवति धर्मवित्।

(Once that a man distinguishes between truth and falsehood, he becomes a knower of *Dharma*.)

(4) सत्यं ब्रह्मेत्युपासीत।

(One should worship *Satya* as *Brahma—Shatapatha Brahmana.*)

(5) नास्ति सत्यात्परो धर्मो नानृतात्पातकं परम्।
स्थितिर्हि सत्यं धर्मस्य तस्मात्सत्यं न लोपयेत्।।

(There is no *Dharma* higher than *Satya* and no *Pataka* other than falsehood; *Dharma* is, indeed, firmly established in *Satya*, and so, one should not transgress *Satya.*)

(6) सत्यमेवानृशंस्यं च राजवृत्तं सनातनम्।
तस्मात्सत्यात्मकं राज्यं सत्ये लोकः प्रतिष्ठितः।।

(Only pure *Satya* is the all-time state policy; a state is therefore one that has *Satya* as its very soul. The glory of the world lies in *Satya.*)

(7) सत्यस्य वचनं श्रेयः सत्यज्ञानं तु दुष्करम्।
यद्भूतहितमत्यन्तं एतत्सत्यं ब्रवीम्यहम्।।

(Words of *Satya* lead to bliss and yet knowledge of *Satya* is difficult to be had. I therefore describe the nature of extreme good of living beings.)

It is clear that according to Gandhiji, Truth and God are more or less synonymous terms, and so, his ultimate aim in saying 'Truth is God' instead of 'God is Truth' is to give a doctrine that will be almost universally acceptable. "Whereas he used to say formerly that God is Truth, from a little before 1931, he began to say, Truth is God. The distinction, though subtle, is of a very significant character. With this changed creed, he could easily accommodate as fellow-seekers those who looked on humanity or any other object as their God, and for which they were prepared to sacrifice their all."[40] Even though philosophically, this might lead to so many problems of which probably he might not be conscious, the fact stands that this view has a metaphysical basis. And *Arjuna* is also asked to realize the Truth of life and of all beings, and also to know that the Truth in all beings originates from God the Supreme: "Whatever is glorious, beautiful and mighty, know thou that all such has issued from a fragment of My splendour" (10:41)

So, when Truth becomes one of the very basis of Gandhiji's teachings, it has this support in the *Gita*. However, we cannot claim that Truth as Gandhiji conceives of it is entirely a doctrine of the *Gita* because Gandhiji's concept of Truth is so wide and so unique in its own way that it can be called an original presentation of the ancient doctrine. Truth as Gandhiji conceives of it is not the main problem of the *Gita*. We do not go into a detailed analysis of Truth as Gandhiji conceives it. It is beyond the scope of the persent Thesis. We may, however, add that Gandhiji has made his conception of Truth so wide, both in theory and practice and it is so all-embracing that it is almost indefinable. Yet Gandhiji rightly states that the *Gita* is a sure and constant guide in man's search after Truth. Gandhiji has brought about a unified concept of truth in life, truth in action, truth in conduct and also spiritual truth. It is this unified concept of Truth that leads him to state that शठं प्रति सत्यं कुर्यात् (one shall resort to truth even towards the cunning), and also that Truth and *Ahimsa* are mutually dependent, or, complementary, or say in the highest state, they are almost synonymous. The सत्य (*Satya*) of the *Gita* when he refers to it in the above mentioned verse, is purely a philosophical concept and not as wide as it is with him.

Several writers and scholars have referred to the grand concept of Truth in Gandhiji. To quote just one: "Bereft of Truth, untethered to Truth, the Gandhian teaching is indeed a jumble of unrelated ideas, falling apart like a necklace of pearls of which the thread has snapped. The *sutra* of truth is the thing."[41] Of course Gandhiji's conception of truth is deep rooted in the ancient Indian tradition, but it is rooted more in the *Mahabharata, Ramayana*, *Upanishads*, etc., rather than the *Gita*, inspite of the fact that the *Gita* has been his *Kamadhenu* and it has inveitably answered all his questions and has thus become his infallible guide.

Gandhian Ethics and *Gita*

This will bring us next to Gandhiji's ethics, and the influence of the *Gita* on it. The *Gita* is for Gandhiji a book of daily reference, a sure guide in the conduct of life. We also know that to Gandhiji, means is more important than the end and so, ethics is more important than attainment. It is therefore quite natural that the *Gita* should become his book on ethics of life. Actually to Gandhiji, means itself is almost the end and so, ethics of life for its own sake is the end. For a very long time in his life, he trained himself, to equip himself for higher rise. For a very long time next, he tried to lift the Indian masses higher in attainment and so in ethical attainment, but in the last years when he saw that the masses lag behind far too much, he concentrated mainly on his own ethical attaiment and spiritual rise.

(a) Gandhian Ethics

In order to get a clear perspective of how far the *Gita* has influenced Gandhiji's ethics we should, first of all, know Gandhiji's ethics in brief.

To Gandhiji, a saint and a prophet of peace that he is, religion, ethics and spiritualism are all one. He is in addition to this, a *Hindu* and a *Vaishnava* and Hinduism and Vaishnavism refuse to conceive of religion, ethics and spiritualism in isolation from each other. In a way we can say that according to Gandhiji, religion and ethics are for life and they form a sort of means to the spiritual attainment in form of self-realization that is the end. But as the entire approach of Gandhiji in the realm of spiritualism is through life, he has laid greater stress on religion and ethics than on spiritualism. Gandhiji's approach in this matter is not exactly in line with the view of the Hindu tradition expressed in these words:

प्रयोजनमनुद्दिश्य न मन्दोऽपि प्रवर्तते।

(Even an idler will not become active without reference to the end)

Gandhiji is consistent therefore in his view that all men consciously or unconsciously are seekers after *Moksha* and so, each man should seek perfection; this should be the ultimate aim of his life. This is in line with the famous view of the *Brihadaranyaka Upanishad* that,

न वा अरे सर्वस्य कामाय सर्वं प्रियं भवति,
आत्मनस्तु कामाय सर्वं प्रियं भवति।

(Well, everything is not dear for its own attachment but because all men are seekers after *Atma.*) The meaning is that all men are *Atmakama*, and since Gandhiji sees the essential unity of religion, ethics and spiritualism, he says: "To me God is Truth and love; God is ethics and morality; God is fearlessness. God is the source of Light and Life and yet He is above and beyond all these. God is conscience."[42] He expects not only the learned and enlightened to seek perfection, he seeks perfection for the ordinary men and women also, and this speaks for his infinite faith in man and his ultimate goodness and his inner wonderful potentialities. When he says that *Moksha* is freedom from birth by breaking the bonds of flesh, by becoming one with God,[43] he sees to the possibility of application of this to one and all. Any man can, by a gradual rise, a constant process of sublimation, attain to this state of *Moksha*, self-realization as he has called it. In other words, where there is a will there is a way and the way is shown by Gandhiji. The way is Gandhiji's ethics or ethical religion. He has laid down these as the basic doctrines of his ethical religion:

(1) Pervasive Influence of Religion and Morality.
(2) Individual and Good Life.
(3) Celibacy and Non-possession.
(4) Restraint and Rigoristic Duty.
(5) Ordering Life on Certain Moral Principles.
(6) Individual and Social Life.
(7) Self-toil and Bread-labour.
(8) A Life of Service.

Let us now discuss each one at some length.

(1) Pervasive Influence of Religion and Morality

Gandhiji is very clear and firm in his conviction that religion and morality must pervade all walks of life. Man's life has as its ultimate aim self-realization and self-realization is possible only through a religious and moral life. That explains the all-pervasive influence of morality on man's life. Gandhiji is again clear in his view that the same religious and moral standards are applicable to man's whole life, be it private or public. Man can have no double standards in life. To illustrate, there cannot be different standards of religion and morality in man's personal life and say, in his business. There cannot be double standards in one's family life and say, in politics. If one accepts the principle शठं प्रति सत्यं कुर्यात् as Gandhiji puts it in reply to Tilak's शठं प्रतिशाठ्यं कुर्यात्, it will apply to all phases of life. No life is conceivable without religion and morality on which stands man's life as a human being. And a similar verse in Sanskrit says the same thing when it distinguishes man from an animal:

आहारनिद्राभयमैथुनं च
सामान्यमेतत्पशुभिर्नराणाम्।
धर्मो हि तेषामधिको विशेषो
धर्मेण हीनाः पशुभिः समानाः।।

(Food, sleep, fear and sex-these are common to animals and humans. But in human beings *Dharma* is an added trait, distinction. Men devoid of *Dharma* are on a par with animals.) Similar is the view in the famous line.

धारणाद् धर्ममित्याहुः धर्मो धारयति प्रजाः।

(*Dharma* is sustenance; *Dharma* sustains human beings.) This shows that *Dharma* (i) always supports man as a human being, (ii) it saves man from degenerating into an animal.

(2) Individual and Good Life

When religion and morality pervade man's whole life and his entire existence, it is natural that man will lead a good life, and, in Gandhiji's opinion, a good life is life led on the precepts of *Ahimsa* together with a constant service to the people, to the society. Life is worth living only when it is a life of service to God. And when a man serves society with faith in God, in Truth, it is bound to be a life based on *Ahimsa* that demanded extreme suffering and extreme love for one's fellow men and for all living beings. This is *Ahimsa*. It is known that when Manu gives the general code of conduct —सामासिक धर्म as he calls it— to the Aryas comprising all the four *Varnas*, the first is *Ahimsa*. He says:

अहिंसा सत्यमस्तेयं शौचमिन्द्रियनिग्रहः।
एतं सामासिकं धर्मं चातुर्वर्ण्येऽब्रवीन्मनुः।। (10-63)

(Abstention from injuring (creatures,) veracity, abstention from unlawfully appropriating (the goods of others), purity, and control of the organs, Manu has declared to be the summary of the law for the four castes.)

(3) Celibacy and Non-possession

Now, for a good life based on *Ahimsa* and service to the people, the basic need is twofold: Celibacy (ब्रह्मचर्य) and non-possession (असंग्रह), two factors, the absence of the cultivation of which leads man to a very ordinary, worldly, selfish life full of mortal attachments. The absence of it also drives man away from the very purpose of his life as a human being. Gandhiji took to complete *Brahmacharya* at the age of 37 and in connection with this he writes:

> "*Brahmacharya* means control of the senses in thought, word and deed. Everyday I have been realizing more and more the necessity for restraint . . . There is no limit to the possibilities of renunciation even as there is none to those of *Brahmacharya*. Such *Brahmacharya* is impossible of attainment by limited effort."[44]

He expected all his ideal *satyagrahis* to follow this life of celibacy. Yet, with unique sympathy for the grave limitations of man, he permitted marriage to others though he insisted on restraint in their case also and insisted on absence of carnal enjoyment. He stated that the purpose of sex-life is only procreation and when the purpose is absent, there shall be no sexual enjoyment. This is again in line with the view of *Dharmashastras* as for the married men, Manu writes:

> ऋतुकालाभिगामी स्यात्स्वदारनिरतः सदा।
> पर्ववर्जं व्रजेच्चैनां तद्व्रतो रतिकाम्यया।। (3:45)

"Let (the husband) approach his wife in due season, being constantly satisfied with her (alone); he may also, being intent on pleasing her, approach her with a desire for conjugal union on a religious day excepting the *parvạns* (religious or auspicious days)". He wants such a man to become a *Brahmacharin* in married life. Gandhiji also gives the same view. He calls it 'Married *Brahmacharya*.' He writes: "Thus marriage must be considered to be a sacrament imposing discipline upon the partners, restricting them to the physical union only among themselves and for the purpose only of procreation when both the partners desire and are prepared for it."[45] He is thus in line with the Hindu view, and he takes it logically further when he expresses his strong opposition against the use of contraceptives for birth-control and insists that birth control can be brought about only by self-control.

It is perfectly a moral, religious and idealistic view. It is consistent with his personality and outlook.

(4) Restraint and Rigoristic Duty

Now cultivation of this *Vrata* of celibacy and non-possession in case of *Satyagrahis* and observance of married *Brahmacharya* are not easy. Hindu *Shastras* have constantly preached self-control and Manu, knowing the weakness of man and woman writes:

न जातु कामः कामानामुपभोगेन शाम्यति।
हविषा कृष्णवर्त्मेव भूय एवाभिवर्धते।। (2-94)

(Desire is never extinguished by the enjoyment of desired objects; it only grows stronger like fire (fed) with clarified butter,) and,

अविद्वांसमलं लोके विद्वांसमपि वा पुनः।
प्रमदा ह्युत्पथं नेतुं कामक्रोधवशानुगम्।। (2-218)

(For women are able to lead astray in this world not only a fool, but even a learned man, and (to make) him a slave of lust and anger.) Gandhiji states that for celibacy and married *Brahmacharya* both to be possible, restraint and self-control is absolutely necessary and this will become possible only by rigoristic performance of duty. If a man indulges in constant activity and that too in the nature of duty, i.e., purposeful work and gets almost lost in service to others, this control or restraint is possible. Man becomes man by this control, man will become divine and bathe in favour of God by this. It is clear that this is a real *Purushartha* in life and it makes life really worth living.

(5) Ordering Life on Certain Moral Principles

All this again will be possible only if an individual orders his life according to certain definite moral principles, and, for the sake of clear understanding, Gandhiji bases these on the famous eleven *Vratas* that he has given in accordance with the needs of modern times. If man is clear on these, if he follows these scrupulously, he is a grand success in self-control and that will lead him to success in the higher pursuits of life and he will remain constantly on the path of self-realization. His life will naturally be very simple and a life full of prayer. He will be alert in his restraint and ever humble before God and praying Him ever to be helpful. Such *Vratas* are given by our *Dharmashastras* and when Gandhiji lays down a more rigorous and hard life for the *Satyagrahi*, we find a parallel of it in the more rigorous *Vratas*—duties that Manu lays down for the *Snataka Grihastha*—the educated householder, who has the minimum of rights and enjoys the maximum of duties.

(6) Individual and Social Life

Gandhiji expects that when men follow this way of life and these *Vratas*, naturally enough the relations between individual and individual and individual and society will be most cordial and there will be the minimum of conflicts. It will give rise to a society in which individual and social life will be in tune with each other. Gandhiji believes that if men are more conscious of their duties and less of their rights, there will be no conflict. The ideal of life laid down by Gandhiji is that of all consciousness only of duties. Rights are shared by all if all remain conscious of their duties. But vice versa is not true. The Hindu *Dharmashastras* that describe only duties of man, only his *Dharma*, talk on the same lines. He says: "In *swaraj* based on *Ahimsa* people need not know their rights, but it is necessary for them to know their duties. There is no duty that but creates a corresponding right, and those only are true rights which flow from a due performance of one's duties."[46]

(7) Self-toil and Bread-labour

Naturally this brings in Gandhiji's ideal of self-toil and bread-labour. Gandhiji wanted to establish unity, he wanted to eradicate untouchability, and for this, one programme was dignity of physical labour that leads to self-help. The ideals of self-toil and implied bread-labour are in line with this. Let man not hoard wealth—let the society have no idlers and parasites. All must work and earn their bread by the sweat of their brow. If all work, distinctions between rich and poor, higher and lower, touchable and untouchable, good and bad occupations can be wiped out. Gandhiji of course agrees that any day a *Brahmin* is superior in learning to a *Bhangi*, but this does not establish the all-time superiority of *Brahmin*. This was a revolutionary idea in

India, since it came after centuries. But the idea finds expression in the *Dharmashastras* when Manu lays down dignity of labour and the ideal that man should take the minimum from the society and give the maximum in return. He says:

कुसूलधान्यको वा स्यात्कुम्भीधान्यक एव वा।
त्र्यहैहिको वापि भवेदश्वस्तनिक एव वा।। (4:7)

(He may either possess enough to fill a granary, or a store filling a grain-jar; or he may collect what suffices for three days, or make no provision for the morrow.)

(8) A Life of Service

This is possible only in case of a man whose life is for service to humanity without any sense of high and low. Gandhiji gives a unique ideal when he says: "The human body is meant solely for service, never for indulgence. The secret of happy life lies in renunciation. Renunciation is life. Indulgence spells death."[47] Man see on others as he sees on himself. 'Love thy neighbour as thyself' says the Bible and a famous mantra says:

आत्मत्सर्वभूतेषु यः पश्यति स पश्यति।

(A man who visions all living beings as his own self is the real seer.) And naturally enough this life will lead man to the realization of Truth that is God, and the purpose of his existence as man will be fulfilled. When all behave in this way under the guidance of religion and morality, naturally this will be *Ramarajya* which means in his opinion, sovereignty of the people based on pure moral authority. It is natural that a man whose life is guided by this ethics, will be a real *Purusharthi*, he will remain firm like a rock in the midst of all pains, sorrows, evils and sufferings.

With this discussion on Gandhian Ethics, we now come to the *Gita* and see how far it has influenced Gandhiji's ethics.

(b) Gandhiji's Ethics and *Gita*

When it is claimed that the *Gita* is a dictionary of daily reference, it is clear that it must answer questions of man in matters religious, ethical and also spiritual. "The *Gita* is not an aphoristic work; it is a great religious poem," says Gandhiji and adds: "The deeper you dive into it, the richer the meanings you get. It being meant for the people at large, there is pleasing repetition." This religion is religion of life, an ethical religion. The *Gita* wants that the world order should go on. It states:

एवं प्रवर्तितं चक्रं नानुवर्तयतीह यः।
अघायुरिन्द्रियारामो मोघं पार्थ स जीवति।। (3:16)

(He who does not follow the wheel thus set in motion here below, he, living in sin, satiating his senses, lives, O Partha, in vain,) because world order is divinely ordained. Krishna says:

विष्टभ्याहं इदं सर्वमेकांशेन स्थितो जगत्। (10:42)

(With but a part of Myself I stand upholding this universe,) and

उत्तमः पुरुषस्त्वन्यः परमात्मेत्युदाहृतः।
यो लोकत्रयमाविश्य बिभर्त्यव्ययमीश्वरः।। (15:17)

(The Supreme Being is surely another—called *Parmatma*, who, as the Imperishable *Ishvara*, pervades and supports the three worlds.) The *Gita* again, accepts the four-fold Varna system as a creation of God when it say:

चातुर्वर्ण्यं मया सृष्टं गुणकर्मविभागशः। (4:13)

(The order of the four Varnas was created by Me according to the different *gunas* and *karmas* of each.) It is therefore natural that for man duties are divided according to the Varna. Every man should follow his Varna-duties. We are again told:

स्वधर्ममपि चावेक्ष्य न विकम्पितुमर्हसि। (2:31)

(Again, seeing thine own duty thou shouldst not shrink from it,) and,

स्वधर्मे निधनं श्रेयः परधर्मो भयावहः। (3:35)

(Better is death in the discharge of one's duty; another's duty is fraught with danger.) All this shows that life, society and everything is a creation of God and life should go on. The *Gita* is thus a book of life and it teaches religion and ethics of life. The first rule of ethics of the *Gita* therefore is that the world – order should go on and every man as a rule should contribute to its running and progress by strictly adhering to one's duties as a member of the four-Varna-system that are the most natural to him. When Arjuna the *Kshatriya* is in a predicament, he is asked to offer a heroic fight, to fight his so-called kith and kin. If a Brahmin had been in a similar predicament and had sought Krishna's advice he would have been asked to offer a similar heroic fight but as a Brahmin.

The next ethical rule of the *Gita* is that every one should act first in a spirit of duty, next with detachment that means non-expectation of fruit and then in a spirit of service to the society so that there is unity of mankind. He should in the end become just an instrument in the hands of God and act in a spirit of complete dedication to the Divine. But act one must, be he *a Karma*yogi, *Jnanayogi, Bhakta* or a *Samnyasin*. "Act, one should constantly act, and rise in spiritualism", this is the *Karma* doctrine of the *Gita*. Rightly does Sri Aurobindo state that: "Krishna is his authority in all matters, religious and ethical and it is noticeable that Krishna lays far more stress on action and far less on quienscence than any other Hindu philosopher. Quienscence in God is with him as with others the ultimate goal of existence, but he insists that quienscence must be reached through action, and, so far as this life is concerned, must exist in action...."[48]

The third important doctrine is the cultivation of a spirit of detachment. This establishes that if all were to work only in selfish interest, there would be no happiness in the world and God's work will not go on. One and all, to the best of his or her ability, work in a spirit of detachment from which naturally Gandhiji derives the principle of service to others. If all work in this spirit, all are happy and all attain to bliss and so, this is a law of life. It is an important ethical priniciple.

The next important principle on the basis of this is that for man in the world, work is worship. Self-help, mutual co-operation and interdependence of man on man and man on Gods is the basis on which the Universe works. There should be no disorder, no anarchy and the world should go on from progress to progress. This is possible if men take to the ideal 'work is worship'. Question of course arises as to what the word 'work' means. Gandhiji would call it physical labour, bread-labour and so on. Gandhiji emphasized physical labour because it was looked down upon. But to the *Gita* actually, work can be of all types including intellectual work, and every individual works in accordance with his inherent nature and instincts and rises through them. That is the reason why the *Gita* gives the principle of *Yajna*, of sacrifice that is expected to inspire man to be worshipful in his work and always to remain conscious of the other men in the world for whom he works in addition to working for himself. This is the meaning of

भुञ्जते ते त्वघं पापाः ये पचन्त्यात्मकारणात्। (3:13)

(But the wicked who cook for them-selves eat sin.) All the senses that different scholars arrive at will ultimately come to this: 'work is worship.'

Now the principle 'work is worship' will be successful only if men preferred self-control to indulgence. The ideal laid down by the *Gita* will be successful only if men cultivate a spirit of self-control, the control of the working of the three *Gunas*. It is interesting that the highest stage to be attained in this rise of man is, getting over even the *Sattava Guna*.

त्रैगुण्यविषया वेदा निःस्त्रैगुण्यो भवार्जुन। (2:45)

(The Vedas have as their domain the three *gunas*; eschew them, O Arjuna). After this man controls all dualities and then attains to the stage of समता, the stage of equanimity, and we are told:

समत्वं योग उच्यते। (2:48)

(Even-mindedness is *yoga*.) This is necessary for man's gradual rise as also for the good of the world and it is possible through the cultivation of the spirit 'work is worship'. That is the reason why for this *Yoga* we are told:

योगः कर्मसु कौशलम्। (2:50)

(*Yoga* is skill in action.) The *Gita* again and again talks of self control, the control of the *gunas* and so on.

But this spirit is not easy to attain for all men. That is the reason why, to the ordinary and average man of the world, *Vratas* more than twenty in number, are given. These *Vratas* are described in the sixteenth *Adhyaya*. These are *Vratas* for the uplift of man's personality, for the progress of the world—order, for making man attain to a stage when he will deserve to enter the realm of the spirit. These *Vratas* are necessary partly even after man has risen to the stage of समत्व (Even-mindedness), they are necessary for all who worship God. Krishna says:

> चतुर्विधा भजन्ते मां नराः सुकृतिनोऽर्जुन।
> आर्तो जिज्ञासुरर्थार्थी ज्ञानी च भरतर्षभ।। (7:16)

(Four types of well-doers are devoted to Me. O Arjuna; they are, O *Bharatarashabha*, the afflicted, the spiritual seeker, the material seeker, and the enlightened.)

This attitude is necessary because everyone is expected to fight to protect Truth and *Dharma*, in his own way, under the guidance of one's nature, and with adherence to one's *Varna*-duties,—i.e., duties as a member of the four-*Varna* system. But one must contribute to protect the two great principles of life—truth and *Dharma*. It might mean constant study and teaching and sacrifice etc. for the *Brahmana* and it might mean physical warfare for the *Kshatriya*. We have already seen that *Ahimsa* or *Himsa* is not the problem of the *Gita*, the problem is protection of world-order and for that, protection of Truth and *Dharma*. If a *Kshatriya* gets a chance to fight a *Dharmayuddha*, he must fight it and fight it heroically. The fight is not at all times allegorical.

The cultivation of the spirit of 'work is worship', the spirit of sacrifice and service to all, creates a unique unity of life. That unity is necessary for all individual men, for all society, for man's rise to the Divine. This is लोकसंग्रह (Lok-Sangraha) (welfare of the world) and it is necessary for the welfare of all. And it should be noted that while the *Gita* applies its *Karma-yoga* to all, no one is expected to give up his nature and work. A *Samnyasin* or a *Bhakta*, a *Jnani* or a *Karmi*, any and every man resorts to his own path in a spirit of sacrifice and contributes according to his own nature and with the spirit of *Karma-yoga* asociated with it. In a way this will mean double *Yoga* for all, his *Yoga* of birth and *Varna* and the *Yoga* of *Karma*. For the लोकसंग्रह (Lok-Sangraha) the world needs all the four *Varnas* and *Samnyasins*, *Jnanins*, *Bhaktas* and all. Man is thus to contribute to world-order, to this लोकसंग्रह (Lok-Sangraha) only in accordance with work as per his nature. The concept of *Karma* in the *Gita* is very wide, wide enough to embrace the whole universe.

At the end of all this comes the personal rise of man to self-realization, to *mukti*, and the *Gita* has shown the path of gradual rise of the individual. If we were to treat the *Gita* only as a spiritual or philosophic work as Shankara, Aurobindo etc. do, we will have to concede wrongly that the *Gita*-doctrine applies only to the individual. But we have seen that the *Gita* applies to all, individually, socially and universally and hence this ethics. The ethics of life shown by the *Gita* and to be followed by all individuals, means the rise of man through life to the highest bliss. And even the modes of worship, *Sadhana* and the consequent rewards are varied. This is because the *Gita* enfolds the whole of humanity in its doctrine. To the *Gita*, no creature, howsoever low socially, culturally or intellectually, is lost. All have a right to the blessings of God and by gradual rise to attain to divinity.

If we were to compare this ethics of the *Gita* with that of Gandhiji, we will easily see that the basis of Gandhiji's ethics lies in the *Gita*. The very great value that he attaches to it, the great veneration in which he holds it, is due to this. Even though Gandhiji's is a very great spiritual force, he has yet laid greater stress on religion, ethics and morality. And naturally enough, being the means to the end in form of self-realization, it is derived from the *Gita*. All new things that we find in Gandhiji and do not find in the *Gita*, are due to Gandhiji's peculiar interpretation of the *Gita*. To illustrate, since Gandhiji accepts that the *Gita* teaches *Ahimsa*, when his conception of a religious and good life is that which is based on *Ahimsa*, the doctrine of the ethics can be said to have been based on the *Gita*. To illustrate again, in Gandhiji's ethics, service to humanity as a *Yajna* and the necessity of physical labour and bread-labour find a prominent place. He has read all these in the *Gita* and so, we can say that they are based on the *Gita*.

But we have also seen that Gandhiji's ethics finds many and important parallels in the *Dharmashastra*, the *Manusmriti* in particular. We can therefore say that Gandhiji's ethics has on it a deep stamp of the doctrine of the *Gita* and it is also influnced by the *Dharmashastra* works.

Gita helps Gandhiji

With this discussion we now proceed to examine how and in what conflicting situations and experiences in life the *Gita* has come to Gandhiji's help and has answered all his questions. Actually the *Gita* was his all-time guide and he actually lived the *Gita* we can say, of course as he understood it. But a few important events and situations in which the *Gita* helped Gandhiji may be noted with interest and this might lead us to a better understanding of Gandhiji's interpretation of the *Gita* and also his teachings.

As we proceed in the matter, we may start with a clarification. It is noted that he lived or tried to live according to the teaching of the *Gita*. It would therefore be difficult directly to point out certain incidents of his life in which the *Gita* can be said to have helped him. No incident in his life is bereft of the help of the *Gita*. Again, except for one specific reference, Gandhiji does not point out incidents in which the *Gita* helped and guided him. Still we try to point out a few glaring incidents of the type.

As we have already noted, he got a clear answer from the *Gita* with reference to the problem of untouchability. His mental question was: Was untouchability sanctioned by the *Shastras*? Answers were on both the sides. It is there that the *Gita* gave a clear cut answer to him on the basis of statements like.

स्त्रियो वैश्यास्तथा शूद्रास्तेऽपि यान्ति परां गतिम्। (9:32)

(Women, *Vaishyas*, and *Shudras* too reach the supreme goal,) and also,

समोऽहं सर्वभूतेषु न मे द्वेष्योऽस्ति न प्रियः।
ये भजन्ति तु मां भक्त्या मयि ते तेषु चाप्यहम्।। (9:29)

(I am the same to all beings; with Me there is none disfavoured, none favoured; but those who worship Me with devotion are in Me and I in them.) And also,

अपि चेत्सुदुराचारो भजते मामनन्यभाक्।
साधुरेव स मन्तव्यः सम्यग्व्यवसितो हि सः।। (9:30)

(Even the most sinful, if he turns to Me with undivided devotion, must indeed be counted a saint, for he has settled resolve,) and Gandhiji adds: "The message of the *Bhagavadgita* is: Treat the *Brahmin* and the *Bhangi* alike, if you would but know God. But how are they alike? A *Brahmin* is any day superior to the *Bhangi* in learning, and how am I to treat them both alike? The *Bhagavadgita* says that you should treat them even as you would wish to be treated by them, or even as you would treat yourself:

आत्मवत्सर्वभूतेषु यः पश्यति स पश्यति।''[49]

Here the *Gita* told him that all men are equal, all men deserve the supreme blessings of God, the *Gita* bars no one from divine attainment that he calls self-realization (परां गतिम् here.) This spirit that he derived from the *Gita* made him a life-time servant of and upholder of the rights of the untouchables in particular and the down-trodden of the society in general. He rightly opined that untouchability is a blot on Hindu society and religion and he prided in calling himself a *Bhangi*. Eradication of untouchability is one of the greatest works of Gandhiji and for this he derived justification from the *Gita*.

Extending the argument further, we can say that he became a champion of the rise and rights of women and he did the best he could to make them equal of men by due education, understanding, creation of self-confidence, fearlessness and so on. The *Gita* promises पर गति (higher state of self-realization) to women also.

He was always feeling sorry that now and then he had ill-treated his wife, Kasturaba, though he was always a loving husband. He of course expected the highest sense of sacrifice and detachment from her; a sense of utter service and non-possession from her because she was his wife. But he was extremely kind and fully considerate towards women. He always wanted India''s womanhood to rise to realize its due status, work and duty in society. He wanted women to have due education. He wanted them to become real partners in the lives of their husbands and family; he wanted women to play a leading role in the *satyagraha* movements and in reconstruction of the country and so on. So many of his activities were guided by these ideas. Gandhiji got inspiration for all this probably from the *Gita* that refuses to distinguish between caste and caste as also between man and woman. Its central word is

यो मद्भक्तः स मे प्रियः। (12:14)

(The devotee (*Bhakta*) of Mine is dear to Me.)

He again rushed for service wherever he found sorrow and backwardness; wherever he found the lowly and lost. He embraced them and all the while he was conscious that he was following the word of the *Gita*.

This is not to underrate the other influences, that of Christianity in particular in this work, and of Tolstoy and Thoreau in looking upon all as equals. But it is clear that the greatest and the deepest is the influence of the *Gita* and it is an influence that grew deeper and deeper while the other influences gradually lessened. The story of Gandhiji's life is in a way that of winning back to the Hindu fold a great Hindu, an ideal Hindu, and in this, greatest is the contribution of the *Gita*. He was a *Vaishnava* and as a *Vaishnava* he had a heart that was full of love. He read the same *Vaishnava* doctrine more or less in the *Gita* and with that, both *Ahimsa* and love towards all humanity were natural offshoots. But here, in his grand effort at eradicating untouchability and also championing the cause of the lowly and lost, he gave a new meaning and glory even to Vaishanavism, that was the creed of his birth. Dr. S. Jaiswal states: "However, in the *Gita*, *bhakti* is not simply adoration of the God in utter humility; it is also intellectual conviction and faith. Faith is the basis of religious devotion, so *Bhakti* is devotion which arises out of faith. Hence the godhead declares in the *Gita* that no matter what one believes in, as long as one has faith, he grants him firm devotion and fulfills his desires through the same faith."[50] And it is thus as a *Vaishnava* of first rank that he reads in the *Gita* his coveted doctrine of *Ahimsa* based on love that is the very basis of the life of a *Vaishnava*. This is inspite of the fact that even scholars of Vaishnavism and *Vaishnava*s might refuse to read Gandhiji's doctrine of *Ahimsa* in the *Gita* and state that: "The *Bhagavadgita* mentions it (i.e. *Ahimsa*) thrice (13:7; 16:2; 17:14) as an attribute of knowledge, and a virtue of those who are born to divine estate. But since the main theme of the work is devotion to God, it does not pay much attention to the principle of *Ahimsa*. Perhaps the setting of the poem militated against it, for it is supposed to be an exhortation to a sanguine war and the preaching of non-violence would have been most inopportune."[51]

A real ideal Bhakta who has renounced his whole self, with all his actions in favour of God the Supreme, with all love and devotion, will naturally base his life on a faith that even the worst of the experiences in life cannot shake. The *Gita* had built and nourished that faith in Gandhiji. As a result of this he became firm in his convictions and firm in his faith in God. In fact, he became more and more firm as his faith was tried more and more and Gandhiji suffered, after 1945, experiences that would have shaken to the roots the faith of any man in the world. But Gandhiji nourished greater and greater faith and adoration and love to God, 'Rama' as he called Him, and every bad experience made him conscious of this supremacy of God. This is real *Bhakti*, it is *Bhakti* par excellence and it came to him from the *Gita* and not only made him firm like *Vajra* (Indra's weapon) under all odds, it always showed him way out of the odds. Dr. Jaiswal states: "In the *Bhagavadgita Bhakti* is pure affection for the highest being, who, although he has the whole world within him and is inconceivable, has also a physical adorable form, with whom the devotee may experience a feeling of close intimacy comparable to that between friend and friend, father and son, lover and beloved; but there is no tinge of emotional love. In his fond adoration of the God, the devotee is fully conscious of the God's transcendence and majesty, and craves for his indulgence in all humility. The *Gita* breathes in an atmosphere of awe and respect for the deity, who has a terrific form but condescends to assume a more bearable one for the benefit of his worshipper."[52] Again, she adds: "In the early stages of Vaishnavism, a sense of the devotee's lowliness is an essential ingredient of the concept of *Bhakti*, and seems to reflect the ideology of the ruling classes. The ruling classes of the *Gupta* period express their *Bhakti* to the God in an attitude of service, described as *dasyabhava* (the state of servitude) by later theologians, and generally the relationship of the master and the slave is established between the deity and the devotee."[53] Gandhiji never claimed to become *Brahman* himself. He did not find

ब्रह्मविद् ब्रह्मैव भवति।

(the knower of *Brahman* becomes *Brahman* himself) to be the teaching of the *Gita* when the *Gita* says:

मय्येव मन आधत्स्व मयि बुद्धिं निवेशय।
निवसिष्यसि मय्येव अत ऊर्ध्वं न संशयः।। (12:8)

(On Me set thy mind, on Me rest thy conviction, thus without doubt shalt thou remain only in Me hereafter,)
and,

तस्मात्सर्वेषु कालेषु मामनुस्मर युध्य च।
मय्यर्पितमनोबुद्धिर्मामेवैष्यस्यसंशयः।। (8:7)

(Therefore at all times remember Me and fight on, thy mind and reason thus on Me fixed, thou shalt surely come to Me,) and,

अन्तकाले च मामेव स्मरन् मुक्त्वा कलेवरम्।
यः प्रयाति स मद्भावं याति नास्त्यत्र संशयः।। (8:5)

(And he who, at the last hour remembering Me only, departs leaving the body, enters into Me; of that there is no doubt,) and even,

ब्रह्मार्पणं ब्रह्महविः ब्रह्माग्नौ ब्रह्मणा हुतम्।
ब्रह्मैव तेन गन्तव्यं ब्रह्मकर्मसमाधिना।। (4:24)

(The offering of sacrifice is *Brahman*; the oblation is *Brahman*, it is offered by *Brahman* in the fire that is *Brahman*; thus he whose mind is fixed on acts dedicated to *Brahman* must needs pass on to *Brahman*). In his opinion these verses do no refer to complete identity of *Atma* with *Brahman* but refer to the *Atma* finding an eternal place in the favour of the Lord. It is, we might say 'bathing in sublimity'. By self-realization Gandhiji never meant anything more than this. Even in the last years of his life, he was thoroughly conscious of this and claimed only the eternal favour of God the Supreme. When he said he wanted no rebirth, he meant *Moksha* just in this *Vaishnava* sense. He wanted ever to be conscious of the living presence of God within himself and to work constantly with Him as the witness. He therefore said: "As days pass, I feel this living presence in every fibre of my veins. Without that feeling, I should be demented."[54] And he said: "Inspite of my numerous failings and shortcomings, of which I am but too well aware, my faith in God is burning brighter every day. If it did not, I would. . .commit suicide."[55] And he was confident that: "God is not a person. He is the all-pervading, all-powerful spirit. Anyone who bears Him in his heart has accession of a marvellous force or energy comparable in its results to physical forces like steam or electricity, but much more subtle."[56] All this shows that he did not claim absolute identity with God, he did not want to become God, he could not even conceive of it. The whole attitude as it is, comes from the unique inspiration of the *Gita*, of the *Bhakti-marga* in the *Gita* in particular. This speaks for the new confidence, faith, perfect self-control and a unique personality that the *Gita* gave to Gandhiji.

This is how it helped him and in his life the *Gita* became a unique guide, an unfailing guide, a loving mother that invariably answered to all his calls.

As time passes and there are greater and greater conflicts, more and more trying and shameful incidents, Gandhiji becomes firmer and firmer in his convictions because these convictions have come to him mainly from the *Gita*. Gandhiji becomes more humble and more devoted to God, because the *Gita* taught him to be so. Gandhiji's submission to the Divine comes to its climax with the worst of incidents because the *Gita* taught,

सुखदुःखे समे कृत्वा लाभालाभौ जयाजयौ।
ततो युद्धाय युज्यस्व नैवं पापमवाप्स्यसि।। (2:38)

(Hold alike pleasure and pain, gain and loss, victory and defeat and gird up thy loins for the fight; so doing thou shalt not incur sin,) and he had reached the highest stage of the rise of the *Sthitaprajna* and with this attitude of *Samatva* he fought the fiercest battles of life as a warrior without weapons but in no way lesser than Arjuna. He rose to those heights when he tried to experience that,

आत्मौपम्येन सर्वत्र समं पश्यति योऽर्जुन।
सुखं वा यदि वा दुःखं स योगी परमो मतः।। (6:32)

(He who, by likening himself with others, senses pleasure and pain equally for all as for himself, is deemed to be the highest *yogi*, O Arjuna,) and he tried hard to scale those heights of *Yoga*. His mind was constantly engrossed in God the Supreme and his firm resolve to be absolutely devoted to Him was his supreme happiness. He experienced:

सुखमात्ययन्तिकं यत्तद् बुद्धिग्राह्यमतीन्द्रियम्।
वेत्ति यत्र न चैवायं स्थितश्चलति तत्त्वतः।। (6:21)

(Where he experiences that endless bliss beyond the senses which can be grasped by reason alone; wherein established he swerves not from the Truth) and he was never shaken from that *tattva*. All this attitude came in his life from the *Gita*, and the result of all this was that the conflicts of the worst type, the failings of the saddest order were no conflicts or failings ultimately because he was practising the doctrine and the way of life of the *Gita*. His Krishna or Rama or Allah or Almighty was the supreme ruler of the Universe, the very root of man's humanity. The centre of all activity of man in life was the one to whom he had handed over in entire submission and in perfect humility, his entire self.

That was precisely the reason why Gandhiji stated that: "But if He or It is not this, He or It is. If we exist, if our parents and their parents have ever existed, then it is proper to believe in the Parents of the whole creation. If He is not, we are nowhere. And that is why all of us with one voice call one God differently as *Paramatma, Ishwara, Shiva, Vishnu, Rama*, Allah, Khuda, Dada Hormuzda, Jehovah, God and an infinite variety of names. He is one and yet many. He is smaller than an atom, and bigger than the Himalayas."[57] This is in line with the famous Upanishadic mantra

एकं सद्विप्राः बहुधा वदन्ति।

(God is one and expressed variously by the learned.) And with all faith in Krishna, the Mahatma worshipped Him as this one and called Him '*Rama*', in his last years in particular, though his heart was presided over by the *Gita*. This spirit of wide outlook on God and through Him on humanity at large, his unstinted devotion and adoration for God and through Him his all-embracing love for humanity at large was mainly the inspiration of the *Gita*. The *Gita* in one reference states:

अव्यक्तं व्यक्तिमापन्नं मन्यन्ते मामबुद्धयः।
परं भावमजानन्तो ममाव्ययमनुत्तमम्।। (7:24)

(Not knowing My transcendent, imperishable, supreme character, the undiscerning think Me, who am unmanifest, to have become manifest,) and also,

मया ततमिदं सर्वं जगदव्यक्तमूर्तिना।
मत्स्थानि सर्वभूतानि न चाहं तेष्ववस्थितः।। (9:4)

(By Me, unmanifest in form, this whole world is pervaded; all beings are in Me, I am not in them,) and in that crowning mantra,

उत्तमः पुरुषस्त्वन्यः परमात्मेत्युदाहृतः।
यो लोकत्रयमाविश्य बिभर्त्यव्ययमीश्वरः।। (15:17)

(The Supreme Being is surely another called *Paramatman*, who, as the Imperishable *Ishwara* pervades and supports the three worlds.) Gandhiji, through the inspiration of the *Gita* and through the constant practice of the *Gita* doctrine came to have a unique devotional faith and a spirit of complete unhesitating submission to this God. Gandhiji's

God made Gandhiji what he is and gave to his teachings the value that they hold for India and for humanity at large.

NOTES

1. 'Young India', 6-8-1925.
2. 'Harijan', 24-8-1934.
3. 'Last Glimpses of Bapu', Manubehn Gandhi, 13-1-1948.
4. 'Young India', 6-8-1925.
5. 'Harijan', 24-8-1934.
6. T.K. Mahadevan in 'An Approach to the Study of Gandhi'.
7. The translation is very much free in the last two lines.
8. 'My Experiments with Truth', pt. 1., Ch. 20.
9. 'Young India', 6-8-1925.
10. 'Young India', 25-9-1925.
11. 'Young India', 6-10-1921.
12. 'In Search of the Supreme', Vol. III, p. viii
13. 'My Experiments with Truth', pt. 1., ch. 20.
14. 'Speeches and Writings', p. 338.
15. 'Harijan', 5-12-1936.
16. 'Harijan', 13-1-1940.
17. 'Harijan', 26-9-1936.
18. 'Young India', 22-9-1927.
19. 'Press Report', 4-4-1946.
20. 'Yeravada Mandir', Ch. xv.
21. 'Harijan', 24-2-1946.
22. 'Harijan', 6-2-1937.
23. 'Harijan', 7-4-1946.
24. 'Last Glimpses of Bapu', p.286.
25. 'Harijan', 5-1-1947.
26. 'Harijan', 14-4-1946.
27. In 'Gandhi Memorial Peace Number', Ed. Kshitish Roy, p.13.
28. 'Nehru on Gandhi', Ed. R.J. Walsh, p.23.
29. 'Harijan', 23-6-1946.
30. 'The Lonely Pilgrim', p. 126.
31. 'Last Glimpses of Bapu', p.6.
32. 'Last Glimpses of Bapu', p. 109.
33. 'Harijan', 23-3-1940.
34. 'Harijan', 5-12-1936.
35. 'Young India', 1-10-1925.
36. 'Young India', 9-4-1925.
37. 'Young India', 21-5-1928.

38. 'Last Glimpses of Bapu', on 23-1-1948, p. 245.
39. 'Gandhian Ethics', B.C. Ray, p. 21.
40. 'Studies in Gandhism', N.K. Bose, p. 269.
41. T.K. Mahadevan.
42. 'Young India', 5-3-1925.
43. 'Young India', 20-11-1924.
44. 'My Experiments with Truth'.
45. 'Young India, 20-11-1924.
46. 'Harijan', 25-3-1939.
47. 'Harijan', 24-2-1946.
48. 'Vyasa and Valmiki', p. 41.
49. 'Young India', 13-1-1927. The verse is not found in the *Gita*.
50. 'Origin and Development of Vaishnavism', p. 113.
51. Vide supra, p. 115.
52. Vide supra, p. 112.
53. Vide supra, p. 113.
54. 'Bapu's Letters to Mira', p. 268.
55. 'Harijan', 17-11-1946.
56. 'Harijan', 14-7-1946.
57. 'Young India', 21-1-1926.

EIGHT

Gandhiji's Views Deduced from *Gita*

"All through the long history of mankind the world has been kept from ultimate tragedy and despair of prophetic and symbolic men. Their great and creative function is to see in vision the coming new day whilst the spiritual sleep of the many is still unbroken; and to acclaim the new life whilst others still perceive naught save darkness."

Carl Heath[1]

"Let the *Gita* be to you a mind of diamonds as it has been to me. Let it be your constant guide and friend on life's way. Let it light your path and dignify your labour."

Gandhiji

"The only virtue I want to claim is Truth and non-violence. I lay no claim to superhuman powers. I want none. I wear the same corrupt flesh that the weakest of my fellow-beings wear and I am therefore liable to err as any."

Gandhiji

Introductory

In our discussion in the last three chapters, we examined (i) Gandhiji's Interpretation of the meaning of the *Gita*, (ii) the part that the *Gita* and Hinduism played in his life and how the world got the great man that he became, and, (iii) how at most critical and conflicting times the *Gita* came to his rescue and guided him and how it has answered his questions. We now come to some very important views that he has read in the *Gita*. We have referred to his *Vaishnavism* and discussed it in details. Very often he referred to his *Vaishnava* heritage. To give one such illustration: "What was the explanation of his strength of character? Gandhi told my husband of his *Vaishnava* mother and of her influence on his life."[2] As a follower of Vaishnavism in theory and practice he read his views in the *Gita*; he has also read and derived from the *Gita* his favourite and basic principle of *Ahimsa*. He has also stated that the works like the *Mahabharata*, *Ramayana*, *Gita* etc., should be read as allegories. The views are mutually dependent. Again, his definition of the ideal *Bhakta* is uniquely original. To him, the *Sthitaprajna*, *Jnani*, *Karmayogi*, *Bhakta* and *Trigunatita* are all the same. Of all these words however, he has again and again preferred to use the word '*Sthitaprajna*' as expressing his ideal. He refuses to worry about the technical and minute distinctions amongst these. Even for the votary of *Ramnama* that he became, particularly in his last years, he held the same view. A devotee of *Rama* in the real sense of the term, was to him a *Sthitaprajna*. To put in his own words: "Thus a devotee of *Rama* might be said to be an embodiment of the ideal of *Sthitaprajna*—man with steady and balanced intellect—described in the *Gita*."[3]

We now examine these and some other minor but important views in the light of the *Gita* itself and examine how far Gandhiji's views stand the test of correctness and exactness from the viewpoint of the *Gita* as it is. For his whole life, he again and again approached the *Gita* to ascertain the correctness of his views. We follow the same method and see what the *Gita* has to say on his views. He was consciously trying and striving to come nearer to the ideal of the *Bhakta* and *Sthitaprajna* of the *Gita*. To illustrate from 'The Last Phase': "A couple of days ago he had waked up earlier than usual owing to some mental worry." Referring to it he remarked: "I did not like it. It only shows how far I am from the ideal of unruffled equipoise described in the *Gita*. But I feel I am daily nearing it."[4]

We examine his views in the following order:

(i) *Mahabharata*, *Ramayana* and *Gita* are allegorical.
(ii) The *Gita* teaches *Ahimsa*.
(iii) Bread-labour and *Gita*.
(iv) Other minor questions.

We study these in detail and after first laying down each view from the point of view of Gandhiji, examine it from *Gita*'s point of view.

Mahabharata, *Ramayana* and *Gita* are allegorical

Tradition has known the epic works *Mahabharata* and *Ramayana* as '*Itihasa*, history' even though it is too well-known that India has not given any work that is historical in the real sense of the term, even in the sense of the word '*Itihasa*' itself, when we analyse it as '*Iti ha asa*," "So it was." Fact and fiction have always been combined and inseparable in these two works and besides the grand exaggeration that results from the lofty imagination of the sage poets *Vyasa* and *Valmiki*, particularly about the *Mahabharata* it is known that so much of matter has continued to be added to the original, whatever it was, that even if the original work '*Jaya*' was composed by the fictitious and mythological sage *Vyasa*, it is now impossible to separate this '*Jaya*' from the vast ocean that the *Mahabharata* is, with its high mountain tops and deep valleys from the viewpoint of literary merit. But with all this, scholars acknowledge that some sort of history is there in the background; that some battle, may be on a lesser scale, was actually fought and it is also known that *Krishna*, *Bhishma*, etc., are characters that can be traced even in the remote Vedic literature. This shows that there is historical element in the *Mahabharata* and so, in the *Ramayana*.

(a) The *Mahabharata*

Gandhiji specifically refuses to look upon these works as historical and insists on interpreting the two as allegories. To express in his own words: "But to me, the *Mahabharata* is a profoundly religious book largely allegorical, in no way meant to be a historical record. It is the description of the eternal duel going on within ourselves, given so vividly as to make us think for the time being that the deeds described therein were actually done by the human beings. Nor do I regard the *Mahabharata*, as we have it now, as a faultless copy of the original. On the contrary, I consider that it has undergone many amendations."[5] That the present *Mahabharata* is not the original and that it has undergone many amendations is a matter beyond doubt and tradition as also scholars accept this. It is also accepted by scholars that besides amendations, countless additions of all sorts have taken place in it, so much so that it covers up almost all knowledge of the ancient days and tradition has glorified the work with unique remarks. But Gandhiji goes a step further and says that the *Mahabharata* is not a historical work in any way, and he is so firm on his stand that he adds: "But if it was proved to me that the *Mahabharata* is history in the same sense that modern historical books are, that every word of the *Mahabharata* is authentic and that the *Krishna* of the *Mahabharata* actually did some of the acts attributed to him, even at the risk of being banished from the Hindu fold, I should not hesitate to reject that *Krishna* as God-incarnate."[6] This shows Gandhiji's revolutionary spirit and insistence on following only what his conscience accepts. It also shows that Gandhiji's conception of *Krishna* is far higher.[7] And we have seen that without any hesitation whatsoever, Gandhiji gives his revolutionary or new views whenever he should. But in the present context, for our purpose, the important fact is that Gandhiji is not prepared to read the *Mahabharata* as history. It is also true that in the *Mahabharata*, history is intermixed with fiction, and that tradition has accepted *Mahabharata* as authentic, and has accordingly played a very important part in shaping the cultural life of India, is something that cannot be denied; even Gandhiji would not deny it. He in another reference again adds: "*Mahabharata* is neither fiction nor history commonly so called. It is the history of the human soul in which God, as *Krishna*, is the chief actor."[8] He has again stated that "The *Mahabharata* and the *Puranas* are neither history nor simple religious maxims. They appear to me to be wonderfully designed to illustrate the religious history of man in a variety of ways."[9] So, it has been his constant stand that "The *Mahabharata* and the *Ramayana*, the two books that millions of Hindus know and regard as their guides, are undoubtedly allegories as the internal evidence shows. That they, most probably, deal with historical figures does not affect my proposition. Each epic describes the eternal duel that goes on between the forces of Darkness and of Light. Anyway, I must disclaim any intention of straining the meaning of Hinduism or the *Gita* to suit any preconceived notion of mine. My notions were an outcome of a study of the *Gita*, *Ramayana*, *Mahabharata*, Upanishads, etc."[10] Actually, the claim of not straining the meaning of the *Gita* to suit their preconceived notions is made by all the *Acharyas*, (commentators) beginning from Shankara, and Gandhiji is just in line with the other great commentators. All claim to interpret *Gita* the best and originally and so does Gandhiji put his claim: "I ascribe to the *Gita*, a totally different meaning from that ordinarily given. I do not regard it as a description of, or an exhortation to, physical warfare. And, in any case, it is God the All-knowing, who descends on the earth to punish the wicked."[11] And even earlier he had stated that: "I venture to submit that the *Bhagavad Gita* is a Gospel of non-co-operation between the forces of darkness and those of light. If it is to be literally interpreted, *Arjuna*, representing a just cause was enjoined to engage in bloody warfare with the unjust *Kauravas*."[12] Unfortunately Gandhiji has not given his internal evidence when he refuses to accept the *Mahabharata* either as history or fiction and only as an allegory and a work intended by the poet to be an allegory. He has, however, tried to give one or two hints in his statement that: "I do not regard the *Mahabharata* as a historical work in the accepted sense. The *Adiparva* contains powerful reference in support of my opinion. By ascribing to the chief actors superhuman or subhuman origins, the great *Vyasa* made short work of the history of kings and their peoples. The persons therein described may be historical, but the author of the *Mahabharata* has used them merely to drive home his religious theme."[13] But he has given many statements to show what that allegory means to him. Gandhiji's is not the method of a scholar being guided by historical and other evidence and following critical and analytical method. It cannot be expected to be so, he is not trained that way. But the finest thing about his views is that he speaks what his conscience accepts and he speaks in no unclear terms. This is the method of a saint, a prophet, and not that of a trained philosopher. He explains the allegory in this way. In explaining the allegory in the *Mahabharata*, he first of all asks: "And who are *Dhritarashtra* and *Yudhishthira* and *Arjuna*? Who is *Krishna*? Were they all historical characters? And does the *Gita* describe them as such?"[14] He then proceeds to answer the question thus: "I regard *Duryodhana* and his party as the baser impulses in man, and *Arjuna* and his party as the higher impulses."[15] So the *Mahabharata*, as a grand religious work describes the battle of life, the battle between right and wrong, the battle between truth and untruth, the battle between *Dharma* and *Adharma*. Gandhiji is particularly interested in the sum total of its teaching. He therefore states: "The heroes described therein are all imperfect mortals, even as we are; the difference being one of degree only. Their alleged actions are not infallible guides for us. The *Mahabharata* sums up its teaching by declaring emphatically that Truth outweighs everything else on earth."[16] So, in the fight, in the eternal duel that is described in the *Mahabharata*, Gandhiji holds the supreme faith that ultimately Truth will win, and that is precisely the reason why he values the *Mahabharata* very greatly. He states: "It is a mine which needs to be explored, which needs to be dug deep and from which diamonds have to be extracted after removing much foreign matter."[17] Gandhiji is naturally interested in the diamonds and not the foreign matter and he strives hard to extract the diamonds. He therefore elaborates the point in these words: "The *Mahabharata* depicts for all time the eternal struggle that goes on daily between the forces of good and evil in the human breast and in which, though good is ever victorious, evil puts up a brave show and baffles even the keenest conscience. It shows also the only way to right action."[18] Similar is the view of Manu who asks man to resort to *Dharma* at all costs, when he says:

> अधर्मेणैधते तावत्ततो भद्राणि पश्यति।
> ततः सपत्नान् जयति समूलस्तु विनश्यति।। (4.174)

(A man grows by *Adharma* and then sees good; then he conquers his enemies, but (in the end) he is destroyed to his very roots.) And this is because,

> नाधर्मश्चरितो लोके सद्यः फलति गौरिव।
> शनैरावर्तमानस्तु कर्तुर्मूलानि कृन्तति।। (4.172)

(Unrighteousness, practised in this world, does not at once produce its fruits, like the earth; but, advancing slowly, it cuts off the roots of him who committed it,)

and,

> यदि नात्मनि पुत्रेषु न चेत्पुत्रेषु नप्तृषु।
> नत्वेव न कृतोऽधर्मः कर्तुर्भवति निष्फलः।। (4.173)

(If (the punishment falls) not on (the offender) himself, (it falls) on his sons, if not on the sons, (at least) on his grandsons; but an iniquity (once) committed, never fails to produce fruit to him who wrought it.)

The view reflects the eternal faith, the unstinted faith, that sages and prophets have in the ultimate goodness of man, and their unique hope that at last, man will be on the right path and there will be eternal peace and universal brotherhood on earth; the earth will become heaven itself. When it is stated in the *Gita* that,

> ऊर्ध्वं गच्छन्ति सत्त्वस्थाः मध्ये तिष्ठन्ति राजसाः।
> जधन्यगुणवृत्तिस्थाः अधो गच्छन्ति तामसाः।। (14:18)

(Higher rise those steady in *Sattva*, they stray in the middle who are governed by *Rajas* and through association with the lower traits, those under the influence of *Tamas* go down in darkness,) this depicts the reality of human nature. But to the sages, even if this be the truth, it is only transitory and a day will come, when, with the blessings of God, men will rise higher and higher in divine blessings and there will be eternal bliss. That explains man's faith in God, his devotion and all higher pursuits that he resorts to; that also explains the words of the 'Holy Bible'—"Man does not live by bread alone but by every word that proceedeth from the mouth of God"; that explains how man is nearest to God and far higher than the animal world.

Gandhiji feels that the belief in incarnation and the perfect incarnation of *Krishna* are indicative of this spiritual ambition of man. To put in Gandhiji's words: "This belief in incarnation is a testimony of man's lofty spiritual ambition. Man is not at peace with himself till he has become like unto God. The endeavour to reach this state is the supreme, the only ambition worth having. And this is self-realization."[19] And the *Mahabharata* is naturally an allegory on these lines. Its purpose is to take man to these divine heights. It is quite natural of the personality and outlook of Gandhiji that he must read this and only this in the work ascribed to *Vyasa*, the sage of all sages. He would read the same in the *Ramayana*.

And for the great sage *Vyasa* it is stated rightly by a famous Sanskrit poet:

> व्यासः क्षमाभृतां श्रेष्ठः
> वन्द्य सः हिमवानिव।
>
> (नलचम्पू 20)

(*Vyasa* is the best of the supporters of the earth, he is venerable like the Himalayas).

It is natural that Gandhiji should read this noble allegorical meaning in the valued works of these great sages.

(b) The *Gita*

Once that Gandhiji takes the *Mahabharata* as an allegory, it is natural that he should take the *Gita* also as an allegory. He states: "Even in 1888-89, when I first became acquainted with the *Gita*, I felt that it was not a historical work, but that under the guise of physical warfare, it described the duel that perpetually went on in the hearts of mankind, and that physical warfare was brought in merely to make the description of the internal duel more alluring."[20] The whole interpretation in '*Anasaktiyoga*', Gandhiji's translation and most of his other writings take this stand. He has clarified and elaborated the view time and again. He states: "It deals with the eternal duel between good and evil. And who does not, like *Arjuna*, often quail when the dividing line between good and evil is thin and when the right choice is so difficult?"[21]

Catlin elaborates the matter thus: "Others, and the *Mahatma* is among these, have seen the *Gita* as a spiritual allegory. The conflict to which *Arjuna* is urged by the Lord *Krishna* is a spiritual conflict against the ranks of the evil passion. They are his own, within a man's own breast; and it is his duty to fight them, against this which is part of his very self."[22] To Gandhiji therefore, just like the *Mahabharata*, the *Gita* is also a work that is allegorical and meant to give the same lesson that such works give. He therefore defends this interpretation now and again. He claims that he is rightly interested in the spirit of the work and not the letter. He says: "Many of us make the very serious mistake of taking literally what is accepted as scriptures, forgetting that the letter killeth and the spirit giveth life."[23] He has, throughout his life and consistently too, resorted to the spirit of all the scriptures that he read and not the letter. His conscience thus rejects so many things from these various scriptures and yet, due to their spirit he glorifies them. Consistently with his personality, he even revises his views and fearlessly accepts corrections on himself whenever found necessary. This attitude also helps him in finding out the best in the scriptures. So, after taking this stand on the *Gita*'s allegory, he elaborates the argument thus: "All the names given in the first chapter of the *Gita* are, in my opinion, not so much proper nouns as names of qualities. In describing the eternal warfare between the heavenly and the devilish natures, the poet has personified them as the characters in the *Mahabharata*."[24]

And here Gandhiji's approach is of faith and conscience and acceptance first by the heart. It is likely that the approach might not always be found rational, critical and analytical by scholars. But Gandhiji frankly states: "I know that ultimately one is guided not by the intellect, but by the heart. The heart accepts a conclusion for which the intellect subsequently finds the reasoning. Argument follows conviction. Man often finds reason in support of whatever he does or wants to do."[25] Gandhiji can adopt only this attitude because all that he reads, understands and accepts is for adoption in action life. To him religion, ethics and philosophy are not only for study but for adoption in life, and not merely for belief and opinion. He has his own peculiar heritage and he has lived in an environment that has shaped his convictions, which have been strengthened by a prayerful study of scriptures of different religions of the world. Ultimately he has accepted only what his faith and conviction approve. Gandhiji after this, is adept in finding out arguments in support of his views. It is therefore natural of him to say that: "I regard *Duryodhana* and his party as the baser impulses in man and *Arjuna* and his party as the higher impulses. The field of battle is our own body. An eternal battle is going on between the two camps and the poet-seer has vividly described it. *Krishna* is the Dweller within, ever whispering in a pure heart. Like the watch, the heart needs the winding of purity or the Dweller ceases to speak."[26] Consistent with this attitude, Gandhiji explaining the first verse of the *Gita* states: "The human body is the battle-field where the eternal duel between Right and Wrong goes on. Therefore it is capable of being turned into the gateway to freedom. The Kauravas represent the forces of Evil, the Pandavas of good. Who is there that has not experienced the daily conflict within himself between the forces of Evil and the forces of Good?" (*Gita* According to Gandhi, p. 132). He has also stated in another context: "The *Gita* is not a historical discourse. A physical illustration is often needed to drive home a spiritual truth. It is not the description of war between cousins but between the two natures in us—the good and the evil". (Quoted by Mahadev Desai, p. 133). The position taken clarifies that from Gandhiji's point of view, the physical warfare is not important, Arjuna is not just an individual, the *Gita* is not written to exhort Arjuna to fight the physical battle; actually the *Gita* has much more to state. The *Gita* takes man at the unique moment of unparalleled conflict when he is at the cross-roads between right and wrong due to several attachments. He is unable to decide as to what course of action he should adopt. It is here that the *Gita* becomes a guide-book on life; a true and all-time guide in matters pertaining to religion, ethics and spiritualism. He says: "But it is well-known that I have never looked upon the *Mahabharata* as a mere record of earthly warfare. In the garb of an epic the poet has described the eternal warfare within the individual as well as in society, between Truth and Untruth, Violence and Non-violence, Right and Wrong".[27] This clarifies his stand on the matter fully.

(c) The Analysis

If the *Gita* were to be written only to exhort Arjuna to fight, it would better have not been written at all, or, Krishna could have adopted any other method to force him to battle. Again, it is Krishna, accepted by Hindu cultural tradition as a *Poorna Avatara*, who is the speaker, the Guru, who is there to save Arjuna at the most critical juncture of his life. The *Gita* has a long discussion between Arjuna the pupil and Krishna the teacher, that has nothing to do with war and everything to do with religion, ethics and spiritualism, or, to state in brief, with philosophy of life. *Acharyas* and scholars are therefore always inclined to take the other meanings, and Sanskrit scholars and pundits accept it as an allegory. We might even say that there is an allegory in the *Gita* and even that the allegory is more important than fact, than history; this would be rather going too far and even twisting the facts. Facts testify that Arjuna and Krishna are constantly before our eyes, we always remember that we are on the battle-field. But to that we shall refer in detail in the next section. Here it would be enough to state that the allegory is there and the facts on which it is based are also there. One of the purposes of Krishna is to make Arjuna fight,. but only after he has been sublimated to the highest philosophical heights.

The physical warfare therefore, and the reality of life—may be history or fiction or partly history and partly fiction—cannot escape our eyes. If at the end of the teaching, Arjuna as a *Kshatriya* has not fought the physical battle, in a spirit of detachment, as a duty, as an order of the Divine, in a spirit of submission to the Divine will, in the spirit only to protect the right and Dharma, then, it is a fact that the whole teaching has gone in vain. So, even if the allegory is there, reality of life or history and fiction modelled on reality of life is there glaringly before our eyes. The *Gita* is not just an allegory and that only.

This stand is all the more important with reference to the whole of the *Mahabharata*. That it is fiction is a matter beyond doubt. It is also true that countless later stories by poets of higher or lower calibre have been added to the bulk of the original, whatever it was. As we saw earlier, the work has developed and expanded in such a way that it is not possible to find out the original, named by tradition as 'Jaya' and ascribed to the fictitious sage Vyasa, from the vast ocean. The characters of the *Mahabharata* are so well-known and found in so many works even other than the *Mahabharata* and the family of the *Kauravas* is such that the work is history. If it is not, it is definitely fiction and the most probable fact is that it is fact and fiction combined, or, it is an exaggerated poetic account of some lesser history. It is possible that the account of the *Mahabharata* has, in its background, some sort of war that did actually take place. In those old days when these historical epics were written, history was supposed to be as the basis. We might therefore concede that the *Mahabharata* is not history in the modern sense; but we must also concede that history is, in all probability at the root of the narration. There is of course no harm in taking the *Mahabharata* as an allegory, but it should be taken as an allegory based on both. Taking the work as an allegory, as some others have also hinted, it should not make us devalue the highly imaginative and lofty work of fiction that the *Mahabharata* is. Again, simply because the work is ascribed to a great sage of the hoary past, the fictitious Vyasa, it should not compel us into the belief that he intended the work to be only an allegory by which he intends to give a lesson about life. The allegorical meaning cannot be contradicted, but probable history and definite fiction can also not be stated not to exist. Vyasa as a sage no doubt intends to give a unique vision of life when he creates the worst of tragedies that the world has ever known; he intends that man should take a lesson from it. But actually he wants, as it seems, to stress: "This is life with all its tragedy and complete lack of self-control and non-cultivation of ennobling virtues;" he tells man as if, "Man, know thyself." Even the victor is put by Vyasa in such a dreadful plight that all the charm of victory is robbed of him, and Gandhiji is right in stressing that: "The author of the *Mahabharata* has not established the necessity of physical warfare; on the contrary, he has proved its futility. He made the victors shed tears of sorrow and repentance, and has left them nothing but a legacy of miseries."[28] But for all this, it is necessary that we accept the *Mahabharata* as describing the real battle of worldly life together with all its tragedy. It is necessary that we take the *Mahabharata* as either history or as fiction based on some reality of life. For deriving all that we do from the *Mahabharata*, we have to take this stand.

(d) Further Analysis

Again, it is difficult to accept Gandhiji's argument that "the *Adiparva* contains powerful evidence in support of my opinion. By ascribing to the chief actors superhuman or subhuman origins, the great *Vyasa* made short work of the history of kings and their peoples. The persons therein described may be historical, but the author of the *Mahabharata* has used them merely to drive home his religious theme." Merely because superhuman or even subhuman origin or even superhuman powers are ascribed to certain of the persons described, it would be too much to say that the author of the *Mahabharata* intends to use history not as history but only as an allegory. This is because it was the tendency on part of poets of all sorts in those days to exaggerate matters and even to write what might be unbelievable or inconceivable. Valmiki, Kalidasa, and others in India in those days and the Greek poets in ancient days have done the same and yet we do not take their works merely as an allegory or even allegory based on fact. Allegorical interpretation cannot be given to all, at the cost of reality.

And even if we do not insist on reading the *Mahabharata* only as an allegory, the work continues to be a religious poem. Actually, it is necessary that we read the work as reality of man's life, be it history or fiction based on reality, in order to bring home to man the lesson that the author wants to give. Even if we read this as a religious poem, it is a religious poem based on reality of life and, as Sanskrit poetics states, epic works like the *Mahabharata*, *Ramayana*, etc., give lessons to man like a friend unlike the Vedas etc., ordering like masters and great poetic works giving lessons of good behaviour in life like a beloved wife. We read the *Ramayana* and automatically take a lesson

"We should behave like *Rama* and not like *Ravana*,

रामादिवद्वर्तितव्यं न रावणादिवत्।" (काव्यप्रकाश-1)[29]

and so take a lesson "We should behave like the Pandavas and not like the Kauravas." For this, we have to treat the *Mahabharata* as reality.

And actually Gandhiji has accepted more than once that the works *Mahabharata* and the *Gita* can be works referring to historical characters. To put in his own words: "Not that actual physical battle is out of the question." (Young India, 6-8-1931) and "This does not imply a refusal to believe that an actual battle took place at *Hastinapur* between the Pandavas and the Kauravas. I hold that the poet took some such actual event as the thread upon which to hang his discourse. Again, if all the names given are the names of real historical characters, the poet has done nothing improper in giving the list at the historical beginning." (Diary of Mahadev Desai, p. 172) And, "That they, most probably, deal with historical figures does not affect my proposition."

So, with reference to the allegory in the *Mahabharata* and the *Gita*, we should better take the following stand in order to be nearer to reality:

(i) The works can be interpreted as allegories.

(ii) But the author also, probably mainly, intends to depict them as history and reality of life.

(iii) Accepting the *Mahabharata* as history and reality is necessary to bring out the religious lessons and the lessons about life that the author wants to give.

(iv) As we shall see later, even for deriving the lessons intended to be given by the author as Gandhiji reads them, it is necessary that we accept *Mahabharata* as history and reality.

(v) For understanding the exact preaching of Krishna to Arjuna, we have to understand and appreciate the stand that he takes. For this, we have to understand the conflict that he is placed in and for this we have to take the battle of the *Mahabharata* in the first chapter of the *Gita* as reality.

(vi) So, the author intends to give this work as reality, though it can be interpreted as an allegory as Gandhiji does. But the fact stands that the author did not mean to give it *only* as an allegory as Gandhiji contends.

Gita and *Ahimsa*

"We shall be able to appreciate your meaning of the message of the *Gita*, only when we are able to study a translation of the whole text by yourself, with the addition of such notes as you may deem necessary. I do not think it is just on your part to deduce *Ahimsa* etc., from stray verses." So said Swami Anand to Gandhiji and accepting the rightness of his argument, Gandhiji started his translation to which later on he also added his *Anasaktiyoga* written in almost sutra-style. (Introduction to *Anasaktiyoga*, *Gita according to Gandhi*–p. 125) In this introduction to his translation Gandhiji states: "But it may be freely admitted that the *Gita* was not written to establish *Ahimsa*." He yet hurries to add that "it was an accepted and primary duty even before the *Gita* age." He has argued out his view of the lesson of the *Gita* and has, after accepting this, stated: "The *Gita* had to deliver the message of renunciation of fruit. This is clearly brought out as early as in the second chapter." But he opines that it is possible to deduce *Ahimsa* from the *Gita* and also that in order to follow the doctrine of detachment or renunciation of the fruit of action, man has to accept the principle of *Ahimsa*. He therefore says: "Thinking along these lines, I have felt that in trying to enforce in one's life the central teaching of the *Gita*, one is bound to follow Truth and *Ahimsa*. When there is no desire for fruit, there is no temptation for untruth or *himsa*." In his opinion, as enunciated in his *Anasaktiyoga* thus, the *Gita* has indirectly accepted the principle of *Ahimsa*, or, to put it otherwise, the *Gita* in its enunciation of the teaching, basically takes for granted the ancient and all-time principle of *Ahimsa*. It is an essential part of the very teaching of the *Gita* in Gandhiji's opinion, and a very important one at that.

Gandhiji and *Ahimsa*

But, before we go into the details of Gandhiji's stand with regard to reading the doctrine of *Ahimsa* in the *Gita*, we should proceed to understand the word *Ahimsa* from Gandhiji's point of view. Various religions and cultures have defined the word *Ahimsa* variously. To illustrate, the implications of the word are different in Hinduism, Buddhism and Jainism, and so in Christianity. We know that in Christianity non-violence is an important doctrine. Actually the presence of a sheep in company of Lord Jesus Christ should indicate non-hurt to and absolute non-violence towards all animals and also at large to all living beings. But in Christianity, the doctrine is unfortunately confined to the world of human beings and when the Bible states "Love thy neighbour as thyself" and gives its fine definition of the neighbour in the famous 'Parable of the Good Samaritan' and so on, this non-violence is confined to man not hurting man in any way, though general non-violence towards animals is also referred to. Again, when we get unique utterings of the type: "If anyone smites thee on thy right cheek, turn to him the other also" (in 'The Holy Bible') and so on, this attitude of self-sacrifice and experiment of change of heart through self-suffering also refers to the general non-violence in the world of human beings. The story of the 'Prodigal Son' would refer to a feast given by the father in honour of his son with the roasting of a sheep and other illustrations may also be cited.

The life of *Mahavira* is an ideal illustration for the Jainas in not only not resisting evil, but also in loving the enemy and wishing him well and experimenting on bringing about a change of heart in the most unenlightened and downtrodden. Absolute non-violence in all walks of life and universal love for all living beings are where Jainism is far ahead of Christianity that advises men in their relation with men "Ye, resist not evil" and "Love your enemies, bless them that curse you" and so on. That is why the ideal mental state to be reached by a man practising non-violence is the stage of *Samyaktva*. "According to Jainism, a person who has *Samyaktva*, always abstains from causing evil, suffering, pain and harm to others. He answers the vehemence of evil, by good and love."[30] This is the other extreme that shows the non-violence of and love towards all the living beings—the lower ones in particular—in Jainism and this has gone a long way in giving to Gandhiji his concept of non-violence. He yet goes far ahead of Jainism, to the extent of making non-violence, Truth, and love almost synonymous terms, even though to him Truth is superior to non-violence and he has passed his whole life in a constant quest after Truth. To put in his own words: "Truth is the same thing as *moksha*. Anyone who does not display *agraha* for *moksha* is no man; he is only a brute,"[31] and, "As I proceed in my quest for truth, it grows upon me that truth comprehends everything. I often feel that *ahimsa* is in truth, not vice versa—out of truth emerges love and tenderness."[32]

He of course in later life and particularly in his last years found Truth and non-violence to be almost identical. He stated once: "When I look for *ahimsa* truth says, find it through me. When I look for truth, *ahimsa* says, find it through me."

Buddhism is also very near this approach of not resisting evil that Gandhiji has interpreted as resisting evil by good, an approach that makes *Ahimsa* a positive approach, an approach of love and tenderness towards all who are God's creation, i.e., creation of Truth. To put in his own words: "Resist not evil meant that evil was not to be repelled by evil, but by good; in other words, physical force was to be opposed not by its like but by soul-force." (*Speeches and Writings of M.K. Gandhi*, p. 99). This is nicely described in that fine verse from *Dhammapada*:

अक्कोधेन जिने कोधं असाधूं साधुना जिने।

(One should conquer anger by absence of anger and a bad man by goodness).[33]

This naturally goes further than what Tolstoy states: "'Resist not him that is evil' means 'never resist him that is evil' that is, never do violence, never do an act that cannot but be contrary to love, and if they then insult you, bear the insult and still do not inflict violence on anyone else."[34]

Now, just like Gandhiji's conception of Truth, his conception of *Ahimsa* is also almost indefinable. Just as Truth is not only philosophical and theoretical, so his conception of *Ahimsa* is not just philosophical but also experimented upon in life. It is far wider a concept than we can ordinarily suppose it to be. It is thus very difficult to know as to from where exactly Gandhiji derived this concept. Gandhiji is a *Vaishnava* and "Vaishnavism asks its followers to meet evil by good. We all know how Chaitanyadeva, an apostle of Vaishnavism, exclaimed when violently struck by a ruffian, 'But I shall offer you my love.' The history of Vaishnavism is a chequered career of evils appearing on the path of good but melting away at its very touch."[35] So, Vaishnavism has definitely inspired him. Yet, Gandhiji's *Ahimsa* does not end here. It goes far ahead and embraces the mundane world, the mental world and also the spiritual world. It is physical, mental, emotional and spiritual non-violence to the full. It applies to the whole life not only of man but the entire world of living beings. It therefore becomes easy for all religions to claim to have inspired Gandhiji in his creed of *Ahimsa*. But it is too well-known that not only Hinduism, but also Jainism and Buddhism did not prevent kings from waging wars or punishing the criminals. We can hardly cite the illustration of any ascetic or saint to have asked a king not to wage war, or not to punish criminals or anything of the kind. In addition to being a general policy of non-hurt to animals and human beings in the normal course of life, the doctrine of *Ahimsa* in Hinduism, Jainism and Buddhism has been a doctrine that is mainly spiritual and therefore mainly applicable to the *Samnyasins* and sages. Even though both Jainism and Buddhism strongly protested against animal sacrifice that the Hindu *shastras* taught, the creed has been mainly spiritual in both religions. Not so with Gandhiji, who denies to a really non-violent man, not only all non-vegetarian food, but goes to the extent of refusing even milk to himself on the ground that even milk is a non-vegetarian food. Hinduism states:

अद्रोहेणैव भूतानामल्पद्रोहेण वा पुनः।
या वृत्तिस्तां समास्थाय विप्रो जीवेदनापदि।। (मनु 4-2)

(A *Brahmana* must seek a means of subsistence which either causes no pain or at least little pain (to others) and live by that except in times of distress.)[36] This implies that in times of crisis like starvation, man might resort to any means of maintenance. Gandhiji would of course reject this altogether, and whether in normal times or in times of crisis, he would desire to practise non-violence. But here also, as in the other doctrines, Gandhiji bases himself on the ancient Hindu tradition, as we can guess from the manner in which he associates *Ahimsa* with Truth that is God, and the conception of Truth and God is known to have been derived by Gandhiji from his *Vaishnava* heritage plus the great works like the *Mahabharata*, *Ramayana*, *Upanishads* and the *Gita*. Here also, he is a *Hindu* as he is in all other respects. It can be stated that Gandhiji has synthesised the doctrine of *Ahimsa* to be found in Hinduism, Jainism and Buddhism, but its main spring of inspiration is Hinduism at its best and noblest no doubt. T.K. Mahadevan is therefore right when he states that: ". . .The Gandhian teaching belongs strictly within this main stream (of ancient Indian tradition) and any superficial resemblance it may have to western Christian tradition can only be accidental."[37] Gandhiji has also specifically stated that: "It is good fortune or misfortune of Hinduism that it has no official creed. In order therefore, to protect myself against any misunderstanding, I have said that truth and non-violence is my creed. If I were asked to define the Hindu creed, I should simply say: Search after truth through non-violent means. A man may not believe in God and still call himself a Hindu. Hinduism is a relentless pursuit after truth,"[38] and, "The fundamental principles of Hinduism are absolute belief in truth and non-violence. Therefore use truth as your anvil, non-violence as your hammer; and anything that does not stand with *Ahimsa*, reject as non-Hindu.[39]

If we were, first of all, to give his basis of firm belief and practice of *Ahimsa*, these words clarify Gandhiji's position in the matter: "I shall not fear anyone on earth. I shall submit to no injustice wherever it might be, I shall conquer untruth with truth. While conquering untruth with truth, hate with love, injustice with justice, I shall put up with all suffering quite cheerfully and with goodwill towards all." This is *Ahimsa* in practice which implies that: (i) *Ahimsa* is not a negative doctrine but a positive one and it is meant to awaken the humanity ingrained in the other party; (ii) *Ahimsa* is very near Truth and Truth is God; (iii) *Ahimsa* bases itself on love towards all; (iv) *Ahimsa* is perfect equanimity (*Samata*) of the mind and this can result only from perfect self-control; (v) *Ahimsa* is preparedness for suffering with love and patience and so it means perfect fearlessness, it is a weapon of the brave and heroic; (vi) The good of all humanity is at the basis of this ideal of *Ahimsa*; (vii) Unstinted faith in God as also in the ultimate goodness of man and the rightness of man's conscience is the very basis of *Ahimsa*.

Gandhiji has elaborated all these views on *Ahimsa* at various stages in life in his various utterances. And this is sufficient to show how wide and all-embracing this doctrine of *Ahimsa* is. It is agreed that his views on *Ahimsa* grew along with his life and his experimentation, but it is to this stage that *Ahimsa* comes in its implication. It covers up, as we have seen, all the planes—the mundane, mental, emotional and spiritual, and Gandhiji expects all men to follow *Ahimsa* on all these planes. Thus, it means physically no injury of any kind, not only to other human beings but also to all the living beings, and this further implies non-resistance to all physical attacks, or, to state more clearly, it implies resistance of the non-violent type. He had set before himself the ideal of not resisting even scorpions and snakes—an ideal that was very difficult to attain and he had confessed that he had not attained it. *Ahimsa* also means non-resistance by the mind, that is, not wishing evil of evil by the mind also, and loving and wishing well to all enemies and all evil. This would mean having no enmity towards others and having love and regard for all. It also means a complete absence of emotional excitement that may be revealed or concealed and it also means a complete absence of coercion of all types. As it is, this implies a spirit of non-injury to the offender even mentally and further, loving the offender and hoping that ultimately God will guide him also as a human being on the right path. It is easy to understand what a big challenge it is to mankind, but it can also be understood that it is a challenge based on optimism and unstinted faith in the basic and ultimate goodness that humanity is. Spiritually it means acceptance of unity of life and its oneness with God, and this would lead to man's constant rise in spirit to come to a stage of highest self-realization. In the end it means acceptance that God in all that He does to man, is kind and merciful and that he has created the universe ultimately for good. It also implies the acceptance of the ideals of eternal peace and universal brotherhood. Surely, when this ideal is put into practice, it faces countless difficulties and problems. Gandhiji first saw the possibility for all people following this path of non-violence but by and by realised the glaring limitations of human nature and also that perfect *Ahimsa* is impossible for a man in flesh and blood. He never claimed to have completely reached this ideal of *Ahimsa* though he clung to it more and more firmly as time passed and the worst ordeals followed. He saw his doctrine of *Ahimsa* fail, and he knew that the doctrine was not at fault but human nature. Man is naturally violent and it is absolutely necessary that he conquers his violence. For this, he laid down a very high ideal and realised that a full attainment of this ideal of *Ahimsa* is not possible for the soul being in flesh and blood, i.e., the body. Flesh is a definite hindrance with all its implications in the full realisation of this ideal of *Ahimsa*, and Gandhiji has again and again accepted the limitations of flesh. This means indirect acceptance of the fact that the highest ideal of *Ahimsa* can be attained only by a *Jivan-mukta*, a man who has attained salvation while in life. Gandhiji practised *Ahimsa* on the moral and worldly plane and the utter impossibility of following the ideal came on the surface. We agree that the doctrine is not at fault but man's nature for which the *Gita* has rightly stated:

प्रकृतिं यान्ति भूतानि निग्रहः किं करिष्यति।। (3:33)

(All creatures follow their nature; what then will constraint avail?)

But, "A *Jivanmukta* has transcended all evil and good, all suffering and pleasure. He alone is completely non-violent." And Hinduism has again and again stressed both the points. We are told that जीवो जीवस्य जीवनम् and also that only the *muktatma* can attain the highest ideal of *Ahimsa*. Gandhiji realised the truth of this, in later life and then he clung to the ideal with all the steadfastness at his command and more and more talked of "my *Ahimsa*" rather than *Ahimsa*. Thus, after a life-time effort of all-sided practice of *Ahimsa* and an attempt to make people of the world practise it individually and on a mass scale and after partial success in this, he came to the realisation that Hinduism had basically accepted and Buddhism and Jainism also accepted in practice that *Ahimsa* in perfection can be attained only by a *samnyasin* who is a *muktatma*.

Ahimsa on Mass Scale

Of course, even the partial success of *Ahimsa* on a mass scale and its results as also long-term implications can, in no way, be underestimated. He propagated the practice of non-violence in order (i) to awaken the common masses from their slumber of centuries, (ii) to make them conscious of their individual existence and self-sacrifice for gaining the independence of Mother India and so on. He called his movement *Satyagraha*, that can have no word of the same sense in English; passive resistance can not be the proper word for it because, "Passive resistance, as commonly understood in the West in its historical setting and as understood by us now, is a weapon of the weak, of the unarmed and helpless. It does not eschew violence as a matter of principle but only because of lack of means of violence or out of sheer expediency. It would use arms if and when they are available or when there is a reasonable chance of success."[40] *Ahimsa* is the very basis of this *Satyagraha* which means firmly resorting to Truth and readiness to sacrifice one's self for it. It is a soul-force for which the basic requisite is full faith in God. To put in his words: "He or she must have a living faith in non-violence. This is impossible without a living faith in God. A non-violent man can do nothing save by the power and grace of God. Without it he won't have the courage to die without anger, without fear and without retaliation."[41] No doubt very few of his followers and *Satyagrahis* understood the exact significance of his concept of Truth, non-violence and *Satyagraha*. But there were thousands who joined the bands of *Satyagrahis* and in several movements, died bravely and without retaliation. Now and then retaliation also took place and after the communal riots and after India was divided, all faith of the masses was lost. But the weapon did work considerably and on one side, the masses awoke and became alert with all their self-respect and on the other side, the British Raj in this country was completely exposed. *Ahimsa* did work on the mundane plane and considerably was its purpose served. But the ideal *Ahimsa* that Gandhiji conceived of remained, as the ancient seers knew and explained, a full ideal that only the *muktatmas* could resort to. The experiment of making it a weapon in the hands of the common masses did not succeed much, but the experiment was unique and great in its own way.

Ahimsa and *Gita*

We have now to see how far this grand concept of *Ahimsa* is really given by the *Gita* as Gandhiji opines again and again. He of course agrees that: "But it may be freely admitted that the *Gita* was not written to establish *Ahimsa*. It was an accepted and primary duty even before the *Gita* age. The *Gita* had to deliver the message of renunciation of fruit." (In *Anasaktiyoga*) Thus, Gandhiji contends that the primary purpose of the *Gita* is to teach *Anasaktiyoga*, as he defined it, for the ultimate purpose of self-realization. But, with reference to the *Gita* and *Ahimsa*, his stand is that the Gita takes for granted the basic principle of *Ahimsa* as we have already noted. It is much earlier in Hinduism and his further contention is that an ideal *Anasakta*, be he a स्थितप्रज्ञ (*Sthitprajna*) or a त्रिगुणातीत (*Trigunatita*), be he a ज्ञानी (*Jnani*) or a भक्त (Bhakta), must of necessity accept *Ahimsa* as the very basic doctrine of life and this is all the more so because the mental attitude of an *Anasakta* is that of perfect equilibrium and *Samnayasa*, both of which are possible only for a man who adopts and practises the principle of *Ahimsa* to the full. In his *Anasaktiyoga* he specifically states that: "Thinking along these lines, I have felt that in trying to enforce in one's life the central teaching of the *Gita*, one is bound to follow Truth and *Ahimsa*." So, in the first instance Gandhiji has conceded that the principle of *Ahimsa* is not directly discussed in the *Gita* but is to be derived as a basic principle accepted by the *Gita* without argument.

After basing his stand on this argument, Gandhiji has elaborated it in various ways and in various statements. If we try to evolve a systematic thought from these varied statements, very difficult though it is, the position taken by Gandhiji would come to this:

(i) The first and very important argument put forward by Gandhiji is with reference to the singer of the *Gita*. The singer of the *Gita* is God the Supreme in the form of Krishna who is known as *Purna Avatara* as also *Yogeshvara*. If Krishna is *Purna Avatara* and if He is *Yogeshvara* and again, if He is God the Supreme, Gandhiji argues, what can He teach other than *Ahimsa*, when He is expounding before Arjuna, and through him to humanity at large, the ideal of religion, ethics and spiritual attainment of life. When He is exhorting Arjuna to undertake his duty in the most dispassionate manner, or, to express better, in a spirit of detachment that will gradually lead to *Samnyasa*? Gandhiji in no unclear terms states that Krishna can teach only *Ahimsa*. To put in his words: "But if we study the whole of the *Gita* and examine its descriptions of *Sthitaprajna*, *Brahmabhuta*, *Bhakta* and *Yogi*, we can reach only this conclusion that the Krishna of the *Gita* was the very incarnation of *Ahimsa*, and his exhortation to Arjuna to fight does not detract from its greatness. On the other hand, if he had given him different advice, his knowledge would have been proved inadequate and he would not have been entitled to be called *Yogeshwara* (The Prince of Yogis) and *Purna Avatara* (the Perfect Incarnation)."[42]

(ii) The next important argument rests on the contents of the second chapter in which *Krishna* gives instruction to *Arjuna*, first from the point of view of *Jnana*

एषा तेऽभिहिता सांख्ये बुद्धिर्योगे त्विमां श्रुणु। (2:39)

(Thus have I set before thee the attitude of knowledge; hear now the attitude of Action) and then, while defining *Yoga*, he defined

Sthitaprajna. The whole definition of *Sthitaprajana* suited very well the mind of Gandhiji and he found in it an attitude only of *Ahimsa*. He therefore opines that the second *Adhyaya* directly and specifically supports *Ahimsa* and the rest of the *Adhyayas* are in line with it. To put in his words: "And when after finishing the first chapter of the *Gita* we enter upon the second, we find that it teaches *Ahimsa* pure and simple,"[43] and "That the central teaching of the *Gita* is not *Himsa* but *Ahimsa* is amply demonstrated by the subject begun and summarized in the concluding Eighteenth chapter. The treatment in the other chapter also supports the position."[44] Again, "Its second chapter, instead of teaching the rules of physical warfare, tells us how a perfect man is to be known. In the characteristics of the perfect man of the *Gita*, I do not see any to correspond to physical warfare. Its whole design is inconsistent with the rules of conduct governing the relations between warring parties."[45]

(iii) Again, *Arjuna* is asked by *Krishna* to rise to sublime heights and come to a stage of perfect detachment in action, to become a *Yogi*,

तस्माद्योगी भवार्जुन। (6:46)

(. . .Therefore be thou a *Yogin*, O *Arjuna*!), to become only an instrument in God's hands,

निमित्तमात्रं भव सव्यसाचिन्। (11:33)

(Be thou no more than an instrument, O *Savyasachin*!), to be associated with *Yoga*,

तस्मात् योगाय युज्यस्व। (2:50)

(Gird thyself up for *Yoga*, therefore), etc. In other words, he should raise his personality far above the ordinary and look at his actions only as duty and that too in a spirit of perfect submission of his entire self to the divine will.

मय्येव मन आधत्स्व मयि बुद्धिं निवेशय।
निवसिष्यसि मय्येव अत ऊर्ध्वं न संशयः।। (12:8)

(On Me set thy mind, On Me rest thy conviction, thus without doubt shalt thou remain only in Me hereafter.)

Surely this is a stage for absolute self-control, a stage in which no

Himsa is possible. To put in Gandhiji's words: "*Himsa* is impossible without anger, without attachment, without hatred and the *Gita* strives to carry us to the state beyond *Sattva*, *Rajas* and *Tamas*, a state that excludes anger, hatred, etc."[46] This will be supported by looking upon the battle only as symbolical, only as an allegory hinting at the constant war that wages in the human heart between right and wrong, justice and injustice, *Dharma* and *Adharma* and so on. And even if Arjuna actually fought the physical war, Gandhiji would contend that in those old days, even though *Ahimsa* was the basic law of Hinduism, people were not clear about its application, and so on.

(iv) Yet the next and an important argument is derived by Gandhiji on the basis of the general tone of the writer of the *Mahabharata*. We know that Vyasa is a *muni* (मननात् मुनि: or मौनात् मुनि: or मौनी) and in the *Mahabharata* he has shown the worst of tragedies of human slaughter. It meant total annihilation of humanity for ages to come; it is total annihilation of humanity in *Aryavarta*. The Kauravas were killed and even though the Pandavas survived and won the battle, they are equally or probably more unhappy. The *Svargarohana Parva* shows that even the victors have wept and repented. Evidently *Vyasa* shows the futility of war and thereby suggests peace that can be the outcome only of an attitude of *Ahimsa*, that is, to Gandhiji, a mightier weapon than *Himsa*. If this could be the teaching of the *Mahabharata* as a whole, surely it must be the teaching of the *Gita*. Gandhiji states the position thus: "The author of the *Mahabharata* has not established the necessity of physical warfare, he has proved its futility. He has made the victors shed tears of sorrow and repentance, and has left them nothing but a legacy of miseries."[47]

(v) The matter is further elaborated in the fact that *Arjuna* is asked to take his whole life in a spirit of *Yajna*. Gandhiji gives a peculiar meaning to the word *Yajna* even when he understands it as 'Sacrifice'. He defines *Yajna* thus: "*Yajna* means an act directed to the welfare of others, done without desiring any return for it, whether of a temporal or spiritual nature. . . And the *Gita* teaches, and experience testifies, that all action that cannot come to the category of *Yajna*, promotes bondage."[48] So, sacrifice would mean service to others to the extent of sacrificing even one's life for others. When the *Gita* lays down this *Yajna*, surely it can be a *Yajna* of a man who has accepted only *Ahimsa*, because service to others in this spirit can be the outcome only of love and it would promote love. And where there is love, surely there can be no *Himsa*. To put in Gandhiji's words again: "'Sacrifice ye for the Gods, and pleased they will give you the reward of your sacrifice,' says the *Gita*. To proceed a little further, sacrifice means laying down one's life so that others may live. Let us suffer, so that others may be happy, and the highest service and the highest love is wherein man lays down his life for his fellowmen. That highest love is thus *Ahimsa* which is the highest service."[49] And the basis of this *Yajna* is faith in God and his working. Just as there can be no *Satyagraha* without faith in God, there can be no *Yajna* without this faith in God. And a man who is guided in this service through love for all living beings, will naturally be guided by *Ahimsa*. If I have faith in God, I would accept that all living beings are His creation and surely I would not even think of hurting His creation. Gandhiji specifically stated: "The human body is meant solely for service, never for indulgence. The secret of happy life lies in renunciation. Renunciation is life, indulgence spells death,"[50] and, "So long as we believe that all is from God, we should have no cause for perturbation. The only condition is that whatever we do, we should do with God as witness. It is He who makes the world go and we only reap the consequences of our actions. Therefore ours is only to obey His law and then be indifferent as to the result."[51] All this is possible only through *Ahimsa*.

Gandhiji has no doubt developed the whole argument about reading the doctrine of *Ahimsa* in the *Gita*, in the most systematic manner and in the manner of an *Acharya* of first rank. If we were to elaborate the argument further, since he has read only Truth and *Ahimsa* in Hinduism, naturally he reads the same two doctrines in the *Gita* that is the most authentic work in Hinduism. And he is consistent, systematic and rational behind his conviction. He has accepted that *Ahimsa* can be proved to be *Gita*'s basic doctrine along with Truth in an indirect manner. Actually *Ahimsa* is included in *Anasakti* that is the main doctrine read by Gandhiji in the *Gita*.

NOTES

1. 'Gandhi' p. 10
2. In 'Gandhi—Man of God' by W.H. Fisher in 'Incidents of Gandhiji's Life', Ed. C. Shukla, p. 53.

3. 'Harijan', 2-6-1946
4. 'The Last Phase', Pyarelal, p. 171
5. 'Young India,' 1-10-1925
6. 'Young India', 1-10-1925
7. 'Young India', 9-4-1925
8. 'Young India', 21-5-1928
9. 'Young India', 15-12-1927
10. 'Harijan', 3-10-1936
11. 'Young India', 9-4-1925
12. 'Young India', 25-8-1920
13. 'Young India', 6-8-1931
14. 'Young India', 12-11-1925
15. 'Young India', 12-11-1925
16. 'Young India', 15-12-1927
17. 'Young India', 21-5-1928
18. 'Harijan', 5-9-1936
19. 'Young India', 6-8-1931
20. 'Nalachampu', 1-12
21. 'Young India', 7-5-1925
22. 'In the Path of Mahatma Gandhi', p. 290
23. 'Young India', 15-12-1927
24. 'Diary of Mahadev Desai', p. 172
25. 'Young India', 12-11-1925
26. 'Young India', 12-11-1925
27. 'Harijan', 18-8-1940
28. 'Young India', 6-8-1931
29. 'Kavyaprakasha of Mammata'—Ullasa I.
30. 'Gandhian Ethics', B.G. Ray, p.25
31. 'Letter to Mahadev Desai', 15-9-1919
32. 'Letter to Jamnalal Bajaj', 16-3-1922
33. 'Dhammapada', 1-4
34. 'What I Believe', Leo Tolstoy, ch. 2
35. B.C. Ray in 'Gandhian Ethics', p. 25
36. 'Manusmriti', 4-2
37. 'Approach to the Study of Gandhi', an Article.
38. 'Young India', 24-4-1924
39. Speech in Madras, 22-3-1925
40. R.R. Diwakar in 'Satyagraha – Its Technique and History', pp. 2-3
41. 'Non-violence in Peace and War', Vol. I, p. 238
42. 'Diary of Mahadev Desai', p. 93
43. 'Diary of Mahadev Desai', p. 105
44. 'Young India', 12-11-1925
45. 'Young India', 6-8-1931

46. 'Young India', 12-11-1925
47. 'Young India', 6-8-1931
48. 'Yeravada Mandir', ch. xiv
49. 'Young India', 8-9-1927
50. 'Harijan', 24-2-1946
51. 'Harijan', 23-6-1946

NINE

Gandhiji's Views Deduced from Gita *(Continued)*

"Calamity and happiness in all cases are men's own seeking."

Mencius II.

"I have endeavoured, in the light of a prayerful study of other faiths and in the light of my own experiences in trying to live the teaching of Hinduism, to give an extended meaning to Hinduism as a living faith."

Gandhiji

"The teaching of Lord Krishna is that the man of duty will grasp eternal things and will know that fighter and fought against, victor and victim, are merely passing phenomena of history."

George Catlin[1]

Gita and *Ahimsa*—Analysis

Now, in order to examine whether the doctrine of *Ahimsa* can be really read in the *Gita* as Gandhiji does, the following points should, first all of, be stressed as facts:

(i) Arjuna came to the battle-field with the intention to fight his kinsmen, with the consciousness that right is on the side of the *Pandavas* and that the battle is actually forced on them. He comes with a thorough dislike towards the *Kauravas* as also Dhritarashtra, as can be seen clearly from his words:

धार्तराष्ट्रस्य दुर्बुद्धेः युद्धे प्रियचिकीर्षवः। (1:23)

(Anxious to fulfil in battle perverse Duryodhana's desire.)

(ii) Just at the critical juncture, when he is about to start fighting, when weapons are about to start falling

प्रवृत्ते शस्त्रसम्पाते. . . . . (1:20)

(And flight of arrows about to begin,)

he sees his elders and kinsmen face to face. Here, we are told that through attachment towards his kinsmen, the elders in particular, he feels a sort of indescribable sorrow that shakes him to his very roots and he experiences as if this dolour dries up his very senses

. . . यच्छोकमुच्छोषणमिन्द्रियाणाम्। (2:8)

(The anguish that shrivels up my senses.)

But it is not only attachment that we have to see here, but also that behind the would-be total desruction of the two armies, he sees almost a total annihilation of all Aryan values, all culture, of *Aryatva* itself!

This is equally important even though, not realising the depth and genuineness of his sorrow, Krishna tells him—

क्लैब्यं मा स्म गमः यार्थ नैतत्त्वयुपपद्यते।
क्षुद्रं हृदयदौर्बल्यं त्यक्त्वोत्तिष्ठ परंतप।। (2:3)

(Yield not to unmanliness. O Partha; it does not become thee. Shake off this miserable faint-heartedness and arise, O Partha!) Then is Krishna convinced of the depth and genuineness of his sorrow and realises that he is just on the first step to knowledge and higher realization, even though Arjuna has come to this stage through attachment to the elders. Krishna then gives the higher religion, ethics and philosophy of life, so that Arjuna comes to the highest stage of mental development, gets over his attachment and then fights.

(iii) During the whole process of discussion, Arjuna is again and again asked to fight.

तस्माद्युध्यस्व भारत। (2:18)

(Fight, therefore, O Bharata!) and so much so that even when he is told,

तस्माद्योगी भवार्जुन। (6:46)

(...Therefore be thou a *Yogin*, O Arjuna!) it seems to mean, "Become a *Yogi* and fight." The fact of the battle can never be lost sight of.

Such is the setting and atmosphere throughout. Even when we were to take the *Gita* and the battle in it as an allegory, its setting is in reality a battle and it is indicative of the battle between right and wrong, *Dharma* and *Adharma*, good and evil that man has to face and fight again and again. No allegory can be there without its basis in reality. Here in particular, the basis in reality can never be lost sight of.

(iv) With the verse

स्वधर्ममपि चावेक्ष्य न विकम्पितुमर्हसि। (2:31)

(Again, seeing thine own duty thou shouldst not shrink from it;) and ending in

सुखदु:खे समे कृत्वा लाभालाभौ जयाजयौ।

etc., in the second *Adhyaya*, there is a very clear reference to the physical battle which is to be fought and no verse in it will support the allegorical meaning that Gandhiji has derived. It is a clear cut and straight reference to the physical battle to be fought by Arjuna. This is in consonance with the famous verse

स्वधर्मे निधनं श्रेय: परधर्मो भयावह:। (3:35)

(. . . better is death in the discharge of one's duty, another's duty is fraught with danger.) This is a clear reference to *Varna* duties and it is always the duty of the *Kshatriya* to fight and protect the right, the good and *Dharma* from the wrong, the evil and *Adharma*. And even when Arjuna is asked to fight, he is asked to cultivate an attitude of *Samata, Samatva, Yoga* and being indifferent to, or taking as the same, happiness and sorrow, loss and gain, victory and defeat, he is asked to fight the battle.

सुखदु:खे समे कृत्वा लाभालाभौ जयाजयौ।
ततो युद्धाय युज्यस्व नैनं पापमवाप्स्यसि।। (2:38)

(Hold alike pleasure and pain; gain and loss, victory and defeat, and gird up thy loins for the fight; so doing, thou shalt not incur sin.)

(v) In the 11th *Adhyaya*, when Arjuna is asked to become a *nimitta* and just that and kill his enemies under divine order, it is an order to Arjuna to fight the physical battle. Verses 33 and 34 run as follows:

तस्मात् त्वमुत्तिष्ठ यशो लभस्व
जित्वा शत्रून् भुङ्क्ष्व राज्यं समृद्धम्।
मयैवैते निहताः पूर्वमेव
निमित्तमात्रं भव सव्यसाचिन्।।

(Therefore, do thou arise, and win renown! Defeat thy foes and enjoy a thriving kingdom. By Me have these already been destroyed; be thou no more than an instrument, O *Savyasachin*!)

द्रोणं च भीष्मं च जयद्रथं च
कर्णं तथान्यानपि योधवीरान्।
मया हतांस्त्वं जहि मा व्यथिष्ठा
युध्यस्व जेतासि रणे सपत्नान्।।

(Drona, Bhishma, Jayadratha and Karna, as also the other warrior chiefs—already slain by Me—slay thou! Be not dismayed, Fight! Victory is thine over thy foes in the field.)

No commentator has taken or even suggested an allegorical meaning of this. Actually it is not possible to interpret that way.

(vi) In verse 18:72, Krishna puts before Arjuna the following question:

कच्चिदेतच्छ्रुतं पार्थ त्वयैकाग्रेण चेतसा।
कच्चिदज्ञानसंमोहः प्रणष्टस्ते धनंजय।।

(Hast thou heard this, O Partha, with a concentrated mind? Has the delusion, born of ignorance, been destroyed, O *Dhananjaya*?) Arjuna's ignorance was in his refusal to fight those whom he took to be his kith and kin and the resultant total annihilation that he could foresee. He was therefore terribly frightened and refused to become instrumental in this total annihilation. Krishna inquires of Arjuna whether this ignorance of his has disappeared and this is as good as inquiring whether he is prepared to fight the physical war.

(vii) In reply to this Arjuna says:

नष्टो मोहः स्मृतिर्लब्धा त्वत्प्रसादान्मयाच्युत।
स्थितोऽस्मि गतसंदेहः करिष्ये वचन तव।। (18:73)

(Thanks to thy grace, O *Achyuta*, my delusion is destroyed. My understanding has returned. I stand secure, my doubts all dispelled. I will do thy bidding.)

Arjuna's ignorance is dispelled, i.e. his attachment and worry about the total annihilation and the personal factor in it are dispelled. He has regained his memory and this is memory of his duty as an ideal *Kshatriya* to fight for the protection of and reinstating of right, good, *Dharma* and so on. When he says: 'I shall act according to your words', we know that again and again Krishna has asked him to fight, the basic instruction being in 11:33-34, to act only as an instrument in the hands of God. Arjuna is thus no authority to decide his own course of action and everything that is happening in the world is ordained by God. Krishna has specifically stated that:

विष्टभ्याहमिदं सर्वमेकांशेन स्थितो जगत्। (10:42)

(With but a part of Myself I stand up holding this Universe.) This specifically shows that the reference to physical warfare cannot be lost sight of, war and destruction of the enemies of Arjuna is what God wishes and wishes to execute through Arjuna. Gandhiji has accepted that God the Supreme is above violence and non-violence both and he states: "I believe in Krishna. But my Krishna is the Lord of the Universe, the creator, preserver and destroyer of us all. He may destroy because he creates."[2] He wants man to reduce himself to zero and he adds: "One who thus reduces himself to zero will always be absorbed in His work."[3]

This is all that can be stressed as internal evidence to show that even if we interpret the *Gita* as an allegory, the fact of physical warfare cannot be lost sight of and it would not be logical or rational to reject physical warfare in favour of the allegory. The actual position is that even for stressing the sorrows of Arjuna and for suggesting how man at certain critical junctures in life is at cross-roads and he is not able to decide his course of action, he falters, he feels pained and he resorts to inaction, the physical warfare is to be accepted as reality. Actually, the physical warfare is too much with us and in the face of facts, it is difficult to prove that the *Gita* preaches *Ahimsa* of the concept of Gandhiji.

It can be argued that even after all his doubts are dispelled, Arjuna does not cease to be a man of the world, he is a heroic fighter for the protection of just, good etc. His doubts about the justness of war are dispelled and he is conscious now that he is on a far higher plane of mental development from which he sees that (i) he, as a *Kshatriya*, has to do his duty, be it even physical warfare, with perfect detachment and with hatred or attachment towards none, and, (ii) ultimately he is acting only as an instrument in the hands of Providence that wills to put an end to *Adharma* incarnated as the Kaurava army in the battle-field. The *Gita* teaches that man has, as per the Divine will, to contribute towards moving the wheel of *samsara*, (3:16) that is set in motion by God, and, even if as a *Kshatriya*, he were to resort to inaction, Krishna says; "Your nature will inspire you, force you to act:"

प्रकृतिस्त्वां नियोक्ष्यति। (18:59)

and of course he will act as a *Kshatriya* because the *Gita* has accepted even *chaturvarnya* as divinely created. From this point of view also, the *Gita* does not teach *Ahimsa.*

The Actual Position

Actually, *Himsa* or *Ahimsa* is not a problem with the *Gita*. The problem is how a man is to act in life, as a *Samsarin*, as he resorts to ideal religion, ethics and spiritualism. The *Gita* teaches *Dharmayuddha* of the highest order and the श्रेय (*Shreya*) of a *Kshatriya* is a *Dharmayuddha* as we are told in:

धर्म्याद्धि युद्धाच्छ्रेयोऽन्यत्क्षत्रियस्य न विद्यते। (2:34)

(. . . For there is no higher good for a *Kshatriya* than a righteous war.) The *Gita* is a book of religion, ethics and spiritualism, for the common man and in his gradual rise to the Divine, by slow but sure steps. This is inspite of the fact that the basic question of Arjuna is war or no war and he has actually resorted to a refusal to fight. Actually we cannot say that Arjun resorts to non-violence because it is through deep attachment to his elders that Arjuna refuses to fight. Even the picture of a horrible destruction and total downfall of all cultural values, of *Aryatva* that he has visioned—and we know that in the end the horrible vision did come true—is not the result of genuine awakening and enlightenment but a flash as if of the future happenings, through his attachment and sorrow. Arjuna is rightly told that

अशोच्यानन्वशोचस्त्वं प्रज्ञावादांश्च भाषसे। (2:11)

(Thou mournest for them who thou shouldst not mourn, and utterest vain words of wisdom.)Arjuna is under the deep influence of *Rajoguna* and so, his refusal to fight is not non-violence. As Gandhiji would put it, it is not the non-violence of a hero and therefore it is no non-violence at all. The immediate fact before Krishna is that a *Kshatriya* hero refuses to fight a *Dharmayuddha*, and, even if the instruction that he gives is for humanity at large, for men of all types and at all the stations of life, the fact remains that the person to receive the instruction is a *Kshatriya.*

So, in those days, it was accepted that non-violence is the best policy in life and general non-hurt to all living beings is accepted as a *Vrata* (*Adhyaya* 16:1 to 4). But besides the *Vratas* of life, the other facts are steadiness and progress of social order, keeping intact individual and social morality, giving the best scope to man's inherent instinct to rise higher and higher towards the Divine and so on. Respect for *Dharma* and its due protection is also a problem. So, Krishna takes all these problems, and from all points of view, tries to convince Arjuna of the necessity of fighting evil. The *Manusmriti* specifically states that

शस्त्रं द्विजातिभिर्ग्राह्यं धर्मो यत्रोपरुध्यते। (मनु . 8-348)

(Twice born men may take up arms when (they are) hindered in the fulfilment of their duties,) and if this is true, it is all the more necessary for a *Kshatriya* to resort to weapons for the protection of *Dharma*. It would be unbecoming of Arjuna as a hero of first rank and a *Kshatriya* to refuse to fight. The fact of battle cannot be lost sight of and this cannot go hand in hand with *Ahimsa*.

The main difficulty in the problem is this. Gandhiji is very much against *Himsa* and we agree that the *Gita* is against *Sakama Himsa*. Arjuna is asked to raise himself above all the three *Gunas*, all dualities, and, taking recourse to सत्त्वं (*Sattvam*), reality in form of God the Supreme, to fight without any consideration of his योगक्षेम (*Yogakshema*) also.

He is again asked to become just an instrument of the Divine Will and to fight (11:33, 34.) So, actually निष्काम हिंसा (*Nishkama Himsa*) is preached to Arjuna. If he comes to that stage, he will fight without love or hatred towards his enemies, fight only as a duty, as an instrument in the hands of God. But Gandhiji could not conceive of *Himsa* being *Nishkama*.The actual position is that Arjuna is asked to raise himself to the status of a court judge and to view his duty of fight in a spirit of perfect detachment. Gandhiji cannot conceive of such a state. To put in his own words: "Thinking on these lines, I have felt that in trying to enforce in one's life the central teaching of the *Gita*, one is bound to follow Truth and *Ahimsa*. When there is no desire for fruit, there is no temptation for untruth or *Himsa*. Take any instance of untruth or violence, and it will be found that at its back was the desire to attain the cherished end", (*Anasktiyoga*) and, "And *Anasakti* transcends *Ahimsa*. He who would be *Anasakta* (selfless) has necessarily to practise non-violence in order to attain the state of selflessness. *Ahimsa* is, therefore, a necessary preliminary, it is included in *Anasakti*, it does not go beyond it."[4] But this contradicts Gandhiji's act of killing an ailing calf about which it is stated that: "A calf was lame and had developed terrible sores; he could not eat and breathed with difficulty. After three days' arguments with myself and my co-workers I put an end to its life. Now that action was non-violent because it was wholly unselfish, in as much as the sole purpose was to achieve the calf's relief from pain,"[5] and he adds in the same article: "Some people have called this an act of violence. I have called it a surgical operation. I should do exctly the same thing with my child, if he were in the same predicament." The *Pandavas* had exhausted all avenues of avoiding the terrible bloodshed and the war was actually forced on them; and here Arjuna is asked to fight this *Dharmayuddha* for the protection of *Dharma*, right (truth) and good against *Adharma*, falsehood and evil and he is asked to fight in a spirit of detachment, and without any desire for reward. Can this not be called non-violence? But Gandhiji will not, and we too will not. It is not *Ahimsa* but *Himsa* that is *Nishkama*, and in this complex life of man, even this is possible, it is often necessary. It is therefore clear that, there is no controversy between the actual opinion of Gandhiji and the text of the *Gita* if Gandhiji were prepared to accept that *Nishkama Himsa* is possible in life. This is because,

(i) The *Gita* has rejected सकाम हिंसा (desire-related violence).
(ii) The *Gita* expects the highest *Ahimsa* of Gandhiji from a *Samnyasin* who is on way to self-realistion.
(iii) Even though a *muktatma* is above *Himsa* and *Ahimsa* both, he is expected to be a staunch follower of *Ahimsa*.

But the *Gita* goes a step futher and accepts *Nishkama Himsa* and that is exactly where there is difference of opinion between the *Gita* and Gandhiji. Actually Gandhiji knows of this possible interpretation and possible difficulty and so, ultimately resorts to his own conviction based on practice in life. He states: "Let it be granted, that according to the letter of the *Gita*, it is possible to say that warfare is consistent with renunciation of fruit. But after 40 years' unremitting endeavour fully to enforce the teaching of the *Gita* in my own life, I, in all humility, feel that perfect renunciation is impossible without perfect observance of *Ahimsa* in every shape and form."[6] We can thus see that Gandhiji humbly but firmly challenges the word of the *Gita*, of *Yogeshwara* Krishna, and disagrees with him. But for our present purpose, the fact remains that the *Gita* accepts *Nishkama Himsa* as a necessity in life, and, being constantly worried about and interested in social order and social uplift, it permits of this *Nishkama Himsa*. We might go a step further and say that this *Himsa* is no *Himsa* to the *Gita*.

Contemporary Common Man and Gandhiji

We concede that Gandhiji's is the method of a *Bhashyakara*. Even though the *Bhashyakaras* honestly believed that they were interpreting the meaning of the *Gita* exacly as it should be interpreted, it is a fact that they have read their own peculiar doctrine in the *Gita*, and it is also a fact that they read the meaning of the *Gita* exactly according to the needs of their time. In everything that Gandhiji did and in everything that he spoke and wrote, his eyes were on the contemporary common man, whom he wanted to serve as a symbol of service to God and whose problems were stupendous. When therefore Gandhiji interprets the *Gita*, the common man of India is before his eyes and he intends to give the meaning of the *Gita* as he intends the common man's mind to have it, and that too in the common man's language. Here exactly lies the real difficulty in so far as, from ancient Indian tradition he brought the doctrines of Truth and *Ahimsa* in all their lustre and vitality. But then, with his faith in the ultimate goodness of man and the scope that the ancient scriptures, particularly the *Gita* saw in the rise of man to the Divine, Gandhiji applied these noble ideals to all men, the commonest of the common also. The ancient scriptures were careful in accepting the possibility of the application of these principles in their full sense only to *muktatmas* or *samnyasins* and only in a limited sense to the common masses.

The *Gita* has, in so many verses, shown gradations of man and asserted that man is expected to rise to the higher achievement only by stages. The *Manusmriti* applies this principle of *Ahimsa* as one of the five व्रत (*Vratas*) to all *Aryas* and this is in a general sense of non-hurt to all living beings.

अहिंसा सत्यमस्तेयं शौचमिन्द्रियनिग्रहः।
एतं सामासिकं धर्मं चातुर्वर्ण्येऽब्रवीन्मनुः।। (10-63)

(Abstention from injuring (creatures), truthfulness, abstention from unlawfully appropriating (the goods of others), purity and control of the organs, Manu has declared to be the summary of the law for the four castes) and the *Manusmriti*, with its typically practical outlook on the limitation of man's nature, states:

अनधीत्य द्विजो वेदाननुत्पाद्य तथा सुतान्।
अनिष्ट्वा चैव यज्ञैश्च मोक्षमिच्छन्व्रजत्यधः। (6-37)

(A twice-born man who seeks final liberation, without laving studied the Vedas, without having begotten sons, and without having offered sacrifices, sinks downwards.) This shows that Manu knows that with enlightenment any man can possibly rise to the higher heights of divinity only through stages and the great doctrines of Truth and non-violence as Gandhiji idealises them can be followed by a man only in the last stage, and the *Gita* worries about man in all stages of life.

T.K. Mahadevan states: " . . . like all great men Gandhi had his fair share of what I would call 'great failings'. One of the most disastrous of these was his procrustean tendency to force reality into a preconceived mould and to reach conclusions that were prima facie questionable." This has actually been the case with all saints as also all *Bhashyakaras* in India and this has happened with him when Gandhiji reads his own typical principles of *Satya* and *Ahimsa* in the *Gita* and gives peculiarly original and new meanings to *Samnyasa*, *Yoga*, *Yajna* and so on, to derive his principles of physical labour, bread-labour, *Swadeshi*, etc., from it. As we have already seen, in reading the principle of *Ahimsa* in the *Gita*, he has adopted the attitude and approach of a *Bhashyakara* and he is original and gives new meaning altogether to the *Gita* by his method. He of course wishes that his should be the correct interpretation, and even though it is not the correct interpretation i.e., the interpretation revealing the doctrine of the writer Vyasa, it is still a great, original and interesting interpretation, and no doubt it is one that has been a very much useful interpretation of the religious scripture in life. And who will deny the fact that an interpretation is of real use only when it is useful in life and helps man to rise higher? He states: "But that is nothing. The question is whether it is a reasonable interpretation, whether it carries conviction. If it does, it does not matter whether it is mine or X, Y, Z's. If it does not, it has no value even if it is mine."[7] Whatever the controversy about Gandhiji's interpretation, whether it is correct or not, it is this interpretation followed in practice in life, that has given to us Mahatma Gandhi and that itself speaks for its value.

World of Scholars on *Ahimsa* in *Gita*

And it is interesting to note that in the world of scholars, there is very great disagreement on the problem. Many scholars have discussed the problem and come to varied conclusions on the matter and no conclusion is similar to the one that Gandhiji derives from it. The ancient *Acharyas* understand by this the general *Vrata* of non-harm to animals and no one refers to non-hurt to birds and other living beings, i.e., the lower life. Actually all the prominent *Acharyas* have taken the war of the *Mahabharata* and *Gita* as a fact, as a reality, and when the word '*Ahimsa*' occurs at various places in various contexts in the work, they take it as, अपीडा प्राणिनाम् (non-pain to living beings) or वाङ्मनःकायैः परपीडारहितत्वम् (avoidance of pain to others by speech, thought or action) or, अहिंसनं, प्राणिनां पीडावर्जनम् (avoidance of violence, removal of pain of living beings), etc., the sole exception being Anandagiri on 13:7 when he goes a step further and defines *Ahimsa* as

परापराधस्य चित्तविकारकारणस्य प्राप्तावेव अविकृतचित्तेनापकारसहिष्णुत्वम्।

(*Ahimsa* is the process of toleration of evil with a mind not unsteadied, just when someone else offends and thus gives reason for degenerating change of the mind.) Actually, the *Ahimsa* ideal of Gandhiji will be very close to that of *Yogabhashya* which says:

तत्र अहिंसा सर्वथा सर्वदा सर्वभूतानामनभिद्रोहः। उत्तरे च यमनियमाः तन्मूलाः तत्सिद्धिपरतया एव प्रतिपादनाय प्रतिपाद्यन्ते, तद् वशात्तद्रूपकरणाय एव उपादीयन्ते। तथा चोक्तं स खल्वयं ब्राह्मणः यथा यथा व्रतानि बहूनि समाधित्सते, तथा प्रमादकृतेभ्यः हिंसानिदानेभ्यः निवर्तमानः तामेवाहिंसां अवदातरूपां करोति।

(There '*Ahimsa*' is lack of hurt of all kinds at all times to all the living beings. For later life *Yamas* and *Niyamas* are laid down only to uphold it (i.e. *Ahimsa*). It is therefore stated that just as *Brahmins* follow these *Vratas* more and more, they bring themselves away from instances of *Himsa* resorted to through sluggishness, and thus brings to success this same *Ahimsa*.) But this *Vrata* is also one of old age and not for constant practice in life.

All this should clearly refer to the fact that the *Ahimsa* ideal is very great on its own, it is at its best a spiritual ideal and only *Samnyasins* of first rank who are progressing on their path to *mukti* would be able to practise it, while, for the man of the world, the practice of *Ahimsa* can be only on a limited scale and plane, and if this were to be read in the *Gita*, there would be no objection. But actually in the *Gita* there is no great importance of *Ahimsa* and *Ahimsa* to be practised by men at various stages of life. It is not distinguished. Swami Krishnatmaja, in his '*Gitadohana*' in Gujarati, takes the philosophic, the spiritual aspect of *Ahimsa* as the principal one and feels that on the mundane plane physical, mental and expressed *Ahimsa* would follow as a matter of natural course. *Ahimsa* cannot go the other way round. This too would establish a better understanding of human nature and also acceptance of the fact that *Ahimsa* as an ideal would be best suitable to a *Samnyasin*, be he a man of inaction or a man of constant detached action or a man of constant detached action with a spirit of service to humanity.

Radhakrishnan agress that the *Gita* preaches *Ahimsa*, but it is not *Ahimsa* of Gandhiji's ideal and definition. He means to suggest that when a man of action takes to an attitude of *Samnyasa* and does his works in perfect detachment, (i) as a duty, (ii) as social service, (iii) as work of God, be it the worst of its kind, it is *Ahimsa*. Here he accepts that there can be *Nishkama Himsa* but wants to suggest that *Nishkama Himsa* is *Ahimsa*. Gandhiji would not agree with Radhakrishnan who says: "The ideal which the *Gita* sets before us is *Ahimsa* or non-violence and this is evident from the description of the perfect state of mind, speech and body in chapter VII and of the mind of the devotee in chapter XII", and "Krishna advises Arjuna to fight without passion or ill-will, without anger or attachment and if we develop such a frame of mind, violence becomes impossible. We must fight against what is wrong, but if we allow ourselves to hate, that ensures our spiritual defeat . . . We may be obliged to do painful work but it should be done in a way that does not develop the sense of super ego."[8] C. Rajagopalachari, another great scholar on Hinduism and *Gita* did not like the whole process of interpreting the *Mahabharata only* as an allegory and then deriving an argument for *Ahimsa* from it. He says, "It would be a cumbersome process to convert the whole of the *Mahabharata* story into a sustained allegory in order to save the *Bhagavadgita* from being an incitement to violence. We should forget the battle scene when we study the *Gita* as a scripture of *Sanatana Dharma*,"[9] and, ". . . the student should note that the *Gita* as a scripture of Hinduism stands apart from the *Mahabharata*."[10]

Gandhiji's staunch followers, who are first-rank scholars of the *Gita* may be quoted before we end this rather long discussion on Gandhiji's view with regard to *Ahimsa* in the *Gita*.

Kakasaheb is inclined to agree with Gandhiji on the problem, but immediately seems to recognise the difficulties of the proposition, when it comes to the matter of interpretation. He therefore lends himself into contradictions on the matter. But, we may note his statements thus: ". . . the *Geeta* is not at all concerned with physical warfare. It neither supports war, nor opposes it. It makes a distinction between a righteous war of self-defence and a war of unrighteousness and aggression."[11] The real fact is that the *Gita* refers to the necessity of war, not so much for self-defence as for upholding *Dharma* at all costs. The *Gita* stresses that if for protection of *Dharma* and *Satya*, a war is to be fought, it must be fought. Again, he contends: "When war disappears from society, the society lends self into great calamity. The spirit of war (क्षात्र धर्म) and the spirit of renunciation (वैराग्य धर्म) both, keep life healthy, lustrous and saintly. If the spirit of war disappears from the society in the name of *Ahimsa* and if it forgets the spirit of renunciation, then in no time cowardice will spread over its sovereign rule."[12]

Kishorelal Mashruwala, who has been very near the *vaishnava* interpretation when he translates and analyses the *Gita* in two different works, has the following remarks on the problem:

(i) It is the constant effort in life of the *Daivi Prakriti* to strike balance between the unavoidability of the acts of violence and the ideal of *Ahimsa*.

(ii) Even a man of *Daivi Prakriti* is not completely free from violence. But his leaning is constantly to move from greater to lesser *Himsa*, that is, *Ahimsa*.

(iii) Yet, the path of life is so much complicated that life would not possibly run only on *Ahimsa*.

The teaching of the *Gita* is therefore non-jealousy towards all life by the mind and a constant effort to avoid *Himsa* as far as possible, and to follow it without dislike, as calamity, as an un-avoidable fact when if falls on one as unavoidable. A *Kshatriya* will, therefore, constantly try to avoid *Himsa*, but when it falls on him as unavoidable, he will fight war as *Dharmayuddha*, without jealousy or attachment or hatred or any crookedness and thus give expression to his love for *Ahimsa*. This interpretation is nearer to the reality of the *Gita* as also reality of life that finds expression in the *Gita* teaching.

Maganabhai Desai discusses the problem and states that,

(i) The *Gita* teaches the *shastra* of war, it is a *Yuddhagita* of eternal warfare.

(ii) It is not possible to overlook the stark reality of the first *Adhyaya* and the war in it.

(iii) Krishna has set an example of non-violence by renouncing weapons.

(iv) The end of the great heroism in the *Mahabharata* is that there is total destruction following war.

(v) Still, inspite of the fact that nothing is good in war, the first *Adhyaya* stresses that war was unavoidable.

The *Gita* essentially therefore accepts that war is an evil, it deserves to be avoided, it leads to annihilation of culture, etc. But with all this, the *Ahimsa* of the *Gita* is not absolute. Krishna therefore teaches the doctrine that "one should resort to *Ahimsa* as far as possible and when it does not work, one may resort to *Himsa* as unavoidable." He again claimed that in reply to a letter of his in 1933, Gandhiji accepted this stand of his. Unfortunately, there are so many statements of Gandhiji even later, in which Gandhiji firmly stood by the principle of non-violence in the *Gita*. The result is difficulty in accepting Maganabhai's claim.

We have made a detailed study of the problem and that too at far great length because of its great importance. We now go to the next problem.

Bread-Labour and *Gita*

Gandhiji took the *Gita* to be a key to understanding world scriptures. This will naturally be so for a Hindu, as the 'Holy Bible' will be for a Christian and the 'Quran' for a Muslim. Approaching scriptures of the world through the most representative scripture of one's religion of birth is quite in the fitness of things. He has again stated that: "The *Gita* is such a transcendental book that men of every creed, age and clime may read it with respect, and find in it principles of their respective religions."[13] It is therefore quite natural that Gandhiji should be able to read his own principles of life in the *Gita* and one such principle read is that of bread-labour. He got this concept of bread-labour from the works of Leo Tolstoy. He therefore states: "The human body is meant solely for service, never for indulgence. The secret of happy life lies in renunciation. Renunciation is life. Indulgence spells death,"[14] and, "It is only when a man or woman has done bodily labour for the sake of service, that he or she gets any right to live,"[15] In a country like India, extremely backward that it was, he saw not only laziness and a dislike for physical labour and a lack of care to do one's own small jobs on one's own, he also saw that a sense of hatred for physical labour even for one's own needs existed in the society and so, dignity of labour should be established. He also saw that for removing the grave sin of untouchability, the sense of dignity of labour and self-dependence as also keen-ness for service should be established. He therefore insisted even on the millionaires earning their bread by the sweat of their brow and said: "Millionaires who eat without work are parasites. Even they should eat by the sweat of their brow or should go without food. The only permissible exception is the disabled for whom society provides."[16] He very specifically and firmly believes in the necessity of bodily labour becoming a law of life for all. He therefore says: "I do not discount the value of intellectual labour, but no amount of it is any compensation for the common good of all."[17] He further clarifies his view when he says that: "Intellectual work is important and has an undoubted place in the scheme of life. But what I insist on is the necessity of physical labour. No man, I claim, ought to be free from that obligation; it will serve to improve even the quality of his intellectual output. I venture to say that in ancient times Brahmins worked with their body as with their mind. But even if they did not, body-labour is a proved necessity at the present time."[18] The first necessity is bodily labour for earning one's livelihood and the next is a sense of dignity of labour that enhances our self-confidence and takes away from our minds the sense of superiority complex. This is next a part of the programme of eradication of the evil of untouchability. Gandhiji therefore insisted on physical labour by all the inmates of the *Ashram* and every new entrant to the *Ashram* was to start with the cleaning of latrines. He went a step further and prided in calling himself a *Bhangi*. This sort of self-dependence is the first step to service to others, and he has analysed the word '*Yajna*' of the *Gita* to mean service to others and thereby coming to service to God. He says: "*Yajna* means an act directed to the welfare of others, done without desiring any return for it, whether of a temporal or spiritual nature. 'Act' here must be taken in its widest sense, and includes thought and word, as well as deed, 'others' embraces not only humanity but all life. . . And the *Gita* teaches, and experience testifies, that all action that cannot come under the category of *Yajna*, promotes bondage." This is how he has analysed the verse:

यज्ञार्थात्कर्मणोऽन्यत्र लोकोऽयं कर्मबन्धनः।
तदर्थं कर्म कौन्तेय मुक्तसङ्गः समाचर।। (3 :9)

(This world of men suffers bondage from all action save that which is done for the sake of sacrifice; to this end, O Kaunteya, perform action without attachment.)

He elaborates the point further when he says: "And what can be a better inspiration for you than chapter Third? It lays down that God created man, and at the same time imposed on him the duty of *Yajna* or sacrifice. Both these words are derived from roots meaning that which purifies, and the Lord also said that 'By sacrifice shall you propagate your kind.' Sacrifice thus means service, and the *Gita* says that he who works only for himself is a thief, 'Sacrifice ye for the Gods, and pleased they will give you the reward of your sacrifice', says the *Gita*. To proceed a little further, 'Sacrifice' means laying down one's life so that others may live. Let us suffer so that others may be happy, and the highest service and the highest love is where a man lays down his life for his fellowmen."[19]

This will give to us a clear hint as to how Gandhiji derived the noble principle of physical labour and also bread-labour from the *Gita*. For a clear understanding of his view, the following verses of the *Gita* may be read together:

न हि कश्चित्क्षणमपि जातु तिष्ठत्यकर्मकृत्।
कार्यते ह्यवशः कर्म सर्वः प्रकृतिजैर्गुणैः।। (3:5)

यज्ञार्थात्कर्मणोऽन्यत्र लोकोऽयं कर्मबन्धनः।
तदर्थं कर्म कौन्तेय मुक्तसङ्ग समाचर।। (3:9)

सहयज्ञाः प्रजाः सृष्ट्वा पुरोवाच प्रजापतिः।
अनेन प्रसविष्यध्वं एष वोऽस्त्विष्टकामधुक्।। (3:10)

अन्नाद् भवन्ति भूतानि पर्जन्यादन्नसंभवः।
यज्ञाद्भवति पर्जन्यो यज्ञः कर्मसमुद्भवः।। (3:14)

यज्ञशिष्टाशिनः सन्तो मुच्यन्ते सर्वकिल्बिषैः।
भुञ्जते ते त्वघं पापाः ये पचन्त्यात्मकारणात्।। (3:13)

कर्म ब्रह्मोद्भवं विद्धि ब्रह्माक्षरसमुद्भवम्।
तस्मात्सर्वगतं ब्रह्म नित्यं यज्ञे प्रतिष्ठिम्।। (3:15)

एवं प्रवर्तितं चक्रं नानुवर्तयतीह यः।
अघायुरिन्द्रियारामो मोघं पार्थ स जीवति।। (3:16)

"For none ever remains inactive even for a moment; for all are compelled to action by the *gunas* inherent in *Prakriti*." (3:5)

"This world of men suffers bondage from all action save that which is done for the sake of sacrifice; to this end, O Kaunteya, perform action without attachment." (3:9)

"Together with sacrifice did the Lord of beings create, of old, mankind, declaring, by this shall ye increase; may this be to you the giver of all desires." (3:10)

"From food springs all life, from rain is born food; from sacrifice comes rain, and sacrifice is the result of action." (3:14)

"The righteous men who eat the residue of the sacrifice are freed from all sin, but the wicked who cook for themselves eat sin." (3:13)

"Know that action springs from *Brahman* and *Brahman* from the Imperishable; hence the all-pervading *Brahman* is ever firm-founded on sacrifice." (3:15)

"He who does not follow the wheel thus set in motion here below, he, living in sin, sating his senses, lives, O Partha, in vain." (3:16)

The verses have found varied interpretations from different scholars and Gandhiji has his own interpretation to give. On the basis of these verses his observations are as follows:

(i) It is not possible for any man on earth to remain inactive even for a moment. Even if one claims to remain inactive, actually he is not so. This is the law of life, because man must live and progress. He needs food, water, and clothes and so on for his maintenance. *Karma* is thus the law of life. Gandhiji says; "I know that there is a school of philosophy which teaches complete inaction and futility of all effort. I have not been able to appreciate that teaching. In my humble opinion, effort is necessary for one's own growth. It has to be irrespective of the results."[20] From the point of view of the *Gita*, the stand taken by Gandhiji is quite correct because while it is stated that:

यस्त्वात्मरतिरेव स्यादात्मतृप्तश्च मानवः।
आत्मन्येव च संतुष्टः तस्य कार्यं न विद्यते।। (3:17)

(But the man who revels in *Atman*, who is content in *Atman* and who is satisfied only with *Atman*, for him no action exists,)

नैव तस्य कृतेनार्थो नाकृतेनेह कश्चन।
न चास्य सर्वभूतेषु कश्चिदर्थव्यपाश्रयः।। (3:18)

(He has no interest whatever in anything done, nor in anything not done, nor has he need to rely on anything for personal ends,) it is added that there is no freedom from action even for Krishna who is *Yogeshwara* and *Poorna Avatara*.

न मे पार्थास्ति कर्तव्यं त्रिषु लोकेषु किञ्चन।
नानवाप्तवाप्तव्यं वर्त एव च कर्मणि।। (3:22)

(For me O Partha, there is naught to do in the three worlds, nothing worth gaining I have not gained; yet I am ever in action.)

That is the reason why the definition given by the *Gita* for *Samnyasa*,

काम्यानां कर्मणां न्यासं संन्यासं कवयो विदुः। (18:2)

(Renunciation of actions springing from selfish desire is known as *Samnyasa* by the seers,) is the real definition acceptable to the *Gita* and so, to Gandhiji. Even Adi Shankaracharaya, who was a great *Samnyasi* and *muktatma*, performed the best *Sattvika karmas* all through his life without even a moment's respite inspite of his claim that after a certain stage of development on the spiritual path, actions are not necessary.

(ii) When *karmas* are a must in life, they are unavoidable, it is better that man voluntarily and willingly and with enthusiasm indulges in action in form of physical labour for earning one's livelihood. This is what Gandhiji calls bread-labour that is to be conceived of as *Yajna*. Gandhiji says: "But when the *Gita* says that 'rain comes from sacrifice' (verse 3:14), I think it indicates the necessity of bodily labour. The 'residue of sacrifice' (verse 3:13) is the bread that we have won by the sweat of our brow. Labouring enough for one's food has been classed in the *Gita* as a '*Yajna*'."[21] According to Gandhiji all must labour for their own food and earn it. All must be active. He says: "'Earn thy bread by the sweat of thy brow', says the Bible. Sacrifices may be of many kinds. One of them may well be bread-labour. If all laboured for their bread and no more, then there would be enough food and enough leisure for all."[22]

(iii) But Gandhiji does not stop here. Just as one of the five *Mahayajanas* in the *Manusmriti* मनुष्ययज्ञ (*Manushyayajna*) as also भूतयज्ञ (*Bhutayajna*) mean sparing at least an atom for others who are needy from what one earns, similarly now Gandhiji goes a step further and states that man should next undertake all his actions in a spirit of help and service to others. An action will become a sacrifice when man will undertake it for the benefit of others. He therefore next wants every man to undertake this bread-labour in a spirit of sacrifice. This would mean keeping the barest minimum to maintain one's self and giving away the rest to those who are in need of it. Man is in a society in which physical labour and mutual co-operation are necessary. He says: "The *Gita* says that anybody who eats without performing *Yajna*, in Tolstoy's language 'bread-labour, is a thief, eats sin.' But body labour becomes *Yajna* only when it is undertaken in a spirit of service, not of indulgence, as it may easily become when it is done only to develop the animal in man."[23] This is the positive third step in the development of the concept of *Karma* as also singing of the glory of bread-labour as Gandhiji would put it. He finds support for this in *Gita* 3:15 in particular. Similar is the fine verse in the *Manusmriti* that strictly prohibits preparing food, i.e., performing fruitful actions solely for one's self. We are told:

> अघं स केवलं भुङ्क्ते यः पचत्यात्मकारणात्-
> यज्ञशिष्टाशनं ह्येतत्सतामन्नं विधीयते।। (मनु. 3-118)

(He who prepares food for himself (alone), eats nothing but sin; for it is ordained that the food which remains after (the performance of) the sacrifices shall be the meal of virtuous men.)

This is also in line with *Rigveda* 10-117-6 that says:

> नार्यमणं पुष्णाति नो सखायं
> केवलाघो भवति केवलादी।

(One who (prepares food and) eats all alone, does not nourish either a friend or an enemy and so, eats sin.) And this is necessary to keep in motion the *Samsarachakra*, set in motion by God, by providence. The relevant verse in the *Gita* is 3:16. The social order must remain in tact, it should continue to progress. It is therefore necessary that this spirit should be cultivated. It is in the interest of individual and society both and we know that both are mutually dependent. The *Gita* says that this sort of mutual dependence exists between Gods and men also. Verse 3:11 says;

> देवान्भावयतानेन ते देवा भावयन्तु वः।
> परस्परं भावयन्तः श्रेयः परमवाप्स्यथ।।

(With this may you cherish the Gods and may the Gods cherish you; thus cherishing one another may you attain the highest good.) How much more is this relation necessary between men and men! The exact significance of the famous Vedic *mantra*,

> सह नाववतु सह नौ भुनक्तु
> सह वीर्यं करवावहै।
> तेजस्विनावधीतमस्तु
> मा विद्विषावहै।।

(Let us protect ourselves jointly, enjoy jointly, let us perform heroic deeds jointly,) fits in the present context very well.

(iv) The next question is this: Why should man resort to this attitude of taking to actions in a spirit of service to others, that is sacrifice? Why not expect for one's self the reward of one's own action? Why not enjoy it? Here, Gandhiji would give only a philosophical reason and that stresses, in the words of the ancient seers again,

आत्मवत्सर्वभूतेषु यः पश्यति स पश्यति।

(He is the real seer who visions all living beings as one's own self.) I would serve all my fellow men, all human life, all living beings because of the presence of the same soul, the same life-force in all. The *Brihadaranayaka Upanishad* would say:

न वा अरे सर्वस्य कामाय सर्वं प्रियं भवति,
आत्मनस्तु कामाय सर्वं प्रियं भवति।।

(All beings are not to one's liking indeed for their own sake; all beings are liked only through attachment to *Atman*.)

We are all seekers after *mukti*, after perfection, whether we know it or not and so, looking on all as one is the next stage in the sublimation of the concept of *Karma*, that has as its basis the priniciple of bread-labour. That is the reason why Gandhiji says: "Everyone has faith in himself that multiplied to nth degree is God. The sum total of all that lives is God. We may not be God, but we are of God; even as a little drop of water is of the ocean."[24] It is therefore necessary that man should know that service to living beings is service to God. Let a man become conscious that whatever he is doing is God's work and then only will he rise spiritually to the highest. The ultimate stage is explained in the cultivation of this spirit — सर्वं खल्विदं ब्रह्म (Really all this is indeed *Brahman*) and also that ब्रह्मविद् ब्रह्मैव भवति (One who has realized *Brahman* becomes *Brahman*), and the *Gita* says:

ब्रह्मार्पणं ब्रह्महविः ब्रह्माग्नौ ब्रह्मणा हुतम्।
ब्रह्मैव तेन गन्तव्यं ब्रह्मकर्मसमाधिना।। (4:24)

(The offering of sacrifice is *Brahman*, the oblation is *Brahman*; it is offered by *Brahman* in the fire that is *Brahman*; thus he whose mind is fixed on acts dedicated to *Brahman* must needs pass on to *Brahman*). This concept of bread-labour with its religious, ethical and spiritual side thus conceived by Gandhiji and the new meaning thus given by him to the known sense of the word '*Yajna*', is a unique contribution of Gandhiji. Other interesting interpretations are there, but this is an interpretation original in its own way, and Gandhiji has scientifically and systematically argued it out. He again shows his vision as a *Bhashyakara* as he had shown in his concept of *Ahimsa* in the *Gita*.

It is an interpretation peculiarly useful to the modern Indian life as the earlier interpretations of the *Acharyas* have been useful to their own times. While the *Gita* permits all these varied interpretations, the modern one given by Gandhiji may be known as the *Yugadharma* of the modern age. The *Gita* gives expression to the *Yugadharma* of each age and this is the real universality of the scripture. The interpretation given by Gandhiji is as true to the modern Indian life as it was more than twenty years back when Pundit Nehru said: "We are drifting everywhere and I sometimes doubt if we are drifting in the right direction. We live in a state of perpetual crisis and have no grip of the situation,"[25] and Gandhiji in his rare, most painful words had said: "My dreams of an ideal India are being shattered . . ."[26] Of course when we grant that this is a unique interpretation and an interpretation that is very much useful to the modern Indian life, it should not and cannot necessarily mean that this is exactly what the writer of the *Gita* means. If we were to argue out the whole case from the viewpoint of the original writer and give an explanation of the words *Yoga* and *Yajna*, it will mean many things more than 'action in a spirit of service to others' as Gandhiji takes it. The words can be interpreted from religious, ethical and spiritual points of view and each interepretation will depend on the approach that we take. To the *Gitakara*, the three approaches are a unity and so, *Yajna* and *Yoga* can be interpreted from that point of view also. Gandhiji's is not a scholastic and philosophic interpretation; it is an interpretation for the guidance of the common man of his times. The conception of the *Gita* is far higher and nobler than this.

Other Minor Questions

Once that Gandhiji takes this peculiar line of thought, it is natural that he should drive the doctrines of *Swadeshi* and spinning from the *Gita*. He is thoroughly consistent here with his line of interpretation, though this does not mean that he is right. He tries to derive his doctrine of *Swadeshi* on the basis of स्वधर्म (*Svadharma*) as explained in:

स्वधर्मे निधनं श्रेयः परधर्मो भयावहः। (3:35)

(. . .better is death in the discharge of one's duty; another's is fraught with danger,)

and,

स्वधर्ममपि चावेक्ष्य न विकम्पितुमर्हसि। (2:31)

(Again, seeing thine own duty thou shouldst not shrink from it). He states: "In its ultimate and spiritual sense, *Swadeshi* stands for the final emancipation of the human soul from its earthly bondage. . . . A votary of *Swadeshi* therefore, in his striving to identify himself with the entire creation, seeks to be emancipated from the bondage of the physical body", and "That is why the *Gita* says: 'It is better to die performing one's duty or *Swadharma* but *Paradharma*, or another's duty, is fraught with danger.' Interpreted in terms of one's physical environment, this gives us the Law of *Swadeshi*....What the *Gita* says with regard to *Swadharma* equally applies to *Swadeshi*, for *Swadeshi* is *Swadharma* applied to one's immediate environment."[27] No argument is necessary to prove that he is straining the meaning of the word *Swadharma* too much and too far to derive the sense that he wants. Similarly in his comments on verse 6:1:

अनाश्रितः कर्मफलं कार्यं कर्म करोति यः।
स संन्यासी च योगी च न निरग्निर्न चाक्रियः।। (6:1)

(He who performs all obligatory action, without depending on the fruit thereof, is a *Samnyasin* and a *Yogin*—not the man who neglects the sacrificial fire nor he who neglects action,) he makes these remarks: "Fire here may be taken to mean all possible instruments of action. Fire was needed when sacrifices used to be performed with its help...Assuming that spinning was means of universal service in this age, a man by neglecting the spinning wheel would not become a *Samnyasi*." The difficulty about deriving the meaning here is that it is just an assumption based on the assumption that only the spinning wheel is the means of Universal service in this age. Arguing on the method adopted by Gandhiji, any sense can be derived here because we change the means of universal service and a new sense arises. This too is like stretching the meaning of the *Gita* too far, in order to derive the interpretation and meaning that one wants to. It is like reading your own views in the work, rather than reading the views of the *Gita*kara from the work. With all the value that the law of *Swadeshi* and the spinning wheel had in the days of Gandhiji, it is not possible to derive these two from the *Gita* by any reasonable stretch of imagination. And that is the reason why one of his very great admirers, C.F. Andrews has stated: "*Swadeshi* is so intimately linked up with Hinduism in his own mind that it is necessary to bring it here as a part of his religious belief, though many earnest othodox people would not hold it to be an integral Hindu doctrine. Perhaps it should be regarded as an idiosyncracy of Mahatma Gandhiji himself representing his own individual way of expressing one aspect of his Hindu faith."[28]

And Gandhiji lived for the common man, the lonely and the lost. In the service of this humanity he sees service to God, and feels that is his only path. To put in his own words: " I am endeavouring to see God through service of humanity for I know that God is neither in heaven, nor down below, but in everyone."[29] In everything that he did therefore, the common man was before his eyes. Even in his interpretation of the *Gita* the common man is before him and he interprets the *Gita* exclusively for him, though we must concede that he has done this in the manner of a *Bhashyakar*. But Chitale is right when he states: 'But the teaching of *Gita* is not only for the most neglected common man, its teaching applies equally well to the most advanced as well as the least advanced, to the most intelligent and the most ignorant, to the highly meritorious and to the most sinful, young and old."[30] This is the reason why the *Gita* 4:11 says:

ये यथा मां प्रपद्यन्ते तांस्तथैव भजाम्यहम्। (4:11)

(In whatever way men resort to Me, even so do I render to them.) The *Gita* will therefore permit other interpretations applicable to the more advanced, without prejudicing its basic teaching that is bound to remain the same.

The originality of Gandhiji's doctrines is that the *Gita* is interpreted purely from the point of view of the common man. Gandhiji brought the *Gita* from its lofty pedestal of the purely spiritual interpretions to the level of the common man and showed to him that the *Gita* teaches, to all men of all times, the day to day religion and ethics as also shows the noblest path to self-realization and God-realization. When he did this, he has of course in no way undermined the glory of the spiritual teaching of the *Gita* that is a great Upanishad on its own claims (श्रीमद्भगवद्गीतासूपनिषत्सु etc.,) and it is rightly contended about it that:

"The teaching of the *Gita* is based on the philosophic teaching of the older Upanishads,"[31] and "The *Gita* is one of the most authoritative sources of Hindu doctrine and ethics, and is accepted as such by Hindus of all denominations,"[32] and "It sets forth in precise and penetrating words the essential principles of a spiritual religion,"[33] and "My heart and mind both received more nourishment from the *Gita* than my body has from my mother's milk. Where the heart is touched, there is no room for argument."[34]

NOTES

1. 'In the Path of Mahatma Gandhi', p. 289
2. 'Young India', 9-4-1925.
3. 'Diary of Mahadev Desai', p.211.
4. 'Harijan', 1-9-1940.
5. 'Harijan', 20-9-1937.
6. 'Harijan', 6-8-1939.
7. 'Harijan', 21-1-1939.
8. 'Bhagavadgita', Introduction, p. 69.
9. 'Bhagavadgita', p. 13.
10. 'Bhagavadgita', p. 12.
11. '*Gita* as Jivan-*Yoga*', p. 7.
12. Translation from his Gujarati 'Jeevanpradeepa', p. 190.
13. 'Young India', 1-9-1927.
14. 'Harijan', 24-2-1946.
15. 'Young India', 29-9-1928.
16. 'Delhi Dairy', 29-1-1948.
17. 'Young India', 15-10-1925.
18. 'Harijan', 6-2-1947.
19. 'Young India', 8-9-1927.
20. 'Young India', 21-10-1926.
21. 'Ashram Observances in Action', p. 60.
22. 'Harijan', 29-6-1935.
23. 'Young India', 20-9-1928.
24. 'Harijan', 3-6-1939.
25. 'Mahatma Gandhi –Last Phase', p. 3.
26. 'Last Glimpses of Bapu', Manuben Gandhi, p. 115.
27. 'Young India', 18-6-1931.
28. 'Mahatma Gandhi's Ideas', p. 118.
29. 'Young India', 4-8-1927.
30. 'Bhagavat *Gita* and Hindu *Dharma*', p. 28.

31. Vide Supra, p. 22.
32. Rajagopalachari in 'Bhagavadgita', p. 11.
33. S. Radhakrishnan in 'Bhagavadgita', Introduction. p. 11.
34. 'Talks on the *Gita*', Vinoba Bhave, p. 1.

TEN

Place of Gandhiji in the Realm of Interpreters of the *Gita*

"There was a time when he appeared to hover between Christ and his native faith, and when he ultimately stuck to Hinduism, it was to a new Hinduism, revivified and chastened through the crucible of his own thought."

A.R. Wadia[1]

"He was to capture India not as a sage or mystic but as a holy doer, an apostle of action, the trail-blazing *Karma-yogin* of the new dispensation. Krishna's message as taught by Tilak pointed to no one else so decisively. The pupil was almost ready for the master."

Geoffery Ashe[2]

"The process of *yoga* is a turning of the human soul from the egoistic state of consciousness absorbed in the outward appearances and attractions of things to a higher state in which the Transcendent and Universal can pour itself, into the individual mould and transform it."

Shri Aurobindo[3]

"If I did not feel the presence of God within me, I see so much of misery and disappointment every day that I would be a raving maniac and my destination would be the *Hoogli*."

Gandhiji[4]

Introduction

With this long and detailed dicussion, we now come to the summing up and discuss the question of placing Gandhiji at his proper place in the realm of interpreters of the *Gita*. We would thus come to understand and evaluate Gandhiji's originality in his interpretation of the *Gita*.

As we do this, the very first fact to be noted is that Gandhiji is not a scholar or philosopher in either the western or eastern sense of the term as we saw earlier. He is not again, trained in the scholar's methods of interpetation and explanation. He at the same time, does not interpret the *Gita* as a pure academician, scholar or cold philosopher; it is actually not his purpose to do so. He never interpreted the *Gita* merely for the sake of interpretation.

His Purpose

His purpose was twofold when he took up the interpretation of the *Gita*. Besides countless words of wisdom on the *Gita*, he gave his famous translation and *Anasaktiyoga*. The work was interpreted in a scholarly way by Mahadev Desai in his English version, "The Gospel of Selfless Action." The twofold purpose of Gandhiji was:

(i) To show what he himself found in the eternal words of wisdom of *Yogeshvara* Krishna in the *Gita* as he, in his own way, tried to follow the teaching of the *Gita* in life for a period of over forty years. He found that the ultimate aim of this great book on religion, ethics and spirtualism was to show the path of self-realization *through* life and all its actions undertaken in a spirit of detachment at the beginning, to rise to a spirit of total submission to the Divine will, in the end.

(ii) To give to the people of India a handbook of religious, moral and spiritual guidance so that they too may find in the *Gita* what he found and they too may try to live the *Gita* as he did. The second purpose follows from the first and there is nothing in the world that he would not share with humanity. With the second purpose in view, he interprets the *Gita* only in a certain fixed way; in a way that the meaning arrived at will fulfill all the needs of the time and all the needs of man, doing best all the while, so that its central teaching does not change or suffer in his interpretation. Kaka Kalelkar quotes Gandhiji in his preface thus: "It is a fact that *Anasaktiygoa* is an authentic translation; but as it covers up the life-philosophy of us the *Ashramites*, in course of time, this work will be used not as a translation but as an independent holy scripture."[5]

He thus wanted the *Gita* to become a guide to himself, to the *Ashramites*, to the *Satyagrahis* and to the people of the country at large, so that it led to the betterment and gradual rise of all. It was thus not an academic study for its own sake and it could not be so. A metaphysician is defined thus: "Anyone who asks whether the world is actually what it appears to him to be, or whether his sensory impressions or reflections are disortions of reality is a metaphysician." Gandhiji will not be a metaphysician in this sense. Again, philosophy is defined thus: "The word 'Philosophy' is derived from the Greek verb (meaning 'to love') and the Greek noun (meaning 'wisdom'). Wisdom means knowledge which has enriched the personality of the thinker and enabled him to orient himself in the universe of which he is a part. It has thus both a theoretical and practical significance . . .It is also significant that for many of the greatest thinkers, philosophy has been not only a matter of theory but also a way of life."[6] Gandhiji is not a philosopher in this sense and he does not claim to be one, though philosophy of God as a conviction has been a way of life to him. Gandhiji lived philosophy in the sense that he lived in God. Here, his torch-bearer was the *Gita* which he found to be "the book *par excellence* for the knowledge of Truth."[7]

It is thus clear that though he took to the interpretation of the *Gita* in all devotion and faith, he took to it for a practical purpose. He wanted that (i) it should guide him on his path of life and in his constant rise to Divinity, (ii) it should give the life-philosophy of the *Ashramites*, (iii) it should show a unique path of onward progress to God through its religion and ethics to the commonest of the common and through him to the whole of humanity. It should be noted that when he interpreted the *Gita*, the average Indian of his own days, the common man who was bound by slavery, was before his eyes. He wanted him to rise, to improve, to progress in life in this world and in the life hereafter. He thus seeks in the *Gita* answers to the problems of India of his days. This will partly explain his reading in the *Gita* the ideals of *Swadeshi*, trusteeship, spinning, bread-labour and so on, as also his peculiar doctrine of *Karma-Yoga* that is *Anasaktiyoga*. When he wanted the *Gita* to teach the doctrine of *Ahimsa*, he was again seeking a solution to a problem with which India of his days was faced. It was thus an interpretation peculiar to the needs of India of his days. The spirit of the *Gita* is so large and universal that if Gandhiji were to get answers to these in the *Gita*, we cannot say that he is wrong or partial or one-sided in his reading of the *Gita*. In this sense, Gandhiji is right to say about the *Gita* that: ". . . it answers all my difficulties and has been my *Kamadhenu*, my guide, my open seasame, on hundreds of moments of doubt and difficulty. I cannot recall a single occasion when it has failed me."[8]

Actually when Gandhiji puts this value on the *Gita* and inerprets it accordingly, he is revealing a new aspect of the glory of the *Gita*, even though in our study so far, we have conceded that at a few places he seems even to twist the meaning of certain verses or to carry the meaning too far.

His other Purposes and Achievements

But if Gandhiji were to do this and only this in his interpretation of the *Gita*, our long study would have been in vain. Actually he has accepted that: "The *Gita* is not an aphoristic work; it is a great religious poem. The deeper you dive into it, the richer the meanings you get. It being meant for the people at large, there is pleasing repetition. With every age, the important words will carry new and expanding meanings. But its central teaching will never vary. The seeker is at liberty to extract from this treasure any meaning he likes, so as to enable him to enforce in his life the central teaching."[9] What he has done in his interpretation and also translation is that,

(i) He has given new and expanding meanings of certain very important words in the *Gita* in accordance with the needs of the present age. To illustrate, "*Yajna* means an act directed to the welfare of others, done without desiring any return for it, whether of a temporal or spiritual nature."[10] To him, Law of *Yajna* is 'The Law of Service'. In another context, he understands *Yajna* as 'bread-labour'. He says: "The *Gita* teaches that one should perform *Yajna* (bread-labour) and partake of the fruits of that labour."[11] Again, by *Anasakti* he gives a meaning that is in line with the traditional one, but interprets it newly. He says: "By detachment I mean that one must not worry whether the desired result follows from your action or not, so long as your motive is pure, your means correct. Really, it means that things will come right in the end if you take care of the means and leave the rest to Him."[12]

(ii) He has successfully interpreted the *Gita* in new light, in the light of his own thinking. That explains his emphasis on *Anasakti* in the *Karma-yoga*, reading of the war as an allegory, trying to find out the doctrine of *Ahimsa*, interpreting a few verses in such a way that he can derive the doctrine of opposition against untouchability, as also bread-labour, *Swadeshi*, spinning, service to humanity, etc., from the *Gita*.[13]

(iii) He has also stressed the never changing central doctrine of the *Gita* in stressing the final aim of the *Gita* as self-realization, the application of the doctrine of *Karma-yoga* to all, his unique interpretation of *Bhakti* in the *Gita*, his stress on the peculiar meaning of *Samnyasa* in the *Gita*, and so on.

It was said about the ancient *Bhashyakaras* that they would exhibit their scholarship and hold on the *shastras* by deriving the same doctrine from the *Prasthanatrayi*. Kalelkar says: "It is a rule and convention with Indian philosophy that only he is to be considered an *Acharya* and an authority, who unifies the *Upanishads*, the *Brahmasutras* and the *Gita* and is successful in deriving the same philosophy from all the three."[14]

Gandhiji—A Bhashyakara

We may go a step further and say that just like Gandhiji's interpretation of the *Gita*, the interpretation of all the three works by the *Acharyas* are based on their experience, their *Sadhana*, and so, though varied in many respects, there is an inner stream of the same philosophy in all of them. The central doctrine of the *Gita* and the metaphysics of the *Gita* that Gandhiji derives are in line with the *Acharyas*, even though his experience and his *Sadhana* are glaringly different from theirs. And it is known that the needs and leanings and tendencies of the time have influenced the *Acharyas* very deeply in their interpretations. Thus, with due respect to the experience, *Sadhana*, insight and scholarship of these *Acharyas* we can say that what Shankara, Ramanuja, Madhusudana, Madhava, etc. gave, has a stamp of the needs of the times in which they lived.

Gandhiji is therefore in line with the ancient *Bhashyakaras* and the orignality in his interpretation is the originality of (i) his personality, (ii) his experience and *Sadhana*, (iii) his idea about the needs of the man of his time, and all the peculiar traits that we find in the

Bhashyakaras. The different virtues and limitations in their interpretations, the originality that we find in each one of them, will be found to the same extent in Gandhiji's interpretation from of course his own point of view and manner of reading the *Gita* He is thus a *Bhashyakara* and a *Bhashyakara* of no mean achievement on his own right. He is different from Shankaracharya when he refuses to treat of the book, only as a work on philosophy, on spiritual attainment of a *Samnyasi*. Here, Gandhiji concedes that the *Gita* is the most representative Hindu scripture on religion and ethics. He differs from the schools of Ramanuja and Vallabha in that he refuses to take the *Gita* only as a work that glorifies *Bhakti* and *Saguna Upasana*. To him, it is also a work that shows to man the path of self-realization through life, by dissolving the ego and sublimating man's personality to take it to higher and higher heights. Gandhiji has his own say in the meaning that he reads in the *Gita*. Gandhiji yet differs from Tilak and Aurobindo, two other *Bhashyakaras* of first order, who are his contemporaries. Tilak reads only *Karma-yoga* in the *Gita* and when it comes to metaphysics, he accepts Shankara. Gandhiji, however, places greater stress on the means, on *Anasakti*, though he accepts *Karma-yoga* as he should and fuses this ideal of life with spiritual attainment. Aurobindo accepts *Karma-yoga* in its fusion with *Bhakti-yoga* and *Jnana-yoga,* but takes *Karma-yoga* from mundane to spiritual heights and stresses that the *Gita* is purely a spiritual work. Here Gandhiji starts on a more modest ground and makes his *Karma-yoga* and *Anasakti-yoga* those of life at its earthly level from where one has to rise. This is because, to put in his own words: "Therefore, I would urge my friends to keep their feet firm on Mother Earth and not scale the Himalayan heights to which the poet took Arjuna and his other heroes. Any way, I must respectfully refuse even to attempt the ascent. The plains of Hindustan are good enough for me."[15] When thus, three *Bhashyakaras* of the same age, looking to the needs of their age and their own vision, interpret the *Gita* differently, we further stress that their interpretations are guided by their own inner vision plus the need of the age as they conceive it.

The Modern Approach

Under the influence of the western methods of analysis and criticism, Hill, Edgerton, Dasgupta, Ranade, Radhakrishnan, Krishna Prem and others tried to derive from the *Gita* the views of the writer of the scripture. Their work was of course more difficult than that of the *Bhashyakaras*. This is because when one is keen to know the view of the writer of a very old scripture, the first requisite is an unbiassed, impartial mind, clean to the core and ready to receive any impression. This is a very difficult attainment indeed, as can be seen from even the most scholarly views on the *Gita*. The views are generally guided by one's own beliefs and faith and so, if the scholar's mind is not open and clear, he is not likely to fare better than the *Bhashyakaras*, who are guided by a specific purpose.

Another requisite is a thorough study and grasp of the history and the social, religious, ethical, spiritual, cultural and similar background on which the book is written. This is an equally difficult task and a unique achievement on its own. It is surprising and interesting to note that no important modern scholar of the *Gita* probes into the details of this background.

The third and an important requisite is to know the time, the other works and the mind of the writer and also to know the inspirer or inspirers, individuals or works that have preceded. This is also very difficult, with reference to the *Gita* in particular, because we know very little about the date, mind, other works etc., of the author of the *Gita*, whoever he is and we have no information about his sources in the writing of the *Gita*.

The technical terms and their varied senses and the senses in the mind of the author of the *Gita* is yet another difficult problem to solve, and there the modern scholars are not agreed on most of the terms.

These and similar problems are faced like challenges by the modern scholars and they too come to different conclusions about,

(i) the nature of the work,
(ii) the message and principles of the work,
(iii) the spiritualism of the work,
(iv) the basic essence of its principles, and so on.

Modern Approach and Gandhiji

Gandhiji of course claims that his interpretation is not challenged by anyone; he too has followed a fixed method and he does not give twists. The preceding discussion examines these claims and how he interprets the *Gita*. Here we should once more stress that as Gandhiji is not trained in modern scholarship and philosophical discipline, he is not an academician and theorist, he does not give his own interpretation from the modern point of view, he does not make a conscious effort to assess the views of the author of the *Gita*. His guides and torchbearers are: (i) his heritage and *Vaishnava* discipline, (ii) his experience and effort to live the teaching of the *Gita*, and (iii) his firm resolve, inspite of constant prayerful study, to accept as truth only what his reason accepts as valid. With these three guides and aids he has worked and the result is that he is nearer to the *Bhashyakaras* than the modern scholars. It would be better to call him a *Bhashyakara* instead of a scholar in his interpretation of the meaning of the *Gita*. Like Shankara, Ramanuja, Madhusudana, Madhava etc., in his interpretation of the *Gita*, (i) he is guided by a specific external purpose , and (ii) he reads his own views in the *Gita* rather than the views of the author out of it. This is exactly the method adopted by the ancient *Acharyas* in their *Bhashyas* on the *Gita*. We can further state, without hesitation, that the purpose with which he writes and interprets is thus fulfilled. We may not agree with the devotees of Gandhiji that only he lived the *Gita* because almost all the ancient *Acharyas*—Shankara, Ramanuja, Madhava, Madhusudana, led very noble ascetic-like lives, they almost lived the *Gita* and their heritage and outlook left a deep mark on their interpretation of the *Gita*. Ramakrishna, Vivekanada etc., are modern ascetics who have lived in the spirit of the *Gita* and they have been first-rank ascetics as also *Karma-yogins*. Similar is the status of Jnaneshwara, Aurobindo and even Tilak who have lived in the spirit of the *Gita*, and these three have read the doctrines of their own lives in the *Gita*. The *Gita* has shaped and bettered and also sublimated their lives and their teaching. Gandhiji is in line with these *Acharyas* and *Bhashyakaras*.[16]

But as we have seen, Gandhiji's approach to the *Gita* as a *Bhashyakara* is unique in its own way and it has uniquely succeeded in bringing out the universality of the *Gita* as a scripture of religion, ethics and spiritualism—all combined into one. No other *Bhashyakara* had the whole of humanity before his eyes as Gandhiji had, even though he had covered up the whole of humanity through the common man of India of his days,[17] the common man who had lost his self-respect and his soul and Gandhiji wanted him to struggle to regain both. It is stated that: "Perhaps the most wonderful thing about the *Gita* is that it is a source of guidance to everyone. For the simplest of men, who have not the understanding of any intricate or far-reaching doctrine, as well as for the most advanced mystic, the path is clearly indicated."[18] Again it is added that: "The inertia of the mass and the inevitability of control in few hands in any scheme of things, brings to the forefront the point which is stressed in the *Gita* over and over again, viz., the necessity of setting a good model to the mass of the people and the desirability of the cultivation of the *Sattva* attribute by the leaders of any human group."[19] Gandhiji was of clear opinion that the *Gita* was mainly, if not entirely meant for the common man. He therefore interpreted it from his point of view and set himself as a model and leader. He was a leader not as one who only commanded; he set himself as an example, the best living example who led his life exactly in accordance with the doctrine of the *Gita* and explained the *Gita* accordingly. This is a unique and original contribution of Gandhiji, whether or not we agree with some of his views.

A Question

A question might arise here. Which interpretation of the *Gita* should we take as more authentic and therefore prefer, the interpretation of the *Bhashyakara* or that of the scholar; the view of the *Bhashyakara* or the view of the original author? It must be conceded that all *Bhashyakaras* honestly believed that they were giving the correct expression to the doctrine of the *Gita* and Gandhiji falls in line with them. The attempt at knowing the view in the mind of the original author by modern critical and analytical method is something that we have learnt from the west and Gandhiji has not taken any serious interest in it. And we have already explained in our Introduction as also elsewhere how the peculiar structure of the *Gita* as a scripture permits of so many interpretations, and all the interpretations that scholars read in the *Gita* find support in the various verses of the work. The *Gita,* inspite of the great value of its purely academic, scholarly and theoretical study, is mainly a work for practice in life and so, there is scope for varied interpretations with every individual and with every age, and no interpretation can be stated to be wrong till it satisfies man's conscience and spiritual needs. Each interpretation is therefore valuable in its own way. We can even go a step further and say that greater the personality of the man who follows the spirit of the *Gita* and interprets it, greater is its value. Gandhiji's interpretation has its value likewise due to the grand ascetic personality of the man. And if we were to say of great ascetics like Shankara, Vivekananda and Aurobindo that: "He who chooses the Infinite has been chosen by the Infinite. He has received the divine touch without which there is no awakening, no opening of the spirit; but once it is received, attainment is sure, whether conquered swiftly in the course of one human life or pursued patiently through many stages of the cycle of existence in the manifested universe,"[20] This will equally be true of Gandhiji to whom these words of Tagore rightly apply: "The word 'Mahatma' means the liberated ego which rediscovers itself in all other souls, that life no longer confined in individual human beings, the comprehensive soul of the *Atman*, of the spirit. In this way the soul becomes 'Mahatma', by comprehending all souls, all spirit in itself."[21]

All this will show that Gandhiji's interpretation has a place of its own in the realm of interpretations of the *Gita* and his is in many respect an original contribution. It is unfortunate that it has not commanded attention that is justly its due. Ours is here the first ever all-sided study of Gandhiji's interpretation together with its influence on Gandhiji's life and his teachings.

NOTES

1. 'The Philosophy of Mahatma Gandhi and Other Essays', p. 9.
2. 'Gandhi—A Study in Revolution', p. 139.
3. 'Synthesis of Yoga', p. 7.
4. 'Young India', 6-8-1925.
5. Preface to Gandhiji's 'Anasaktiyoga' in Gujarati. Translation is mine.
6. 'Philosophy of Religion', Patterson, p. 15.
7. 'My Experiments with Truth', pt. 1. Ch. 20.
8. 'Harijan', 30-1-1937.
9. 'Young India', 6-8-1931.
10. 'Yeravada Mandir', Ch. xiv.
11. 'Young India', 8-9-1927.
12. 'Delhi Diary', p. 390. 29-1-1948.
13. 'Harijan', 7-4-1946.
14. Preface to Gandhiji's 'Anasaktiyoga' in Gujarati. Translation is mine.

15. 'Young India', 21-5-1928.
16. Incidentally it may be noted here that when it came to discussing as to who interprets the *Brahmasutras* of sage Badarayana the best, scholars of first rank have discussed the problem but ultimately found the interpretations of their own sects the best. Even in the interpretation of the *Gita* by the Indian scholars, this has happened with many.
17. It would be better to say that surprisingly enough, no scholar has taken due interest in Gandhiji's interpretation and studied it as elaborately as we have done here.
18. '*Gita* Explained'—Manu Subedar, p. 27.
19. '*Gita* Explained'—Manu Subedar, p. 22.
20. 'Synthesis of Yoga'—Aurobindo, p. 2.
21. Tagore quoted by Rene Fullop Miller in 'Gandhi—The Holy Man' p. 8-9.

Bibliography

English

1.	Bhagavad Gita	Prabhavananda and Isherwood
2.	Bhagavad Gita	Colliers Encyclopedia
3.	Bhagavad Gita	Telang
4.	Bhagavad Gita	C. Rajagopalachari
5.	Bhagavad Gita	Swami Nikhilanand
6.	Bhagavad Gita	S.K. Belvalkar
7.	Bhagavad Gita	S. Radhakrishnan
8.	Bhagavad Gita—An Exposition	Vasant Rele
9.	Doctrine of Bhagavad Gita	Pt. Bhavanishankar
10.	Gitanjali	Rabindranath Tagore
11.	Gita Rahasya	B.G. Tilak
12.	Shrimad Bhagavad Gita	Balaram D. Sopan
13.	The Bhagavad Gita	W.D.P. Hill
14.	The Bhagavad Gita	Dr. S.R. Shastri
15.	The Bhagavad Gita	Swami Swarupananda
16.	The Bhagavad Gita	Swami Chinmayanand
17.	Song Celestial	Edwin Arnold
18.	Song Celestial	Raman Maharshi
19.	Age and Origin of Gita	J.N. Farquhar
20.	Bhagavad Gita—A Fresh Approach	P.M. Modi
21.	Bhagavad Gita and Hindu Dharma	M.P. Chitale
22.	Bhagavad Gita—The Song of God	Aldous Huxley
23.	Bhagavad Gita and Modern Life	K.M. Munshi
24.	Bhagavad Gita—As a Philosophy of God-Realization	R.D. Ranade

25. Discourses on the Gita	M.K. Gandhi
26. Ramanuja on the Bhagavad Gita	J.A.B. Van Buitenan
27. Essays on the Gita	Shri Aurobindo
28. Gita the Mother	M.K. Gandhi (Ed. J.P. Chandar)
29. Gita Letters	Swami Avinashananda
30. Gita Explained	Manu Subedar
31. Gita as Jivan Yoga	K. Kalelkar
32. Gita and the Gospel	J.N. Farquhar
33. Gita Sandesh	Swami Ramdas
34. Gita Meditations	Swami Shivananda
35. Glimpses of Bhagavad Gita and Advaita Vedanta	M.W. Burvey
36. Gospel of the Gita	T.V. Kapalishastri
37. Introduction to Bhagavad Gita	Shri Yatindra Ramanujadas
38. Introduction to Bhagavad Gita	V.K. Ramanujacharya
39. Krishna and the Gita	Sitanath
40. Permanent Lessons of the Gita	J.N. Farquhar
41. Quest for Original Gita	G.S. Kher
42. Talks on the Gita	Vinoba Bhave
43. Gita According to Gandhi	Mahadev Desai
44. The Teaching of the Gita	Ed. A.T. Hingorani
45. The Gita and Indian Culture	J.G. Wadiyar
46. The Gita and the Quran	Sunderlal
47. Thoughts on the Gita	Swami Vivekananda
48. The Yoga of Bhagavad Gita	Krishna Prem
49. A Week with Gandhi	Louis Fisher
50. Delhi Diary	Mahadev Desai
51. Gandhi	G. Ramachandra T.K. Mahadevan
52. Gandhi—The Holy Man	Rene Fullop Miller
53. Gandhi—As Saint and Statesman	Sayud Hossain
54. Gandhi's Discovery of Religion	Nikam
55. Gandhian Ethics	B.C. Ray
56. Gandhi's Emissary	Sudhir Ghosh
57. Gandhi Sutras	D.S. Sharma
58. Gandhi's Life, Thoughts and Philosophy	R.R. Diwakar

59. Gandhi Lives — Marc Edmund Jones
60. Gandhi Memorial Peace Number — Ed. Kshitish Roy
61. Gandhi's Philosophy in Life and Action — K.M. Munshi
62. Philosophy — C.E. M. Joad
63. Gandhism—An Analysis — P. Spratt
64. Gandhism — N.C. Bandopadhyaya
65. Gandhi's View of Life — Chandrashankar Shukla
66. Gospel of Gandhi — K. Santhanam
67. In the Path of Mahatma Gandhi — George Catlin
68. Incidents of Gandhiji's Life — Chandrashankar Shukla
69. Last Glimpses of Bapu — Manubehn Gandhi
70. Legacy of Gandhiji — Rajendra Prased
71. Lenin and Gandhiji — R. Fullop Miller
72. Lessons from Gandhiji's Death
73. Mahatma Gandhi — Haridas T. Mazumdar
74. Mahatma Gandhi — J. Nehru
75. Mahatma Gandhi — Polak, Brailsford, P. Lawrence
76. Mahatma Gandhi — R. Rolland
77. Mahatma Gandhi — Vincent Sheean
78. Mahatma Gandhiji's Ideas — C.F. Andrews
79. Mahatma Gandhi and Kavi Rajachandra — (Trans.)
80. Mahatma Gandhi—The Early Phase — Pyarelalji
81. Mahatma Gandhi—The Last Phase — Pyarelalji
82. M.K. Gandhi: An Indian Patriot in South Africa — Joseph. J. Doke
83. My Days with Gandhi — Nirmal Kumar Bose
84. My Gandhi — J.H. Holmes
85. Nehru on Gandhi — R.J. Walsh
86. Satyagraha—Its Technique and History — R.R. Diwakar
87. Selections from Gandhi — N.K. Bose
88. Selected Writings from M.K. Gandhi — Ronald Donal
89. Studies in Gandhism — N.K. Bose
90. Teachings of Mahatma Gandhi — J.P. Chandar
91. The Diary of Mahadev Desai — —
92. The Gandhian Way to World Peace — S.C. Gangal

93. The Gandhian Way — J.B. Kripalani
94. The Lonely Pilgrim — Manubehn Gandhi
95. The Philosophy of Mahatma Gandhi and Other Essays — A.R. Wadia
96. The Unique Christ and the Mystic Gandhi — P.V. George
97. The Weaponless Warrior — S.H.S. Thapar
98. Tolstoy and Gandhi — Kalidas Nag.
99. Yeravada Mandir — M.K. Gandhi
100. Bapu's Letters to Mira — M.K. Gandhi
101. Upanishad 48 — V. Sheean
102. A Source Book in Indian Philosophy — S. Radhakrishnan and C.A. Moore
103. A Synthetic View of Vedanta — P.N. Srinivasachari
104. Atmabodha — Swami Chinmayanand
105. Autobiography — J. Nehru
106. A Week on the Concord and Merrinal Rivers — H.D. Thoreau
107. Base of Yoga — Shri Aurobindo
108. Conquest of Violence — John V. Bondurant
109. Dhammapada (Trans.) — S. Radhakrishnan
110. Doctrine and Argument in Indian Philosophy — Ninian Smart
111. God and Reality — R.J. Kreyche
112. Early Indian Thought — S. Rangacharya
113. Ends and Means — Aldous Huxley
114. Epics and Puranas — A.D. Pusalkar
115. Epics, Myths & Legends of India — P. Thomas
116. Essays and Reflections — R.D. Ranade
117. Hindu Philosophy — Theos Bernard
118. History of Indian Philosophy, Vol. II — S.N. Dasgupta
119. History of Indian Philosophy — J.N. Sinha
120. Holy Bible
121. Ideal of A Karmayogi — Shri Aurobindo
122. India—A World in Transition — Beatrice P. Lamb
123. Indian Philosophy Vol. 1 — S. Radhakrishnan
124. Indian Thought and Its Development — Albert Schweitzer

125. Indian Antiquary (Intro. To Bhagavad Gita) — Garbe
126. Indian Philosophy Vol. II — S. Radhakrishnan
127. Indian Wisdom — Monier Williams
128. Kalki — S. Radhakrishnan
129. Introduction to Vedanta — P. Nagaraja Rao
130. Kabir—The Great Mystic — I.A. Ezekiel
131. Law of Manu — G. Buhler
132. Lead Kindly Light — Vincent Sheean
133. Miscellaneous Letters & Essays — Leo Tolstoy
134. On the Vedas — Shri Aurobindo
135. On the Meaning of Life — Will Durant
136. Origin and Development of Vaishnavism — Suvira Jaiswal
137. Outline of Indian Philosophy — M. Hiriyanna
138. Out of Dust — D.F. Karaka
139. Patiala University Messages
140. Perennial Philosophy — Aldous Huxley
141. Philosophy of India — H.A. Zimmer
142. Philosophy of Religion — Editors: George L. Abernethy, Thomas A. Longford
143. Philosophy of the East — J.M. Kennedy
144. Philosophy of Beauty — E.F. Carrit
145. Radhakrishnan — Ed. W.R. Inge, etc.
146. Religion Culture and Society — Ed. Louis Schneiden
147. Religious Consciousness — G.S. Ghurye
148. Renaissance India — Shri Aurobindo
149. Sankara's Advaita
150. Satyagraha—Its Technique and History — R.R. Diwakar
151. Science and Human Values — J. Bronowski
152. Science and the Modern World — A.H. Whitehead
153. Studies in Vedanta — V.J. Kiritikar
154. Submission in Suffering — H.H. Rowley
155. Synthesis of Yoga — Shri Aurobindo
156. The Encounter of Man and Nature — Sayyed H. Nasr

157. The Great Philosophers — E.W.F. Tomlin
158. The Hindu View of Life — S. Radhakrishnan
159. The Meaning of Life in Hinduism and Buddhism — Floyd H. Ross
160. The Portable Nietzsche — Walter Kaufrnann
161. The Religion of India — Max Weber
162. The Supremental Manifestation — Shri Aurobindo
163. The Varieties of Religious Experience — William James
164. This is My Philosophy — Ed. Whit. Burnett
165. Lectures on the Vedanta Philosophy — Max Muller
166. Vedanta Through Letters — Swami Chinmayananda
167. Vyasa and Valmiki — Shri Aurobindo
168. Walden — H.D. Thoreau
169. War Without Violence — K. Shridharani
170. What I Believe — Leo Tolstoy
171. What Vedanta Means to Me — Isherwood
172. Why I am not a Christian — B. Russell
173. Yoga — Ernest Wood
174. Satyagraha — M.K. Gandhi
175. Ramanam — M.K. Gandhi
176. Uttararamacaritam — Ed. G.K. Bhatt
177. Manusmriti—with six commentaries — V.N. Mandlik
178. Shakuntalam — Ed. A.B. Gajendragadkar
179. One Hundred Poems of Kabir — Rabindranath Tagore
180. Akshara — P.M. Modi
181. History of Dharmasastra (All Vols.) — P.V. Kane
182. Markandeya Purana — Pargitor
183. Philosophy of Religion — Patterson
184. Quran — E.H. Palmer
185. Hinduism — K.N. Sen
186. Religion in Modern Life — Hackmann Negley—Nikander
187. Self Restraint Vs. Self Indulgence — M.K. Gandhi
188. My Philosophy of Life — Ed. A.T. Hingorani
189. God is Truth — M.K. Gandhi

190. In Search of the Supreme V. 1 & 3	M.K. Gandhi
191. Ethical Religion	M.K. Gandhi
192. Unto This Last & Other Essays	John Ruskin
193. India of My Dreams	M.K. Gandhi
194. Religious Knowledge	P.F. Schmidt
195. Manusmriti—A Fresh Approach	R.S. Betai
196. The Hindu Theology	Tatia
197. God Exists	Shivananda
198. Karma and Redemption	A.G. Hogg
199. Hindu Gods and Hidden Mysteries	G.K. Pillai
200. India's Message of Peace	A.M. Purohit
201. Hindu Polytheism	Alain Daniel
202. Hinduism	C. Rajagopalachari
203. Krishna	Bhagavan Das
204. Shri Krishna	A.S.P. Ayyer
205. Eastern Lights	M.N. Sircar
206. Autobiography	B. Russell
207. The Varieties of Religious Experience	William James
208. Gandhi and Some of His Thoughts	S.Devas
209. Gandhi—a Study in Revolution	Geoffery Ashe
210. Gandhi and Tagore	Gurdial Malik
211. Gandhi	Carl Heath
212. Facets of Gandhi	Ed. B.K. Ahluwalia
213. An Approach to the Study of Gandhi	T.K. Mahadevan
214. The Gandhi Reader	Homer A. Jack
215. The Gandhian Way	J.B. Kripalani
216. Non-Violence in Peace and War	M.K. Gandhi
217. My Non-Violence	M.K. Gandhi
218. Philosophy	C.E. M. Joad
219. The Unseen Power	M.K. Gandhi
220. What Religion is?	Swami Vivekananda
221. Hinduism	R.C. Zaehner
222. Hinduism and Buddhism	Anand K. Coomaraswamy
223. Essence of Principal Upanishads	Swami Shivananda
224. The Gospel of Life	F.T. Brooks
225. An Afterword	Paramananda Yogananda

226.	A Constructive Survey of Upanishadic Philosophy	R.D. Ranade
227.	Vaishnavism, Shaivism	Bhandarkar
228.	Aitreya Upanishad	Swami Chinmayananda
229.	Atma Bodha	Swami Chinmayananda
230.	Kathopanishad	Swami Chinmayananda
231.	Ishavasyopanishad	Swami Chinmayananda
232.	Ishopanishad	Shri Aurobindo
233.	Kaivalyopanishad	Swami Chinmayananda
234.	Kenopanishad	Swami Chinmayananda
235.	Mandukya Upanishad	Swami Chinmayananda
236.	Mundakopanishad	Swami Chinmayananda
237.	Prasnopanishad	Swami Chinmayananda
238.	Shrimad Bhagavata	S.S. Cohen
239.	Thousand Ways to the Transcendental Vishnu Sahasranama	Commentary by— Swami Chinmayananda
240.	Taittiriya Upanishad	Swami Chinmayananda
241.	Vedanta Through Letters	Swami Chinmayananda
242.	Gandhiji's Teachings and Philosophy	C. Rajagopalachari
243.	The Power of Non-violence	Richard B. Gregg

Hindi and Sanskrit

1.	श्रीमद् भगवद्गीता	शांकरभाष्यसंहिता
2.	श्रीमद् भगवद्गीता	गीताप्रेस, गोरखपुर
3.	श्रीमद् भगवद्गीता	विद सिक्स कमैन्ट्रीज़
4.	गीतालोचन	स्वामी दिगंबरजी
5.	श्रीमद् भगवद्गीता विशेषांक	गीताप्रेस, गोरखपुर
6.	भारतीय धर्मों का इतिहास	आर. डी. भंडारकर
7.	भारतीय दर्शनशास्त्र का इतिहास	हिरियण्णा
8.	भारतीय नीतिशास्त्र का इतिहास	भीखनलाल आत्रेय
9.	भारतीय संस्कृति और अहिंसा	धर्मानन्द कोसाम्बी
10.	भारतीय दर्शनसार	बलदेव उपाध्याय
11.	भारतीय दर्शन के मूल तत्त्व	डा॰ रामनाथ शर्मा
12.	भारतीय संस्कृति कोश (3)	
13.	मनुस्मृति	निर्णयसागर

14. महाभारत (शांति, सभा,भीष्म, अनुशा., स्वर्गा. पर्व.)
15. महाराष्ट्रीय ज्ञानकोश
16. माण्डूक्योपनिषद् — गीताप्रेस, गोरखपुर
17. मुंडकोपनिषद् — गीताप्रेस, गोरखपुर
18. ऐतरेयोपनिषद् — गीताप्रेस, गोरखपुर
19. रामचरितमानस
20. रामानुजाचार्य और उसका विशिष्टाद्वैत — भक्तिदर्शन
21. केनोपनिषद् — गीताप्रेस, गोरखपुर
22. धम्मपद
23. नारदस्मृति — निर्णयसागर
24. सामाजिक विचारों का इतिहास — शुभरत्न त्रिपाठी
25. श्रीमद् भागवतम् — गीताप्रेस, गोरखपुर
26. शतपथब्राह्मणम्
27. शाकुन्तलम् — कालिदास
28. विवेकचूडामणि — शंकराचार्य
29. रघुवंश — कालिदास
30. याज्ञवल्क्यस्मृति — निर्णयसागर प्रेस
31. भगवद्गीता (हिन्दी अनुवाद सहित) — बेलवालकर
32. श्रीमद् भगवद्गीता — (मधुसूदनीव्याख्यासंहिता)
33. मार्कण्डेय पुराण
34. शांकरभाष्य — हनुमानदास शास्त्री
35. अग्निपुराण
36. भागवतपुराण
37. देवीभागवत
38. रामायण

Gujarati

૧. શ્રીમદ્ ભગવતગીતા—સરળ ભાષાંતર — પ્ર. મો. મોદી
૨. શ્રીમદ્ ભગવદ્ગીતા — સ્વામી ચિદ્ઘનાનંદજી
૩. રોમહર્ષણી — સું. ગો. બેટાઈ
૪. શ્રીમદ્ ભગવદ્ગીતા — મ. ન. દ્વિવેદી
૫. શ્રીમદ્ ભગવદ્ગીતા — નાનાલાલ
૬. ગીતામંજરી — જુગતરામ દવે
૭. ગીતાદર્શન — સંતબાલ
૮. ગીતાધર્મ — કાકાસાહેબ કાલેલકર

૯. ગીતાધ્વનિ	કિશોરલાલ મશરૂવાલા
૧૦. ગીતામંથન	કિશોરલાલ મશરૂવાલા
૧૧. સંકલિતા ભગવદ્ગીતા	કાકાસાહેબ કાલેલકર
૧૨. ભગવદ્ગીતા—એક અભિનવ દૃષ્ટિબિંદુ	પ્ર. મો. મોદી
૧૩. ગીતાબોધ	ગાંધીજી
૧૪. ગીતાદોહન	સ્વામી કૃષ્ણાત્મજ
૧૫. ગીતાપ્રસ્થાન	મગનભાઈ દેસાઈ
૧૬. અનાસક્તિયોગ	ગાંધીજી
૧૭. આપણો ધર્મ	આ. બા. ધ્રુવ
૧૮. ઈશાવાસ્ય ઉપનિષદ્	એ. જી. ભટ્ટ
૧૯. કેવલાદ્વૈતના પરિપાકરૂપે ભગવદ્ગીતા	મ. ન. દ્વિવેદી
૨૦. ગીતાપદાર્થકોશ	ગાંધીજી
૨૧. જીવનદીપ	કાકાસાહેબ કાલેલકર
૨૨. ગીતાપ્રવચનો	વિનોબા ભાવે
૨૩. ગીતાશોધન	કિશોરલાલ મશરૂવાલા
૨૪. જૈન ધર્મનો પ્રાણ	
૨૫. દેવી ભાગવત	(ગુજરાતી અનુવાદ)
૨૬. મધુકર	વિનોબા ભાવે
૨૭. મનુસ્મૃતિ	ગુજરાત પ્રિન્ટીંગ પ્રેસ
૨૮. મનુસ્મૃતિ	સસ્તું સાહિત્ય કાર્યાલય
૨૯. મહાભારત (શાંતિ અને અનુશાસન પર્વો)	
૩૦. વ્યાપક ધર્મભાવના	દેવરાજ
૩૧. સર્વોદય દર્શન	ગાંધીજી
૩૨. સ્વતંત્ર ચિંતન	
૩૩. હરિજનબંધુ	(વિભિન્ન અંકો)
૩૪. સ્થિતપ્રજ્ઞદર્શન	વિનોબા ભાવે
૩૫. હિંદુ વેદધર્મ	આ. બા. ધ્રુવ
૩૬. રામનામ	મો. ક. ગાંધી
૩૭. મારા સ્વપ્નનું ભારત	મો. ક. ગાંધી
૩૮. સત્ય એ જ ઈશ્વર છે	મો. ક. ગાંધી
૩૯. વર્ણવ્યવસ્થા	મો. ક. ગાંધી

૪૦. ગોસેવા — મો. ક. ગાંધી
૪૧. ત્યાગમૂર્તિ — મો. ક. ગાંધી
૪૨. નીતિનાશને માર્ગે — મો. ક. ગાંધી
૪૩. આપણે સૌ એક પિતાનાં સંતાન — મો. ક. ગાંધી
૪૪. આશ્રમજીવન — મો. ક. ગાંધી

Glossary One

(Important technical terms In Hindu philosophy and metaphysics)

Adharma	अधर्म	Opposite of Dharma
Adhimanas	अधिमनस्	Overmind
Ahambhava	अहंभाव	Egoism
Ahamkara	अहंकार	Egoism
Akshara	अक्षर	The indestructible, Immortal, The supreme
Amrita	अमृत	Immortal, Liberation, Bliss
Ananda	आनन्द	Supreme delight, Supreme pleasure
Anasakta	अनासक्त	Unattached, Detached
Anasakti	अनासक्ति	Non-attachment, Detachment, Selflessness
Apara Prakriti	अपरा प्रकृति	Primordial matter,
Apara Vidya	अपराविद्या	Knowledge leading to God, Knowledge of God, Highest Knowledge
Asakta	असक्त	Same as Anasakta
Asuri Sampat	आसुरी संपत्	The devilish traits, Demoniac traits
Atma	आत्मा	The Self, Individual soul
Atmajnana	आत्मज्ञान	Knowledge of the Self, Philosophical knowledge
Atimanas	अतिमनस्	Supermind
Atmaupamya	आत्मौपम्य	Comparing with oneself, Taking as similar to oneself

Avidya	अविद्या	Nescience, Ignorance, Leading to illusion
Avyakta	अव्यक्त	Not manifest, Primary matter, Above the senses, God
Brahma, Brahman	ब्रह्म	God, God the Supreme
Brahmanirvana	ब्रह्मनिर्वाण	Dissolution in Brahman, Liberation
Brahmi Sthiti	ब्राह्मीस्थिति	State of oneness in God, The supreme bliss, Liberation
Bhakti-yoga	भक्तियोग	Yoga of Devotion
Buddhi	बुद्धि	Intellect, Alertness and steadfastness of mind
Cit, Chit	चित	Perception, Spirit, Soul
Daivi Sampat	दैवीसंपत्	Godly or noble traits in human nature
Dama	दम	Self-restraint
Dehi	देही	The emobdied Soul
Dharma	धर्म	Righteousness, Humanitarianism, Religion
Divya Purusha	दिव्यपुरुष	The Divine Being, God
Dhyana Yoga	ध्यानयोग	Yoga of Concentration
Guna	गुण	Threefold traits in living beings, Ingredients of nature, Characteristics of all substances
Gunatita	गुणातीत	One above Gunas
Indriyah	इन्द्रियाः	Senses—Five of cognition or perception and five of action
Indriyanigraha	इन्द्रियनिग्रह	Control over the senses
Ishvara	ईश्वर	God, the all powerful
Jnana-yoga	ज्ञानयोग	Yoga of Knowledge
Jiva	जीव	The active soul, Life force in the body
Kama	काम	Worldly desires, Passions, Attachments
Karma-yoga	कर्मयोग	The Yoga of action

Kavayah	कवयः	Sages, Seers, Poets (of Vedas)
Kshara	क्षर	Destructible, Mortal
Mahat	महत्	The great principle, Intellect
Moksha	मोक्ष	Salvation, Bliss. Dissolution of the Self in Divine, Freedom of the soul from body
Muktasanga	मुक्तसंग	Free from worldly attachments, Free from attachment of the senses
Muktatma	मुक्तात्मा	Liberated Soul
Mukti	मुक्ति	Same as Moksha
Mumukshu	मुमुक्षु	One desiring salvation
Muni	मुनि	Sage, Seer, Man of philosophical learning and practice, a *Samnyasin*
Navadvarapura	नवद्वारपुर	City with nine gates or body
Nihshreyasa	निःक्षेयस	Final liberation, Bliss, Supreme joy
Nirakara	निराकार	God the Supreme, Spirit without form or above form, Above appearance, Subtle
Nirguna	निर्गुण	Without traits, Above traits
Nirvana	निर्वाण	Extinction, Dissolution, Emancipation from Matter, Salvation, Liberation
Nistraigunya	निःस्त्रैगुण्य	State of being above Gunas
Niyati	नियति	Destiny, Providence
Parabrahma	परब्रह्म	God the Supreme
Param-gati	परम–गति	Highest State, Liberation, Bliss

Parashanti	पराशान्ति	Highest peace, Supreme Quietude.
Param-purusha	परमपुरुष	Highest spirit, Supreme Principle, God the Supreme
Paraprakriti	पराप्रकृति	The eternal principle
Paravidya	पराविद्या	Knowledge leading to God, Knowledge of God, Highest knowledge
Prakriti	प्रकृति	Nature, Primary Matter, Original source of material world, The first *tattva* in *Samkhya* Philosophy
Prana	प्राण	Life-force in the body
Preya	प्रेय	Worldly attractions, Attachments
Purnavatara	पूर्णावतार	Highest Incarnation, Perfect Incarnation
Purusha	पुरुष	Soul, God, the Supreme being, God the Supreme
Purushottama	पुरुषोत्तम	A name of Vishnu, the Supreme Purusha, God the Supreme
Rajas	रजस्	Emotions, Activity, Cause of activity
Saguna	सगुण	Qualified, Having attributes (God the Supreme)
Sakara	साकार	Having form,Expressed through form
Samadhana	समाधान	Profound meditation, Deep contemplation, Composure
Samatva	समत्व	Evenness, Equity
Samnyasa	संन्यास	Renunciation, Self-control
Samnyasi	संन्यासी	Self-controlled man, Sage, One who has renounced

		the world (physically and/ or mentally)
Sat	सत्	Existence, Original existence
Sattva	सत्त्व	The good or goodness, Noble, Elevating, One of the Gunas, Purity
Satya	सत्य	Truth, Knowledge of Truth, Knowledge of God, God the Supreme
Sham	शम	Tranquillity, Calmness
Shanti	शान्ति	Peace, Quietude, Supreme peace, Bliss
Shiva	शिव	One leading to welfare, One for highest good, God
Shreya	श्रेय	Bliss, Welfare
Sthitaprajna	स्थितप्रज्ञ	Man of detached intellect, Man of firm intellect, Sage
Sundara	सुन्दर	The beautiful (a trait of Brahman)
Tamas	तमस्	Darkness (mental), Error, Ignorance, Illusion, Stagnancy
Titiksha	तितिक्षा	Endurance, Forbearance
Uttama Purusha	उत्तमपुरुष	Highest Reality, God the Supreme.
Vidya	विद्या	Knowledge
Yoga	योग	Concerntration of mind, Contemplation of the Supreme spirit
Yogi, Yogin	योगी	Sage, Seer, One engrossed in Yoga

Glossary Two

(For interested readers whose knowledge of Sanskrit is limited)

Achar	आचार	Conduct, natural decent human behviour
Acharan	आचरण	Conduct, behaviour
Acharya	आचार्य	One who teaches Vedic lore, one who teaches highest philosophy
Adhyatmavadin	आध्यात्मवादिन्	One who has faith in and practices spiritual knowledge
Adhyaya	अध्याय	Chapter, dialogue, discourse
Ahimsa	अहिंसा	Non-violence, non-hurt to all living beings
Aradhana	आराधना	Propitiation, prayer
Asakti	आसक्ति	Worldly attachment, mental attachment
Asteya	अस्तेय	Non-stealth, non-covetousness (one of the vows-vratas)
Ashram	आश्रम	Stages of life (four in number), stages of the development of human personality
Atmakama	आत्मकाम	One who desires to know the self (soul), one who puts in effort to have knowledge of the self

Avarana	आवरण	Covering, obscuring
Avatara	अवतार	Incarnation of God (Vishnu) in a worldly form
Bhagawan	भगवान	The Divine, Divinity
Bhakta	भक्त	Devotee of God, devotee who adopts or accepts Bhakti as the path of blessedness or salvation
Bharatarshabha	भरतर्षभ	A lion amongst the Bharatas, Arjuna
Bhashya	भाष्य	Detailed doctrinal commentary or analysis of a rather tough work
Bhashyakara	भाष्यकार	Writer of Bhashya or detailed analysis of a topic or work
Brahmasakshatkara	ब्रह्मसाक्षात्कार	Visualization of God the Supreme, realization of Atma as Parmatma
Dharma-Yuddha	धर्मयुद्ध	Battle for righteousness, for right or ethical cause or great values
Gitakara	गीताकार	Writer or singer of Gita, Lord Krishna
Himsa	हिंसा	Violence, hurt to living beings—physical, mental, emotional or spiritual
Hathayoga	हठयोग	A type of Yoga—of rigorous meditation
Jnana	ज्ञान	Knowledge of reality, knowledge of soul, of God, knowledge of the Supreme
Jnana-nishtha	ज्ञान निष्ठा	Being engrossed in spiritual knowledge
Jnani	ज्ञानी	Man of knowledge, man of spiritual knowledge, learned one

Kalyana	कल्याण	Good or welfare of humanity, service to humanity
Karmya	कर्म्य	Desired, coveted
Kartratva	कर्तृत्व	Performance of action or duty
Keval-Jnana	केवल ज्ञान	Absolute knowledge, knowledge of supreme reality, highest knowledge
Kevaladvaita-rupa	केवलाद्वैतरूप	Of the nature of absolute oneness or non-dualism
Lila/Leela	लीला	Divine sport
Lokasangraha	लोकसंग्रह	Welfare of the world or welfare of humanity or good of the living beings
Naishkarmya	नैष्कर्म्य	Absence of worldly activity
Narayana	नारायण	God the Supreme, Lord Krishna
Nishkama-Karma	निष्काम कर्म	Action resorted to without desire or covetousness of reward
Rasa	रस	Interest in, attachment to
Sadhak	साधक	Propitiator
Sadhana	साधना	Fulfilment, means, instrumental cause
Samanvaya	समन्वय	Sequence, mutual connection
Samsara	संसार	External world, mortal world, world of the living
Shastra	शास्त्र	Philosophy, science, doctrine, principle
Shraddha	श्रद्धा	Faith
Tapas	तपस्	Penance, religious austerity, mortification
Tarkapada	तर्कपाद	A work on logic

Tattva	तत्त्व	True state or condition, true or essential nature, real nature of the human soul
Uprati	उपरति	Abstaining from sexual enjoyment, indifference to attachment
Upasana	उपासना	Propitiation, worship, adoration, religious meditation
Vaidik-dharma	वैदिक धर्म	The path or way of life laid down by the Vedas, sacred and authentic path of duties and conduct
Vaikuntha	वैकुण्ठ	Higher or blessed world, heaven
Vasishtha	वसिष्ठ	One of the most renowned sages of old
Vibhuti	विभूति	Magnificence
Yati	यति	An ascetic
Yogakshema	योगक्षेम	Worldly maintenance, worldly joys and happiness
Yoga Vasishtha	योगवसिष्ठ	A Sanskrit work on the science of Yoga
Yogeshvara	योगेश्वर	Lord of all Yogas, Lord Krishna

Index I (English)

M

N

O

P

W

Y

Note: The following words come on so many pages and are therefore not given separately in the Index.

Gita, Gandhiji, Yoga, Yogin, Karma, Karma-yoga, Karma-yogin, Dhyana, Dhyana-yoga, Jnana, Jnana-yoga, Dhyana-yogin etc.

Index II (Sanskrit)

SELECT PUBLICATIONS OF THE NATIONAL GANDHI MUSEUM

Title	Author	Price
1. Birth of Free India's National Anthem: A Gift from Netaji Subhas Bose	Y.P. Anand (Comp.)	25.00
2. The Essential Relationship between Netaji Subhas Bose and Mahatma Gandhi: The Supreme Martyrs in India's Freedom Struggle	Y.P. Anand (Comp.)	25.00
3. What Mahatma Gandhi Said about the Atom Bomb	Y.P. Anand (Comp.)	5.00
4. Into the Sun: An Autobiography	Ramadevi Choudhuri	100.00
5. Pietermaritzburg Railway Station: The Start of the Journey from Mohandas Karamchand Gandhi to Mahatma Gandhi	National Gandhi Museum	20.00
6. The Little Princess and the Birds	National Gandhi Museum	20.00
7. Exploring Gandhi (Reprint)	Manmohan Choudhuri	90.00
8. Mahatma Gandhi the Journalist (Reprint)	S.N. Bhattacharyya	225.00
9. Gandhi's Social Philosophy: Perspective and Relevance (Reprint)	B.N. Ganguli	450.00
10. In Defence of Freedom: Exciting Times and Quiet Meditations	Amlan Datta	125.00
11. Gandhiji's Lost Jewel: Harilal Gandhi	Nilam Parikh Tr. by Kalpana Palkhiwala	135.00
12. गांधीजी किस प्रकार इस निष्कर्ष पर पहुंचे कि अन्तर्जातीय विवाह से जाति प्रथा का उन्मूलन करना होगा	मार्क लिन्डले, सं.	20.00
13. पीटर मेरित्सबर्ग रेलवे स्टेशनः एक यात्रा जिसने मोहनदास करमचन्द गांधी को महात्मा गांधी बना दिया	राष्ट्रीय गांधी संग्रहालय	20.00
14. महात्मा गांधी ने अणु बम के बारे में क्या कहा	वाई.पी. आनन्द, सं.	5.00
15. नन्ही राजकुमारी और हजार पक्षी	राष्ट्रीय गांधी संग्रहालय	20.00
16. कामरेड रामकिशनः व्यक्तित्व और विचार	वी.पी. गुप्त एवं मोहिनी गुप्ता, सं.	250.00
17. राजकोट सत्याग्रह का ऐतिहासिक महत्व	बालुभाई वैद्य, अनु. हसमुख व्यास	65.00
18. गांधी जी का खोया हुआ धनः हरिलाल गांधी	नीलम परीख, अनु. योगेन्द्र परीख	135.00

Gandhi Literature Centre
NATIONAL GANDHI MUSEUM
Rajghat, New Delhi 110002
Tel.: 3328310/3310168 Fax: 91-011-3311793
E-mail: gandhimk@nda.vsnl.net.in
Website: www.gandhimuseum.org